Thomas Paine's American Ideology

Thomas Paine's American Ideology

A. Owen Aldridge

Newark: University of Delaware Press
London and Toronto: Associated University Presses

Associated University Presses
440 Forsgate Drive
Cranbury, NJ 08512

Associated University Presses
25 Sicilian Avenue
London WC1A 2QH, England

Associated University Presses
2133 Royal Windsor Drive
Unit 1
Mississauga, Ontario
Canada L5J 1K5

Library of Congress Cataloging in Publication Data

Aldridge, Alfred Owen, 1915–
Thomas Paine's American ideology.

Bibliography: p.
Includes index.
1. Paine, Thomas, 1737–1809. Common sense.
2. Paine, Thomas, 1737–1809. 3. United States—Politics and government—1775–1783. 4. Political science—History—18th century. 5. Monarchy. I. Title.
E211.P153A43 1984 973.3′11 83-40239
ISBN 0-87413-260-6

Printed in the United States of America

That no proud privilege from birth can spring,
No right divine nor compact form a king.

Joel Barlow, *The Columbiad*

Contents

Preface

Thomas Paine has been the subject of at least ten biographies during this century, but little attention has been devoted to his ideas. The only portion of his broad intellectual interests which scholars have treated in any depth is his polemic with Edmund Burke in *Rights of Man,* and even here much remains to be said. *Common Sense* has been universally praised for its effectiveness as propaganda, but there exists no thorough analysis of its contents. Nor has Paine's American ideology as a whole ever been adequately explained or fully stated.

Paine's writing does not belong exclusively to American literature and culture, or even to English and American traditions combined, but to the Enlightenment as a broad international movement. His pregnant statement in *Common Sense* concerning ethnic strains in the colonies has equal application to culture: "Europe, and not England, is the parent country of America." Paine's thought, which embodies, in his own words, "a new system of government," not only contributed directly to the ideologies of later revolutions in France and Latin-America, but also raised issues of social relationships which are still being debated.

In this book I shall make very little effort to assess the efficacy of *Common Sense* in converting the majority of the British colonists to a sentiment in favor of independence. Deciding whether ideology or socioeconomic forces had priority in the colonists' desire for independence is like dealing with the proverbial chicken and the egg. Both ideology and self-interest are part of the record and both need to be accounted for.

Nor shall I attempt to reinforce Bernard Bailyn's well-known opinion that "the American Revolution was above all else an ideological, constitutional, political struggle and not primarily a controversy between social groups undertaken to force changes in the organization of the society or the economy." Unlike Bailyn, I shall be dealing with Paine as an individual thinker rather than with the ideology of America as a whole. In attempting to provide a summary of Paine's intellectual career between the years 1775 and 1783, I shall consider the entire spectrum of his ideological concerns, not merely—or even primarily— his attitude toward independence. Paine's fundamental goal was the creation of a just and ordered society through reason and choice instead of passive submission to accident and force, and toward this end he developed such essential themes as the inherent nature of man, the meaning of virtue, and the identity of American character.

The following pages are devoted exclusively to the intellectual content of Paine's writings between 1775 and 1787. They analyze the productions of his apprenticeship as a magazine editor, sketch the publishing history of *Common Sense,* explain its major philosophical doctrines and historical issues, and indicate the relations of these ideas to earlier manifestations in such forerunners as Locke, Montesquieu, and Rousseau. No attempt is made to impose later ideologies upon Paine's system of thought.

As part of the polemics over *Common Sense,* Paine wrote a pamphlet, which has never before been ascribed to him, applying some of the issues of national government to Pennsylvania politics. This pamphlet is here shown to be the fulfillment of Paine's promise in the last of his "Forester" letters to explain the distinction between a government and a constitution.

The following pages also investigate the intellectual content, of *The Crisis* and of Paine's newspaper writings concerning particular issues of the American Revolution, including the Pennsylvania Constitution of 1776 and the Bank of America. A final section explores Paine's theories of the relationship of the United States to Europe and the possibility of international peace through a process described by Paine as completing "the circle of civilization."

During the period of the American Revolution Paine published a number of purely occasional pieces, including personal satires on British officials, a series of essays on the Silas Deane affair, another series on taxation in Rhode Island, and a pamphlet concerning the disposal of western lands in Virginia. The ideological significance of these pieces is negligible, however, and for this reason they are not taken up in this book.

These purely occasional pieces aside, Paine's writings on the American Revolution may be placed into sharply distinctive categories according to the classes of readers to whom he appealed and the responses which he hoped to produce. *Common Sense* emphasizes abstract political concepts of universal application, but is, nevertheless, designed to bring about immediate political action throughout the entire American continent. *The Crisis,* in contrast, focuses upon local events and particular occasions, but is likewise intended to produce instantaneous action and is regarded by its author as being of interest to all humanity. Paine's newspaper essays concerning Pennsylvania politics contain, on the other hand, relatively few principles of universal application and are oriented toward the provincial community. Finally, Paine's *Letter to the Abbé Raynal* associates abstract philosophical principles with the American Revolution as a historical movement and attempts to impress public opinion on an international rather than a local or even a continental scale.

Research for this book was carried out at the British Museum, the New York Public Library, the New York Historical Society, the University of Illinois, and the American Philosophical Society. I wish to express my gratitude to all of these institutions and particularly to the staff of the Library of the American Philosophical Society and to its Director, Whitfield J. Bell, Jr., for their undeviating graciousness and courtesy. All materials from the Colonel Richard Gimbel Thomas Paine Collection in the American Philosophical Society are quoted with kind permission.

My greatest debt is to the National Endowment for the Humanities for a Senior Fellowship which made it possible for me to devote an entire academic year to research and writing.

Thomas Paine's American Ideology

PART I

Writing and Publication of *Common Sense*

1

Common Sense and the History of Ideas

The view that ideologies are primarily the political expression of ideals is of particular relevance to Thomas Paine. Any discussion of his ideology must take into consideration the moral fervor of *Common Sense,* the work which he considered to be his greatest contribution to the American Revolution. In title pages of his later publications he proudly identifies it as his own; he describes himself in his will as "author of the work entitled Common Sense" and asks to have these same words engraved on his tombstone along with his name and age. He even disclosed just before his death that he believed that in a future state he would be conscious of his authorship.[1]

Common Sense is generally admitted to be a superb propaganda weapon in the struggle for independence and a masterpiece of world literature. It is all this and more. It constitutes a summary of a large segment of the ideology of the American Revolution as well as a substantial contribution to that very ideology. The foregoing statement implies that Paine's political ideas harmonized in general with prevailing public opinion during the American Revolution, but it does not suggest either that Paine reflected the majority sentiment or even that any of his particular thoughts molded the attitudes of a majority of his contemporaries.

The concept of ideology has so many varied significations that it is essential to state exactly what meaning is intended by referring to this aspect of Paine's writings. In a broad sense, ideology consists of "an empirical belief system held in common by the members of any collectivity," but it may also designate a system of beliefs held by "a sub-collectivity of one" either conforming to the main culture of the society or deviating from it.[2] Essentially the body of beliefs which Paine set forth in *Common Sense* should not be considered as a formal ideology in the sense of an integrated series of doctrines which taken together represent a unified intellectual system. At the time that he wrote his stirring pamphlet, Paine had not completely organized his various concepts into a systematic order, as he later attempted to do in *Rights of Man.* But whether his principles in January 1776 were unified or discrete, whether a system of political philosophy or merely separate arguments based on abstract theory, *Common Sense* must be interpreted as embodying an ideological structure, the essence of which was fundamentally ethical. This structure was not pervasive, however, in the sense that the presence of one doctrine would automatically imply the existence of related ones, as it does, for example, in eighteenth-century Calvinism or twentieth-century Marxism. Paine's pattern of ideas resembles a group of avenues with connecting alleys rather than a network of intertwining strands. His system would remain functional even with the removal of some of its parts, but a true ideological network would collapse with the cutting away of any of its constituent links.

From this perspective, the major ideas of the American Revolution may be said to constitute a political system, but not an ideology. The philosophy of the American Revolution consists in that body of notions and concepts concerning human behavior, society and government which led directly to the separation of the British colonies in America from the Empire, to the consequent adoption of the Declaration of Independence, and to the framing of the Federal Constitution. Paine cannot of course be given credit for writing the Declaration of Independence, and he was not even in America during the working months of the Constitutional Convention, but his *Common Sense* calls for the drawing up and promulgation of both documents and it foreshadows many of the major doctrines which they set forth. This masterpiece of persuasion either sketches or suggests, moreover, such notions as the state of nature, the theory of progress, the evolution of social structures, the distinction between natural rights and civil rights, the impropriety of allowing one generation to legislate for future ones, and the means of attaining international peace.

Paine's primary appeal in *Common Sense* and in his other major writings of the Revolution was moral rather than economic. His later *Rights of Man* is not a bit more radical than *Common Sense* in its basic ideology, but merely applies identical principles to a fresh set of circumstances in a dissimilar social environment and on a more extensive scale. Sir Thomas Erskine, who defended Paine in England for publishing *Rights of Man,* based his case on the ideological identity of the two works. The charge in the indictment was simply "seditious libel," but the prosecution sought to portray Paine as having mounted a treasonable attack on national institutions. Erskine argued that the accusation of treason was ridiculous, since *Common Sense,* which "contains every one principle of government, and every abuse in the British constitution, which is to be found in the *Rights of Man,*" had "been sold without restraint in every shop in England."[3] Paine himself affirmed in 1802 that the "principles" of the two works were "the same" and that the only difference between them was "that the one was adapted to the local circumstances of England, and the other to those of America."[4] The conclusion of *Common Sense,* moreover, anticipates the social philosophy of Paine's later work by defining a good citizen as an open friend and virtuous supporter "of the RIGHTS OF MANKIND and of the FREE AND INDEPENDENT STATES OF AMERICA." Throughout his life,

Paine never wavered in his belief that social and political rights are inseparable.

This was the century of the Englightenment, the period in which rational inquiry into all aspects of human knowledge was initiated by zealous philosophers and in varying degrees tolerated, if not promoted, by rulers and officers of state. As a great innovation, government was recognized as being the most influential source of social change. The theory that government controls or conditions all phases of social relationships and even human nature itself is the theme of two of the most famous eighteenth-century treatises of intellectual history, Montesquieu's *Spirit of the Laws* and Voltaire's *Essay on Manners.* The theories of both men are suggested in the opening sentence of *Common Sense:* "Some writers have so confounded society with government, as to leave little or no distinction between them."

The concept of social change conflicted in the eighteenth century with another widespread notion of the period—the neoclassical doctrine that human nature is invariable or unchanging in all times and places. Voltaire resolved the conflict by observing, "Men are born everywhere more or less the same; . . . it is government which changes manners, which elevates or debases nations."[5] Rousseau was even more precise in asserting that human nature everywhere is fundamentally good, but that government brings out the worst in mankind. Paine, in *Common Sense,* reflects both of these principles. He defines government as a "necessary evil," but at the same time presents a model for political association which he considers ideal.

In regard to the abstract concept of the original nature of man, that is, whether man is inherently good or evil, *Common Sense* is somewhat ambivalent, but Paine's phraseology certainly suggests the doctrine of original sin: government, he says, is needed because of "our wickedness" and is "the badge of lost innocence." Also the "impulses of conscience" are not "clear, uniform, and irresistibly obeyed." In *Rights of Man,* however, his language is Rousseauistic rather than Calvinistic: "man, were he not corrupted by governments, is naturally the friend of man, and . . . human nature is not of itself vicious."[6] The question of man's moral nature was crucial to many of the problems confronting the Revolutionary generation and to those presented in *Common Sense,* for example, whether man is impelled by gregariousness or by violence into society, whether checks are needed by one set of individuals in government upon another, and whether an appreciable degree of progress is possible in human relations.

Probably most of the contemporary readers of *Common Sense* were not aware of the ideological traditions on which it rested, concerned as they were with the practical exigencies of the moment. Even Paine himself may not have been cognizant of the ultimate source of many of his concepts, but he did realize that *Common Sense* was based as much upon abstract ideas as upon considerations of national self-interest and practical advantages. In the concluding pages he declares: "We have it in our power to begin the world over again. A situation, similar to the present, hath not happened since the days of Noah until now. The birthday of a new world is at hand."[7] Paine repeated these statements and amplified their meaning in *Rights of Man.* Separation from England would probably have occurred as a historical process, he later affirmed, even without the particular events of the American Revolution, but the significant consideration for mankind was that the Revolution as it had actually taken place represented a philosophic movement. In Paine's words, "it was the *principle,* at *that* time, that produced the independence; for until the principle spread itself abroad among the people, independence was not thought of, and America was fighting without an object."[8]

The concept that the American Revolution was fought for an ideology—that a system of political philosophy was at stake—was also the main point of another of Paine's Revolutionary pamphlets, his *Letter to the Abbé Raynal,* published in 1782.

To be sure, Paine's mere affirmation that the American Revolution was a philosophical movement does not constitute proof that it was, but it is possible to show that his *Common Sense* is based upon a set of ideas of international scope and significance which transcend the immediate circumstance of a conflict of interest between Great Britain and her American colonies. The most sophisticated of Paine's contemporary readers, moreover, realized the ideological significance of his pamphlet. In the very month after its publication, a New York newspaper quoted an admiring comment that *Common Sense* "introduces a new system of politics as widely different from the old, as the Copernican system is from the Ptolemaic. . . . This extraordinary performance . . . contains as surprising a discovery in politics as the works of Sir Isaac Newton do in philosophy."[9]

Because of the tendency of the exponents of ideological systems to take extreme positions and maneuver themselves into irreconcilable confrontations with their opponents, some historians have argued that American culture from colonial times to the present has shown a consistent resistance to ideological conflict and that basic issues have been settled through pragmatic compromise. The proponents of what is called the consensus interpretation of American history accept the role of public opinion and debate, but maintain that pragmatic solutions have in the long run carried more weight than rigid ideologies. It is true that pragmatism has been an important element in American thought, in colonial times as much as in any other. The wisest and most respected American of that period, Benjamin Franklin, was also a great pragmatist. But this does not mean that Franklin distrusted ideas. Indeed he devoted most of his political career from his middle years to old age writing and circulating propaganda essays for the press.

Franklin deeply loved and admired the British Empire, that "fine and noble China Vase," as he called it, and he did not advocate independence until the months just preceding the publication of *Common Sense.* But as soon as he had made up his own mind in its favor, he realized that the struggle would fail unless public opinion could be swayed in the same direction. It was Franklin, therefore, who suggested to Paine the writing of a propaganda "history of the present transactions."[10] This accounts for the paradox that, *Common Sense,* the outstanding ideological pamphlet of the American Revolution, grew out of a proposal by that movement's leading pragmatist.

American historiography during the last eighty years has vacillated from one extreme to another on the matter of intellectual influences in the American Revolution. The classical nineteenth-century historian Moses Coit Tyler described the conflict with Britain as "preeminently a revolution caused by ideas, and pivoted on ideas."[11] Just the opposite perspective appeared in the 1930s in the works of Charles A. Beard, who maintained that socioeconomic relationships were paramount and that the constitutional and philosophical arguments of Paine and other pamphleteers, together with the broad principles in the Declaration of Independence, were secondary and intended for effect. According to Beard and his disciples, the true motives for the Revolution were "the realistic features of economic conflict, stress and strain."[12] Even the pioneer of American intellectual historians, Vernon L. Parrington, maintained in 1926 that Paine's major argument concerned the "economic consequences to America of the English connection" and that he saw independence as "only a question of expediency" which "must be determined in the light of economic advantage."[13] Although a later Progressive historian, Arthur M. Schlesinger, carried on the thesis that pamphlets of the Revolution consisted of rhetoric rather than substance and that the chief advocates of the patriotic cause swayed from one position to another in response to changing conditions, the view that the patriot position was insubstantial and inconsistent was challenged by Edmund S. Morgan, who traced in regard to the Stamp Act the development and consistent affirmation by the colonists of well-defined constitutional principles. A group of historians of the 1950s, now known as the neo-whigs, similarly interpreted the Revolution as having more to do with political, legalistic, and constitutional issues than economic or social ones. These neo-whig historians, in the words of Gordon S. Wood, came "full circle to the position of the Revolutionaries themselves and to the interpretation of the first generation of historians."[14] In the 1960s, Bernard Bailyn sought to disentangle the ideas which the patriots set forth from the motivations which drew them into the conflict. He portrayed the partisans of the American cause, however, as not fully aware of the ramifications of the ideas they expressed nor able to foresee the directions in which these ideas would lead later events. In his words, "the familiar meaning of ideas and words faded away into confusion, and leaders felt themselves peering into a haze, seeking to bring shifting conceptions somehow into focus."[15] As Gordon S. Wood has expressed it, Bailyn "ended by demonstrating the autonomy of ideas in phenomena, where the ideas operate, as it were, on the heads of the participants."[16] Bailyn also declared flatly that the American Revolution was in no obvious sense undertaken to bring about extensive social change. No one, he stated, "deliberately worked for the destruction or even the substantial alteration of the order of society as it had been known."[17]

More recently, the notion of the autonomy of ideas has come under sharp attack as an elitist concept, irrelevant to the major concerns of society. Intellectual history as practiced by Parrington and his successors has been accused of concentrating on a few dominant major thinkers and deriving from them a meaningless consensus. The method known as the history of ideas, although just the opposite in its stress on minor writers and currents, has been charged by the same critics with abstracting ideas from the flow of actual life. In the words of one of them, "the infatuation with consensus; the vogue of a disembodied 'history of ideas' divorced from considerations of class and other determinants of social organization; the obsession with 'American studies' which perpetuates a nationalistic myth of American uniqueness—these things reflect the degree to which historians have become apologists, in effect, for American national power in the holy war against communism."[18]

One may argue against this position that ideas are no more disembodied than are literary works whose authors have died. Even ideas which were once powerful, but are no longer taken seriously, have as much historical reality as any past physical event; for example, the notion that this is the best of all possible worlds. By the same token, ideas which are today considered of fundamental significance, for example, the concept of human rights, have even more contemporary reality than any past battle or parliamentary debate. It is still a valid aim of historical and literary studies to account for the origin and influence of ideas.

A type of historical inquiry which is currently in vogue attempts to trace ideologies to social antecedents, attributing, for example, the political and economic radicalism in the works of revolutionary theorists to their proletarian birth and early hardships. This kind of sociological ideology dominates a study of Paine by Eric Foner entitled *Tom Paine and Revolutionary America*. The author argues that the understanding of Paine "involves less a study of ideas (although Paine's thought certainly merits careful analysis) than a social history of intellectual endeavor and political communication."[19] According to the unifying thesis of this book, Paine's writing reflects his own class origins and appeals primarily to other members of that same social class. Foner concentrates, therefore, on the artisans of Philadelphia under the assumption that "Paine's brand of republican ideology struck its deepest chords among the artisans."[20]

It is reasonable to assume that Paine's works did not appeal to Tories or other readers sympathetic to the British Crown, but there is no evidence whatsoever to indicate that responses to his ideas were divided in any way by social class. His ideology, to the contrary, cuts across class lines. It would be very difficult, moreover, to prove that an inherent relationship exists between any person's ideology and his social status. To be sure, a person's language and his nominal religion come to him from the country in which he is born, but similar assumptions cannot be made about particular ideas. One needs but to ask questions such as the following: Do all poor people believe in God? Do all rich ones disbelieve? Are all farmers individualists? Do all city dwellers believe in cooperation? Do all factory workers advocate socialism? Do all capitalists want laissez-faire individualism? Certainly it is true, as Paine himself remarked, that "a man's ideas are generally produced in him by his present situation and condition,"[21] but situation and condition are not equivalent to social class. And social classes do not necessarily produce homogenous political and philosophical ideologies. Several years before the publication of Foner's book, valid objections were raised to the method of relating "ideas or sets of ideas directly and functionally to the alleged interests of certain classes." Under this reductionist treatment, it was said, "the intellectual disappears as an individual with a personal and unique contribution to make, and becomes merely the symbol of a class or interest."[22]

In specific reference to Paine, it is perfectly true, as Foner argues, that Paine came up from the working classes, that he was for a brief time an artisan before becoming a serious author, and that much of his writing portrays a fascination with pragmatic science. It is also true that he associated himself politically with radical social movements and mirrored their ideals in his works. Both of these statements are valid, but it is a fallacy to assume that the second is a consequence of the first. In other words, a working-class background does not necessarily lead to the adoption of a radical social ideology.

Paine's ideas were not based on economic interest nor did they seek to abolish distinctions in social classes, even though they tended to condemn privilege. His system was firmly and consciously based, in his own words, on his personal "moral and philosophical principles," which, in turn, despite his later reputation as a foe of institutional religion, were essentially Christian. The arguments in *Common Sense* to which Paine gives greatest prominence have nothing to do with economic advantage, but are based on abstract principles of government, and he repeated them later in *Rights of Man,* a work begun several years after the independence of America. *Common Sense* contains absolutely no references to social class; indeed Paine unequivocally affirms in it that "the distinctions of rich and poor, may in a great measure be accounted for . . . without having recourse to the harsh, ill-sounding names of oppression and avarice." In a pamphlet published shortly after *Common Sense,* which will be for the first time identified as Paine's in a subsequent chapter of the present book, he specifically accepted the prevailing class structure, declaring forthrightly that "no reflection ought to be made on any man on account of his birth, provided that his manners rise decently with his circumstances, and that he affects not to forget the level he came from."

Whatever historians may say on the subject, it is a matter of conjecture alone whether colonists were motivated primarily by ideologies, social pressures, or economic necessity. The actual appeals used in *Common Sense,* however, can be measured objectively, and these certainly were not primarily economic in nature. Despite the interpretations of Parrington and others, the arguments to which Paine gives greatest prominence are those based on abstract principles of government, precisely those repeated in *Rights of Man.* These have as much relevance to England as to America and for the most part have nothing to do with the economic grievances of America growing out of its colonial status.

To be sure, at least two-thirds of *Common Sense* consists of pragmatic arguments—those based on the feasibility and practicability of independence and the actual means of bringing it about. Only one-third of the work consists of ideology—that is, of arguments based on abstract theory or of reasoning from the authority of the Old Testament. Yet these abstract arguments, precisely those to be repeated in *Rights of Man,* were presented in the opening pages of *Common Sense,* and it was this ideological section which its readers found most challenging, to judge by the evidence of the rejoinders and supporting documents it inspired. Many contemporary commentaries passed over the practical and pragmatic sections to concentrate on theory.

The major contribution of *Common Sense,* moreover, was not so much in calling for the independence of the American colonies as it was in advocating a republican form of government, which was by no means a necessary concomitant of separation from Great Britain. Various monarchies, for example, were later set up in the western hemisphere during the nineteenth century, and after Lexington and Concord a new ruling family could easily have been installed in the former British colonies. Many patriots such as John Adams, and perhaps even Washington himself, would have been favorably disposed toward such a monarchy.

Common Sense transcended the personalities and issues of the moment, and for this reason it continued to be debated and discussed for years after American independence was proclaimed. In the words of one of Paine's early nineteenth-century admirers:

> it taught a whole people to understand the quality and exercise of their natural and civil rights—their moral and social duties: it pointed out to a misguided and wrangling world, the origin and end of all governments, the first and fundamental objects of all kinds of restraint imposed by

laws; the elementary principles of justice, making clear to the humblest perceptions, the rational road to freedom and happiness.[23]

If Paine's contemporaries could see in *Common Sense* a kind of prospectus for a new social order, it is certainly valuable two hundred years later as a register of the ideas which appealed to the people of the times. Paine himself, in his introduction, specifically affirmed the universal relevance of his thought. "The cause of America," he stated, "is in a great measure the cause of all mankind. Many circumstances have, and will arise, which are not local, but universal, and through which the principles of all lovers of mankind are affected, and in the event of which their affections are interested."

Paine clearly believed that considerations of ethics overbalanced those of self-interest in the behavior and thinking of the American people. He expressed this opinion in his *Crisis* No. 11 in relation to the alliance with France. "Could I convey a thought that might serve to regulate the public mind," he stated, "I would not make the interest of the alliance the basis of defending it. All the world are moved by interest, and it affords them nothing to boast of. But I would go a step higher, and defend it on the ground of honor and principle."[24] A few sentences later he affirmed, "Character is to us, in our present circumstances, of more importance than interest." Paine also indicated somewhat later that just prior to writing *Common Sense,* when his thoughts had turned toward matters of government, he had seen the need to "form a system . . . that accorded with the moral and philosophical principles" in which he had himself been educated.[25]

This revelation suggests that Paine in *Common Sense* had sought to justify independence as a legitimate moral enterprise before proposing it as either desirable or feasible. Only after undertaking this moral justification as a preliminary step, did he proceed with his efforts to convince his readers that independence was also the most expedient solution to their problems and to demonstrate that they possessed the military and economic resources necessary to gain it. In other words, he offered abstract philosophical arguments concerning the origin and function of government as the foundation for pragmatic arguments based on the particular circumstances of the American colonists. Imbued as they were with normal self-interest, they, like Paine himself, possessed from their religious heritage—whether evangelical, puritanical, or latitudinarian—a strong sense of collective moral rectitude forceful enough to keep them from any major concerted action which seemed to be contrary to their traditions of right and wrong. Paine realized the strength of this collective ethical consciousness, and in the early pages of *Common Sense* demonstrated that the solution of independence he was proposing for the grievances of his fellow citizens was a goal which could be defended on moral grounds. In this particular objective as well as in several others Paine's pamphlet was a necessary preparation for the Declaration of Independence of July 1776. *Common Sense* provided the colonists with a feeling of moral justification in their decision to separate from Great Britain. The Declaration which followed was a further means of proclaiming this moral rectitude to the world.

2
Paine's Political Writing before *Common Sense*

Practically every editor and biographer of Paine has felt obliged to vindicate him for declaring in *Crisis* No. 2 and repeating the assertion to a committee of the Continental Congress in October 1783 that "in England I never was the author of a syllable in print"; whereas in actuality he had published in 1772 four thousand copies of a pamphlet, *Case of the Officers of Excise,* describing the economic hardships of employees in the British service to which he at the time had belonged.[1] When this early publication was exposed in 1791 by George Chalmers in his *The Life of Thomas Paine, the author of Rights of Man,* John Adams and others considered the revelation a confirmation of their opinion that Paine's word could not be relied upon. Paine's admirers and disciples have defended his statement by maintaining that the *Case of the Officers* should not be considered an example of authorship since it had been printed merely for private circulation. Few, if any, writers on Paine have drawn attention to his parallel declaration in *Crisis* No. 7, in which he states that at the time he arrived in America the world could not have persuaded him that he would be either a soldier or an author. "If I had any talents for either," he wrote, "they were buried in me, and might ever have continued so, had not the necessity of the times dragged and driven them into action."[2] In *Crisis* No. 13 he affirmed, "It was the cause of America that made me an author," and more than twenty years later he also maintained "the pamphlet Common Sense" to be "the first work I ever published."[3] According to John Adams, writing in his autobiography, Paine made oral as well as written protestations of his inexperience in publishing. "He was extremely earnest to convince me, that common Sense was his first born: declared again and again that he had never written a Line nor a Word that had been printed before Common Sense." Adams, however, "cared nothing" for these protestations and remained silent.[4]

Paine's multiple affirmations of literary inexperience leave the impression that his creative talent developed almost overnight, and his statement that "it was the cause of America that made me an author" implies that his ideological tendencies were also a late development. It has been argued convincingly, however, that his English excise pamphlet clearly foreshadows his later radicalism, William Cobbett going so far as to maintain that the shabby treatment he received in the Excise service "was the real cause of the Revolution in America."[5]

Within four or five weeks after his arrival in Philadelphia, Paine entered upon a professional literary career as managing editor of a monthly periodical, the *Pennsylvania Magazine,* which the enterprising printer Robert Aitken had just begun to publish. This literary apprenticeship, however, had very little relevance to politics or to "the necessity of the times," perhaps because of the policy of the publisher Aitken, who had promised in his proposals for printing the magazine that it would avoid matters of religious and political controversy.

In addition to working as an editor, Paine contributed a number of poems and essays of his own to the magazine. Some pieces can be positively identified, but there are problems with others which seem in one way or another to be linked to Paine, but lack conclusive ties.[6] The only one which bears Paine's recognized pseudonym "Atlanticus" and which also concerns the dispute between Great Britain and the colonies is a poem, "Liberty Tree," which when reprinted in editions of Paine's works many years later bore the subtitle, "A Song Written Early in the American Revolution." Even though almost nobody believed that a revolution was in progress in July 1775, when the poem initially appeared in the *Pennsylvania Magazine,* one of its stanzas complains of the colonists going unrewarded for their support of British maritime power and another, quoted below, warns of the British threat to colonial freedom.

> But hear, O ye swains ('tis a tale most profane),
>   How all the tyrannical powers,
> Kings, Commons, and Lords, are uniting amain
>   To cut down this guardian of ours.
> From the east to the west blow the trumpet to arms,
>   Thro' the land let the sound of it flee;
> Let the far and the near—all unite with a cheer,
>   In defense of our *Liberty tree.*

The nature of the threat to liberty is not even suggested, however, and the only direct criticism of Britain comes in the phrase "tyrannical powers." In later editions the phrase "Kings, Commons, and Lords" was changed to "Kingcraft and Priestcraft." This is a direct echo of *Common Sense,* where Paine observes that "there is as much of kingcraft as priestcraft in withholding the scripture from the public in popish countries."[7]

The introductory essay to the first number of the *Pennsylvania Magazine,* entitled "To the Public," January 1775, also is signed "Atlanticus," and other evidence indicates that it is by Paine.[8] Although not connected with the immediate antecedents of the American Revolution, the essay touches on two major intellectual themes of the Enlightenment which reappear in Paine's later political writings, the literary quarrel of the ancients and the moderns and the notion of biological degeneration in the West. Paine enlists himself on the side of the moderns by ridiculing the vanity of the ancients for attributing to themselves the honor of inventing everything of value in the arts and sciences and for assuming that these subjects are as a consequence exhausted. "The divine mechanism of creation reproves such folly," according to Paine, "and shows us by comparison, the imperfection of our most refined inventions." Combining the philosophical notion of the perfectibility of man with the theological doctrine of the millenium, Paine affirms that "improvement and the world will expire together." The times of antiquity had greater vanity than the present, he states, "and so unwilling were our ancestors to descend from this mountain of perfection, that when any new discovery exceeded the common standard, the discoverer was believed to be in alliance with the devil."

With the same vigor with which he defends the present against the past, Paine repudiates the notion of Buffon and some other French philosophers that all plants and animals, including men, lose their strength and vitality when transplanted to the Western Hemisphere. Axiomatically Paine assures his readers, "Degeneracy is here almost a useless word." Ingeniously he completely turns around the notion of degeneration by affirming that it was vices imported from Europe which lost their vigor in the atmosphere of America, while the good qualities grew and thrived. "Those who are conversant with Europe," he affirms, "would be tempted to believe that even the air of the Atlantic disagrees with the constitution of foreign vices; if they survive the voyage, they either expire on their arrival, or linger away in an incurable consumption. There is a happy something in the climate of America, which disarms them of all their power both of infection and attraction." This doctrine of the salubrious environment of America and its topographical superiority over Europe was to become one of the dominant themes of *Common Sense*.

From the perspective of Paine's later theories of social welfare, the most relevant article in the *Pennsylvania Magazine* is a brief essay in the June issue bearing the pseudonym "Amicus.".

A recent biographer has revealed that during Paine's youth in the English town of Lewes he belonged to a group "convened regularly in order to administer grants to the needy, as well as to levy rates and provide for town needs such as roads and lighting."[9] It is only natural that Paine's concern for the relief of economic distress should continue in Philadelphia. Parallels in language and idea between the "Amicus" essay and Paine's later writing suggest that "Amicus" was another of his pseudonyms. In this brief essay, hardly more than a note, "Amicus" promises to contribute to a future issue of the *Pennsylvania Magazine* details of a plan to raise a fund for portioning off young people "with a reasonable sufficiency to begin the world with" and another fund "for the purpose of supporting us in our old age." These promised hints failed to appear in any subsequent number of the *Pennsylvania Magazine.* Perhaps the notion of public assistance for private needs was incompatible with the individualistic thinking of colonial America. Even such an outstanding humanitarian as Benjamin Franklin believed that "giving mankind a dependance on anything for support, in age or sickness, besides industry and frugality during youth and health, tends to flatter our natural indolence, to encourage idleness and prodigality, and thereby to promote and increase poverty."[10] A detailed plan to attain objectives very similar to those outlined by "Amicus," however, appeared in Paine's *Rights of Man* nearly two decades later. "It is easily seen," Paine remarks in the latter work, "that the poor are generally composed of large families of children, and old people unable to labor. If these two classes of people are provided for, the remedy will so far reach to the full extent of the case, that what remains will be incidental."[11] The rest of the chapter in which he announces this program unfolds the practical measures proposed to bring it about.

Seven years after *Rights of Man,* Paine refurbished his welfare scheme and announced it to the world in language almost identical to that of key phrases in the "Amicus" article. This duplication of language appears in the title of a pamphlet by Paine which in traditional eighteenth-century fashion summarizes the contents of the entire work: "*Agrarian justice, opposed to agrarian law, and to agrarian monopoly, being a plan for meliorating the condition of man, by creating in every nation, a national fund, to pay to every person, when arrived at the age of twenty-one years, the sum of fifteen pounds sterling, to enable him or her to begin the world! And also, ten pounds sterling per annum during life to every person now living of the age of fifty years, and to all others when they shall arrive at that age, to enable them to live in old age without wretchedness, and go decently out of the world.*"[12] The similarity of language is too close to be the result of coincidence alone. "Amicus" had also proposed joint funds for providing the young "with a reasonable sufficiency to begin the world with" and "for the purpose of supporting us in our old age."

The identification of Paine as "Amicus" indicates that when writing *Common Sense* he had at the back of his mind the social philosophy which he later unfolded in *Rights of Man,* and that it was not the French Revolution which released his progressive and humanitarian impulses, but that they had been in existence, although dormant, for many years. It suggests, moreover, that he did not proceed further to develop or publicize his social welfare schemes in the New World because the climate of opinion in colonial America, unreceptive to projects of social assistance, had prevented him from doing so. Political scientists have in recent years taken from Paine the distinction of being a pioneer in social planning by demonstrating that principles similar to those in *Agrarian Justice* had been expounded by European reformers in the two decades previous to it.[13] Taking account of the

"Amicus" proposal in 1775 restores to Paine his priority over these European authors as a proponent of government-sponsored social welfare schemes.

Paine's most recent editors have attributed to him an essay in the July issue of the *Pennsylvania Magazine* signed "A Lover of Peace," which vindicates defensive warfare against the Quaker opposition to the shedding of blood.[14] In a style resembling that of *Common Sense,* the author argues that political and spiritual freedom are intimately related and that active warfare may be necessary to acquire and retain either one. This essay cannot conclusively be attributed to Paine, but the probabilities of his authorship are high. "I am thus far a Quaker," he declares, "that I would gladly agree with all the world to lay aside the use of arms, and settle matters by negotiation; but unless the whole will, the matter ends, and I take up my musket and thank heaven he has put it in my power."

The essay is essentially an answer to a speech by Lord Sandwich in the House of Commons. According to Paine's interpretation, the British Lord has exhorted the royal troops to fight "not for the defence of their natural rights, not to repel the invasion or the insult of enemies, but on the vilest of all pretenses, gold." Sandwich had affirmed that the Americans would not fight back because of their religion or their cowardice: "they either *cannot* or *dare not* defend; their property is open to any one who has the courage to attack them." In essence, Paine in his essay accuses the English lord of maintaining that might makes right, and he argues that self-defense is the only protection of the peaceable part of mankind against vile opportunistic avarice. In *Common Sense* he similarly observes that "'Tis not in the power of Britain or of Europe to conquer America, if she doth not conquer herself by *delay* and *timidity.*"[15] As the "Lover of Peace," Paine invokes higher motives than the mere defense of property—he appeals to the inseparable grounds of political and religious liberty. "Political liberty is the visible pass which guards the religious," and conversely "spiritual freedom is the root of political liberty." Not above playing upon anti-Catholic prejudices, he cites the history of Mary Stuart to support his principle that "the popish world at this day by not knowing the full manifestation of spiritual freedom, enjoys but a shadow of political liberty." Although he does not directly accuse "the present government of popish principles," he asserts that it cannot "be clearly acquitted of popish practices." This is a clear foreshadowing of the implication in *Common Sense* that monarchical governments deliberately limit the enlightenment of their people, one of the inescapable inferences of the statement in that work that "monarchy in every instance is the popery of government."[16] The essay by "A Lover of Peace" was apparently one of the most widely read in the *Pennsylvania Magazine,* for the "Notes to Our Correspondents" section in the following month informed interested readers that offprints were to be obtained at "two coppers" each.

Paine's first publication in America under his own name consisted of a brief explanation of a process for making saltpeter to be used for ammunition. Signed jointly by himself and an officer in the Continental Army, Thomas Prior, it appeared in a newspaper, the *Pennsylvania Journal,* 22 November 1775. In the next issue Paine and Pryor added further details concerning their saltpeter experiments, beginning with a statement characteristic of Paine: "Nature, properly speaking, is the only Salt-Petre maker, and the process used by us, or any others, is only *to get* or *extract* it from the holes or corners, dirt and rubbish, in which she is pleased to hide it."[17] This comment embodies one of the themes uniting *Common Sense* and *Rights of Man,* the notion that science and politics rest on an identical foundation of natural law and that rational procedure in either area consists in discovering and following this natural law.

In the same issue of the *Pennsylvania Journal* which printed Paine's first communication on saltpeter, a letter appeared under the pseudonym "A Lover of Order" concerning the Second Continental Congress and the manner in which delegates to it should reflect the popular will. This letter foreshadows particular sections of *Common Sense* and, despite the conservative connotations of the pseudonym "A Lover of Order," suggests the policy of independence. The pen name "Lover of Order" is parallel to that of "Lover of Peace," which had appeared previously in the *Pennsylvania Magazine,* and like the previous pseudonym it attempts to gain the confidence of those holding opposite views from the author by appearing to share their attitudes. The essay by a "Lover of Order" has never been attributed to Paine, but parallel passages link it to *Common Sense,* passages which are much closer than those uniting *Common Sense* and the essay by "Lover of Peace."

The "Lover of Order" expressed his feelings during the period when the Continental Congress was in session but when the authority and responsibilities of that body were still ambiguous, as were the methods of selecting its delegates. In October, the regular election was held to choose members of the Pennsylvania Assembly, and in the following month the new Assembly selected nine delegates to the Continental Congress, including Franklin and John Dickinson. A committee of the Assembly thereupon issued a set of moderate instructions to the delegates, affirming in essence that since the problems and affairs of the Congress were hopelessly diverse it would be impractical for the committee to set forth the precise policies to which the delegates should adhere. But in a subsequent section completely in violation of this principle, the committee explicitly instructed the delegates to "dissent from, and utterly reject, any propositions, should such be made, that may cause, or lead to, a Separation from our Mother Country, or a Change of the Form of this Government." Paine, if he were the "Lover of Order," was indignant at this interdiction, which, he charged, was "couched in terms amounting to a command." He protested that the members of the House of Assembly had no authority over the delegates to the congress since this authority rested in the people whom the delegates represented. In Paine's words, "When I voted at the last Election for a representative in the House in which you now sit, I never meant to invest any of you with such a power, and I protest against your assuming it. The Delegates in Congress are not the Delegates of the *Assembly* but of the *People,*—of the Body at large. For convenience sake only, we at *present* consent to your nominating them; but we may as well be without Delegates if they must act solely under your influence, and thus circumstanced they can only set there as cyphers."[18] In *Common Sense* Paine makes exactly the same point by putting "as a question to those, who make a study of mankind, whether representation and election is not too great a power for one and the same body of men to possess."[19] In his newspaper article Paine based his protest on the illegality of the powers assumed by the Pennsylvania Assembly, but the major source of his opposition was the substance of the instructions it had issued, requiring the delegates to dissent from any proposition leading to a separation from England.

Paine emphasized the enormity of the Assembly's action by describing it as illegal even by English standards, a device enabling him to emphasize the rift between America and the mother country. "The Constitution of England, decayed, and complicated as it is, never suffers one House to instruct the other; neither doth it permit a person to sit in both Houses." Further, Paine expressed the hope that he would never see the day when the continent would be without a congress but that he would "in proper season . . . see a Congress chosen by the people—which may as easily be done as the choosing an Assembly; by which means not only every colony, but every part of it will be represented." To this theme of direct representation, Paine added that of continental unity as opposed to provincialism. As an individual, he wished that the delegates to Congress would "*lay aside all private interest and connection, and consider themselves not acting PROVINCIALLY but CONTINENTALLY, That as men, they will disregard all undue influence—and as Fathers, That they will think for Posterity.*" This is a foreshadowing of the warning in *Common Sense* that "the continental belt is too loosely buckled,"[20] and his reminder "that our strength is continental, not provincial."[21] It looks ahead, moreover, to his admonition in *Crisis* No. 1 that a "generous parent" would say, "If there must be trouble, let it be in my day, that my child may have peace."[22]

Paine's implied advocacy of independence did not pass unnoticed. His letter was denounced in a subsequent issue of the *Pennsylvania Journal* by a writer under the pseudonym "Pennsylvania Associator," who accused the "Lover of Order" of entertaining "the pernicious hope of seeing Great Britain and America in a state of separation" and of being "much more offended" with the substance or content of the instructions given to the delegates than with the Assembly for taking upon itself to issue instructions.[23] In the next issue of the *Pennsylvania Journal* another correspondent, "Independent Whig," accused the "Associator" of being "more offended with the 'Lover of Order's' latent inclination to independency, than with any other thing in his performance." Paine himself then answered the "Associator" by assuming in the issue of 6 December 1775 the identity of "A Continental Farmer," a pseudonym which probably reminded readers of John Dickinson's "Pennsylvania Farmer" while it stressed the theme of intercolonial unity. Paine's authorship may be established by a number of parallels to *Common Sense* as well as by an admission of the "Continental Farmer" himself that he was also the "Lover of Order." The "Associator" had suggested that the instructions issued by the House members were legitimate since they were excellent from the perspective of content. Paine replied that the excellence of the instructions—even if demonstrated—would make the procedure of accepting them all the more dangerous since "he who doth a *right thing,* not having a *right* to do so, may hereafter do a *wrong one* under sanction of the precedent." But beyond this, Paine affirmed that the instructions were not only illegal, but also deficient in both literary style and ideology.

As a literary composition, Paine derided the instructions as "mystical, contradictory, and absurd." "The preamble and the conclusion are in opposition. The head disowns the tail, the tail the head, and the body belongs to neither." The lack of precision and logic sufficiently convinced Paine that "cunning can never acquire the rectitude of wisdom." According to Paine's analysis, the preamble speaks of a great and difficult trust, alludes to the many reasons why the instructions could not be made precise, and suggests that new and unforeseen circumstances might arise; whereas the conclusion, flatly rejecting as it does any proposition leading to separation, shows that the degree of trust is not a prime consideration, incorporates positive instructions, and lays down a prejudgment of future circumstances.

Paine objected also that the language of the instructions ordering the rejection of any proposition which would "lead to a separation from our Mother Country" was "dark and equivocal" regardless of its superficially "absolute and positive air." Various delegates, according to Paine, might have differing notions about the circumstances which might lead to separation and thus vote against completely contrary measures. One might think that arms would lead to separation, another that petitioning might do so. "Another thinks that nothing will reconcile us like fighting it out, wherefore, he is for spirit and resolution. Another thinks that nothing will *lead to a separation of our animosities* like separating the dependence, wherefore in obedience to the same instruction, he votes point blank for independence; and makes his report to the house accordingly."

Mistakenly assuming that Joseph Galloway had drafted the instructions, Paine suggested that he had done so in order to win favor with the "Mother

Country," hoping to be rewarded with a governorship.[24] Paine argued, moreover, in absolute contradiction to the spirit of the Assembly's instructions, that most recent events in Pennsylvania were leading directly to independence. The instructions were, therefore, faulty by restraining the delegates' judgment, "for until every matter hath had a fair hearing, and all the circumstances thereof duly weighed and considered, no man can tell what he ought to do, or what ought to be done." In conclusion, Paine reverted to the theme of his preceding letter—the need for a continental rather than a provincial perspective. "I despise the narrow idea of acting PROVINCIALLY, and reprobate the little unworthy principle, conveyed in the following words, *'In behalf of this colony,'* and the more so, because by a late resolve, all Colony distinctions are to be laid aside. 'TIS THE AMERICAN CAUSE, THE AMERICAN CONGRESS, THE AMERICAN ARMY, &c. &c. Whom God preserve."

Paine, in *Common Sense,* repeated the essence of this criticism of the ambiguous and illogical language of the Assembly's instructions and the abuse of authority which this document represented, strong supporting evidence of his multiple identity as "A Lover of Peace," "A Lover of Order," and "A Continental Farmer." His comments in *Common Sense* concern the potential dangers implicit in the behavior of the House Assembly of Pennsylvania. Looking back upon "the unwarrantable stretch . . . which that house made in their last sitting, to gain an undue authority over the delegates of that province," he considered the maneuver as a warning to "the people at large, how they trust power out of their own hands." He charged that a "set of instructions for their delegates were put together, which in point of sense and business would have dishonoured a school-boy, and after being approved by a few, a very few, without doors, were carried into the house, and there passed *in behalf of the whole colony;* whereas, did the whole colony know with what ill will that house had entered on some necessary public measures, they would not hesitate a moment to think them unworthy of such a trust."[25]

Another parallel between the "Continental Farmer" and *Common Sense* is to be found in the valedictory phrases in both works. "A Continental Farmer" closes his letter after a reference to the Continental Congress with the pious invocation "Whom God preserve." In *Common Sense,* Paine ends a proposal for a national congress in the same liturgical style, "Whose peace and happiness, may God preserve." He likewise subscribes *Crisis* No. 3 as "Written this fourth year of the UNION, *which God preserve.*"

Despite the aggressive tone of Paine's politically inspired writings up to this point and the parallels to his later thought which they definitely possess, they reveal few signs that within a matter of weeks he would compose *Common Sense,* one of the most powerful political tracts in the history of the Anglo-Saxon peoples.

3

A Runaway Best Seller

Even though a survey of Paine's literary apprenticeship reveals that his political principles during this period of his life embodied a high degree of humanitarianism, such a survey gives no indication whatsoever of when he first conceived the notion of independence for the American colonies.

Indeed rumors that Paine originally opposed separation from Britain were circulated during the Revolution by John Witherspoon, a prominent Presbyterian clergyman and one of the signers of the Declaration of Independence. Witherspoon, who cherished serous literary aspirations of his own, was a frequent contributor to the *Pennsylvania Magazine.* It may be that his accusation that Paine lacked complete dedication to colonial freedom grew out of an unsatisfactory contributor-editor relationship. At any rate, when Paine in 1779 was being considered for the post of secretary to the Committee for Foreign Affairs of the Congress, Witherspoon opposed the nomination with slurs on Paine's loyalty. He alleged that when Paine "first came over he was on the other side, and had written pieces against the American cause; . . . afterwards . . . finding the tide of popularity run rapidly, he had turned about."[1]

In the aftermath to the Silas Deane affair, moreover, Paine was accused in an article in the Philadelphia press in the summer of 1779 of seeking to prolong the war. It was also suggested in this article that on his arrival in America he had at first vainly opposed the measures taken by the colonists "for public liberty and safety" and that he had suddenly, but insincerely, become a convert to the opposing side.[2] This line of attack was continued in another article maintaining that he had not changed from a Tory to a Whig until "some time after the commencement of hostilities" and that he had been discharged by his employer Aitken on account of his "inveterate hatred to every thing produced in favor of the liberty of these states."[3] Another newspaper published the following scurrilous dialogue

Who is an Englishman? Tom P——
Who was a Tory? Tom P——
Who maintains Tom P——? Nobody knows
Who is paid by the enemy? Nobody knows
Who best deserves it? Tom P——.[4]

These attacks constitute a well recognized and often-practiced technique of condemning one's enemy for one's own crimes. Paine's friend and political ally, the painter Charles Willson Peale, immediately rose to his defense by declaring from personal knowledge that Paine had "done more for our common cause than the world, who had only seen his publications, could know."[5]

Two years later when Colonel John Laurens was appointed as envoy extraordinary to France, Paine's nomination as secretary to accompany him was blocked by Witherspoon and two or three other similarly prejudiced members of Congress. At the end of the war, Paine affirmed that Witherspoon's opposition arose out of the publication of *Common Sense* and its author's "going a step beyond him in literary reputation." Witherspoon, according to Paine, "went so far as to tell Colonel Laurens, that he doubted my principles, *for that I did not join in the Cause till it was late.*"[6]

Benjamin Rush, who in later life came to dislike Paine for his religious ideas and consequently made no attempt to be complimentary in his reminiscences, not only does not bear out Witherspoon and the supporters of Deane, but testifies almost the opposite, that shortly after their first meeting Paine "realized the independence of the American Colonies upon Great Britain, and that he considered the measure as necessary to bring the war to a speedy and successful issue."[7] He implies that Paine had for some time recognized the appropriateness of independence, despite the "immense mass of prejudice and error relative to it" in the public mind.

Rush himself had been an early proponent of separation from Great Britain, but had not been willing to submit himself to public fury by revealing his own radical views. Apparently his medical practice had been almost ruined by adverse reaction to an antislavery pamphlet he had published a few years previously. He pointed out in conversation, however, that Paine "had nothing to fear from the popular odium" to which unorthodox opinions "might expose him, for he could live anywhere." In the same conversation, Rush explained that his own profession and connections tied him to Philadelphia, "where a great majority of the citizens . . . were hostile to a separation of our country from Great Britain," and thereby inhibited him from coming forward as "a pioneer in that important controversy." According to Rush, Paine read to him "every chapter of the proposed pamphlet as he composed." He intended to call it *Plain Truth,* but Rush suggested instead *Common Sense.* Rush reports in addition that after *Common Sense* had been completed, he advised Paine to show it to Franklin, David Rittenhouse, Samuel Adams, and James Wilson. Samuel Adams was in Philadelphia attending the meetings of the Continental Congress, and the other three were permanent residents of the city. Rush also affirms that Paine did show the manuscript to Franklin, who presumably struck out the passage, "A greater absurdity cannot be conceived of, than three millions of people running to their seacoast every time a ship arrives from London, to know what portion of liberty they should enjoy."[8] Franklin's participation is also alleged in a note in William Duane's edition of *Memoirs of . . . Benjamin Franklin* (Philadelphia, 1818). The writer of this note, probably Duane himself, claims that he had been told by Paine "that the suggestion of the papers Common Sense was made to him by Dr. Franklin," and "that one or two papers were revised by the doctor, but with very few alterations."[9]

It is doubtful that Paine showed Franklin any part of his manuscript, however, or even revealed that he was at work upon one, for in *Crisis* No. 3 he specifically states that, hoping to surprise Franklin, he had turned over his work to the press as fast as possible and had sent Franklin the first copy to be printed. More than a month after the appearance of the work in print, moreover, Franklin wrote to Gen. Charles Lee that Paine was "the reputed and, I think, the real author of 'Common Sense.'"[10] He would hardly have been this tentative had he known the facts of composition for certain. Paine himself says that David Rittenhouse, "a gentleman of known principles," was "one of the very few to whom the author of Common Sense showed some part thereof while in manuscript."[11]

A quarter of a century after its appearance, Paine publicly declared, "In my publications, I follow the rule I began with in 'Common Sense,' that is, to consult nobody, nor to let anybody see what I write till it appears publicly. Were I to do otherwise the case would be that between the timidity of some, who are so afraid of doing wrong, that they never do right, the puny judgment of others, and the despicable craft of preferring *expedient to right,* as if the world was a world of babies in leading strings, I should get forward with nothing."[12] This individualistic claim is plausible, revealing both Paine's undeniable independent cast of mind and his literary vanity. His perennial self-esteem probably kept him from seeking advice on any of his manuscripts. Even though we now know that he received payment from French diplomatic sources for writing some of his *Crisis* papers, he probably did not submit the text of even these commissioned works for approval before publishing them.

One cannot be sure exactly when Paine began thinking in terms of independence, but he says himself in *Common Sense* and several other places that the turning point in his thought was news of Lexington and Concord. His exact words: "No man was a warmer wisher for a reconciliation than myself, before the fatal nineteenth of April, 1775, but the moment the event of that day was made known, I rejected the hardened, sullen-tempered Pharaoh of England for ever."[13] In his "Forester" Letters, Paine maintained that even before this fateful day he had already made up his mind that the republican form of government was preferable to the monarchical, but that he had remained silent in order not to perplex his neighbors with his private opinions. Presumably he felt that the outbreak of war changed the nature of the society in which he was living and removed his scruple against speaking out.

In a letter to Franklin in May 1778, he indicated that he had not been exactly happy with the turn of events upon his arrival in America, even though these circumstances had afforded him the opportunity of promulgating his political notions. "I thought it very hard," he declared, "to have the country set on fire about my ears almost the moment I got into it."[14] Six months later he repeated the metaphor almost verbally in the passage of *Crisis* No. 7 in which he says that he had not expected to become either a soldier or an author. "When the country, into which I had just set my foot, was set on fire about my ears, it was time to stir."[15] At the war's end, moreover, in appealing to Congress for recognition and recompense of his services, he similarly declared, "Scarcely had I put my foot into the Country, but it was set on fire about my ears."[16] According to Rush, he remarked that he "was at a loss to know whether he was made for the times or the times made for him."[17]

In an autobiographical letter to Henry Laurens, President of Congress, in January 1779, Paine provides a somewhat fuller explanation of the birth of his sentiments concerning independence and a slightly later date for his first expression of them.[18] Here he says that in May 1775, he had written to his English friend George Lewis Scott, who had introduced him to Franklin, specifically declaring, "Surely the ministry are all mad; they never will be able to conquer America." Paine further informs Laurens that his actual decision to write *Common Sense* came as a result of the refusal of the British government to respond to the last petition of the Continental Congress. This intransigent action of the Crown, Paine declares, put it past doubt that the British were resolved upon total conquest, "on which I determined with myself to write the pamphlet."

In *Rights of Man,* Paine maintains that the smooth operation of affairs in the colonies after British control had been cut off demonstrated to him the superiority of government on a simpler plan, and he accordingly based *Common Sense* on this principle. "During the suspension of the old governments in America," he states, "both prior to and at the breaking out of hostilities, I was struck with the order and decorum with which everything was conducted; and impressed with the idea, that a little more than what society naturally performed, was all the government that was necessary, and that monarchy and aristocracy were frauds and impositions upon mankind."[19] Paine discusses the origins of *Common Sense* even in *Age of Reason,* further proof of the importance he attached to his earlier work. He declares that "I saw, or at least I thought I saw, a vast scene opening itself to the world in the affairs of America; and it appeared to me that unless the Americans changed the plan they were then pursuing with respect to the government of England and declared themselves independent, they would not only involve themselves in a multiplicity of new difficulties, but shut out the prospect that was then offering itself to mankind through their means."[20]

Shortly before his death, Paine affirmed that he had realized the deficiencies of monarchy even before embarking for America. "It was," he declared, "the absurd expression of a mere John Bull in England, about the year 1773, that first caused me to turn my mind to systems of government. In speaking of the then King of Prussia, called the Great Frederick, he said, *'He is the right sort of man for a king for he has a deal of the devil in him.'* This set me to think if a system of government could not exist that did not require the devil, and I succeeded without any help from anybody."[21]

Paine had originally intended to publish *Common Sense* as a series of letters in the newspapers.[22] Since his previous literary experience had been with periodicals, this is quite understandable. Perhaps this intention explains why the work is divided into four separate parts. Paine changed his mind about the periodical publication of separate letters, however, when he realized "the impossibility of getting them generally inserted." Presumably this means that they would have been accepted by some Philadelphia paper such as the *Pennsylvania Journal,* but there could be no guarantee that they would be reprinted by other papers throughout the colonies—as were most of Paine's later *Crisis* papers and several of his other pieces. There is no reason for believing that he decided against periodical publication in order to obtain literary continuity, for even in its pamphlet form, continuity is one of the stylistic qualities notably lacking in *Common Sense.*

Paine described the circumstances of publication in an open letter printed 27 January 1776 in the *Pennsylvania Evening Post.* Here he affirmed that one of his friends, "a gentleman of the city," arranged with the printer Robert Bell for the work to be produced as a pamphlet. In a later letter, 21 April 1783, he states that it was on the recommendation of Rush that he entrusted his manuscript to Bell. This letter was designed to furnish Congress with an example from his own experience to illustrate the necessity of passing a copyright law which was then being considered. The relevant section, never before published, is printed below.[23]

> On the recommendation of Doctor Rush I gave the Manuscript Copy of the pamphlet Common Sense to a certain printer of this city, and as I did not intend to have any trouble with the work after it was printed, and had conceived it proper towards supporting the reputation of the principles the pamphlet contained, that no part of the profits arising from the sale, should come into my hands. I therefore, gave one half the clear profits to the printer over and above his charge of printing—and the other half, I gave by an order under my own hand, to Mr. Thomas Prior and Mr. Joseph Dean both of this city, to be received by them and disposed of to any public purpose they might chuse, the particular thing mentioned was to purchase woolen mittens for the soldiers then going on the Quebec Expedition—The printer not only kept the *whole* profits of

the first edition, which he still retains but in the course of two or three days printed a second edition, and on my expressing some surprize at his doing it without my knowledge, as I intended making additions to it, he very bluntly told me—I had no business with it.

In his communication in the *Pennsylvania Evening Post,* Paine indicated that when news arrived in Philadelphia of the repulse of colonial troops at Quebec on 31 December, the death of General Montgomery and the wounding of Arnold, Paine arranged to have his own half of the profits donated "for the purpose of purchasing mittens for the troops ordered on that cold campaign" and he secured Bell's written promise for payment of this portion to two members of the Continental Army. Bell charged two shillings for a single copy and eighteen shillings for a dozen.[24]

The date of publication has traditionally been given as Saturday, 10 January 1776, but the discovery of an advertisement in the *Pennsylvania Evening Post* for Friday, 9 January, has caused some doubt. The advertisement reads in part:

> This day was published, and is now selling by Robert Bell, in Third-street (price two shillings) COMMON SENSE addressed to the INHABITANTS OF AMERICA.

This advertisement in itself does not demonstrate that the pamphlet appeared on Friday the ninth rather than Saturday the tenth, for periodicals in colonial America often appeared after the date printed on them. This is unlike twentieth-century American newspapers, which are frequently sold on the eve of the date which they bear. The April number of the *Pennsylvania Magazine,* for example, could not have been printed prior to 19 April since it refers internally to the battles of Concord and Lexington, which had taken place on that date. At present, therefore, there is insufficient evidence to consider either 9 or 10 January as the conclusive date for the publication of *Common Sense.*

After the entire edition of one thousand copies sold out in a week (an enormous number for the time and place), Bell told an incredulous Paine that there were no profits whatsoever. Paine thought there should have been sixty pounds, not including expenses. This is probably an unreasonable expectation. If Bell had received the retail price of two shillings for each copy, his gross receipts would have been one hundred pounds, and if he had averaged only one shilling, his gross would have been only fifty pounds. Still it is hard to believe that there were no profits at all.

Paine thereupon severed his relations with Bell—or thought he was doing so—in order to handle his own financing. He contracted with two other printers to print six thousand more copies and gave them to another bookseller, W. & T. Bradford, at 8½ d. each with the understanding that they would be sold at one shilling, a minimal price to assure maximum circulation. To this edition, Paine added an Appendix and an Address to the Quakers. Bell in the meantime revealed that he had no intention of parting with a valuable literary property once he had it in his hands, and he advertised "a new Edition" of *Common Sense* in the *Pennsylvania Evening Post* (20 and 23 January). On 27 January he announced in the same newspaper that it was now off the press.

This edition, which may be called the second, is notable by revealing on the title page "Written by an Englishman." From the contemporary perspective, this information was useful in giving some clue to the authorship of the pamphlet. Conjectures had naturally been made, and Franklin, Rush, Samuel Adams, and John Adams had all been considered as possible authors. The ascription to an Englishman narrowed the field considerably. From a twentieth-century perspective, the fact that Paine himself did not apply the phrase "Written by an Englishman" to his work but that it was added by another hand suggests that he did not consider himself as belonging in a different class from the other citizens of Philadelphia. There is absolutely nothing in the text of *Common Sense,* moreover, which reveals the antecedents of the author. In an introduction to later editions Paine affirmed that the only relevant matter is "the *Doctrine itself,* not the Man." He, nevertheless, added that "he is unconnected with any Party, and under no sort of Influence public or private, but the influence of reason and principle." Certainly Paine was not writing from the point of view of an Englishman, and criticism is off the mark which argues that vehement denunciation of Great Britain from an Englishman would have had greater force than the same doctrine from a native American. Paine did maintain, however, that his past knowledge of English politics combined with his present experience of the American situation gave him an unusual advantage. "In writing *Common Sense,*" he observed at the conclusion of the war, "however easy it may appear now it is over, the necessity of knowing both countries was so material, that no person who had reflected only on one could have sufficiently succeeded in a proposition for their political separation; and though that pamphlet has much to say respecting England, it has never been attacked in that country on the score of error or mistake, which scarcely would have happened had the writer known only one side of the water."[25] At the time Paine made this observation, October 1783, it is true that no English complaints of factual errors had been raised, but, as we shall see, at least one major discrepancy was later alleged.

In between Bell's announcement of a "new edition" on 20 and 23 January and its appearance on 27 January, now described on the title page as a "second edition," Paine through an advertisement by Bradford in the same newspaper, *Pennsylvania Evening Post,* 25 January, advised the public that Bell's new edition was being printed without the author's consent and that it did not include the additional material in Bradford's. Bell continued the war of advertisements some days later by maintaining that it was he who had severed relations with the ostensible author because of the latter's "capricious disposition," "dishonest malevolence," and "reprehensible cunning." Bell based these charges on the author's reducing "a price which himself had a share in making," and his attempting "to destroy the reputation of his own first edition, by advertising intended additions before his earliest and best customers had time to read what they had so very lately purchased."[26] Since Bell had nothing to offer comparable to Bradford's added materials of an *Appendix* and an *Address to the . . . Quakers,* he concentrated on appearance and predicted that Bradford's edition because of its "smallness of print and scantiness of paper" would resemble his own second edition "as much as a British shilling in size and value resembles a British half crown."[27]

During these newspaper polemics Paine carefully maintained his anonymity, being uniformly described in Bradford's advertisement merely as "the author." Bell ridiculed this posture in a further blast against him as a "self-conceited Englishman" in the *Pennsylvania Evening Post,* of 1 February. "You say you wanted to remain unknown (prudence dictated the thought in speculation) but, in practice, yourself telling it in every beerhouse, gives the direct LIE to the assertor of such a falsehood."[28] This sentence indicates that Bell probably knew that Paine was the author of *Common Sense* from the very beginning. Paine's name was actually published for the first time in connection with the controversy over independence a few weeks later, on 30 March 1776, to be precise.[29] Bell's sentence is also significant as a public reference to Paine's fondness for alcohol almost at the outset of his career in America. It is true that Aitken, who had been Paine's employer in the previous year, later asserted that Paine never wrote without the stimulus of brandy, but Aitken did not divulge this detail until shortly before his own death. At this time he told Isaiah Thomas, a famous Massachusetts printer, that the material Paine "penned from the inspiration of the brandy, was perfectly fit for the press without any alteration, or correction."[30] Bell's accusation that Paine, while drinking, freely acknowledged his paternity of *Common Sense* is quite credible in view of Paine's later career, in which he continually boasted of his literary achievements.

A poem, *Sketches of the Times,* published in 1804, brings together both aspects of Paine's personality, his fondness for drink and his vanity.[31]

> Paine takes a sling, and gives a lift.
> For though, when sober, Tom is dull,
> Stupid, and filthy as a gull,
> Yet give him brandy, and the elf,
> Will talk all night *about himself;*
> And whilst his patron stands amaz'd,

Waiting to hear himself be-prais'd,
The drunken sot does nought but cry,
And sing, and write, of Mr. I.

Bradford's edition, which may be called the third, containing Paine's *Appendix* and *Address to the . . . Quakers,* appeared on February 14 and was advertised the same day in Bradford's newspaper the *Pennsylvania Journal.* The new materials were said to have increased the work upwards of one third in size. As soon as it appeared, Bell brought out a new collection which he entitled *Large Additions to Common Sense.* The only part in it which was by Paine, however, consisted of the *Appendix* and the *Address to the People called Quakers,* which Bell had pirated from Bradford's edition. The other six pieces, taken from newspapers, consisted of the following:

1. The American Patriot's Prayer [a poem later erroneously attributed to Paine for many years]
2. American Independancy defended, by Candidus
3. The Propriety of Independence, by Demophilus
4. A review of the American Contest, with some Strictures on the King's Speech. Addressed to all Parents in the Thirteen United Colonies, by a Friend to Posterity and Mankind
5. Letter to Lord Dartmouth, by an English American
6. Observations on Lord North's Conciliatory Plan, by Sincerus[32]

Bradford, probably at Paine's instigation, warned prospective buyers in later advertisements for his own edition that these were "Pieces taken out of News Papers, and not written by the Author of COMMON SENSE." But Bell, nevertheless, seemed to be offering the greater bargain since his edition contained everything in that of Bradford and these six pieces in addition, and each publisher now charged the same price of one shilling. Still, it was *Common Sense* which was the great attraction to potential customers, not the appended pieces, for none of the latter has aroused any important measure of interest either during the Revolution or later.

Bell had the last word in the newspaper controversy, publishing a further blast in the *Pennsylvania Evening Post* on 22 February, still in the form of a paid advertisement. Referring to Paine as "the envious Mr. ANONYMOUS," Bell accuses him of once more creeping "into the field to ROB and to DESTROY the reputation of authors, whose literary abilities OUT-SHINE his, as far as the blaze of a torch OUT-SHINETH the glimmering of a candle." Bell also suggests that *Common Sense* is based on borrowed materials and portrays Paine as "the would-be-author" and as a "go-between" or intermediary between the writers of original materials and the bookseller. Bell gives his own version of the beginning of his relations with Paine. "When the work was at a stand for want of a courageous Typographer, I was then recommended by a gentleman nearly in the following words, 'There is Bell, who is a Republican Printer, give it to him, and I will answer for his courage to print IT.'"

According to Bell, he had done fifty pounds worth of work and had received only twenty for it, and it was through his "knowledge in business" that "the pamphlet was made respectable." Bell maintained that as soon as Paine realized "the success of the sale and of the sentiment," he "formed the disgraceful intention to circumvent the real bookseller" by publishing the Bradford edition. Bell, thereupon, to protect his own interest "determined to out-jockey if possible" by producing the enlarged third edition. Paine, according to Bell, "immediately fell into a fit of ill-natured, ostentatious, and pretended generosity, [donating his profits to buy mittens for the troops] which would most certainly have carried him to Bedlam or a p——n, had he not in the midst of his debasement recollected it was not yet impossible for him to arise again, by touching public money, and to attain to be the MASSANELLO among authors and booksellers, at least for one DAY."[33]

In April 1776 Paine estimated that 120,000 copies of *Common Sense* had been printed and sold ("Forester" No. 2), and three years later he raised the figure to 150,000.[34] If we make allowances for Paine's ample self-esteem and tendency to exaggerate, we are probably safe in assuming that by the end of the eighteenth century at least 100,000 copies had been printed. Other evidence indicates that the work had a more extensive reception than that represented by the actual number of copies sold. Apart from the probability of a high multiple readership of each printed copy, there were handwritten copies and summaries made and circulated.[35] Also the *Connecticut Courant* printed the whole of *Common Sense* in its issue for 19 February 1776, and there may have been other newspapers which did the same. A French traveler in America, Brissot de Warville, specifically attributed the tremendous influence of Paine's work to its circulation in newspapers. In his words, "*Common Sense* had such a prodigious effect only because it was a hundred times cited and reproduced in these gazettes, devoured with avidity by the artisan, the farmer, and the man of all classes."[36] The best way of conceiving the vogue of *Common Sense* is to compare its publishing history with that of the other most important pamphlets of the Revolution. Thomas Randolph Adams, who has done exactly that, states that *Common Sense* "was a runaway best seller" and that "the next ranking pamphlet went through less than half as many American editions."[37]

Even the theater, limited as it was in Philadelphia during 1776, echoed Paine's message. A five-act play produced in February or March of that year, *The Fall of British Tyranny; or, American Liberty Triumphant,* refers to *Common Sense* in both its Prologue and its Epilogue.

> Blest Continent, while groaning nations round

> Bend to the servile yoke, ignobly bound,
> May ye be free—nor ever be opprest
> By murd'ring tyrants, but a land of rest!
> What say ye to't? what says the audience?
> Methinks I hear some whisper COMMON SENSE.
> [From the Prologue]
>
> Let's act in earnest, not with vain pretense,
> Adopt the language of sound COMMON SENSE,
> And with one voice proclaim INDEPENDENCE
> [From the Epilogue]

The preface to the printed edition of *The Fall of British Tyranny,* which was published in Philadelphia, with subsequent editions in Boston and Providence, ends on an encouraging note: "Happy then for America in these fluctuating times, she is not without her Solomons, who see the necessity of heark'ning to reason, and listening to the voice of COMMON SENSE."[38] Paine himself later called the press the "tongue of the world,"[39] but it was *Common Sense* which first gave him proof of its power and range.

4
Theories of Government

The meaning of the title *Common Sense* may perhaps now seem obvious, and even mentioning the subject may appear banal, but one of the published answers to Paine's pamphlet brings up two different interpretations: that the author intends to convey "that his Opinion is the Common Sense of all America, or that all those who do not think with him are destitute of Common Sense."[1] This is a valid distinction between common sense as a belief shared by a majority of people in a given culture (consensus or general opinion) and common sense as the mental processes by which an opinion is reached unhindered by prejudice or other obstacles (sound reasoning). The second seems to be the signification which Paine intends. He uses the phrase in this connection in the following sentence from the pamphlet itself: "Common sense will tell us, that the power which hath endeavoured to subdue us, is of all others, the most improper to defend us."[2]

The phrase *common sense* has a long history in its Latin form, *sensus communis,* and it was thus used early in the eighteenth century in the signification of sound reasoning by an early deist, Lord Shaftesbury, as the subtitle of one of the sections of his *Characteristics* (1711). Shaftesbury explains that the phrase may mean not only a standard of rational behavior, but also a "sense of public weal, and of the common interest; love of the community of society, natural affection, humanity, obligingness, or that sort of civility which rises from a just sense of the common rights of mankind, and the natural equality there is among those of the same species."[3] After Shaftesbury, the term was given further currency in France by Buffier and in Scotland by Thomas Reid in his *Inquiry into the Human Mind on the Principles of Common Sense* (1764), an attack on the skeptical conclusions which Berkeley and Hume had drawn concerning the reality of human perception. As a result, a number of like-minded writers in Scotland appropriated the methods and vocabulary of common sense to oppose the skeptical philosophy of the age.[4] For the sophisticated reader in Paine's times, therefore, the notion of common sense was associated with a protest against metaphysical subtleties and intellectual concepts out of touch with reality. Paine was in no way original in applying the phrase *common sense* to government and society, for it had thus appeared as part of the title of an anonymous English work concerning political conditions in America, *Common Sense: in nine conferences . . . tracing the several causes of the present contests between the mother country and her American subjects* (London: J. Dodsley, 1775).[5]

The advertisements for the earliest editions of Paine's *Common Sense,* including the first, incorporated two lines from James Thomson which were also used as an epigraph in the pamphlet itself.

> Man knows no master save creating HEAVEN,
> Or such as choice and common good ordain.

These lines come from Part 4 of *Liberty* (lines 636–37). They serve to summarize the antimonarchical theme of Paine's argument and to make it respectable by associating it with one of Britain's most admired poets. The passage from Thomson concerns the bold Britons, "careless sons of Nature," who, taught by the Druids, resisted the invasions of the conquering Romans. The sentiments in this section of Thomson's poem correspond not only to Paine's antimonarchical theme but also to his individual portrayal of the state of nature, a concept which Paine adopted from a major tradition in the political thought of his century.

In a short Introduction to his pamphlet, Paine makes the somewhat grandiloquent declaration that "the cause of America is in a great measure the cause of all mankind." He may have taken a hint from the first of John Dickinson's Farmer's *Letters,* which affirm in reference to the individual colonies that "the cause of one is the cause of all." The concept was so striking that even Franklin took up Paine's phrase shortly after arriving in France on his mission to enlist the French government in the war against the British. In a letter to Samuel Cooper on 1 May 1777, he reports, "'tis a Common Observation here, that our Cause is *the Cause of all Mankind,* and that we are fighting for their Liberty in defending our own." It is somewhat strange that Franklin should associate this sentiment with France rather than the colonies in writing back to Cooper in New England. Franklin must have encountered it originally in *Common Sense,* for, as we shall show in a subsequent chapter, he read Paine's pamphlet in Philadelphia shortly after its appearance.

Paine opens the main part of his work with the blunt statement that society and government, although traditionally considered identical, are actually separate entities with different origins. In a radical pronouncement, incorporating the fundamental tenet of anarchistic philosophy, he next affirms that society is good and government bad, although softening the shock by admitting that government, bad as it is, is a necessary evil. If all men acted according to an interior conscience unerringly pointing to right behavior, his argument runs, no exterior supervision would be necessary, but since men do not so conduct themselves, they voluntarily accept the sanctions of government. They surrender part of their "property," which seems to mean for Paine freedom of action as well as material possessions, in order to guarantee the safe proprietorship of the rest.

According to Paine, "government, like dress, is the badge of lost innocence; the palaces of kings are built on the ruins of the bowers of paradise."[6] Here he clearly associates the Christian doctrine of the fall of man with popular eighteenth-century notions of primitivism. The ignoble fig leaf, symbol of Adam's transgression, is made to serve as well for the institution of government. The more complex the government, Paine suggests, the greater the amount of evil or rebellion against the divine will. Paine is not far away from Madison's later observation in *The Federalist* No. 51 that government is "the greatest of all reflections on human nature." "If angels were to govern men," Madison suggests, "neither external nor internal controls on government would be necessary."[7]

To show the origin of society, Paine asks his readers to assume "a small number of persons settled in some sequestered part of the earth" symbolizing "the first peopling of any country, or of the world." He does not follow tradition to the letter by using the term "state of nature" to describe this situation, but speaks of the "state of natural liberty." Since one man in this condition could not erect a house or create any substantial amenities through his single unaided efforts, individuals have learned to cooperate in small groups. "Four or five united would be able to raise a tolerable dwelling in the midst of a wilderness, but one man might labour out the common period of life without accomplishing any thing; when he had felled his timber he could not remove it, nor erect it after it was removed; hunger in the mean time would urge him to quit his work, and every different want call him a different way."[8] Paine's theory of cooperative effort in building a house is in keeping with the spirit of Voltaire, who, unlike Paine, opposed primitivism and like Paine considered the modern world much to be preferred over the ancient. In a dialogue affirming the superiority of the moderns, Voltaire argues that cooperation and mutual aid are the products of instinct and judgment, themselves "elder sons of nature." As an example, he cites two old cardinals, both dying of hunger, who come together under a plum tree: "they would instinctively help each other to climb up the tree in order to pick the plums."[9] Paine affirms that as long as individuals remain perfectly just in their mutual relationships a primitive society such as he has described could remain without government, but the influence of vice—an inevitable accompaniment of human character—renders some form of control necessary.

To illustrate the origin of government, Paine calls once more upon the imagination of his readers, asking them to conceive of a group of people recently joined in society coming together under a tree to form a parliament. Every man in this miniature state will at first have a voice in lawmaking, and public esteem will be the only sanction for enforcement. But as this primitive settlement grows in size, its population will be too numerous and its territory too extended for every individual to participate personally in the governing body. Representatives will then be elected to express the will of the various parts of the society. Shifting almost imperceptibly in his perspective from what presumably had taken place in primitive times to what should take place ideally, Paine then affirms that elections should be held at frequent intervals to assure the regular return of representatives to learn the will of their constituents. And this frequent interchange between individuals and representatives, rather than a mystique of kingship, provides "the strength of government and the happiness of the governed." Paine is not saying, as many of his critics later improperly maintained, that all social groups started out with a compact; instead he is saying that ideally all of them should have.

After this relatively pragmatic prescription, Paine returns to theory by describing government as "a mode rendered necessary by the inability of moral virtue to govern the world" and its "design and end" as the attaining of "freedom and security." He then somewhat irrelevantly informs us that his notion of government is based on a general principle in nature, "that the more simple any thing is, the less liable it is to be disordered." The one thing that can be said in favor of absolute governments, he argues in an aside, is that they are simple.

Although Paine later became known as the foremost exponent in the Anglo-Saxon world of the theory of the rights of man, he significantly says nothing in *Common Sense* about rights as a reason for entering into a system of government. His only motives are "freedom and security." This is in sharp contrast to the Declaration of Independence, which specifically affirms that governments are instituted in order to secure the inalienable rights of "Life, Liberty, and the Pursuit of Happiness."

There seems to be some element of contradiction in Paine's portrayal of man in the state of nature as requiring government to check his perversity and viciousness, but at the same time being impelled into society by rational processes and virtuous sentiments. Had Paine himself been challenged to explain this presumed inconsistency he might have contended that man in the state of nature and the earliest stages of society was guided by his rational and virtuous instincts and that his vicious and selfish impulses developed as society grew more complex and, therefore, required the restraints of government. Such an explanation still does not reconcile Paine's formal definition of government as a system of restraint "to supply the defect or moral virtue" with his description of the parliamentary process in which government appears merely as a means of carrying out the general will. The inconsistency cannot be completely resolved.

A similar contradiction is implicit in Richard Hooker's *Laws of Ecclesiastical Polity*, 1593, a work which Paine probably did not know, but which was quoted frequently by Locke and was accepted as the ultimate authority in the Anglo-Saxon protestant milieu in which Paine matured. Although attributing man's uniting himself into society to "a natural inclination, whereby all men desire sociable life and fellowship" (bd. 1, chap. 10, sec. 1), Hooker still believes that all civil laws are improper "unless presuming the will of man to be inwardly obstinate, rebellious, and averse from all obedience unto the sacred laws of his nature; in a word, unless presuming man to be in regard of his depraved mind little better than a wild beast" (bk. 1, chap. 10, sec. 2).

Another major inconsistency in *Common Sense* concerns the power and efficacy of human thought. Although Paine assumes that reason strikes the mind with instantaneous and overwhelming force, it does not occur to him that the arguments of his opponents—often completely at variance with his own—were also arrived at through use of the rational powers. In regard to his theory of the origin and rise of government, he apodictically declares, "however our eyes may be dazzled with show, or our ears deceived by sound; however prejudice may warp our wills, or interest darken our understanding, the simple voice of nature and of reason will say, 'tis right."[10] Yet several pages later he affirms with equal certainty, "It is but seldom that our first thoughts are truly correct."[11]

Paine's fundamental principle that government and society are separate entities also seems to be contradicted in a newspaper letter comprised in one of his *Crisis* series (3 April 1782) proclaiming that "Government and the people do not in America constitute distinct bodies."[12] This assertion he bases on the operation in America of the principle of common interest. "Members of Congress, members of Assembly, or Council, or by any other name they may be called," he says, "are only a selected part of the people. They are the representatives of majesty, but not majesty itself. That dignity exists inherently in the universal multitude, and, though it may be delegated, cannot be alienated. Their estates and property are subject to the same taxation with those they represent, and there is nothing they can do, that will not equally affect themselves as well as others." This doctrine, we shall see in a later chapter, has some resemblance to Rousseau's theory in the *Social Contract* that the sovereign is only a collective being and that sovereignty is merely the exercise of the general will. Paine presumably believed that he was free from contradiction since he meant that all governments except that of America were at that time distinct from society, and that only in America was government made up of the people. Obviously, however, if government and society are merged in any particular country or situation, they cannot as an abstract principle be declared to be separate and distinct entities.

Paine greatly expanded his concept of organized society in a letter to Henry Laurens published in the New York *Public Advertiser*, 30 May 1807, and never reprinted until now. In this letter Paine accepts the principles of the Physiocrats, which he may have absorbed during the French Revolution through direct contact with idéologues such as Condorcet or earlier through the intermediary influence of Franklin. If these Physiocratic principles came from Franklin, they may have already been in Paine's mind at the time of the composition of *Common Sense.* Of special interest in his letter which follows is his reference to himself as a "Farmer of thoughts."

> . . . The first useful class of citizens are the farmers and cultivators. These may be called citizens of the first necessity, because every thing comes originally from the earth.
>
> After these follow the various orders of manufacturers and mechanics of every kind. These differ from the first class in this particular, that they contribute to the accommodation rather than to the first necessities of life.
>
> Next follow those called merchants and shopkeepers. These are occasionally convenient but not important. They produce nothing themselves as the two first classes do, but employ their time in exchanging one thing for another and living by the profits.
>
> . . . I believe . . . I am of the first class. I am a *Farmer of thoughts,* and as all the crops I raise I give away, I please myself with making you a present of the thoughts in this letter.

In 1778 Paine set forth a similar ranking of the means of obtaining wealth, in which he included some methods even less productive than those of merchants and shopkeepers. Here his categories consisted of cultivation, trade, and professional employments. Both agriculture and trade, he indicated, could "neither be too large, too numerous, or too extensive," but professional employments may be all three. As an example, he cited authors and lawyers, both of whom are capable of doing either harm or good.[13] Paine's conception of the economic structure of society has no direct connection with his theories of the formation of government in America, but it seems to support the principle that society and government are separate rather than the contrary.

Paine next in *Common Sense* turns his attention to what he calls "the so much boasted constitution of England."[14] This is a verbal echo of a sentence in one of the few books cited in his pamphlet, a well known political tract by James Burgh, entitled *Political Disquisitions; or, An Enquiry into Public Errors, Defects and Abuses. Illustrated by, and Established upon Facts and Remarks Extracted from a Variety of Authors, Ancient and Modern* (London, 1774–75). In this book, Burgh, after a vigorous diatribe against rotten boroughs and political venality, raises the question, "Is this the universally admired and universally envied *British* constitution?"[15] This verbal echo is stressed not to reveal a textual similarity—although it is certainly a significant one—but to show that Paine was not, despite the assertions of several historians, the first author to subject the British constitution to hostile analysis.[16] Indeed Burgh presents a far more comprehensive and devastating attack on the British constitution than does Paine. The latter's only direct reference to the *Political Disquisitions* comes in a later section of *Common Sense* in which he states merely that "those who would fully understand of what great consequence a large and equal representation is to a state" should read that work. Paine, in addition to exposing some of the weaknesses of the British constitution, devised an acceptable substitute. He may have been following in Burgh's footsteps, but in doing so he constructed an intellectual highway for his contemporaries.

According to Paine's analysis, the king and the House of Lords represent the remains of monarchical and aristocratical (i.e., oligarchical) tyranny respectively, and the Commons represents new republican materials, on the virtue of which "depends the freedom of England." Without reference to Montesquieu, Paine derides the theory of checks and balances as farcical: the notion of "an *union* of three powers, reciprocally *checking* each other," he proclaims, is either meaningless or self-contradictory. The system alternately supposes one branch wiser than the other, "a mere absurdity."

Paine repudiates the explanation, which he attributes to "some writers," that the king and the people are two entities, with the House of Lords working in behalf of the king and the Commons in behalf of the people. Not only does this structure represent "a house divided against itself," in Old Testament terminology, but it leaves unexplained the fundamental question of how the king came by his power, "which the people are afraid to trust, and always obliged to check." In this section, Paine anticipates one of the major objections to the democratic system made in the nineteenth century by Alexis de Tocqueville, that the notion of a mixed government is illusory and that one or the other of the three powers will inevitably gain the upper hand. Paine, with imagery drawn from natural science, insisted that no matter what importance is ascribed to balance in theory, "the greater weight will always carry up the less, and as all the wheels of a machine are put in motion by one, it only remains to know which power in the constitution has the most weight, for that will govern." In England, he adds, "the crown is this overbearing part." Tocqueville makes exactly the same point: "Accurately speaking, there is no such thing as a *mixed government,* in the sense usually given to that word, because in all communities some one principle of action may be discovered which preponderates over the others."[17] At the time he was writing, Tocqueville described England as an aristocratic state. This passage occurs in a section of his work devoted to "the tyranny of the majority." This phrase, with its full connotative strength, had also been prefigured in a similar phrase of Paine's, not in *Common Sense,* but in his later *Dissertations of Government; The Affairs of the*

Bank; and Paper Money (1786). Here he condemns "the despotism of numbers, for despotism may be more effectually acted by many over a few, than by one man over all."[18]

Paine changed his mind about the value of checks and balances, later accepting them as valid devices in regard to the American constitution of 1787. Even in *Common Sense,* it was not because he felt that men were like angels and, therefore, needed no control upon political agencies that he objected to mutual restraints. His point was simply that a system of checks and balances was inefficient and self-defeating. This is also one of the reasons why he preferred a unicameral legislature over a bicameral one.

In *Common Sense,* Paine admits that individuals are safer in England than in some other countries and the Crown less oppressive, but he points out that "the *will* of the king is as much the *law* of the land in Britain as in France," with the difference that in England it is expressed in the more formidable form of an act of Parliament.[19] If the English Crown is less oppressive than Turkish absolutism, Paine continues, this condition is a result of the constitution or temper of the people, not of the constitution of the state. To most Anglo-Saxons as well as to Paine, this would have seemed to be a plausible explanation. One of his earlier opponents was to ask sardonically, however, if the moderate temper of the English people furnishes their well being, why did it not "afford them superior safety" during the tyrannical reigns of Richard III and Henry VIII?[20]

Paine introduces his second section, entitled "Of Monarchy and Hereditary Succession," with the axiom that men were originally brought forth as equals in the order of creation, and consequently he admits as valid distinctions only those between male and female and between good and bad, describing the first as distinctions of nature, the second, as those of heaven. The artificial distinction in monarchical countries between kings and subjects, Paine insists, is based upon neither nature nor religion. Because of his theological background (he may even have been a kind of itinerant preacher in England), it is quite possible that Paine was consciously or unconsciously echoing the dichotomies in Galatians 3:28, which says: "There is neither Jew nor Greek; there is neither slave nor freeman; there is neither male nor female; you are all one in Christ Jesus."

To justify his affirmation that the distinction between king and subjects is not supported by religion, an important area in the thinking of the pious majority of his readers, Paine proceeds with an original interpretation of the Christian Scriptures. The earliest generations in the scriptural record were happy ones, he asserts; the people of these times had no kings, but instead patriarchs, who presided over a quiet and rural society. Their government was a kind of republic "administered by a judge and the elders of the tribes."[21] Kings, he maintains, were an invention of the heathens, not accepted by the Jews until almost three thousand years after the creation of the world, according to the Mosaic chronology. Paine declares that the Scriptures not only disapprove of government by kings but even denounce monarchy as a sin for the Jews. Accusing royalist writers of glossing over the passages which condemn the autocratic system, Paine proposes to elucidate the scriptural ban against monarchy. This he does by means of an original interpretation of history as found in the first book of Samuel. According to his exposition, the children of Israel, elated by Gideon's victory over the Midianites, proposed to make him a hereditary monarch, but Gideon not only declined the honor, but denied that the Israelites had a right to bestow it: "I will not rule over you, the Lord shall rule over you." More than a century later, the children of Israel, under the influence of the idolatrous heathens, asked Samuel to provide them with a king so that they could emulate other nations. Samuel, troubled and displeased by their perversity, prayed to God for guidance. The Lord thereupon consoled Samuel by observing that "they have not rejected thee, but they have rejected me, that I should not reign over them." The Lord instructed Samuel to warn the Israelites in detail of the baleful consequences they would suffer if they should persist in their perverse desire for a king, evils such as the impressing of their sons for military service, the seizure of one-tenth of their national product as tribute, and, in general, oppression, expense, luxury, bribery, corruption, and favoritism. The people refused to listen to Samuel's warning, but persisted in their obstinate resolve to have a king. Samuel threatened to call upon the Lord to send as a punishment thunder and rain to destroy their harvest; they still refused to listen and the Lord accordingly subjected them to the threatened disasters. Finally, the people recognized their folly and admitted "we have added unto our sins this evil, to ask a king." Either the Scripture is false, Paine concludes, or "the Almighty hath entered here his protest against monarchical government." For this reason, Paine suggests, kings have been in league with priests in "popish countries" in withholding the Scripture from the public. This gives him the opportunity for a cogent phrase, "monarchy in every instance is the popery of government."[22]

Paine next turns to the related evil of hereditary succession, which he refutes by natural reason instead of scriptural authority. Here he reintroduces the principle that all men are created equal, but treats it as an axiom rather than a step in a formal argument. After an introductory allusion, he affirms that the principle of equality by extension precludes any man's having the right at birth to set up his own family in perpetual preference to all others, no matter what title to personal honors he may have earned. The principle also restrains a bestower of public honors from the "power to give away the right of posterity," since such a power would place succeeding generations in danger of being governed by a rogue or a fool. All reasoning justifying hereditary power, Paine adds, presupposes that kingship originated from the attaining of honor; whereas, only too probably its source was of a completely contrary character, that is, plunder, depredation, or chicanery. Later kings, Paine speculates, may have been accepted merely to avoid disorders among rival candidates. The hereditary principle which was thus originally submitted to as a convenience was subsequently claimed as a right. As a single example from English history, which comprises many bad and very few good kings, Paine cites William the Conqueror, who had absolutely nothing of "divinity" in his career, as he landed from a foreign country with a horde of "armed banditti" and set himself up against the will of the natives.[23]

Paine then returns to speculation concerning the ultimate origin of kings, dogmatically affirming that only three explanations are possible: that they had been established by lot, by election, or by usurpation; Paine conveniently ignores the view taken by Robert Filmer in the seventeenth century and still held by some of Paine's contemporaries that kings had originated through divine appointment. Logically Paine is required to take notice of the divine right theory since his immediately preceding pages appeal extensively to the authority of Scripture. His failing to do so emphasizes the fact that his actual method consists in large measure of affirming as being already proved one of the points which is in the process of being debated. Having established his three categories, Paine next asserts that if the first king were appointed by either lot or election, a precedent has been established for selecting subsequent kings by the same method and hereditary succession is thus firmly excluded. Usurpation Paine portrays as so dishonorable that nobody at all would defend it, and he then points out that the succession of the English monarchy is based on the usurpation of William the Conqueror, "a French bastard."

Ingeniously joining arguments based on the state of nature with those based on the Judeo-Christian Scriptures, Paine draws a parallel between divine right and original sin, a relationship which is suggested in his earlier reference to government, as being, like dress, "the badge of lost innocence." At first glance, the parallel between divine right and original sin would seem to support hereditary monarchy, particularly for any readers who might believe in the literal truth of the Scriptures and also be disposed to accept the political arguments of the patriarchal tradition (which even today are considered by some commentators as strong in themselves as well as being respected for their great antiquity).[24] A traditionalist of this type (fundamentalist in religion, royalist in politics) would argue that in Adam all sinned; Adam was the father of mankind; therefore, all men are tainted with Adam's sin and properly subjected to the dynasties of temporal rulers succeeding him. Paine's contrary handling of the parallel is based on reasoning no sounder than this. He also accepts the premise that in Adam all sinned, but argues as his next step that since sin is evil, anything inherited from Adam, including monarchy, is also evil and should be shunned. In a sense, Paine sets up a "political Adam," to use a phrase which Paine himself later used against Burke in a different context.[25] "Dishonorable rank! inglorious connection!" are his words.[26] Paine does not even recognize the problem of explaining how man can cast off hereditary monarchy if he is still inexorably bound by original sin.

Paine proceeds with a series of somewhat disjointed practical objections to the institution of hereditary monarchy. He observes that kings through their superior position became insolent or oppressive and are not even aware of the true interests of mankind. A throne may also be inherited by minors of very tender age or by senile men. Paine is not willing to grant even the most "plausible plea" in favor of kings, which is that they preserve order and protect a nation from civil strife. The history of England, according to Paine's perspective, has been devastated by eight civil wars and nineteen rebellions during the reigns of thirty kings and two minors. After reviewing this apparently irrefutable evidence of the havoc which the kings of England have wrought, Paine concludes by portraying the reigning monarch, George III, as having few functions to exercise which are both legitimate and useful. In absolute monarchies, he observes, kings control all civil and military affairs, but in countries where monarchs are not absolute they have no business to occupy them.

Paine admits to some bewilderment over how the government of England should be described: he is not willing to call it a republic, despite the powers held by the House of Commons. He points out that the king, because of various perquisites and the right of appointing many crucial officers, is able to engross or dominate the Commons and magnify his own powers. The English king, in Paine's final appraisal, is neither a judge nor a general, and he does little else except declare war and give away places. Paine does not attempt to explain why these functions are objectionable or whether they should be exercised by other bodies in the state. Instead he concludes rhetorically, "A pretty business indeed for a man to be allowed eight hundred thousand sterling a year for, and worshipped into the bargain! Of more worth is one honest man to society, and in the sight of God, than all the crowned ruffians that ever lived."[27]

In both *Common Sense* and later works, Paine ferociously attacks the institution of monarchy, but in his personal opinion he did not always consider it to be the worst of the three parts of a mixed government, that is, one comprising king, lords, and commons. In a private letter to Thomas Walker of Rotherham, 16 January 1789, he affirmed that "tho' the people exercise a power in making a King and in electing a house of Commons, they exercise none in the creation or dissolution of a House of Peers—and that therefore the monarchy is nearer related to the people than the Peers are." In the same letter he maintains that aristocracy "of all forms of government is the worst."[28] This was not a unique opinion at the time. The poet Charles Churchill, for example, a member of the Wilkes faction, declaimed in a well-known poem, "The Farewell," (1764):

> Let not, what other ills assail,
> A damned ARISTOCRACY prevail.
>
> [11. 363–64]

Paine was a reader of Churchill, and he quoted another of the latter's poems as an epigraph to *Crisis* No. 2.

It has never been sufficiently emphasized that Paine says very little against the evils of hereditary aristocracy in *Common Sense.* Nearly all of his fulminations against the hereditary principle apply to the monarch alone. One of the reasons for his concentration on kingship may be that no titled aristocracy of any kind existed in the colonies, and the only members of the nobility to be encountered there were occasional English and European travelers and British royal governors, not all of whom were titled.[29]

But even though it be granted that Paine leaves the British aristocracy relatively untouched, this does not mean that people of wealth and social pretensions in the colonies remained insensitive to his ringing defense of political equality and to his denunciation of privilege. John Adams shrewdly made note of this class reaction. In reference to North Carolina, he wrote in April 1776, "The Gentry are very rich, and the common People very poor. This inequality of Property, gives an Aristocratical Turn to all their Proceedings, and occasions a strong Aversion in their Patricians to Common Sense."[30] This distaste for the doctrines of political equality led many Tories to remain loyal to the Crown throughout the struggle and some to leave the country at its conclusion. It is obvious, on the other hand, that some men of wealth and position felt that their commercial interests were being infringed by legal restrictions, and they naturally applauded Paine's forthright appeals for autonomy. The prevailing opinion among the disaffected minds in the colonies, however, was that Parliament rather than the king was responsible for their grievances. The colonists consistently pledged loyalty and devotion to George III and in public messages right up to the moment of the Declaration of Independence called upon royal authority to protect their rights against the heavy hands of Parliament. Paine's strategy, therefore, was designed to draw attention to the evils emanating from the king rather than to those associated with Parliament. Since most of his fellow colonists were already fully disillusioned with the behavior of Parliament, his best means of increasing a sentiment of independence was to widen the area of responsibility for colonial woes to include the king.

Here his strategy was quite different from that of Franklin, who until the outbreak of hostilities considered Parliament exclusively responsible for the repressive measures taken against the colonies. Franklin developed, moreover, a private theory that the King, not Parliament, was the only coordinating link between the colonies. From a long and thorough consideration of the subject, he wrote to his son in 1773, "I am indeed of opinion that the Parliament has no right to make any law whatever, binding on the colonies, that the King, and not the King, Lords, and Commons collectively is their sovereign; and that the King, with their respective Parliaments, is their only legislator."[31] This theory that only the king possessed authority over the colonies had been enunciated as early as 1766 by Richard Bland in a tract published in Williamsburg, Virginia, and developed by James Wilson in 1774.[32]

For Franklin, the real villain in the plight of the colonies was Parliament, and in condemning the hereditary principle he specifically attacked the House of Lords. As the aftermath of a visit to that body during a session when a proposal by Pitt for withdrawing troops from Boston had been defeated, Franklin scornfully observed of hereditary legislators that there would be more propriety "in having (as in some University of Germany) Hereditary Professors of Mathematicks."[33] *Common Sense* has not even a hint of this scorn of the Lords. Even *Rights of Man* bears harder upon a hereditary monarchy than upon a hereditary legislature. Paine seems to have adopted Franklin's witticism, however, by declaring in the latter work a hereditary governor to be as inconsistent as a hereditary author. "I know not," he says, "whether Homer or Euclid had sons; but I will venture an opinion, that if they had, and had left their works unfinished, those sons could not have completed them."[34]

The absence of reflections upon royal governors or other titled officials in *Common Sense* shows that personal grievances were not at the root of the dissatisfaction which Paine sought to create in the minds of his readers. Indeed, he touches on surprisingly few of the restrictive acts of Parliament which traditional historians tells us were major causes of the Revolution, the duties on tea, glass, and paper and the prohibition of various manufactures. He dismisses the subject by declaring that "the taking up arms, merely to enforce the repeal of a pecuniary law, seems as unwarrantable by the divine law, and as repugnant to human feelings, as the taking up arms to enforce obedience thereto."[35] Paine's targets were the system of hereditary monarchy in the abstract and the personage of George III in particular.

He realized that the Parliament was already so unpopular in the colonies that little further need be said against it. It was the theory of the king as the constitutional link holding the colonies to the empire which kept the desire for independence in check. Instead of attacking this political theory, however, Paine adopted the much more radical device of denouncing the institution of monarchy itself. This was the startling originality of *Common Sense* and one of the reasons for its phenomenal success in molding public opinion.

5
The State of American Affairs

The first two parts of *Common Sense,* which together constitute somewhat less than a third of the entire work, comprise most of its theory. Judged by resulting polemics in the thirteen colonies and repercussions in other nations in the world, these parts were also considered the most significant. The third and fourth parts, entitled respectively "Thoughts on the Present State of American Affairs" and "Of the Present State of America, with Some Miscellaneous Reflections," are concerned with practical matters requiring immediate action, but still not the bread and butter considerations of the average colonist. These two parts are scarcely distinguished from each other.

Paine himself underscores the transition from abstract reasoning to practical considerations by affirming that in Part 3 he offers "nothing more than simple facts, plain arguments and common sense." Although superficially parts 3 and 4 seem to lack order and coherence, they are not actually as miscellaneous as they appear. The third part consists primarily of a demonstration of the disadvantages of reconciliation and of the weaknesses inherent in the structure of the British Empire; the fourth part stresses the urgency of immediate action in proclaiming independence.

The theme of time emerges as the predominant leitmotif in both parts. At the outset of Part 3, Paine reports an admittedly apocryphal comment by the late Henry Pelham, former chancellor of the exchequer. Pelham allegedly defended the weak and unsubstantial measures he had instituted by saying, "They will last my time." Paine denounces this selfish and defeatest attitude as fatal and unmanly. Several paragraphs later he urges his readers collectively and symbolically to "take our children in our hand, and fix our station a few years farther into life."[1] In *Crisis* No. 1, to expose the ignominy of preferring present comforts at the cost of sacrificing posterity, he uses the same image of the dependent small child. Here he shifts the scene to describe an American Tory, standing at his door holding "as pretty a child in his hand . . . as I ever saw," and uttering the ignoble words, "Well! give me peace in my day."[2] This utterance is probably as apocryphal as Pelham's. Paine uses both attitudes as symbols of unworthy temporizing, which he successfully derogates as criminal.

Paine insists that the fundamental problems facing his readers are not temporary nor are they confined to the American colonies. In his words, "'Tis not the affair of a city, a county, a province, or a kingdom; but of a continent—of at least one-eighth part of the habitable globe. 'Tis not the concern of a day, a year, or an age; posterity are virtually involved in the contest, and will be more or less affected even to the end of time by the proceedings now."[3] Then in a dramatic reversal of perspective, shifting from the future to the present, he affirms, "Now is the seed-time of continental union, faith and honor." Later in the work he again uses the biblical metaphor of "seed-time" to refer to the formation of good habits in the youth of nations as well as individuals.[4] The relationship which Paine brands as temporary is the authoritarian control of Great Britain over America, which he predicts must sooner or later come to an end.[5] That which is called "the present constitution," Paine declares, has no stability. Those parents who live in America, among whom Paine rhetorically includes himself, "can have no joy, knowing that *this government* is not sufficiently lasting to insure anything which we may bequeath to posterity." And touching on one of the most important principles later to be developed in *Rights of Man,* he argues, "as we are running the next generation into debt, we ought to do the work of it, otherwise we use them meanly and pitifully."[6] This statement is a precursor of an argument developed in several of Paine's later writings that no generation has the right to control subsequent ones or, in Paine's own words, to govern "beyond the grave."[7]

As Paine uses the perspective of time, he portrays the future as inevitably fatal to British control of America, and the present as the opportunity for America to forge its own destiny. In his words, "'Tis not in the power of Britain or of Europe to conquer America, if she doth not conquer herself by *delay* and *timidity.* The present winter is worth an age if rightly employed, but if lost or neglected the whole continent will partake of the misfortune."[8]

For the most part Paine relies on argument and logical reasoning, but occasionally he appeals to the feelings of his readers, for example, when he depicts the small child trustfully holding the hand of her father. His outstanding emotional passage concerns the sufferings of the people of Boston which had been brought upon them by the Boston Port Bill and the destruction by General Howe of one hundred of their houses for use as firewood. Paine introduces this section by observing that many people cannot sympathize with the pain of others unless they witness suffering in person. "It is the good fortune of many to live distant from the scene of present sorrow; the evil is not sufficiently brought to their doors to make *them* feel the precariousness with which all American property is possessed. But let our imaginations transport us a few moments to Boston; that seat of wretchedness will teach us wisdom, and instruct us forever to renounce a power in whom we can have no trust."[9]

Paine thereupon unfavorably contrasts men of dull sensibilities with those of natural feelings. It is the "men of passive tempers" who overlook the offenses of Great Britain and call for the renewal of friendship; whereas those who experience the normal "passions and feelings of mankind" commiserate with the inhabitants of Boston. Paine asks a series of rhetorical questions designed to shake from their torpor all those still not sufficiently aroused by British atrocities. "Hath your house been burnt? Hath you property been destroyed before your face? Are your wife and children destitute of a bed to lie on, or bread to live on? Have you lost a parent or child by their hands, and yourself the ruined and wretched survivor?" Any man who could answer these questions affirmatively and still fraternize with the British has, according to Paine, "the heart of a coward, and the spirit of a sycophant." Denying that he is exaggerating matters, artificially inflaming passions, or exhibiting horrors to provoke a spirit of revenge, Paine states that he is simply bringing the actual state of affairs into contact with "those feelings and affections which nature justifies, and without which we should be incapable of discharging the social duties of life."[10] He is seeking to rouse his readers "from fatal and unmanly slumbers."

Paine's emphasis on feeling is related to a trend in British moral philosophy during the preceding hundred years to vindicate the affections. The movement originated with latitudinarian clergymen of the late seventeenth century, acquired respectability with Shaftesbury's *Characteristics* and Hutcheson's *Essay on . . . the Passions,* and spread out into imaginative literature with such novels as Henry MacKenzie's *The Man of Feeling,* Sterne's *A Sentimental Journey,* and Goldsmith's *The Vicar of Wakefield.* It is almost certain that Paine had read the last two novels, but there is no evidence that he was acquainted with the more formal psychological expositions of Shaftesbury or Hutcheson. The tradition of sentimentalism was strong throughout the eighteenth century, and it could easily have penetrated his literary awareness through periodical essays similar to one signed "Cupid and Hymen" which had appeared in the *Pennsylvania Magazine.* In *Common Sense* all of Paine's emphasis on feelings is upon the benevolent affections—he later specifically rejects the opposing ones; "I am not induced," he says, "by motives of pride, party, or resentment."[11]

One of the widespread attitudes which Paine had to destroy was that of faith in the power and efficiency of the British Empire. Most Americans as well as Englishmen felt both pride and a sense of security in belonging to Britain's worldwide administrative network, or as Franklin called it, "that fine and noble Chinese vase."[12] Paine attributed this pride in the Empire to "ancient prejudices and . . . superstition." The argument had been advanced that the "united strength of Britain and the colonies" enabled them in conjunction to bid defiance to the world. Paine retorted that the issue of war could never be predicted with a certainty and that Americans would never send masses of its inhabitants to foreign wars. Their interest was not in setting the world at defiance, but in trading peacefully with all nations.

Paine refuted another line of reasoning which maintained that since America had done well in the past under British rule a continuation of the relationship was requisite for the future. "I have heard it asserted by some," Paine remarks, "that as America hath flourished under her former connexion with Great-Britain, the same connexion is necessary towards her future happiness, and will always have the same effect. Nothing can be more fallacious than this kind of argument. We may as well assert that because a child has thrived upon milk, that it is never to have meat, or that the first twenty years of our lives is to become a precedent for the next twenty."[13] This metaphor had been used and developed even more extensively by a writer in the *Pennsylvania Packet* six months previously. This author not only compares the growth of the American colonies to the ripening process from childhood to maturity, but also, like Paine, rejects the opinion that happiness under one condition of life is a necessary prescription for its continuance under another.

> New systems of government advance gradually towards perfection. Man may be free and happy without knowing in what freedom and happiness consist. It is a misfortune to think too highly of a nation as well as of individuals, in as much as we are often led thereby to copy their imperfections along with their excellencies. This hath been too much the case in our attachment to Great Britain. In our veneration for her constitution and laws, we have lost sight of those evils which now press down her liberties and spread desolation and slavery through every part of the empire. We thrived upon her wholesome milk during our infancy. She then enjoyed a sound constitution. I will not say that it is high time we should be taken from her breasts, but I will say, that she has played the harlot in her old age, and that if we continue to press them too closely, we shall extract nothing from them but disease and death.[14]

Paine goes to much greater lengths than this author, however, to demolish the image of Britain as the parent country of America, perhaps in order to take advantage of his previous sentimental passages describing a father holding a little child by the hand. The phrase "*parent* or *mother country,*" Paine asserts, has been "jesuitically adopted by the king and his parasites, with a low papistical design of gaining an unfair bias on the credulous weakness of our minds." Paine derides the image for its absolute inappropriateness by declaring that "even brutes do not devour their young, nor savages make war upon their families."[15] A New York loyalist in replying to *Common Sense* indignantly pictured this attack on Britain as comparable to the behavior of a "rash, froward stripling, who should call his mother a d—mn—d b——ch, swear he had no relation to her, and attempt to knock her down."[16]

After affirming that America had now come of age and could take care of herself, Paine would not even admit that the past British connection had been necessary, but argued that America's capacity for producing food for European markets would have in itself guaranteed its prosperity. Whatever protection Britain had afforded, Paine contended, had been provided through interest, not attachment, and the military campaigns which had taken place in America had been against the enemies of Britain, not those of America.

For Great Britain, the European continent consisted of past and potential enemies; for Paine it represented potential friends to America. He repudiated the opinion that the colonies had "no relationship to each other but through the parent country," by denying forthrightly that England should be considered their sole progenitor. "Europe, and not England," he declared, "is the parent country of America."[17] Maintaining that not even one-third of the inhabitants of Pennsylvania were of English descent, he branded references to England as the single mother country as "false, selfish, narrow, and ungenerous."

In rejecting the theory of ethnic solidarity, Paine discoursed on human nature in general, ignoring for the moment the burning question of British domination. In his opinion, people recognize a kinship in their common national origins only when they find themselves in a foreign environment.

> It is pleasant to observe by what regular gradations we surmount the force of local prejudice, as we enlarge our acquaintance with the world. A man born in any town in England divided into parishes, will naturally associate most with his fellow-parishioners (because their interests in many cases will be common) and distinguish him by the name of *neighbour;* if he meet him but a few miles from home, he drops the narrow idea of a street, and salutes him by the name of *townsman;* if he travel out of the county, and meet him in any other, he forgets the minor divisions of street and town, and calls him *countryman, i.e. countyman;* but if in their foreign excursions they should associate in France or any other part of *Europe,* their local remembrance would be enlarged into that of *Englishmen.* And by a just parity or reasoning, all Europeans meeting in America, or any other quarter of the globe, are *countrymen;* for England, Holland, Germany, or Sweden, when compared with the whole, stand in the same places on the larger scale, which the divisions of street, town, and county do on the smaller ones; distinctions too limited for continental minds.[18]

A similar passage describing social relations in a gradually expanding perspective is to be found in Bernard Mandeville's *Fable of the Bees,* published more than fifty years earlier. "Two Londoners, whose business oblige them not to have any commerce together, may know, see, and pass by one another every day upon the Exchange, with not much greater civility than bulls would: let them meet at Bristol, they will pull off their hats, and on the least opportunity enter into conversation, and be glad of one another's company. When French, English, and Dutch, meet in China, or any other Pagan country, being all Europeans, they look upon one another as countrymen, and, if no passion interferes, will feel a natural propensity to love one another."[19]

Paine and Mandeville seem to have the same objective of demonstrating that people recognize their common origins only in the surroundings of an unfamiliar geographical setting. But this similarity is merely superficial. Mandeville's primary concern is to refute the notion that men are inherently drawn to each other through social benevolence. Paine is not at all concerned with this notion in this section of *Common Sense,* and, if anything, the theory of government which he develops in his opening pages actually tends to support the notion of benevolent instincts, in opposition to Mandeville. In dealing with the widening circle of social relations, Paine is rejecting the notion of nationality or kinship based on territorial boundaries, a notion completely irrelevant to Mandeville's argument. It is possible—indeed highly probable—that Paine had read *The Fable of the Bees,* and it may be that he had subconscious memories of the passage concerning national identities, but there is no reason for assuming that he is imitating it in *Common Sense.*

Even though Paine regards the continent of Europe rather than the island of England as the natural link between the New World and the Old, he rejects, a few paragraphs later, the prospect of forming alliances, diplomatic or military, with the European continent, warning against the continual wars and power struggles which are there fomented: "Europe is too thickly planted with kingdoms to be long at peace." Paine's main argument is that "any submission to, or dependence on, Great Britain, tends directly to involve this continent in European wars and quarrels."[20] Paine's corollary principle as seen from the perspective of subsequent American history, however, is far more important, that is, the view that since Europe is the market for the American produce, "we ought to form no partial connection with any part of it." This is, of course, a clear statement of the doctrine of isolation, or the policy of noninvolvement in the political affairs of Europe. It was expressed by Paine in *Common Sense* almost a quarter of a century before Washington's Farewell Address, the document with which isolationism has traditionally been associated. Indeed Paine preached the doctrine even before the United States had become a political entity able to isolate itself from anyone. This section contains the germ of a concept later to be expressed in the *Crisis* and in *Rights of Man* that no nations or peoples in the world are destined by nature to be either enemies or friends to each other.[21]

The British Empire, Paine further maintained, was no more efficient in operation than legitimate in origin. It could not do justice to the needs of America, and it could not dispose of weighty and intricate business because of the great distance separating the colonies and the metropole. Paine's actual words are "if they cannot conquer us they cannot govern us," but the reverse seems to fit his argument better, that is, "if they cannot govern us they cannot conquer us." Paine ridiculed the lack of efficiency in being always required to run "three or four thousand miles with a tale or a petition, which, when obtained, requires five or six more to explain it in."[22] This sentence is closely related to the one which Rush alleges was in the manuscript copy of *Common Sense,* but which was omitted in the printed version, "A greater absurdity cannot be conceived of, than three millions of people running to their seacoast every time a ship arrives from London, to know what portion of liberty they should enjoy." In the published version, Paine found the element of absurdity "in supposing a continent to be perpetually governed by an island." He drew a parallel with the world of science, observing that since in nature a satellite is never larger than its primary planet, England and America must belong to different systems. Even in Paine's day, this must have seemed one of the weakest points in his argument since cities, relatively small in geographical area, have traditionally exercised control over large empires. Weak also is Paine's companion principle that "even the distance at which the Almighty hath placed England and America is a strong and natural proof that the authority of the one over the other, was never the design of heaven. Propinquity has seldom been considered a requirement for political control nor distance a reason against it.

Further developing the concept of divine providence—a concept which in the eighteenth century was as much deistical as Christian—Paine observes that the "Reformation was preceded by the discovery of America: As if the Almighty graciously meant to open a sanctuary to the persecuted in future years, when home should afford neither friendship nor safety." Paine is here touching on a notion of the privileged status of America which later scholarship has described by such terms as exceptionalism, historical uniqueness, and millenialism. The doctrine itself, however, is not exclusive to American thought. Campanella, in the late Italian Renaissance, suggested in his utopia, *City of the Sun,* that the Spanish conquered the New World in order that all nations could be gathered together under Christian law.[23] Paine's exact words echo the later affirmation of Jonathan Edwards in *Some Thoughts concerning the Present Revival of Religion in New England* that "America was discovered about the time of the Reformation, or but little before: which Reformation was the first thing that God did toward the glorious renovation of the world, after it had sunk into the depths of darkness and ruin under the great antichristian apostasy. So that as soon as this new world is (as it were) created and stands forth in view, God presently goes about doing some great thing to make way for the introduction of the church's latter day glory, that is to have its first seat in, and is to take its rise from that new world."[24] In Edwards, this doctrine of divine intervention is one hundred percent theological; in Paine it is theological with political applications.

Many other seventeenth- and eighteenth-century clergymen believed that God had specifically appointed the discovery and exploration of

America as stages in a carefully devised plan for humanity. Cotton Mather, for example, in his *Magnalia Christi Americana* portrayed the "*American Strand*" as the arena in which "Divine Providence hath *Irradiated* an Indian Wilderness." Somewhat earlier, John Winthrop set forth possible *Reasons to be considered for justifieing the undertakers of the intended Plantation in New England.* After portraying the corruption and desolation of the church in Europe, he queried, "whoe knowes, but that God hath provided this place to be a refuge for many whom he meanes to save out of the generall calamity."[25] A quarter of a century after *Common Sense,* David Humphreys, the first American poet to attain any degree of international celebrity, expressed the millenial notion in the advertisement to his poem "On the Future Glory of the United States of America." In words combining Paine's patriotic fervor with millenial theology, Humphreys suggested that "America, after having been concealed for so many ages from the rest of the world, was probably discovered, in the maturity of time to become the theatre for displaying the illustrious designs of Providence, in its dispensations to the human race."[26] Paine did not necessarily accept all the ramifications of millenialism, "rising glory," and *translatio studii,* but each of these notions is encompassed in his declaration in *Common Sense* that America is a privileged land, especially marked by providence "as a sanctuary to the persecuted" and an asylum for freedom.

In developing his theory of inherent differences between America and Europe, Paine reinforces his appeal to natural forces. "It is repugnant to reason," he affirms, "to the universal order of things, to all examples from former ages, to suppose that this continent can long remain subject to any external power. . . . Nature has deserted the connection, and art cannot supply her place." Paine crystallizes his opposition to the restoration of former conditions by means of a quotation from Milton, "Never can true reconcilement grow where wounds of deadly hate have pierced so deep." Strange to say, not a single one of Paine's editors or commentators on his works until this day has identified this quotation. Probably since Paine printed the passage as prose, it has universally been assumed that it comes from one of Milton's political tracts, and the task of locating it has seemed too arduous for the rewards involved. Actually the quotation comes from *Paradise Lost* (4. 98–99) and is part of a speech by Satan exhorting his followers against resubmission to God. In a sense it is somewhat anomalous for Paine to cite as bulwarking his original arguments against reconciliation with Britain the words of Satan opposing reconciliation with the forces of good. The contemporary opponents of *Common Sense* failed to take advantage of the opportunity to portray Paine as a spokesman for Satan, perhaps because he might have then retorted that Milton's Satan is purely imaginary and that it is possible for evil characters to express truths in their utterances.

The situation of the colonics, as Paine portrays it, however, is not quite parallel to that of Satan and God. In *Paradise Lost* it is the rebel Satan who rejects reconciliation because of his own festering wounds of hatred; whereas in *Common Sense,* it is England, the ruling power, rather than America, the subject, which is tormented by rancor and bitterness. Kings, according to Paine, are confirmed in their vanity and obstinancy by having petitions repeatedly offered to them, and this circumstance in itself contributes to their becoming absolute. As examples, he cites the kings of Denmark and Sweden, referring to the ill-fated Charles XII of Sweden and to Frederick IV of Denmark, characters whom he may have encountered in Voltaire's *History of Charles XII,* a work which seems to be reflected also in a passage of *The Crisis.*[27]

Paine continues to stress the concept of time as he reveals how "the massacre at Lexington" brought about a change in his personal attitude from one of seeking reconciliation to one pursuing independence. In April 1775, he had "rejected the hardened, sullen-tempered Pharaoh of England for ever."[28] From an intercolonial perspective, he argues, the sacrifices and expenditures in life and property already made have been too great to justify reconciliation or the acceptance of administrative reforms. Even the removal of North or the whole Ministry would be an inadequate return for the millions already expended, and the same principle exists for the repeal of punitive acts of Parliament. " 'Tis as great a folly to pay a Bunker-hill price for law as for land."[29] Since fighting had been going on for months, the goal to be attained had to be in proportion to the sacrifice involved.

Even though some form of reconciliation were to take place, Paine insists, America would be ruined in the process. In such an event the king, who would retain a negative over all American laws, would continue in his resolve to allow no legislation except that which suited his purpose. Paine himself brings forth the anticipated reply to this argument, that the king has a negative as well over all laws made in England, but Paine declines to rest his refutation on the grounds of the absurdity of monarchy as an institution, grounds which he had fully considered in his previous theoretical section. He maintains instead that it is the geographical situation which requires the monarch's despotism to be turned against America and which aggravates his opposition to its prosperity. According to this reasoning, it would be contrary to the king's interest to oppose legislation strengthening the defenses of England, but he would have no reason not to veto similar measures for America. At the same time Paine warns the colonists against any apparent signs of moderation in the king, such as his repealing harsh acts. This would represent an attempt to "accomplish by craft and subtlety, in the long run, what he cannot do by force and violence in the short one."

The best terms which the colonists could hope to obtain through reconciliation, Paine continues, would represent merely a temporary arrangement, and such an interim period before eventual independence would be "unsettled and unpromising." The people as a whole would not respect a government which could not keep order, and eventually some part would break out in open rebellion. Having suggested that a civil war might erupt in a single colony, Paine is forced to settle fears that the same kind of internal turmoil could break out if the colonies were independent. He argues that they have already manifested "a spirit of good order and obedience to continental government," and that since they are equals among equals one colony will not strive for superiority over another. As illustration he observes that the republics of Europe, that is, Holland and Switzerland, are always in a condition of peace.[30]

In the next section, Paine presents a formula for the structure of an American republic. He offers this plan for government, so he says, to enlighten those people who have hesitated to accept the notion of independence merely because they do not know how a new state should be organized. It may be that an underlying reason was his dissatisfaction with the authoritarian manner in which the Pennsylvania Assembly had issued instructions to its delegates to the Continental Congress, a dissatisfaction reflected in his essay as "A Lover of Order." Paine's proposals are simple, and they clearly favor the popular elements of society, particularly a provision for a single, democratically elected legislature, a provision which repelled men of property and conservative instincts. John Adams, for example, forthwith published a pamphlet of his own, *Thoughts on Government,* primarily to set forth the superiority of a bicameral structure.

Paine proposes that each colony have an annual assembly presided over by a president and that its business be entirely domestic and subject to the authority of a continental body, the congress. The latter, he suggests, should be chosen by a wide electorate, each colony being divided for the purpose into a convenient number of districts. Each colony would through this method send at least thirty representatives to the congress. For the selection of a president of this congress, Paine proposes a combination of lottery and election to assure that the presidency would pass in turn to a resident of each of the colonies: the first colony to be so honored would be selected by a lottery, and the presidency would pass in subsequent congresses to the other colonies in turn, each time the choice being determined by lot; the colonies from which a president had already been taken would be omitted in each consecutive drawing until all thirteen had been covered. The lottery would decide merely the colony of each president, but the individual president would be selected by an election in which all the delegates to the congress would vote. All laws passed by this congress would require a three-fifths majority. According to Paine, anyone who would "promote discord, under a government so equally formed as this, would have joined Lucifer in his revolt."

The element in this scheme which seemed most outlandish to Paine's contemporaries was the large number of delegates he proposed, thirty for each colony. One advocate of reconciliation derisively declared, "I have such an aversion to titles and pensions that I would not be one of the three hundred and ninety commissioners, on the plan of the writer of the piece called Common Sense, for all the money that has been made in America since the commencement of the unhappy differences."[31]

The proposal for combining a lottery with election in the selection of a president, although unorthodox in the twentieth century, would probably not have disturbed Paine's contemporaries. A pamphlet circulating in the colonies, for example, looked with approval on the method of selecting magistrates in Venice. These were "chosen, not by a party or majority of the freemen, but by electors drawn by lot out of a larger number previously drawn by lot out of the body of freemen, to nominate them."[32] This system, as well as that for selecting the grand duke, involving as it did four lotteries and four elections, was praised for mixing choice and hazard to eliminate "party-dealing" while still preserving enough choice to allow the best men to be selected.

Paine proposes also a temporary body, which he calls a Continental Congress, to be selected for the purpose of drawing up a continental charter. This amounts essentially to a call for a constitutional convention, parallel to the one which actually came into being in 1787. Paine's suggestions for choosing delegates provide for a cross section of society; each colony would send two of its members already seated in the existing Continental Congress, two members of each house of its assembly or of its provincial convention, and five representatives of the people at large. In this way, Paine takes account of the divisions in society between the conservative and liberal, the vested and the popular interests, or, as he expressed it, "the two grand principles of business, *knowledge* and *power*."[33] It is a puzzle why he felt it necessary to recommend that these two elements of society be represented in the convention for framing a constitution, but not in the actual legislative body which he hoped this constitution would establish. Perhaps if he had observed the binary principle in his prescription for a national legislature as well, Adams would not have felt it necessary to write his *Thoughts on Government.*

The constitution or "Continental Charter" which Paine proposes would fix "the number and manner of choosing members of congress, members of assembly, with their date of sitting," draw "the line of business and jurisdiction between them," and secure "freedom and property to all men, and above all things the free exercise of religion." In words reminiscent of his identity as "A Lover of Order," Paine advises constant remembrance "that our strength is continental, not provincial." And he concludes the paragraph with the benediction, "Whose peace and happiness, may God preserve, AMEN," words reminiscent of those he had used when writing as "A Continental Farmer."

In the following paragraph Paine offers for the consideration of the delegates to his constitutional convention two sentences from an Italian political essay of the eighteenth century, *Treatise on Virtues and Rewards,* 1766, by the marquis Giacinto Dragonetti [*Trattato delle virtù e dei primi*]. "The science of the politician consists in fixing the true point of happiness and freedom. Those men would deserve the gratitude of ages, who should discover a mode of government that contained the greatest sum of individual happiness, with the least national expense."

Even among Italian political theorists, Dragonetti is by no means a significant figure. His work was eclipsed by the universally known and admired *Treatise on Crimes and Punishments* by Beccaria upon which it served as a commentary. Paine later quoted the same two lines from Dragonetti in his *Address to the Addressers,* 1792, one of his polemical tracts growing out of *Rights of Man.*[34] It is not in the least degree likely that Paine had ever read any part of Dragonetti's treatise or that he had ever seen it. Probably he took his two-line quotation from some English political tract, or it may have been among the materials turned over to him by Franklin. The greatest happiness theory embodied in the quotation had already been expressed, moreover, by English moralists such as Francis Hutcheson. In a sense, Dragonetti's view that a mode of government could be an instrument toward the attaining of individual happiness conflicts with Paine's distrust of governing too much and his statement in the early pages of *Common Sense* that "government, even in its best state, is a necessary evil." An Italian scholar has pointed out that Dragonetti, like Beccaria, is a very conservative author and a strange intellectual source for a revolutionary such as Paine.[35]

Immediately after quoting Dragonetti, Paine abruptly poses the problem, "But where, say some, is the king of America?" The only monarch he recognizes "reigns above, and doth not make havoc of mankind like the Royal Brute of Great Britain." In this passage Paine echoes the sentiments of political Puritanism, for example, those of a group of Philadelphia Presbyterians "who as early as 1765 exclaimed 'No King but King Jesus.'"[36] In order to join celebration of the continental charter with homage to the deity, Paine proposes a day to be set apart for proclaiming the charter or constitution. The solemn ceremony he prescribes consists in depositing the charter on the Bible and then placing a crown on the charter. This symbolizes that, for America, the law is king. But lest other symbolic meanings attached to a crown be improperly implied in the ceremony, Paine further proposes that the crown at the conclusion of the ritual "be demolished, and scattered among the people whose right it is." This gives Paine the occasion to revert to theory by means of a forceful axiom, as he observes, "a government of our own is our natural right."[37]

He observes that it is far better to proceed with constitution making in "a cool deliberate manner" than to trust to the vagaries of time and chance. Present action, he warns, is the only means of avoiding anarchy or attempts to establish dictatorship in the future. As an example of a demagogue, he cites an Italian popular hero, Masaniello describing him in a footnote as

"Thomas Anello, otherwise Massanello, a fisherman of Naples, who after spiriting up his countrymen in the public market place, against the oppression of the Spaniards, to whom the place was then subject, prompted them to revolt, and in the space of a day became king." Superficially this note seems to indicate that Paine possessed specialized knowledge of Italian history, but such a conclusion is quite misleading. Aniello, or Masaniello as he is also called, was throughout England and the continent during the seventeenth and eighteenth centuries a symbol for popular uprisings. He was not as well recognized as Machiavelli, or Paine would not have felt the need for identifying him in a footnote, but there is still nothing significant in Paine's being acquainted with him.

Paine closes Part 3 with a burst of inflamed rhetoric against reconciliation, which ties together the twin themes of time and feeling which he had previously emphasized.

> Ye that tell us of harmony and reconciliation, can ye restore to us the time that is past? Can ye give to prostitution its former innocence? neither can ye reconcile Britain and America. The last cord now is broken, the people of England are presenting addresses against us. There are injuries which nature cannot forgive; she would cease to be nature if she did. As well can the lover forgive the ravisher of his mistress, as the continent forgive the murders of Britain. The Almighty hath implanted in us these unextinguishable feelings for good and wise purposes. They are the guardians of his image in our hearts. They distinguish us from the herd of common animals. The social compact would dissolve, and justice be extirpated from the earth, or have only a casual existence were we callous to the touches of affection. The robber, and the murderer, would often escape unpunished, did not the injuries which our tempers sustain, provoke us into justice.[38]

Noteworthy in this passage is Paine's resentment against "the people of England," not only against the King and Parliament. Jefferson, in his draft for the Declaration of Independence, similarly inveighed against the British people. "Manly spirit bids us to renounce for ever these unfeeling brethren. We must endeavor to forget our former love for them, and to hold them as we hold the rest of mankind enemies in war, in peace friends."[39] Both Paine and Jefferson appeal to human feelings. Indeed Paine invokes the benevolent passions (which he had previously used to explain the social contract) to vindicate resentment and inspire wrath despite his prior repudiation of "the motives of pride, party or resentment."

In his final paragraph, Paine converts from poetry to prose a theme which had been widely used throughout the century, that of *translatio studii,* or the geographical progression of an abstraction from ancient to modern times. The progress theme in English poetry ordinarily describes the rise of some concept in ancient Greece and then its historical transfer to Rome, to Renaissance Italy, to Augustan France, and, finally, in contemporary perfection to England. The *translatio imperii* theme extends the process to the western world or portrays the final stages of the passage of empire from Britain to America. Examples of the progress theme are Thomson's "Liberty," from which Paine took his epigraph, and Gray's "Progress of Poetry." The best-known example of the *translatio imperii* theme is Berkeley's "On the Prospect of Planting Arts and Learning in America," with its famous conclusion

Westward the course of empire takes its way.

Paine's prose unites denunciation of the old world with praise of the new. "Ye that dare oppose not only the tyranny but the tyrant, stand forth! Every spot of the old world is overrun with oppression. Freedom hath been hunted round the globe. Asia and Africa have long expelled her. Europe regards her like a stranger, and England hath given her warning to depart. O! receive the fugitive, and prepare in time an asylum for mankind."[40] Instead of the westward movement of the course of empire, we visualize the flight of freedom from the Far East, through Europe, to her final refuge in America. In a later newspaper article in December 1778, Paine continues and amplifies the metaphor by warning his readers that America must treat liberty with the same wisdom extended toward religion. "Never violate her and she will never desert. 'Tis her last residence, and when she quits America she quits the world."[41]

6
"The Time Hath Found Us"

In the fourth section of *Common Sense* entitled "*Of the* present ABILITY *of* AMERICA, *with some miscellaneous* REFLEXIONS," Paine again emphasizes the present moment. He affirms that he has never met a man in either England or America who has not expressed the opinion "that a separation between the countries would take place one time or another." Since there is universal consent that the event will occur eventually, only the time of its taking place is at issue, and this has been abruptly decided, for "the *time hath found us.*" Undoubtedly Paine is exaggerating in his claim of consensus, but he conceals his overstatement by reference to a "general concurrence," and a "glorious union of all things."

His next concern is American military power, and again exaggeration is wrapped in ringing phrases: "It is not in numbers, but in unity that our great strength lies; yet our present numbers are sufficient to repel the force of all the world."[1] The two clauses of this sentence have become among the most quoted phrases from *Common Sense,* the first by its admirers, the second by its critics. The braggadocio of the latter phrase concerning the strength to repel all the world led to its being cited ironically five different times in one pamphlet reply.[2] Paine, in continuing to emphasize the moment at hand, affirms that America will not be better equipped or better prepared at any later period. In the future, England would not allow the construction of naval vessels and the necessary timber would be less available; an increased population, moreover, would mean more people to share trials and suffering rather than to increase military strength.

Paine affirms that America at present has absolutely no debts, but he does not as some commentators have suggested imply that this is necessarily an advantageous condition. He advocates spending, but only for a great or important purpose and only to an amount sufficient to guarantee success. "Whatever we may contract on this account will serve as a glorious memento of our virtue." In saying this he was in tune with his times, for Montesquieu and Hume, who had carried on a correspondence concerning the propriety of a national debt, both agreed that a moderate one could be to the advantage of a republic.[3] The subject intrigued Paine in later life, and he sought to prove in a pamphlet, *Decline and Fall of the English System of*

Finance (1796), that Great Britain had grossly exceeded the limits of moderation and would shortly descend into bankruptcy.

In the original text of *Common Sense* he merely touches on the British monetary system. In an addition to the third edition, however, he compares the British national debt with the value of the Royal Navy, using statistics concerning the size and expense of the fleet from John Entick's *New Naval History* (1757).[4] On the basis of these figures, Paine calculates that the cost of the entire British navy, including armament, in the year when it was "at its greatest glory," was £3.5 million. The date Paine cites is that of the publication of Entick's *History,* 1757, roughly the same time when he himself went to sea in the navy for a brief period, but he does not mention the latter detail. The figure of £3.5 million, Paine considers extremely low and within the reach of the united colonies. He compares this amount to the British national debt, which he calculates at £140 million, bearing an annual interest of more than £4 million. In other words, according to Paine, America could have a navy as large as that of Great Britain for less than the British paid every year in interest.

One of the early replies to *Common Sense,* a pamphlet named *Plain Truth,* the author of which was actually a military expert, called these statistics in question. According to *Plain Truth,* the fleet at the close of the previous war comprised 200 ships of the line and 200 smaller vessels, and the value of naval stores alone in British arsenals was £twenty million.[5] This criticism was answered in the *Pennsylvania Evening Post,* 16 April 1776, probably by Paine himself, in the following terse statement:

> To the Author of a pamphlet unjustly *called* PLAIN TRUTH. Extract from COOPER'S rise, progress, and present state of the British navy, published in the year 1758.
>
> The value of the whole ROYAL NAVY at present is computed at 2,591,397.

Almost twenty years later an English antagonist accused Paine of rigging his figures in order to make the expense of a navy seem much smaller than it actually was. According to this critic, Paine cited Entick's *New Naval History* in such a way as to leave the impression that the estimates and figures it contains represent the state of affairs in 1757, the date of publication of the book; whereas "he carefully kept concealed what was stated in the book itself, that the estimates were of the last century, when the materials and labour of ship-building, were at half the present price."[6] This is a serious charge, and it requires looking into, particularly since Paine in 1783 maintained that *Common Sense* had never been attacked in England on the ground of error or mistake.[7]

On the page cited by Paine, Entick prints in a column the cost of building ships according to the number of guns each contains, the entries starting with 100 and descending in tens to 20 guns. This column is preceded by the explanation that the cost includes "*Masts, Yards, Sails and Rigging, together with a Proportion of eight Months Boatswain's and Carpenter's Sea-stores, as calculated by* Mr. Burchett, *Secretary to the Navy.*" Paine reprints these statistics and the accompanying explanation absolutely verbatim except for changes in capitalizing and italicizing. Entick next affirms in a brief paragraph:

> And from hence it will be easy to sum up the Value or Cost of the whole Royal Navy, according to the List given on page ii, supposing every Ship to be furnish'd as above.

The list on the cited page contains the number of ships, frigates, and sloops in service in 1757 and the number of guns they carry. Directly after the above paragraph, Entick prints four columns, listing the number of ships, the guns they carry, the cost of one ship, and the cost of all. In other words, he multiplies the cost for one unit as supplied in his first table with the number of units as indicated on page ii of his text.

Paine reproduces Entrick's four columns accurately and only slightly changes the wording of the brief introductory paragraph in the following manner:

> And from hence it is easy to sum up the value, or cost rather, of the whole British navy, which in the year 1757, when it was at its greatest glory consisted of the following ships and guns.

Essentially the only change Paine makes is to delete the reference to page ii in Entick and to substitute for it the information that the statistics have reference to 1757 when the navy "was at its greatest glory." Paine is, therefore, following his source faithfully. It is true that the material in Entick immediately preceding these tables of costs consists of naval regulations which were put into force in 1661, and they are so introduced on page xlviii, but Entick clearly indicates that his tables do not refer to this page, but to a much earlier one dealing with 1757. The regulations were "of the last century," but the financial estimates were contemporary. The charge against Paine is, therefore, completely without foundation.[8]

After quoting Entick's statistics, Paine without transition of any kind lists the natural products of America which are needed for shipbuilding and urges the immediate construction of a navy. If it should turn out that the vessels are not needed for combat, he adds, they may be sold for profit, but he makes no statement concerning potential customers—whether in the event of sale these vessels are to be used as warships by other nations or to be kept for use at home in a nonbellicose status.

In keeping with his argument that the cost of a navy is within the reach of the united American colonies, he maintains that the number of experienced sailors required to man a navy is small enough to be readily recruited. This anticipates the objection that since American population was relatively low few men experienced in maritime activities were available to man the ships. In Paine's opinion, it is "not necessary that one fourth part should be sailors." Referring to a ship on the decks of which he may have walked in his youth, the privateer *Terrible,* he points out that it "stood the hottest engagement of any ship last war, yet had not twenty sailors on board, though her complement of men was upwards of two hundred." Presumably the other hands were performing functions not involved with the nautical arts. Paine adds the cheerful and undoubtedly unrealistic prediction that "a few and able social sailors will soon instruct a sufficient number of active landmen in the common work of a ship." Paine leaves the impression that the *Terrible* won an easy victory in her famous battle with the *Vengeance,* but actually over 150 of her crew were killed, including Captain Death and every other officer except one.[9]

Still stressing the need for immediate action, Paine points out that "shipbuilding is America's pride," but because of British restrictions "our timber is standing, our fisheries blocked up, and our sailors and ship-wrights out of employ." America, he says, has all of the natural resources for shipbuilding, an advantage which no other part of the world, including Africa, Russia, and the rest of Europe, can match. A few paragraphs later, Paine specifies the indigenous articles of defense: hemp, iron, saltpeter and gunpowder. Still without envisioning naval warfare on a broad scale, Paine affirms that a fleet is needed to protect American waters against pirates. Then once more considering the condition which would prevail if reconciliation with Britain were to take place, Paine insists that England would not and could not protect American waters.[10]

Returning to his point that the might of the British navy had been greatly exaggerated, he charges that less than a tenth of its vessels are seaworthy; "their names are pompously continued in the list, if only a plank be left of the ship." America, moreover, would never be called upon to face all of the British naval strength at one time. Paine puts forth another original idea by suggesting that premiums be given to merchants for the outfitting of their vessels with guns so that at the conclusion of hostilities the nation would not be burdened "with the evil so loudly complained of in England, of suffering their fleet, in time of peace to lie rotting in the docks." This was a notion favorably received in England. A London newspaper, the *Morning Post* (8 June 1776), although indicating that the idea was the only observation in Paine's "celebrated pamphlet" worthy of any attention, recommended its adoption, "not despising it on account of the quarter it comes from."[11] Another newspaper, however, the *St. James's Chronicle,* printed in August "an extract of a letter from Jamaica, dated June 29, 1776, which asserted that *Common Sense's* recommendations about naval premiums were not borne out by the facts."[12]

Paine reinforces his principle that "the present time is preferable to all others" for breaking loose from Britain by introducing the ambiguity of claims to ownership of the western lands of America. Three colonies, Pennsylvania, Virginia, and Connecticut, were then involved in a dispute over this territory. The opposition between Pennsylvania and Virginia over an area called Indiana in what is now western Pennsylvania was a relatively peaceful affair, mainly involving lawyers, those from Virginia headed by Carter Braxton, who was soon to write against *Common Sense,* and those from Pennsylvania headed by Thomas Wharton, who was to become the state's first president. The contentions between Connecticut and Pennsylvania were more serious since they gave rise to a clash of settlers and actual bloodshed, the situation to which Paine refers in *Common Sense.* He discreetly fails to mention that the Continental Congress had been asked to adjudicate both controversies, but had refused to intervene. Paine shrewdly uses the dispute involving Connecticut as an evidence of weakness in the British administration rather than a potential hazard to American unity. The vacant lands themselves, he sees as a further reason for immediate action. The smaller the population, the more unoccupied land would be available to be used after independence for paying off the debt and the expenses of government. Although it was not apparent at the time, Paine was here touching on an area of great political and economic sensitivity. Even before the fighting came to a halt, Paine became involved in a dispute between the state of Virginia and a group of speculators known as the Indiana Company. In defense of the latter, he published in 1780 a historically oriented pamphlet, *Public Good,* in which he argued in the spirit of *Common Sense* that western lands be used for the advantage of the entire nation rather than a particular local group.[13] In the appendix to *Common Sense* Paine likewise argues against a reconciliation or a return to submission to Britain on the grounds that if the western lands reverted to Crown control they could not then be used to pay off debts already contracted for military action.[14] He suggests that when sold these lands should be under the trusteeship of congress.

The circumstance that American population was small, Paine uses as a favorable indication, and in doing so he goes contrary to generally received opinion everywhere in Europe before Malthus. A great controversy concerning population was waged throughout the eighteenth century, but the point at issue was always how to attain maximum population, not whether it was uniformly desirable.[15] The latter was assumed on the basis of both Scripture and economic theory. Paine draws on one phase of the controversy which had concerned Montesquieu and Hume among others, that of the relative size of population in ancient and modern times. Paine expresses an original concept in relation to America that "the more a country is peopled, the smaller their armies are," a somewhat strange proposition even for the eighteenth century. He argues that "in military numbers, the ancients far exceeded the moderns."[16] The reason he gives, completely different from that of Montesquieu, is that large population results from trade and that "commerce diminishes the spirit, both of patriotism and national defense." Since England is a commercial nation, there is little to be feared from its military.

Swinging back again to the concept of immediate action, Paine insists that "the *present time* is the *true time*" for establishing cooperation and concord between the colonies. Fifty years later varying or conflicting interests might create confusion or worse. The present time, moreover, represents the unique opportunity for the colonies of forming their own government. Most nations have a king first and subsequently adopt a method of ruling themselves. America should begin "at the right end" by deciding first on its political system. Touching only briefly on an assumption which probably influenced most colonial minds, that independence would not mean a new system of government, but merely a new king, Paine warns that unless his fellow citizens "legally and authoritatively" choose the occupant of the seat of government, they are "in danger of having it filled by some fortunate ruffian," who may treat them in the manner William the Conqueror treated the English people. This passage is sometimes construed as referring to potential future dictators, but since the dictator is a nineteenth- and twentieth-century phenomenon, it is much more likely that Paine intended to oppose the setting up of a new ruling dynasty in America, a solution which may at that time have seemed quite realistic for the majority of opponents to the continuation of English sovereignty.

Once more abruptly shifting to another topic, that of religion, Paine expresses his own opinion that it is "the indispensable duty of government, to protect all conscientious professors thereof," that government has no other business with religion, and "that it is the will of the Almighty, that there should be diversity of religious opinions among us."[17] Referring to his suggestions for a Continental Charter, he maintains that this solemn document should protect religion equally with personal freedom and property. This enables him next to discuss principles of representation and specifically to express his displeasure over the manner in which the delegates from Pennsylvania to the Continental Congress had been selected. Expanding the concepts of his "Lover of Order" essay, he insists that there is no political matter more important than the attaining of a large and equal representation. By this he means that the actual number of electors or representatives should be large and that all regions should have an equal voice. In the abstract, Paine's principle of equality seems to be based entirely on geography, not on wealth or social or economic condition, but from the pragmatic perspective of Pennsylvania, which he had in mind, his call for equal representation was based on the grievances of the Philadelphia artisans and the western farmers who were both greatly underrepresented in the Assembly.[18] As an example of the evils associated with inadequate representation he discusses the reception of the "Associators petition" in the Pennsylvania House of Assembly and the instructions for delegates to the Continental Congress which had been drawn up by the same house. Paine objected not so much to the puerile style of the instructions themselves, bad as it was, but to the fact that the instructions had been drawn up by a small number of delegates and passed by the House as representing the whole colony, whereas in Paine's opinion the majority of its inhabitants would not have approved them.

Without making any recommendations of his own, Paine observes that the method of choosing delegates to a future national congress is a matter of utmost concern. Although he does not precisely condemn the method then in use for selecting representatives to the Continental Congress, their being picked by members of the colonial assemblies, he suggests that in future the two bodies be completely separated. He poses the question, "whether *representation* and *election* is not too great a power for one and the same body of men to possess?"[19] To confirm his insistence on a large and equal representation, he quotes the contemptuous reception which Charles Cornwall, one of the Lords of the Treasury, had accorded a petition of the New York Assembly. The trifling number of its members, twenty-six, Cornwall observed, "could not with decency be put for the whole." The democratically inspired Paine thereupon thanks him for "his involuntary honesty." He also refers in a footnote to the discussion of the principles of representation in James Burgh's *Political Disquisitions.*

The relevant pages in Burgh's treatise present statistics concerning "rotten boroughs" and other causes of inequality in England.

> Here we see *(monstrum horrendum, ingens!)* two persons, the lord of the pitiful town of *Newton,* in the isle of Wight, and him of *Old Sarum, Wiltshire,* where there is not a house, send in as many members as the inestimable wealth of the city of *London,* in which the livery, who are the legal electors are 8,000; and the persons who ought to have votes are probably 30,000, and upwards. Here two individuals have equal weight in the state with 30,000!
>
> . . . The *British* government, therefore, taking it according to its avowed state, is neither absolute monarchy nor limited monarchy, nor aristocracy, nor democracy, nor a mixture of monarchy, aristocracy and democracy; but may be called a ptochocracy (the reader will pardon a new word) or government of beggars. For a few beggarly boroughs [that is, economically deprived; many of their voters receiving alms and therefore being influenced by those on whom they depend] do avowedly elect the most important part of the government, the part which commands the purse. It is true this is only the ostensible state of things. The *British* government is *really* a juntocracy (I doubt the reader will now presume I think I presume upon his good nature) or government by a minister and his crew. For the court directs the beggars whom to choose.
>
> Is this the universally admired and universally envied *British* constitution?[20]

This invective is certainly as extreme as that of the most impassioned passages of *Common Sense.*

Paine brings his pamphlet to a close with four soberly stated reasons showing "that nothing can settle our affairs so expeditiously as an open and determined declaration for independence." First, as a result of such a declaration, continental European powers could intercede on behalf of the American nation; second, France and Spain would offer actual assistance, assistance which would be logically denied as long as any sign remains that the breach with England may be healed; third, the status of Americans in international relations would be changed from a dishonorable to an honorable one, from that of rebels to that of combatants; and, fourth, America would receive the sympathy and respect of the rest of the world. In his final paragraph, Paine again stresses the present as the time for action; until independence is declared, the American people will be like a man "who continues putting off some unpleasant business from day to day, yet knows it must be done, hates to set about it, wishes it over, and is continually haunted with the thoughts of its necessity."[21] This is not a very forceful ending from the perspective of rhetorical principles of either the eighteenth century or the twentieth.

Perhaps the weakness of this conclusion helps to explain why Paine added an appendix in the third edition of his work six weeks later. The ostensible reason he gives is that *Common Sense* left the press on the same day on which a particularly immoderate speech by King George III first appeared in Philadelphia. The speech, revealing the monarch's "bloody mindedness," according to Paine, failed in its purpose of intimidation, and instead emboldened the Americans. Although Paine affirms in his appendix that "the chastity of . . . national manners" justifies "silent disdain" of the king's words, he was temperamentally unable to pursue his policy of ignoring the royal address; he therefore labels it "nothing better than a wilful audacious libel against the truth, the common good, and the existence of mankind; and . . . a formal and pompous method of offering up human sacrifices to the pride of tyrants."[22] With these words, Paine was, of course, laying himself open to charges of lese majesty. The body of *Common Sense* might possibly have been overlooked on the grounds that it is concerned with general principles of government, but in this passage George III is personally traduced and maligned. Paine carries on in this vein by further exposing brutality and tyranny in the royal speech and declaring that "he, who hunts the woods for prey, the naked and untutored Indian, is less a Savage than the King of Britain."

As an example of the sycophancy in the British court, Paine quotes Sir John Dalrymple, "the putative father of a whining jesuitical piece, fallaciously called, '*The Address of the people of* ENGLAND *to the inhabitants* of AMERICA.'" Referring to compliments which had been paid to the Rockingham administration, Dalrymple, while not objecting to them, had argued that similar compliments should also be addressed to the king "*by whose* NOD ALONE" the administration was "*permitted to do anything*."

Labeling this attitude "toryism" and "idolatry," Paine affirms that anyone who could accept it would be "an apostate from the order of manhood; and ought to be considered as one, who hath not only given up the proper dignity of man, but sunk himself beneath the rank of animals, and [should] contemptibly crawl through the world like a worm."

Since Paine's major aim in *Common Sense* was to vindicate the moral right of America to break away from England, he next adopts the tactic of accusing the monarch of that nation of unethical conduct. Without providing any specifics whatsoever, Paine affirms that George III "hath wickedly broken through every moral and human obligation, trampled nature and conscience beneath his feet; and by a steady and constitutional spirit of insolence and cruelty, procured for himself an universal hatred." After this undocumented indictment, Paine appeals directly to the ministers and lawyers of the colonies to embrace the doctrine of separation. This he considers "the moral part" of his argument and he leaves the leaders of public opinion to reflect privately upon it.

He then enunciates the "self-evident" proposition that separation is in the interest of America, his first and only reference to economic advantage. No nation can reach material eminence without control of its own affairs, he affirms, and America through assuming self-government may attain opulence. Even England will gain in the process, for it will benefit more by commerce with America than by political domination. The advantages of independence, "like all other truths discovered by necessity," will become clearer every day. Independence, Paine insists is inevitable, but the more it is delayed the more difficult it will be to accomplish.

To answer the argument that a military effort would be more successful if delayed forty or fifty years, Paine points to the experience which the colonists had gained in the French and Indian war. Skilled officers who are now available, he states, would not be around fifty years later. In reference to his doctrine that independence is to be preferred over reconciliation, Paine affirms that "he who takes nature for his guide" always accepts simple solutions over complex ones.[23] Independence represents a single, simple line; whereas reconciliation is a perplexed and complicated process. This is an obvious echo of his "principle in nature" from the first section of *Common Sense* that "the more simply any thing is, the less liable it is to be disordered, and the easier repaired when disordered."[24]

Strangely enough, Paine fails to develop one of the strongest arguments that could have been made at the time—that de facto independence already existed and that nothing more was necessary than a formal declaration to that effect. Instead he exposed the weakest aspects of existing conditions, the colonies being "held together by an unexampled concurrence of sentiment, which is nevertheless subject to change, and which every secret enemy is endeavouring to dissolve. Our present condition is, Legislation without law; wisdom without a plan; a constitution without a name; and, what is strangely astonishing, perfect independence contending for dependence."[25] It might have been far more effective to point to the positive aspects—that the "unexampled concurrence of sentiment" was in itself powerful enough to keep the colonies united and that since "perfect independence" already existed nothing more was needed but a determination to maintain the status quo. This is implied, moreover, by the statements early in his third section that "the period of debate is closed" and that "arms as a last resource decide the contest."

Even though in his previous theoretical section, Paine had praised the smooth operation of society without law and without government, he next portrays as "truly alarming" the present circumstances of America, that is, the first weeks of 1776. The social fabric is flimsily held together by courtesy, but otherwise absolute license prevails. Under such conditions, property is not secure, and no law curtails crime. Paine is concerned, however, with merely a single crime, which had to be specified—the crime of treason toward the new social entity. He affirms, therefore, that a distinction must be made between English soldiers and captured Tories—the former are to be imprisoned and the latter to be executed.

The impunity under which the Tories were able to operate, Paine berates in another of his notable phrases, "The Continental Belt is too loosely buckled."[26] In his opinion, "the king and his worthless adherents are got at their old game of dividing the Continent." As an example of this type of pernicious Tory propaganda, he points to an "artful and hypocritical letter which had appeared a few months ago in two of the New York papers."[27]

The divisive communication to which Paine objected had come out in *Rivington's New-York Gazetteer; or . . . Weekly Advertiser* in the issue for 12 October 1775 under the heading "Extract of a letter from a Gentleman in London, to his friend in this city, dated July 26, 1775." It was reprinted in the following week in the *New-York Gazette and Weekly Mercury,* edited by Hugh Gaine. The gentleman in London attempts to convince his New York correspondent that the problems of the American colonies are being considered sympathetically by the British authorities, that proposals of compromise, beneficial to the colonies, are soon to be offered in precise terms, and that the full rights of Englishmen are to be guaranteed to residents of the colonies. If these assurances had been accepted and believed by newspaper readers in New York, they would have thoroughly undermined Paine's major arguments that the colonies were being treated as a subject people, that the point beyond which the colonies could no longer tolerate political oppression had been passed, and that it was too late to hope for any accommodation from London.

The author of the letter establishes his credentials by affirming that he has "seen the ministry" and "conversed with the first personages near our sovereign." He assures his correspondent that these people have breathed forth the "language of humanity" and that their bosoms have swelled with compassion in considering the American people as afflicted with "unhappy delusion," the common phrase used by the supporters of Parliament against the colonies. According to the letter-writer, Great Britain is prepared to abandon both external and internal taxation, and in place of taxes to require from each colony a fixed amount of money to be used towards the expenses of defending the empire. The main concern of the ministry is not with the money itself, moreover, but rather with obtaining from the colonies a recognition of the right of Parliament to tax them, or in the correspondent's words, "an acknowledgement of that superintending power, always exercised by Great Britain over its external dominions, a superintending power absolutely necessary for promoting the happiness of colonies, so widely differing on commercial interests." Carefully preparing the way for a vindication of British use of force while preserving a tone of impartiality, the correspondent reports as an unshakable condition of affairs "that Parliament has by its constitution certain inherent rights, which it cannot divest itself of," including "that of a supreme legislative power over the extended dominion." The writer then calls on America to "meet England on friendly and equitable ground" and settle the dispute by negotiation rather than civil war. Without actually predicting a victory for the King's forces, the writer suggests that any resort to armed conflict would be a disaster for America. Even though the colonists might take the upper hand in a few hard-fought battles, he warns, "the American trade must suffer, the farmer, the merchant, and the wealthy inhabitants, who by many years industry, have purchased a peaceful retirement from the busy world, must be reduced to the lowest ebb of distress."

According to the letter-writer, American advocates of violence have been deceived by false reports from England, which make them perceive the situation "thro' a false medium: Local politics influence some, others oppose government on any principles, and care not if America was deluged in blood, if their private purposes were answered." Of special interest is the writer's reference to those who "oppose government on any principles," a phrase which anticipates Paine's dictum that "government, even in its best state, is but a necessary evil."[28]

Although Paine deplored the lack of unity among the colonies to which the New York letter alludes, he paradoxically uses this state of affairs as an argument for separation. Those who advocate reconciliation, he suggests in his Appendix, do not realize "how difficult the task is and how dangerous it may prove, should the Continent divide thereon.[29] By this he means that many Americans had already been placed into such a situation that they would reject reconciliation even if it were imposed upon them. Also to be taken into consideration were those who had already lost their lives in defense of their country. "Ill-judged moderation" would render their sacrifice in vain. Paraphrasing an old English proverb, Paine predicts that those who work for reconciliation "are reckoning without their host," that is, they are unrealistic in ignoring the opposition to their attitude, just as a diner in a tavern is not being realistic if he attempts to add up his own bill for a meal he has just eaten.[30]

Paine patiently explains to the advocates of conciliation why the colonies cannot return to the conditions of 1763, which many had talked of. "Put us, say some, on the footing we were in the year 1763." Paine had in mind scores of articles using some variation of this phrase. One such was a correspondent in the *Pennsylvania Journal,* 8 March 1775, who had hotly demanded, "have they not expressly said, and is it not the ground work of their whole proceedings, *place America in the situation she was in before* 1763, and all our complaints will subside?"

Even if Britain were to accept such a solution, Paine insists, there is no way of forcing future parliaments to comply with it. Also there is no way of repairing the destruction of making good the losses which have taken place during the interim. "The Rubicon is passed." By portraying reconciliation as futile, Paine supports his previous argument that nothing less than a major victory will justify the sacrifices which have already been made. From the moment that "the first musket was fired" against America nothing less than independence would satisfy the gravity of the confrontation.

Once more assuming that independence at some time is inevitable, Paine observes that it may be obtained in three ways: through the efforts of congress as the legal voice of the people, through military power, or through mob action. The debate, therefore, should not concern the actuality of independence, but merely the means of accomplishing it. Obviously, according to Paine's presentation, it should come through the first of these means, that is, through congress as the legal voice of the people. "We have every opportunity and every encouragement before us, to form the noblest, purest constitution on the face of the earth. We save it in our power to begin the world over again. . . . The birthday of a new world is at hand."[31]

Of great significance in this passage is the emphasis upon that which is new, for the notion of a fresh start soon became one of the major themes of the Revolution and the emerging republic. It is expressed by the Latin phrase *Novus ordo seclorum* on the Great Seal of the United States. The Latin tag, which is now printed on a one dollar bill, is adapted from a line in Vergil's fourth Eclogue, which prophesies the return of the Golden Age.

> magnus ab integro saeclorum nascitur ordo
> [a great order is being born from the fullness of time]

Vergil presents a theory of history based on cycles rather than on continued progress, for he refers to the "annus magnus," a vast period which will come to an end when all of the heavenly bodies return to the exact positions they occupied at the time of the creation of the world.[32] His reference to a new order, however, has been shown to be a precursor of the American goal of the pursuit of happiness.[33]

In the modern world, the theme of newness acquired a significant cachet of respectability with the proclamation of the New Science early in the seventeenth century. A poem, "The Rising Glory of America," by Philip Freneau and Hugh Henry Brackenridge four years prior to *Common Sense* specifically joined the notion of newness to that of the high worth of America.

> A theme more new, tho' not less noble, claims
> Our ev'ry thought on this auspicious day;
> The rising glory of this western world.[34]

After *Common Sense* the theme of newness was carried over into the Declaration of Independence, which asserts the right of the people "to institute new Government." Both *Common Sense* and the Declaration suggest a relationship between a new government and a new world, even though neither makes the association precise. Two decades later, the French Revolution made its own homage to newness by instituting the revolutionary calendar, the chronology of which assigned the Year One to 1792. Paine himself, in the midst of the French Revolution while looking back upon the preceding one in America, rapturously emphasized, as we have already noticed, that the latter represented "the opportunity of *beginning the world anew,* . . . and of bringing forward a *new system* of government."[35]

In a sense, this emphasis on newness and the rising glory of America marked the beginning of one of the major myths associated with American society—that of its eternal youth. As the historian C. Vann Woodward has pointed out, quoting Oscar Wilde, "'The youth of America is their oldest tradition. . . . It has been going on for three hundred years.' He said that nearly a century ago. Later on, D. H. Lawrence confirmed the perception in a more serious vein. 'That is the true myth of America,' he declared, 'the impulse to go backward, from old age to golden youth' in fantasy."[36]

Paine concluded *Common Sense* with a plea for harmony and internal reconciliation. Even Tories should welcome independence, he argued, for it would at last bring a stable government and offer them protection from the resentment of aggrieved patriots. Independence would also remove from all Americans the stigma of being considered "rebellious subjects." Reasonable men as well as merchants in England would welcome the opportunity of resuming trade with America. Most important, America had the power to withhold consent from any footing less than separation. Paine closed with a plea for harmony and internal reconciliation. The names of Whig and Tory should be blotted out in favor of "those of A GOOD CITIZEN, AN OPEN AND RESOLUTE FRIEND, AND A VIRTUOUS SUPPORTER OF THE RIGHTS OF MANKIND AND OF THE FREE AND INDEPENDENT STATES OF AMERICA."

Another document which upset Paine for reasons comparable to those which led to his denouncing the Tory letter of the *New-York Gazetteer* was a printed statement by a group of Philadelphia Quakers dated 20 January 1776 and entitled "The ANCIENT TESTIMONY and Principles of the People called QUAKERS renewed, with Respect to the KING and GOVERNMENT, and touching the COMMOTIONS now prevailing in these and other parts of AMERICA addressed to the PEOPLE IN GENERAL."[37] The statement incorporated, along with the notions of pacificism for which the Quakers were generally noted, a declaration of loyalty to the reigning family of Great Britain together with a statement of opposition to any colonial resort to arms. The Tory letter from New York suggested that the British would eventually remedy all reasonable grievances of the colonies; the Quaker testimony from Pennsylvania maintained that any military action against the British was immoral. Had the doctrine which these documents incorporated been widely accepted, both would have effectively undercut Paine's argument for independence. It is quite significant that the Quaker "Testimony" is addressed not merely to fellow religionists, but to "the PEOPLE IN GENERAL." It may well have been stimulated by the publication of *Common Sense,* but it contains no direct references to the pamphlet nor to any aspect of the contemporary political situation other than a prayer that the Father of Mercies may grant to those in superior stations, presumably the members of Congress, the wisdom to "guard against and reject all such measures and councils, as may increase and perpetuate the discord, animosities, and unhappy contentions which now sorrowfully abound."

In the third edition of *Common Sense,* Paine replied to the Pennsylvania document with an address "To the Representatives of the Religious Society of the People called Quakers," a fundamental statement of the doctrine of the separation of church and state.[38] The Quaker declaration which it answers seems on the surface to maintain a partial divorce of religion and politics by specifically excepting from the right of the state to control every phase of the lives of its people anything which interferes with the exercise of their religion. Paine, however, maintains that such a doctrine shows a religious sect granting a political power and that the framers of the declaration are thereby using religion as an instrument of secular coercion. He affirms that religion and politics should, to the contrary, be completely separated, that neither should make any attempt to interfere with the business of the other. In Paine's words, "To God, and not to man, are all men accountable on the score of religion."

Paine introduces his remarks on a personal note: "The Writer of this, is one of those few, who never dishonors religion either by ridiculing, or cavilling at any denomination whatsoever." Although he says nothing whatsoever about his own attitude toward Quakers in particular, this is a subject which has interested some of his biographers, since his father is known to have been a member of the Society of Friends. Paine himself, however, in his early years had become alienated by their austere manners and drab life style, possibly because of the influence of his mother, an Anglican. Paine's only personal link to the Quaker religion apart from his father's affiliation consists of his will, in which he expresses a desire to be buried in a cemetery of that faith. There he says, "I know not if the Society of people called Quakers, admit a person to be buried in their burying ground, who does not belong to their Society, but if they do, or will admit me, I would prefer being buried there; my father belonged to that profession, and I was partly brought up in it. But if it is not consistent with their rules to do this, I desire to be buried on my own farm at New Rochelle."[39] Paine also said to one of his friends, "I could be buried in the Episcopal church, but they are so arrogant; or in the Presbyterian, but they are so hypocritical."[40] This remark indicates that his request to the Quakers was not necessarily based upon a great admiration for their creed or behavior.

At the grammar school which he attended, Paine's tutor was an Anglican minister, the Reverend William Knowles. According to the hostile and frequently unreliable George Chalmers, Paine served as a schoolmaster at two different establishments during 1766 and also engaged in itinerant preaching. Chalmers suggests that both Paine's teaching and his preaching were Anglican-oriented. He identifies the first school in which Paine was employed as being conducted by "Mr. Noble, who kept the great Academy in Lemon-street, Goodman's fields," and the second as headed by "Mr. Gardnor, who then taught a reputable school at Kensington."[41] Chalmers further alleges that before his first marriage in 1759, Paine had organized a congregation in his lodgings "to whom he preached as an independent, or a methodist." When he married, the ceremony took place in the Anglican church of St. Peter's in Sandwich, and Paine was described in the church register as a member of the parish. According to Chalmers, his desire of preaching returned to him in the spring of 1767, and he applied to "his old master for a certificate to the bishop of London, of his qualifications." Mr. Noble, however, "told his former usher, that since he was only an English scholar he could not recommend him as a proper candidate for ordination in the church."[42]

Evidence recently brought to light verifies the fact of Paine's teaching during this period but reveals that his orientation was dissenting rather than Anglican. His first employment was at an establishment maintained by "Daniel Noble (1729–1783), elder and minister of the Sabbath-Keeping Baptist Church at Mill Yard, Lemon Street, Goodman's Fields."[43] A letter from Benjamin Vaughan to Lord Shelburne, 28 January 1784, also reveals that Paine's school was neither Anglican nor Quaker: Vaughan reports that "A friend of mine just returned from Philadelphia was surprised upon being introduced to Mr. Paine the author of *Common Sense,* to find that he was an old acquaintance, having been tutor to him at a little dissenting school near Whitechapel."[44] Finally, Methodist sources maintain that in

1758 while engaged as an apprentice corset-maker, he attended chapel with his employer and on one occasion was "requested to conduct a service in default of the appointed preacher."[45] None of this evidence supports in any way the hypothesis that Paine had any affiliation or close association with Quakers in his youth.

No matter what Paine's opinion of the Quakers as a religious group, his reply to the authors of the Philadelphia *Testimony* considers them entirely as a political, not a religious body. He accuses them of playing games of identity by presuming to speak for all the Quakers of Pennsylvania when they represent only a part, and he admits that he is trying to make them aware of their "presumption of character" by adopting their own technique, that is, by elevating himself to be the spokesman for all those whose principles they oppose. In actuality, however, neither he nor they, he says, have any claim to "political representation."

Paine praises "the love and desire of peace" which characterizes the first two of the four pages of the *Testimony.* Peace is an ideal which all men hold high from principles of natural reason as well as religion, he says, and the advocates of an Independent Constitution are equally committed to it. Indirectly condemning the past record of the British Empire, Paine specifically distinguishes the aims of the advocates of independence from those of the British. "We fight neither for revenge nor conquest; neither from pride nor passion; we are not insulting the world with our fleets and armies, nor ravaging the globe for plunder." He also paraphrases a biblical expression which he was to use again in the *Crisis:* "Beneath the shade of our own vines are we attacked." Characterizing the British forces as highwaymen and housebreakers, Paine argues that the Americans are not waging war (an activity reprehensible to Quaker thought) but punishing transgressors (an activity considered acceptable). They are merely using the sword instead of the hangman's halter. Allowing a note of reproach to enter his remonstrance, he suggests that the framers of the declaration lacked sensibility, or as he expresses it in the third section of *Common Sense,* "those feelings and affections which nature justifies." Speaking as throughout for all the advocates of independence, he suggests that "we feel for the ruined and insulted sufferers in all and every part of the continent, with a degree of tenderness which hath not yet made its way into some of your bosoms." The Quaker "coldness of soul" should not be called religion nor their bigotry, Christianity.

Paine in his main argument accepts the right of the Quaker group to express political opinions, but accuses them of being illogical in applying their principles only partially, that is, by objecting to the martial activities of the Americans but not to the equally warlike measures of the British. Paine insists that since the British also bear arms, their depredations should also be deplored. As an example of a logical and straightforward Quaker, he cites Robert Barclay, one of their coreligionists, who in the seventeenth century had preached repentance to Charles II. In the quotation from Barclay's address which Paine gives in a footnote, however, the austere Quaker rebukes his king only on a personal level, not from the political perspective, which Paine was urging upon the Quakers of Philadelphia. Barclay, nevertheless, addresses Charles as an ordinary man, not as a monarch, exhorting him to turn unto the Lord with all his heart and to apply himself to the light of Christ shining within his conscience. Undoubtedly Paine introduced Barclay primarily for effect, for the rest of his comments indicate that he would not have been satisfied with Barclay's kind of simple piety. He really wants the Quakers to ignore the separation of church and state and to join with him in combating English troops.

The particular passage which Paine quotes has been more admired than any other part of Barclay's work by both Quakers and non-Quakers. It had been quoted and given extensive European circulation by Voltaire, for example, almost half a century previously in the third of his *Lettres philosophiques* (1733, 1734). Paine and Voltaire cited it for essentially the same reason, to undermine respect for royalty. In so doing, Paine implicitly rebukes the Philadelphia Quakers for their hypocrisy in complaining of being persecuted for their religion. In Paine's opinion, they were condemned precisely for not living up to their principles, that is, for opposing only one party in the conflict, the patriots, instead of remaining truly neutral and treating both parties equally.

Throughout the eighteenth century both in England and the colonies, opponents of the Quakers commonly accused them of being mercenary and of bending their religion for the sake of material gain. Paine follows this tradition by denouncing their pretended scruples as "made by the same men, who, in the very instant that they are exclaiming against the mammon of this world, are nevertheless, hunting after it with a step as steady as Time, and an appetite as keen as Death." The authors of the *Testimony* had quoted a verse from Proverbs to justify their nonbelligerent status: "when a man's ways please the Lord, he maketh even his enemies to be at peace with him." According to Paine's reinterpretation of this text, it proves that the ways of George III are not pleasing to the Lord, "otherwise, his reign would be in peace."

Paine also quotes a long passage from the Quakers' profession in which they affirm that they have nothing to do with the setting up and pulling down of governments. Paine replies that they fail to live up to their profession, for in practice they sanction everything done by kings. If it is true that they do not wish to act on behalf of one side, they should abstain as well from supporting the other. Paine accuses their principles of reflecting a kind of determinism in regard to monarchy—of approving everything which ever happens to kings as being the work of God. Paine at first has nothing to say against the doctrine except to indicate sardonically that if George III should come to the same untimely end as Charles I, the writers of the *Testimony* are bound by their doctrine to applaud the fact. On a more serious level he denies the intervention of providence in political affairs; if kings are taken away or other changes in government take place, he asserts, these events are brought about solely by "common and human" means. Elsewhere Paine did not consistently adhere to the doctrine of natural causation. The body of *Common Sense* implies that providence has a great deal to do with human events, and when Paine wrote his *Age of Reason* many years later, designed in part to correct and reduce the superstition in Christian theology, he paradoxically traced the influence of providence in his own life.

Paine ridicules the *Testimony* for professing to have nothing to do with governments but still publicly calling "for a share of the business" by stirring up the people to abhor all measures designed to break off the connection with England. This, according to Paine, is gross inconsistency and absurdity. The situation then facing the people of America, Paine ingeniously maintains, has no bearing on either setting up or pulling down a king. The Americans simply want nothing further to do with George III, and Paine therefore wants the Quakers merely to abstain from supporting him.

In summarizing his objection to the Quakers' *Testimony,* Paine makes three concluding points: the document leads to disrespect of religion, for it is socially dangerous to make religion a party in political disputes; it claims that all Quakers favor its principles, whereas only a few do; and it threatens to unsettle the harmony which has been established throughout the continent. In bidding farewell to the authors of the *Testimony,* Paine expresses the wish that they may continue fully to enjoy every civil and religious right, but, more important, he hopes that the bad example they have set "of mingling religion with politics, may be disavowed and reprobated by every inhabitant of AMERICA."

PART II

Intellectual Background and Reception of *Common Sense*

7
Levellers and Puritans

Although Paine condemned the Philadelphia Quakers for mixing religion with politics, it is obvious that much of *Common Sense* appeals to the authority of Scripture, most of it implies that the author is Christian, and nearly all of it makes use of biblical terminology. Even though Paine's later deistical writings have made him a hero of freethinkers in the Anglo-Saxon world, his first work cannot be fully understood without reference to the complicated politico-religious background from which it emerged.

In the history of Great Britain, internal complaints over the power and policies of the ruling dynasty have frequently been associated with opposition to the personal religious profession of the monarch. Especially in the seventeenth century, Presbyterian and Independent clergymen voiced their displeasure with the conduct of Stuart kings, who were either Catholic or Anglican. In the upper reaches of society, the disputes concerned abstract theology and issues of Church government, but independent groups of farmers and laborers insisted that practical issues involving their political liberties and economic welfare be treated as essential matters of Christian belief.

The most radical of these proletarian worshipers were known as Levellers because of their view that men are equal both in the sight of God and in the sight of each other and that class and economic distinctions are contrary to the Scripture. Their opponenets accused them of seeking to bring all men down to their own impecunious state. The literature of the Levellers is relatively sparse, since the members of the movement for the most part lacked education and their doctrines were disseminated by word of mouth in religious meetings or in individual encounters.

Those who would see Paine as a Cromwellian radical returned from the dead naturally look to such groups as the Levellers for resemblances in his thought. According to J. G. A. Pocock, the "Levellers denounced Norman usurpation and looked backwards to Anglo-Saxon liberty." They denied the continuity and sacredness of English common law and talked instead the language of "a golden age, a lost paradise in which Englishmen had enjoyed liberties that had been taken from them and must be restored. If asked by what right Englishmen could claim the liberties they had lost, they could not appeal to the law, but to natural right and reason."[1] Language of this kind is indeed compatible with Paine's theories of the development of society from the state of natural liberty. The anti-Normanism of the Levellers, moreover, is duplicated in *Common Sense* in the passages in which William the Conqueror is labeled a usurper and a "French bastard landing with an armed banditti." This is, nevertheless, scant subservience to the Gothic tradition in comparison with a pamphlet which appeared in Philadelphia a few months after *Common Sense,* lauding *The Genuine Principles of the Ancient Saxon, or English Constitution* and proclaiming that "whatever is of Saxon establishment is truly constitutional; but whatever is Norman, is heterogeneous to it, and partakes of a tyrannical spirit."[2]

It is extremely doubtful that Paine had direct contact with any of the writings of the Levellers, which as a group had minimal influence upon subsequent traditions. According to Julian H. Franklin, "when republican and democratic reformers of the last third of the eighteenth century looked for sources of authority and inspiration, they returned to Locke's *Two Treatises.*"[3] Some attention must, nevertheless, be given to the leveling tradition, that is, to the combination of religion and economic egalitarianism, because of the persistence of Paine's contemporaries, especially his enemies, in associating him with it.

In America, *Common Sense* was seldom openly impugned on the ground of its resemblances to the doctrines of the Levellers, perhaps because nonconforming sects had traditionally occupied a respected position throughout the colonies, particularly in New England. Innuendoes and insinuations in published attacks implied, however, that the sympathies of the author lay with leveling doctrine. At that time, the names Leveller and Independent carried throughout most of the British Empire about the same stigma which has been associated with the terms Communist and Red in the United States during the second quarter of the twentieth century. One British attack on *Common Sense* and its author drew upon English history for proof "that saints of his disposition, tho' more eager to grasp at power than any other set of men, have a thousand times recited the same texts by which he attempts to level all distinctions."[4] *Common Sense* was not accorded a great deal of attention in the British press, but when its major political doctrines were repeated in *Rights of Man,* they were immediately associated with "those Levellers and Republicans, those Robbers of the National Peace and of Englishman's Rights, in overturning the Government, bringing the first *Charles* to the Block, and making their Fellow countrymen miserable." Another critic in the same period similarly complained that *Rights of Man* reflected "the spirit of puritanic malignity," that its language consisted of "the familiar indecent slang of the conventicle." Still another opponent of *Rights of Man* argued that Paine "is a leveller; and his doctrines are not new but obsolete: they were the doctrines of Cromwell's time."[5]

Despite the ideological and linguistic similarities between Paine and some seventeenth-century doctrines of a religious-economic nature, he specifically denies the concept of economic leveling or the equal division of wealth in both *Common Sense* and his most radical English publication, *Agrarian Justice.* In *Common Sense,* he affirms that "the distinctions of rich and poor, may in a great measure be accounted for . . . without having recourse to the harsh, ill-sounding names of oppression and avarice."[6] He accepts economic distinctions even more explicitly in *Agrarian Justice,* the very tract in which he introduces the concept of governmental care of the individual from cradle to grave. Here he says that although personally not seeking great wealth, "I am a friend to riches because they are capable of good. I care not how affluent some may be, provided that none be miserable in consequence of it."[7]

If one is looking for strong language in America appealing to proletarian sentiments, it may be found in the introduction to a pamphlet, *The People the Best Governors,* published shortly after *Common Sense.* According to the anonymous author:

> GOD *gave mankind freedom by nature, made every man equal to his neighbour, has virtually enjoined them, to govern themselves by their own laws. The government which he introduced among his people, the* Jews, *abundantly proves it, and they might have continued in that state of liberty, had they not desired a King. The people best know their own wants and necessities, and therefore, are best able to rule themselves. Tentmakers, cobblers, and common tradesmen, composed the legislature at* Athens. "*Is not the body (said* Socrates*) of the* Athenian *people compos'd of men like these.*"

This remarkable paragraph not only effectively summarizes all of Part 2 of *Common Sense,* but blends into the argument an egalitarian bias completely foreign to the broad appeal of Paine's pamphlet.

Levellers are considered as historically belonging to the Puritan tradition. Although there is almost no reason to believe that Paine's views derive directly from Levellers, some external evidence seems to link his notions to the broader category of political Puritanism. John Adams specifically affirms that the main source of Paine's antimonarchical doctrine was Milton. Reporting a conversation about *Common Sense* over thirty years after it allegedly took place, Adams maintains that Paine visited him in the late spring of 1776. According to Adams, "I told him . . . that his Reasoning from the Old Testament was ridiculous, and I could hardly think him sincere. At this he laughed, and said he had taken his ideas in that part from Milton: and then expressed a Contempt of the Old Testament and indeed of the Bible at large, which surprized me. He saw that I did not relish this, and soon check'd himself, with these Words, 'However I have some thoughts of publishing my Thoughts on Religion, but I believe it will be best to postpone it, to the latter part of Life.' "[8]

It is impossible to confirm or deny that a conversation such as this actually occurred, but is is a relatively simple matter to compare *Common Sense* with the political works of Milton to determine whether a sufficient number of parallels or resemblances exist to warrant the conclusion that Paine was at all indebted to Milton for his political notions. The answer is completely negative. As we have already seen, the only quotation from Milton in *Common Sense* is a passage from *Paradise Lost* rather than from one of his political tracts. Milton's republican enthusiasm and antimonarchical zeal may have been no less extreme than Paine's, but this does not establish a personal relationship. The only subject matter which coincides or overlaps in Milton and Paine derives from the Old Testament narrative concerning the opposition of Samuel to the appointing of a king over the Israelites. Milton cites some of the same passages which figure in *Common Sense,* but his citations are scattered in a number of different works, and he offers no complete version of the episode. Original editions of the tracts in which Milton's references to Saul and Samuel appear are extremely rare today, and it is highly doubtful that they would have been available to Paine in the American colonies. He frequently makes statements in harmony with previous statements of Milton, but this by no means indicates influence or discipleship. One example should suffice. Milton declares in *Pro Populo Anglicano Defensio* (1651):

> *Give then to Caesar,* says he, *the things that are Caesar's.* . . . Our liberty is not Caesar's. It is a blessing we have received from God himself. . . . Being therefore peculiarly God's own, that is, truly free, we are consequently to be subjected to him alone, and cannot, without the greatest sacrilege imaginable, be reduced into a condition of slavery to any man. . . . Absolute lordship and Christianity are inconsistent.[9]

Paine affirms somewhat more caustically:

> "*Render unto Caesar the things which are Caesar's*" is the scripture doctrine of courts, yet it is no support of monarchical government, for the Jews at that time were without a king, and in a state of vassalage to the Romans.[10]

This is an obvious example of two authors drawing upon a common source with no other relationship between them. Paine's narrative of the biblical origin of kingship is closely tied to the Old Testament, but there is no evidence that he relied upon Milton or any other secondary interpretations. This conclusion applies equally to the suggestion that he consulted Joseph Priestley for his political treatment of the Saul-Samuel story.

Another theory which traces Paine's political antecedents to seventeenth-century English puritanism appeared in one of the early answers to *Common Sense* entitled *The True Interest of America Impartially Stated* (1776). The author, a New York Anglican clergyman of strong loyalist sentiments, charges that most of the arguments in *Common Sense* against hereditary succession are borrowed from *The Grounds and Reasons of Monarchy Considered* (Durham, 1650), by John Hall, one of the most vigorous opponents of Charles I. The subtitle of Hall's work, written during the early months of the Commonwealth, indicates that his primary concern is with the Stuarts: *A Review of the Scotch Story, Gathered out of Their Best Authors and Records.* In his preface Hall points out that in the first part of his book he concerns himself with "Kingship" in general and in the second part with "The Instance out of Scottish History." Since Paine in *Common Sense* has nothing to say about the Stuarts, but limits his strictures to William the Conqueror and the eighteenth-century Hanoverian dynasty, only Hall's general section on "Kingship" could be at all relevant.

Hall first of all presents a subjective contrast between "the monarchical" and the "popular" forms of government. "I could never be persuaded," he observes, "but it was more happy for a people to be disposed of by a number of persons jointly interested and concerned with them, than to be numbered as the herd and Inheritance of One to whose lust and madnesse they were absolutely subject."[11] Writing thirty years before Filmer's *Patriarcha,* Hall refutes the major arguments of royalist writers. He observes that instead of concerning themselves with the concrete rights and claims of a particular prince, the royalists ordinarily present nothing but abstract reasoning, attempting to justify monarchy in general.[12] Also in vindicating monarchy, they are not specific about the particular kind they have in mind, "whether absolute, mixt, limited, meerly Law-Executive, or first in order."[13] Hall affirms that the titles of all monarchs then reigning are ambiguous: "Look but three or four stories back, and you will meet either some savage unnatural Intrusion (disguis'd under some forc'd Title or inexistent Cognation) or else some violent alteration, or possibly some slender Oath or Articles—hardly extorted and imperfectly kept."[14] Hall condemns as blasphemous the analogy between the unity of god and the unity of the monarch, as he expresses it, the "Argument that flourishes out Kings as the Eclypes of Divinity, and vainly lavishes some Metaphysicks, to prove that all things have a naturall Tendencie to an Onenesse."[15]

Hall repudiates a number of other arguments in favor of monarchy which are based on analogy: that is, on likenesses with the animal kingdom, with Adam's dominion over beasts, with Old Testament kings, and with military commanders. For each of these he demonstrates that a true parallelism is lacking. The claims of monarchy, he says, are based upon election, force of arms, and inheritance, a somewhat different list, one might observe, from Paine's categories of lot, election and inheritance. Each human being, according to Hall, has natural liberty or the freedom to make his own life as "justly happy and advantageous" as he can. His father can no more dispossess him of this liberty than he can of his understanding or his eyesight, "for these are priviledges which God and Nature" have endued all men with. This analogy is no more realistic than those mentioned above used by the monarchists.

Hall also objects to the manner in which monarchists appeal to the law of nature to justify the superior station of a single man. To justify their contention, he maintains, they must demonstrate that men are endowed with unequal degrees of freedom and that some are selected to rule; whereas it appears on the contrary, that all men naturally are equal, "for though Nature with a Noble variety hath made different the Features and Lineaments of men, yet as to freedome, till it be lost by some externall means, she hath made every one alike, and given them the same desires." If nature had indeed given a certain family illustrious marks for governing, Hall continues, nature would be guilty of a double irregularity, first, by deserting the principle of making everyone free, and, second, by interfering with the harmonious operation of general law, that is, by making "her generall work meerly subservient, and secondary to her particular." If the proponents of monarchy should change their ground and claim that the Law of Nations supports their principles, they must, according to Hall, specify exactly what their Law of Nations is and, thereby, be forced to admit that there are hardly four or five axioms which are universally accepted.

None of the above points is made in *Common Sense,* not even the demonstration that all men are equal, but there are two other concepts in Hall's discourse which do appear in Paine: the difficulty of tracing an unbroken lineage in any royal family, and the possibility that heirs ascending the throne may be incompetent. Hall maintains that no monarch may be found whose crown has come to him by untainted succession, and even if such a one could be discovered, it would not rectify the evils of monarchy. He further charges that the hereditary system puts matters of government "into the hands of Fortune, when a Child uncapable or infirm, under the Regiment of a Nurse, must (possibly) be Supreme Governour, and those whom either their Abilities or vertues fit for it, Subordinate or laid aside." These arguments are so general, however, that absolutely no significance should be attached to their appearing also in *Common Sense,* particularly since other more plausible sources exist. The impossibility of tracing an unbroken line had been treated by Daniel Defoe in a well-known satirical poem, *The True-Born Englishman* (1701), which Paine later quoted in 1805,[16] and the hazards of hereditary power had been exposed by Franklin by means of concepts such as a hereditary professor of mathematics.[17] Hall's small book, moreover, was a rare publication, even in its own day, and there is very little likelihood that Paine ever saw a copy.

Many years after the composition of *Common Sense,* Paine revealed some knowledge of the literary background concerning the Stuart succession, but the author he quotes is Buchanan rather than Hall.

> Several writers before Locke had remarked on the absurdity of hereditary succession, but there they stopped. Buchanan, a Scots historian, who lived more than a hundred years before Locke, reproaches Malcolm II, king of Scotland, and his father, Kenetkus for making the crown of Scotland hereditary in his family, "by which means, says Buchanan, the kingdom must be frequently be possessed by a child or a fool; whereas before, the Scots used to make choice of that prince of the royal family that was best qualified to govern and protect his people."[18]

Paine goes on to say that he knows of no author before *Common Sense* who has attacked hereditary succession on the ground that is is illegal, the strongest argument against it, "for if the right to set it up do not exist, and that it does not is certain, because it is establishing a form of government, *not for themselves,* but for a future race of people, all discussion upon the subject ends at once."

In the polemics which raged over *Common Sense* in the twelve months after its publication, many of Paine's opponents, nevertheless, associated the doctrine of independence with seventeenth-century religious nonconformity. According to an observer in 1776, "Intestine confusions, continued wars with each other, Republicks, and Presbyterian Governments, compose the bugbear of the day, and the very name of them frightens people more than the whole force of Great Britain."[19] Paine has been attacked by quotations from traditional British political authorities such as Sidney, Harrington, and Hooker. The same authorities have also been used in his defense. One of his English supporters, writing after the publication of *Rights of Man,* roundly maintained that "in the celebrated writings of Thomas Paine, there is not a political maxim which is not found in the works of Sydney, Harrington, Milton and Buchanan. These principles have not been confuted."[20]

But parallel doctrines do not necessarily demonstrate influence. Whatever political notions Paine shares with seventeenth-century thinkers, religious or secular, may be explained by a process of transmission through intermediaries. The ideas of Commonwealth writers who espoused republican principles were kept alive by eighteenth-century Whig theorists such as Robert Molesworth, Thomas Gordon, and Thomas Hollis. Their political attitudes could easily have passed into Paine's intellectual milieu by means of debates and friendly discussions in Lewes and London.

The attempt to associate Paine with Levellers and Puritans naturally brings up the question of the relationship of his religious and his political ideas to each other, both at the time he published his notorious deistical work *The Age of Reason,* and more specifically when he wrote *Common Sense.* It has been asserted by various critics that "Paine's political ideas cannot be evaluated apart from his religious attitudes."[21] As a generality this is true, but is is also true that Paine's attitude toward religion in *Common Sense* is completely contrary to that in *Age of Reason.*

Whether or not Paine was himself a believer in orthodox Christianity at the time he wrote *Common Sense,* the work is undubitably written from the Christian perspective. The most obvious indication is the section which cites at length the authority of the Old Testament to prove that "the Almighty hath here entered his protest against monarchical government." In introducing this section Paine respectfully refers to "Scripture chronology" and to "the history of Jewish royalty." Other passages treat Christian doctrine or Christian symbols as accepted standards of authority. "Brotherhood" is claimed "with every European Christian"[22] and England is denounced as "a reproach to the names of men and christians."[23] The real presence of Satan is strongly suggested by statements that no power which needs checking can "be from God,"[24] that monarchy is "the most prosperous invention the devil ever set on foot for the promotion of idolatry,"[25] and that anyone who would promote discord under Paine's proposed system of representation "would have joined Lucifer in his revolt."[26] (Presumably the thought did not occur to Paine that the British ministry at that time would probably have considered him and other advocates of independence as themselves rebellious disciples of Satan.) Finally, in *Common Sense* the operation of providence in human affairs is clearly affirmed: "The distance at which the Almighty hath placed England and America" is seen as "a strong and natural proof" that it was "never the design of Heaven" for one to have authority over the other.[27] "The king of America" is said to reign above,[28] and "unextinguishable feelings for good and wise purposes" are said to be implanted in us by the Almighty.[29] Speaking in his own character, Paine expresses a full and conscientious belief that "it is the will of the Almighty that there should be diversity of religious opinions among us."[30] Strangely enough, in his letter to the Quakers in the third edition of *Common Sense,* Paine seems to repudiate much of this defense of divine providence by affirming, as we have seen, that "kings are not taken away by miracles, neither are changes in governments brought about by any other means than such as are common and human."[31]

Rights of Man by and large ignores the Bible, although Paine does in this work observe "that the genealogy of Christ is traced to Adam" and he also indicates that "the Mosaic account of the Creation" may be "taken as divine authority or merely historical."[32] He also declares that "every religion is good that teaches man to be good; and I know of none that instructs him to be bad."[33] This essential difference between the Christian perspective of *Common Sense* and the secular one of *Rights of Man* is not now pointed out to prove that the two works conflict in any way, for they do not. They present identical principles of government. The important consideration is that the religious references in *Common Sense* are superfluous to Paine's political system, which could stand by itself, as it does in *Rights of Man.* In this sense, there is no essential connection between Paine's religion and his politics.

Common Sense reflects a Christian attitude, *Age of Reason* a stridently deistical one, and *Rights of Man* neither one nor the other. It should be observed, however, that even the *Age of Reason,* which fiercely assails orthodox Christianity, at the same time clearly affirms the existence of a divine being, as well as the working of providence in human affairs.

There is only one reference in *Common Sense* which could possibly be interpreted as a combination of religious and political concepts. This is the remark that "there is as much of kingcraft as priestcraft in withholding the scripture from the public in popish countries,"[34] but even this remark is vastly more political than religious in significance, and would have been just as acceptable to a New England Puritan as to an English deist.

The question naturally arises: how effective in the setting of colonial America in 1776 was Paine's appeal to scriptural authority, particularly in regard to the history of Jewish kings. One might assume that educated men with a background similar to that of John Adams would have agreed with him that Paine's reasoning from the Old Testament was ridiculous. Most of the printed answers to *Common Sense,* however, as we shall see, took this section seriously and attempted to provide counterarguments. More important, Paine did not write *Common Sense* primarily to influence men like John Adams, but rather to appeal to the average mentality of the colonies. The ordinary man did not write tracts in support of Paine's arguments or in retaliation against them, and it is, therefore, impossible to know how his theological reasoning was generally received. Paine obviously expected his Scripture demonstration to be effective. He was probably also prepared to have it associated by both friendly and unfriendly critics with the ideology of Puritans and Levellers.

An English commentator, for example, observed in 1792 that Paine's "scripture politics [in *Common Sense*] are obsolete and superannuated in these countries by an hundred years."[35] His "monstrous nonsense," this critic continued, might "be suited to the fanatics of Boston, where witchcraft was in great vogue the beginning of this century, but here will excite nothing but contempt as a wretched endeavour to arm ignorance and superstition against reason and common sense." Although this critic believed that Paine himself was motivated more by hypocrisy than religious enthusiasm, he took the trouble of replying to Paine's biblical arguments.

> When the Jews, weary of the tyranny of priests, desired governours whose acts not pretending to be commanded by God might be questioned by men, is it enough to prove against the reasonableness of this desire that *the thing displeased Samuel,* when they said Give us a King to judge us? If the people of Rome were at this day to require a civil governour in the place of the Vicar of Christ, I suppose the thing would displease the Pope, but would that prove the folly or wickedness of the request? In truth such stuff is no otherwise worthy of notice, except to

> show the low arts to which this mountebank has recourse, to adapt his drugs to people of all sorts. Provided he can *overturn,* he cares not whether it be by the hand of philosophy or superstition, and it is nothing to him which of the two possess themselves of the ruined edifice.

These strictures lead to a second question: could Paine have really been sincere in appealing to scriptural authority and using Christian symbols in *Common Sense* and, if so, did he experience a drastic change in theological belief before writing *The Age of Reason?* Or was he, on the other hand, already a deist when he wrote *Common Sense* and was he using Christian terminology merely for its effectiveness in appealing to the majority of his readers, who were likely to be orthodox churchgoers? Adams in March 1776 objected to the "artfull Adresses to superstitious Notions" in *Common Sense,* and much later reported that Paine shortly after its publication "expressed a contempt of the Old Testament and indeed of the Bible at large."[36] Adams's latter testimony is unreliable since it came several years after *The Age of Reason* and at a time, as we shall see, when Adams was very much prejudiced against Paine. Much more reliable evidence exists in a letter of Paine himself to Major General Nathanael Greene, under whom Paine had served in 1776 at Fort Lee. In this letter of 17 October 1780 which has never been published, Paine remarks on the sparseness of his correspondence, "Thank God nobody can publish my letters after I am dead for I write none."[37] (The irony of this remark is now apparent.) In the rest of the letter Paine comments on providence and prayer in relation to the desertion from the American cause of Benedict Arnold.

> Good God what an escape have you had! Were I inclined to be superstitious, I should attribute the whole of this discovery to Providence. I see so many changes the Treason had of succeeding and every chance opposed by an uncontrived something, that I almost feel myself a Predestinarian.
>
> But how is it that André who died like a Roman should suffer himself to be taken as a coward would have been taken.—A man on horseback against three on foot had a chance of escaping especially as the pursuit could not have been far or long. Do you think an American officer would have been taken by three Tories within sight almost of his own lines without a struggle for it—but there again comes in the answer, *It was to be*—and so be it.
>
> But why, if Providence had the management of the whole did she let Arnold escape? Perhaps to be hung afterwards by the Enemy for some act of traitorship against them. . . .
>
> Though I do not write much I pray often, if fervency of hoping and wishing can be called prayer and these will constantly [illegible] you on your expedition to the Southern [*sic*] of which I congratulate you. . . .

Unfortunately these remarks are somewhat ambiguous. Paine first of all suggests that belief in providence is associated with superstition, but then he goes on to describe himself as almost a Predestinarian and to ascribe the capture of Major André to providence. Careful consideration indicates, however, that there is no real contradiction. One may label as superstition the excessive ascribing of events to providence while still believing that providence may operate to a limited degree. This seems to be Paine's position in the letter to General Greene and in *Common Sense* as well.

Paine's view of prayer in his letter is also equivocal. After introducing prayer in the conventional sense, he immediately suggests that he means by it nothing but reflection upon a topic and fervent wishing for a particular outcome. The language of *Common Sense* suggests that Paine's views on prayer and similar matters of Christian faith were more orthodox. To this degree, there seems to be an incompatibility between Paine's private and public doctrine. The conclusion is inescapable that he did not personally accept the Scriptures as the inspired word of God at the time that he wrote *Common Sense,* but that he quoted biblical passages as a forensic device in order to conform to the generally accepted traditions of the time and place.

Despite Paine's strategic combining of religion with rhetoric, one must not discount the evidence which indicates that he still retained a sincere conviction of the truth of the doctrine of the depravity of man, which had probably been instilled into him by his evangelical antecedents. His reference in *Common Sense* to "the badge of lost innocence" may be merely a concession to his biblically minded readers, or even a type of poetic license, but there are passages in two of his other works published during the same year which suggest that he held closely related personal convictions. In the third of his "Forester" letters he remarks, "If all human nature be corrupt, it is needless to strengthen the corruption by establishing a succession of kings." Even if this should still be considered rhetoric rather than conviction, the conclusion of subsequent series of letters has the ring of sincerity: "Perfection in government, like perfection in all earthly things, is not to be hoped for. A single house, or a duplication of them, will alike have their evils; and the defect is incurable, being founded in the nature of man, and the instability of things."[38]

Despite these and many other passages with religious overtones published in 1776, it is still possible to discern in *Common Sense* undertones of emotional chafing at the evangelical-Puritan straitjacket. Paine's insistence on reason and the united strength of the American people implies a challenge to the doctrine of human frailty. Even his assertion that "original sin and hereditary succession are parallel" may have a double-edged effect by casting as much doubt upon orthodox theology as upon traditional politics. Although British rule is the main target of Paine's pamphlet, one senses also an underlying dislike of all authority, an antipathy toward omniscient clergymen and clever lawyers as well as despotic governors. This may be one of the reasons why Paine seldom quotes from other writers. He precedes his attack on hereditary succession, moreover, by the charge that monarchical governments have smoothly glossed over parts of Scripture damaging to their case.

Paine's own exegesis of Old Testament texts may imply the divine authority of the Scriptures, but it also illustrates his capacity to beat the established clergy at their own game. Even his charge that "there is as much of kingcraft as priestcraft in withholding the scripture from the public in popish countries" may have been intended to reflect upon dogmatic and autocratic ministers in Protestant America. In one of his most forceful passages, Paine charges his reader to think for himself, or, as Paine expresses it, to "divest himself of prejudice and prepossession, and suffer his reason and his feelings to determine for themselves."[39]

Calvinist theology tended to see political events as the predestined fulfillment of biblical prophecy. Paine, on the other hand, secularized history, portraying it for the most part as a sequence of natural events. Instead of asserting that it would be the divine will which would keep America from remaining subject to any external power, he declared merely that such subjugation would be "repugnant to reason, to the universal order of things, to all examples from former ages."[40] True enough, this declaration seems contrary to the deterministic concept expressed a few paragraphs before that "the Reformation was preceded by the discovery of America, as if the Almighty graciously meant to open a sanctuary to the persecuted in future years." Only the "as if" frees this sentence from the Puritan mold.

In *Crisis* No. 5, Paine makes a complete break with the past as he observes that "mankind have lived for little purpose" if they must constantly go back two or three thousand years for instruction and example.[41] This rejection of ancient authority is clearly foreshadowed in the closing lines of *Common Sense,* "We have it in our power to begin the world over again. . . . The birthday of a new world is at hand." This social rebirth has little in common with the purely spiritual regeneration inculcated by ministers of the gospel. Paine is declaring independence from the ancients in both the pagan and the Christian tradition.

These passages rejecting the concept of continuity inherent in the Puritan view of history and suggesting Vergil's theory of historical cycles, however, do not in themselves provide a sufficient basis to assert that Paine held a cyclical view of history. His writings taken as a whole portray the doctrine of progress—and certain passages even suggest that this progress is guided by providence or an undefined supernatural force. In a later chapter, we shall see how he looked toward the completing of "the circle of civilization," a concept in itself embodying the theory of progress. In conclusion, *Common Sense* combines a vague uneasiness over man's fundamental nature with a fully expressed hope for social improvement in the future. Paine's devout readers could find in its pages, therefore, a comforting reliance on Christian doctrine; his unorthodox ones could read into them an affirmation of reason over tradition.

8
Relations with Locke

In considering next Paine's predecessors in areas other than religion, we encounter three outstanding figures in the history of political thought, Locke, Rousseau, and Montesquieu. These are not only writers in the grand intellectual tradition of the Enlightenment, but also the specific ones whom Paine's contemporaries consistently associated him with and those who keep reappearing in the extensive polemical literature on Paine's theories of government. It may perhaps be argued that Paine was personally and intellectually less compatible with Locke, Rousseau, and Montesquieu than with his eighteenth-century British predecessors, the True Whigs or Real Whigs, ranging from Molesworth and Hutcheson early in the century to Brand Hollis and Mrs. Macaulay at its end. Admitting the possibility of the transmission of ideas through conversation and other indirect means, one cannot affirm that Paine knew any of these writers—British or continental—at first hand with the single exception of James Burgh, and even here, as we have already seen, the indebtedness is not significant. Since the triumvirate of Locke, Rousseau, and Montesquieu is still regarded as a major intellectual force in the Revolutionary milieu, however, it cannot be disregarded in a consideration of Paine.

If we attempt to decide whether Paine drew from these eminent forerunners, we are confronted by some of the most complex problems inherent in the study of literary relationships. It is far more difficult to demonstrate that a writer has not been influenced by a preceding work which is similar to his own than to show that he actually has had some contact with it. Indeed it is impossible to prove the complete absence of influence, granting accessibility and the appropriate chronological relationship. Even though a writer declares that he has no knowledge of a particular author, he may not be telling the truth or he may even have completely forgotten all contact with a work which he has actually read. Indirect influence, which may be suggested by parallelism in theme or idea rather than revealed in specific phraseology, is obviously less concrete than direct influence. It is, therefore, easier to affirm, but equally difficult to disprove. It is important to bear in mind, moreover, that the transmission of thought does not necessarily take place through individual words, no matter how golden, or single sentences, no matter how brilliant. As Irene Samuel has remarked, "only a pedant would lift word after word from another's page, or retain in separate compartments of his mind what he has learned from this source and what from that. . . . In large part the effect of a writer upon any reader cannot be traced back to isolated passages; the spirit of the whole is more likely to remain with him than a series of excerpts."[1]

As far as Paine is concerned, it is hard to believe that he or any other man of literary talents with a strong interest in political theory and living in the British Empire during the last half of the eighteenth century would not have possessed a rudimentary knowledge of the basic theories of Locke, Montesquieu, and Rousseau. John Adams, no great admirer of Paine, suggested that he obtained his revolutionary notions by oral exchanges rather than by study, that he "came from England, and got into such company as would converse with him, and ran about picking what Information he could concerning our Affairs, and finding the great Question was concerning Independence, he gleaned from those he saw the commonplace Arguments concerning Independence: such as the Necessity of Independence, at some time or other, the peculiar fitness at this time; the Justice of it: the Provocation to it: the necessity of it: our Ability to maintain it, &c. &c."[2] To be sure, Adams specifies only the pragmatic arguments concerning American independence rather than the theoretical principles of government in Locke, Montesquieu, and Rousseau, but Paine may very well have derived his ideology as well as his current history through the conversational method. If anything, Adams's emphasis should be reversed; Paine's pragmatic notions reflect for the most part his personal background and original thinking; whereas his abstract ideas could hardly have come into existence without the assistance of at least a moderate acquaintance with the intellectual traditions to which they belong.

Even though the prominence of Locke's *Two Treatises* in colonial controversy "was largely confined to the post-1760 constitutional writings of the highly educated,"[3] a group to which Paine certainly did not belong, the work had a massive influence upon both French and English political thought of the entire century, and it is hard to believe that its major doctrines failed to make an impression upon Paine, either directly or indirectly. Paine makes no declaration whatsoever concerning any knowledge of Locke, Rousseau, or Montesquieu prior to the publication of *Common Sense*. In order to prove a direct influence of any one of them, therefore, it will be necessary to discover parallel passages close enough in idea or phraseology to warrant the assumption that one is based upon the other. This quest for possible influences upon Paine does not in itself represent a denial of his intellectual independence, since the results may be inconclusive or even negative instead of positive.

As we have seen, the most abstract or "philosophical" section of *Common Sense* is the introductory one, which covers only six of the seventy-nine pages in the original edition of January 1776. Under the rather clumsy subtitle "On the Origin and Design of Government in General with Concise Remarks on the English Constitution," it attempts to show how existing political institutions grew out of the mythical state of nature and to distinguish between the powers of the sovereign and the rights of the subject.

Obviously Paine was not the first author to approach these topics, and some of his predecessors had written volumes comprising hundreds of pages in contrast to his own half dozen. Paine, however, had no knowledge of most of these books. Although an original thinker and a forceful phrasemaker, he was not a scholar nor an avid reader. Indeed he read few books of any kind, customarily gleaning his knowledge of the intellectual problems which intrigued him from conversation, newspapers, and magazines. A few months after the publication of *Common Sense,* he proudly proclaimed, "I scarcely ever quote; the reason is, I always think."[4] And toward the end of his life, he specifically denied having read Locke's treatise on government, or even having the work in his hand, dismissing it as a "speculative, not a practical work," with a heavy and tedious style.[5] One may wonder how Paine could categorically judge Locke's style and content without reading as much as a single page of his work. In this regard, we may notice a parallel to Locke himself, who when writing philosophy "'utterly refused to read any books upon that subject' so as to keep other men's notions out of his head."[6]

Another parallel between Locke and Paine is that both denied authorship of at least one of their printed works. We have already noticed that in the *Crisis,* Paine unequivocally declared, "I never troubled others with my notions till very lately, nor ever published a syllable in England in my life," despite the fact that in 1772 while he was an excise collector at Lewes, England, he had written and arranged the printing of four thousand copies of a pamphlet which appealed for better treatment of employees in the service. Locke in a personal letter to the earl of Pembroke, December 1684, no less categorically affirmed, "I here solemnly protest in the presence of God, that I am not the author, not only of any libel, but not of any pamphlet or treatise whatsoever in print, good, bad or indifferent."[7] It is nonetheless a matter of record that Locke's *Fundamental Constitutions of Carolina* had appeared in 1669, his *Letter From a Person of Quality* in 1675, and his *Growth of Vines and Olives* in 1680.

An edition of Locke's *An Essay concerning the True Original, Extent and End of Civil Government* was published in Boston by the printing house of Edes and Gill in 1773, presumably making it available to Paine had he wished to read it. We notice the similarity in phrasing of this title to that of Paine's subtitle, "On the Origin and Design of Government in General with Concise Remarks on the English Constitution." The Boston edition of Locke's *Essay* contains only the second of two parts which had appeared in Locke's original publication in 1690 under the title *Two Treatises of Government.* The first treatise (that which was dropped from the Boston edition) was described on the title page as one in which "The False Principles and Foundation of Sir Robert Filmer, and His Followers are Detected and Overthrown." Filmer was widely known in the seventeenth century as an apologist for the divine right theory of monarchy, and it was his book *Patriarcha; or, The Natural Power of Kings,* 1680, which Locke refutes.

Because of the division of the work into two treatises, it has generally been assumed that Locke wrote the one which is printed first, that against Filmer, not long after the appearance of *Patriarcha* in 1680, and that he wrote the second one, that on civil government, in 1688 as a vindication of the Glorious Revolution, which brought William and Mary to the throne. A modern scholar has presented convincing evidence to show, however, that the book was designed as a whole, not as two treatises; that, if anything, the refutation of Filmer was written after the discussion of civil government; and that both parts were complete before the Glorious Revolution.[8] The work was, therefore, a call for a revolution to take place, not a justification of one which had already occurred, another parallel of sorts with Paine's *Common Sense.*

A much more important parallel exists, however, between the structure of Locke's *Two Treatises* and that of Paine's *Common Sense.* We have already seen the resemblances between the title of Locke's treatise on civil government and the introductory section of Paine's pamphlet concerning the origin of government. It is also noteworthy that the subsequent section of *Common Sense* adopts the identical method of Locke's treatise refuting Filmer. The latter's defense of the theory of divine right had been based on a citation of biblical texts presumably establishing the power of kings as decreed by God. Locke's refutation consists of a reexamination of these and other texts. The second section of *Common Sense,* entitled "On Monarchy and Hereditary Succession," also consists in large measure of an examination of scriptural passages concerning kings and the hereditary principle of sovereignty.

A fundamental contradiction exists in Locke's work, since the method of the second treatise, arguing from a presumed state of nature and subsequent sociological development taking place according to purely natural laws, is incompatible with arguing from scriptural authority and divine institution, the method of the first treatise.[9] *Common Sense* obviously incorporates the same inconsistency. Locke may have been inhibited by the fear of reprisals had he ignored the received theology and rested his case entirely on reasoning from natural law. Bernard Mandeville resolved a similar dilemma in the eighteenth century. Recognizing the problem of presenting social theories based on the assumption of the unhampered operation of natural law in a climate of opinion firmly dominated by belief in divine providence, Mandeville protected himself by affirming that his discussion of the state of nature was completely fanciful. He prudently put his readers on notice that "*when I say Men, I mean neither* Jews *nor* Christians; *but meer Man, in the State of Nature and Ignorance of the true Deity.*"[10] Paine tried to avoid inconsistency by affirming that the institution of monarchy cannot be either "justified on the equal rights of nature" or "defended on the authority of scripture."[11] But this affirmation does not really reconcile the use of both methods. One cannot believe both that social relations developed out of the state of nature and that they were imposed or given by divine will. One must accept one or the other approach. Probably neither Locke nor Paine believed in the complete and literal authority of Scripture when they wrote their respective works, but both pretended to do so since the majority of the public which they were addressing professed to hold such a belief. Like astute politicians of all times, Paine had no compunctions about using one argument to convince one segment of his constituency and a completely different argument, even an inconsistent one, to convince another segment.

Locke's first treatise is designed primarily to refute Filmer's hypotheses, based on scriptural interpretation, that "all Government is absolute Monarchy," that "no Man is Born free," and that "Adam was an absolute Monarch, and so are all Princes ever since."[12] In order to contest these propositions Locke demolishes a series of proofs which Filmer had offered to vindicate the title to universal political sovereignty which he felt belonged to Adam, the first of men. Adam, Locke argued, could not have received such a power by virtue of being the first of the species to be created, since at the time he was created he had no subjects. He did not receive the power through the donation of God, described in Genesis 1 : 28, alloting dominion over "every living thing," for this passage is a reference to inferior creatures, not to other men, and it concerns dominion held in common with all mankind. Nor did Adam receive political sovereignty through the subjection of Eve as recorded in Genesis 3 : 16, "And thy desire shall be to thy Husband, and he shall rule over thee." These words grant merely a conjugal power, not a political one of life and death over Eve or anyone else. Finally, Adam did not receive political sovereignty through "fatherhood" or begetting offspring. The latter is, of course, Filmer's most important doctrine, the basis of his title *Patriarcha.* Locke answers that a father does not really create human life; he is powerless to do so, for he does not even understand the biological process of generation (a statement which remained true all the way through the eighteenth century); God is the creator of all human life, and, therefore, He, not any human father, is the only one to have rights over any progeny.

Having refuted the claims to monarchy based upon the sovereignty of Adam, Locke turns next to the question of the conveyance of title or inheritance. Here Locke argues that even if Adam had been invested by God with universal sovereignty, there was no way by which this title could be passed on to his descendants. Filmer had considered fatherhood (paternal authority based on blood relationship) and property (the father's private dominion) as the twin fountains of sovereignty. Locke demonstrates that fatherhood and property are two distinct titles not always meeting in the same person. If Adam's property (private dominion) descended at his death to his eldest son, his blood relationship (natural dominion through fatherhood) descended equally to all his sons; there came into being, therefore, conflicting titles and dominion, which cannot descend together and may be separated. In subsequent chapters, Locke maintains that a child may inherit his father's property, but not the rule which his father had over other men. As far as modern monarchies are concerned, "if the Agreement and consent of Men first gave a Scepter into any one hand, or put a Crown on his Head, that also must direct its descent and conveyance." As Locke himself summarized his argument, Adam had no dominion over the world either by natural right of fatherhood or by positive donation from God; even if Adam possessed this dominion, his heirs had no right to it; even if his heirs had this right, there was no means of determining the line of succession; and even if such a principle of succession could be determined, the knowledge of which is the eldest line of Adam's posterity has been irretrievably lost.

It is apparent that almost none of this argument reappears in Paine. Although the two writers are obviously treating the same institution of hereditary monarchy, they are approaching it from different perspectives and with different arguments. There do exist, however, two significant parallels in their expositions. The first concerns Adam's original sin, which both Locke and Paine repudiate as a source of monarchical sovereignty. Locke in one of his rare humorous passages observes that if Adam's kingship derives from his sin, then this type of monarchy was a very poor one. "God sets him to work for his living, and seems rather to give him a Spade into his hand, to subdue the Earth, than a Scepter to rule over its Inhabitants."[13] Paine also observes that "hereditary succession can derive no glory" from the authority of Adam. "For as in Adam all sinned, and as in the first electors all men obeyed; as in the one all mankind were subjected to Satan, and in the other to sovereignty; as our innocence was lost in the first, and our authority in the last; and as both disable us from reassuming some former state and privilege, it unanswerably follows that original sin and hereditary succession are parallels. Dishonorable rank! inglorious connection!"[14]

Verbal similarities are quite close, moreover, as the two authors consider the alternative methods by which kings came into being. Locke promises to analyze Filmer's doctrine to "consider how *Inheritance, Grant, Usurpation* or *Election,* can any way make out Government in the World upon his Principles."[15] Paine poses a rhetorical question concerning the origin of kings and replies, "The question admits but of three answers, viz. either by lot, by election, or by usurpation."[16]

These two parallels do not by any means suggest, however, that Paine had read Locke's treatise, for they comprise notions widely discussed in theology and political science, the common stock of serious conversation in the period. Important contextual differences also separate the passages as found in Locke and Paine. The likelihood of direct influence is all the more remote, moreover, because as we have already indicated the edition of Locke's political works which was most probably available to Paine did not reprint the first treatise.

Locke's other essay, that on the end and origin of civil government, begins with a treatment of the state of nature, that illusory land which has never been completely charted in the history of ideas. The notion is prominent in Locke's predecessor, Thomas Hobbes, who considers the state of nature as "the time men live without a common power to keep them all in awe." It represents a state of war, although not necessarily of actual fighting.[17] The related concept of the "law of nature," an understanding of right and wrong independent of human institution, but presumably based on moral sense or informal conscience, has been traced as far back as Sophocles, whose Antigone appeals to the eternal "unwritten and unfailing statutes of heaven."[18] Locke defines the "State all Men are naturally in," as "a *State of Perfect Freedom* to order their Actions, and dispose of their Possessions, and Persons as they think fit, within the bounds of the Law of Nature, without asking leave, or depending upon the Will of any other Man."[19] Unfortunately, this is not all that is necessary for the state of nature, for Locke adds other requirements, particularly a condition of equality and an observance of the law of nature, which, for Locke, is the same thing as the exercise of reason. In order to explain how one man may protect himself against crimes perpetrated or contemplated by another, Locke affirms that in the state of nature "*every one has the Executive Power* of the Law of Nature."[20] At the same time, Locke is careful to distinguish against the prior theory of Hobbes that government "is the product only of Force and Violence, and that Men live together by no other Rules but that of Beasts." According to Locke, a state of war may exist in the state of nature, for example, when one man protects himself against another who is trying to overpower him, but the state of nature is nevertheless not equivalent to the state of war. Indeed, for Locke, one of the reasons men gather into society is precisely to avoid the state of war.

Although Locke does not immediately assign any reason other than the above, it becomes clear from his subsequent discussion that he believes that the principal reason for uniting into society is to safeguard the possession of property. "As Families increased, and Industry inlarged their Stocks, their *Possessions inlarged* with the need of them; but yet it was commonly *without any fixed property* in the ground they made use of, till they incorporated, settled themselves together, and built Cities, and then, by consent, they came in time, to set out the *bounds of their distinct territories*, and agree on limits between them and their Neighbours, and by Laws within themselves, settled the *Properties* of those of the same Society."[21] Locke's concept of property is based on the "labor theory," that is, that anything which man has improved by his own toil, including land, becomes his property. Another important reason which Locke gives for the formation of societies is the need for an umpire to settle disputes. Each individual gives up his natural right or power of punishing offenses against him in exchange for the protection of the legislative and executive power of civil society.[22] Those who are united in one body with a common law and executive power are in civil society; those who have no such common appeal are still in the state of nature. Locke affirms that "Government has no other end but the preservation of Property," although he seems to understand by Property both liberty and security.[23] He also indicates that "the End of Government is the good of Mankind,"[24] as in his first treatise he says that government is "for the benefit of the Governed, and not the sole advantage of the Governors."[25] Man in the state of nature, apart from enjoying innocent delights, has the power to do whatever he sees fit for his own preservation and the power to punish crimes against the law of nature; both of these he surrenders when he joins in a political society. Locke does not exalt monarchy over any other form of government, but suggests that it was the earliest, as it is the simplest and most obvious.

Unlike most other political writers, Locke uses the term "the Golden Age," but it is not clear whether he means by Golden Age the state of nature or the earliest years of government.[26] He describes it as a period before vain ambition and evil concupiscence "had corrupted Men's minds into a Mistake of true Power and Honour." Locke does not specifically describe the process by which men leave the state of nature to enter political society (the establishing of government), but he suggests that it was a process of mutual agreement, and that its purpose was to preserve for each member his liberty and property.[27] The probabilities were that men in ancient times vested the ruling power into a single man's hand "by their own consent" without stipulating the conditions limiting or regulating his power. Locke firmly insists, however, that whatever engagements or commitments a man may make for himself, he "*cannot* by any *Compact* whatsoever bind his *Children* or Posterity."[28] The most he can do is to attach conditions to the land he enjoys as a subject of a commonwealth and pass these conditions along to his posterity.

In discussing the origins of political societies, Locke gives as illustrations of primitive rulers, the Indian "Kings" in America, and the Judges of the Old Testament. The former, he describes as little more than "*Generals of their Armies,*" and the latter "*Captains in War.*" The episode of the Children of Israel in 1 Samuel calling on God to grant them a king who would judge them and fight their battles, Locke considers as evidence that the only business of a monarch in those days was to lead armies. He argues, in addition, that they were elected on a temporary basis and that their authority ceased when the war was over.[29]

The major possible forms of government which Locke mentions are democracy, oligarchy, elective monarchy, and hereditary monarchy, and he devotes most of his discussion to the last-named. He accepts the hereditary principle, but not that of divine right. He clearly states that the ruling dynasty is chosen by the people and that its reign may be dissolved when a prince acts contrary to his trust or to the laws of the land.[30] To the argument that the right of the British monarchy to its sovereign power is based on the Norman Conquest, Locke replies that even if the conquest itself were legitimate, its right "could reach no farther, than to the *Saxons* and *Britains* that were then Inhabitants of this Country."[31]

The foregoing discussion does not, of course, represent a synopsis of the entire reasoning of Locke's essay, but a survey of those points which are relevant to *Common Sense*. I shall now attempt to indicate the degree of resemblance between the two authors.

The point of departure for both writers is the mythical state of nature ("state of natural liberty" for Paine). Paine seems to provide three separate explanations for the formation of governments or political societies. (1) The inadequacy of private morality in primitive society to restrain private vice; (2) the inability of primitive society to guarantee rights of property and liberty; and (3) the inadequacy of primitive society to provide for material needs and amenities. The first two explanations may perhaps be coalesced into a single one. Paine is not explicit, to say the least, but wraps his meaning in metaphorical language. In the second paragraph of *Common Sense,* he writes, "Government, like dress, is the badge of lost innocence; the palaces of kings are built upon the ruins of the bowers of paradise." He then indicates that if conscience operated upon all men in a clear, uniform, and compelling manner, no other lawgiver would be needed, but "that not being the case," man "finds it necessary to surrender up a part of his property to furnish means for the protection of the rest." In his third paragraph he tells us that since "nothing but Heaven is impregnable to vice" the newly arrived emigrants into society "will began to relax in their duty and attachment to each other; and this remissness will point out the necessity of establishing some form of government to supply the defect of moral virtue." Finally, in his seventh paragraph, Paine summarizes the origin and rise of government as "a mode rendered necessary by the inability of moral virtue to govern the world," an attempt, as we have already noticed, to associate the institution of government with original sin or Adam's disobeying of the divine decree. Locke also seems to suggest this doctrine of man's lost innocense in his passage on the Golden Age "before vain Ambition," and *amor sceleratus habendi,* evil Concupiscence, had corrupted Mens minds into a Mistake of true Power and Honour."[32]

This was a period of "more Virtue, and consequently better Governours, as well as less vicious Subjects," but it gave way in later ages to a separation in interests between princes and their people, which was brought on by ambition, luxury, and flattery. Although Paine and Locke use similar language in their references to the past, Paine seems to be talking about a remote period before the existence of any government at all, and Locke seems to have reference to any early stage of government during which the kings reigned with moderation and virtue.

On the question of property as the end of government, Locke is less equivocal than Paine. Apart from the emphasis on the topic in his first treatise, Locke vigorously declares in the second, "The great and *chief end* therefore, of Mens uniting into Commonwealths, and putting themselves under Government, *is the Preservation of their Property.* To which in the State of Nature there are many things wanting."[33] By property, Locke, who devotes an entire chapter to the subject, means as we have seen anything which man has touched by his own labor. Paine, however, in referring to man's need "to surrender up a part of his property to furnish means for the protection of the rest" seems to be referring to rights such as liberty of movement as well as to material goods. No less forthrightly than Locke, he affirms that security is "the true design and end of government," but security, it should be noticed, is hardly identical with the preservation of property.

Paine's reconstruction of the formation of a typical primitive society has no parallel in Locke. Paine imagines four or five aborigines in the wilderness gathering together to fell timber and construct a house, a result which one man by his unaided efforts could never accomplish in a lifetime.[34] By and large the motivations which Locke provides for the gathering into society are negative ones, whereas Paine's are positive. According to Locke, men form societies in order to avoid a state of war or to provide an umpire to settle disagreements. He conceives of government as a means of avoiding the inconvenience of perpetual disputes. Paine's stress on incentives for the formation of government, the social instincts of man, and man's cooperative home building, aligns him with Hobbes's principal opponent in English, Lord Shaftesbury, even though he may never have read a page of Shaftesbury's *Characteristics.* In this work Shaftesbury stresses benevolent and social impulses and denies Hobbes's hypothesis that primitive man was a savage beast. Shaftesbury even denies the existence of a state of nature and argues that if generation, affection, and care of his offspring are natural to man, it follows that "society must be also natural to him" and that he never has or never could exist out of it.[35] It is important to notice that neither Locke nor Paine offers any suggestion that the formation of government is motivated by the need to preserve or guarantee human rights. In the next chapter we shall see how Paine developed a theory that man exchanges natural rights for civil rights by the process of entering into society.

Another major difference between Locke and Paine consists in the power structure which they attribute to the first governments. Locke, like almost every author before Paine to treat the theme, assumes that these governments were monarchical, although he makes no specific declaration to that effect. Paine, however, particularly describes the organization of the community along democratic lines. According to his reconstruction of remote history, policies were determined at first through the deliberation of every member on an absolutely equal basis, and then as physical area and population increased, a legislature based on the representative principle came into being. And on the frequent interchange of opinions between the electors and the elected rather than "on the unmeaning name of king" rests, according to Paine, "*the strength of government, and the happiness of the governed.*"[36]

A very close resemblance between Locke and Paine exists, however, on the subject of the hereditary principle. Locke forthrightly declares that "it was not the natural right of the Father descending to his Heirs, that made Governments in the beginning" and that "whatever Engagements or Promises any one has made for himself, he is under the Obligation of them, but *cannot* by any *Compact* whatsoever, bind his *Children* or Posterity. For this Son, when a Man, being altogether as free as the Father, *any act of the Father can no more give away the liberty of the Son,* than it can of any body else."[37] In similarly forceful terms, Paine declares that "as no man at first could possess any other public honors than were bestowed upon him, so the givers of those honors could have no power to give away the right of posterity, and though they might say 'We choose you for our head,' they could not without manifest injustice to their children say 'that your children and your children's children shall reign over ours forever.' Because such an unwise, unjust, unnatural compact might (perhaps) in the next succession put them under the government of a rogue or a fool."[38] On the surface Locke and Paine seem to be saying exactly the same thing, that a compact made by one generation cannot be enforced upon a succeeding one, but there is, nevertheless, a fundamental difference in their approach to this principle. Locke declares that the posterity of subjects in a kingdom cannot be bound by commitments to a particular king; Paine declares to the contrary that the posterity of a particular king cannot be imposed upon the subjects of a kingdom. The general principle is the same, but the two authors treat it from opposite perspectives.

Among biblical illustrations to disprove the divine right theory of kings Locke includes the episode of the children of Israel calling upon God to provide them a monarch.[39] Paine examines the same episode at much greater length.[40] Once again their treatment of the theme and their conclusions are completely different. Locke uses the episode to show that the judges or kings of Israel were elected on a temporary basis to lead in warfare and that their authority ceased when the war was over. Paine cites the biblical texts to argue that the origin of monarchy was shrouded in vice and that God himself "entered his protest against monarchical government."

The argument of monarchists that the rights of the British ruling family are based on the Norman conquest is also treated by both Locke and Paine. The former replies that even if the conquest itself were legitimate, its dominion "could reach no farther, than to the *Saxons* and *Britains* that were then Inhabitants of this country."[41] The Normans and all their descendants, according to Locke, remained freemen. Paine cites William the Conqueror as an example of the weakness of the claim to hereditary rights maintained by the British throne. In his words, "a French bastard landing with an armed banditti and establishing himself king of England against the consent of the natives, is in plain terms a very paltry rascally original."[42]

Simplicity in government is recognized by implication as being salutary in Locke's *Essay,* and monarchy is described as "being simple, and most obvious to Men."[43] Simplicity, for Paine, becomes not only salutary, but a dominant virtue, according to the principle which he finds in nature, "that the more simple any thing is, the less liable it is to be disordered, and the easier repaired when disordered."[44] On the basis of this principle, he admits that absolute governments "(though the disgrace of human nature) have this advantage with them, they are simple."

The final chapter of Locke's essay, entitled "Dissolution of Government," justifies revolution or the right of the people to react to a breach of trust in the government by grasping absolute power; in these circumstances the people could legitimately resume their original liberty and establish a new political order. Paine does not literally advocate revolution in this sense in which the people of a state cast off their rulers; rather he argues that when one segment of the state is a victim of a breach of trust, this segment has the right to break away or declare its independence of the rest. His argument cannot be said to be supported or justified by Locke, who vindicates a revolution on the part of all of the people of the state, but not of any part of the whole. In this section Locke also makes a distinction "between the dissolution of the society and the dissolution of the government," which suggests, of course, Paine's famous dichotomy between society and government. But since Locke is discussing a government already in place and Paine speculating on the formation of one, there is no real parallel.

There exists in Locke's *Essay* an earlier argument favoring revolution against unjust rulers, which seems to justify individual or class rebellion. In treating the question of individual will in contrast to the law of nature, Locke seems to affirm that a state of war exists between individuals living in a society and magistrates of that society who behave unjustly in their office.[45] Such an argument could have been used to defend the British colonies in declaring their independence of Great Britain, but it nowhere appears in *Common Sense.* This negative evidence, that is, the absence in

Paine of a solid argument which had appeared in Locke, gives considerable weight to Paine's declaration that he had never read Locke.

Finally to be considered is a similarity of phraseology existing in a sentence from Locke's final chapter and one from the introduction to *Common Sense.* In discussing the possibility of the legislative authority being usurped—that is, of a body of men making laws when they have not been empowered by the people to do so—Locke describes this condition as "being usually brought about by such in the commonwealth, who misuse the power they have." Paine affirms that "a long and violent abuse of power, is generally the Means of calling the right of it in question." Although Paine's words are similar to Locke's, they are not close enough without supporting evidence to warrant the conclusion that they derive directly from Locke's treatise.

As we have seen, Locke sets forth at least three different explanations of the function and purpose of the state. The "chief end" of men's forming a government "*is the Preservation of their Property*"; government is "for the benefit of the Governed, and not the sole advantage of the Governors"; and "the end of Government is the good of Mankind."[46] Paine's single explanation does not conflict with those of Locke, but it is, nevertheless, entirely different: he considers "the design and end of government, viz. freedom and security."[47] Nearly all of Locke's argument—abstract and theoretical though it may be—concerns the practical powers which the British monarch held over his individual subjects. Modern students of Locke have been more interested in such questions as the nature of majority rule and the conflict between public good and individual good. These theoretical considerations, which are obviously important for Paine as well, will be treated in the following chapter.

The foregoing comparison of Locke and Paine has revealed a number of agreements in idea and several similarities in expression, but not a single example of a resemblance so close as to suggest the direct influence of the earlier writer upon the later one. In other words, there is not the slightest internal evidence to indicate that Paine had read Locke's essays on government before he wrote *Common Sense.*

This is a point of considerable importance in the assessment of Paine's intellectual background. Toward the end of his life, one of Paine's former political associates who had changed party affiliation, James Cheetham, charged in a New York newspaper which he edited, the *American Citizen,* that "writers on government since the days of Locke, including Mr. Paine, are but the mere retailers of his ideas and doctrines." He also maintained that "On hereditary and *elective* government, Mr. Paine, in his *Common Sense* and *Rights of Man* has followed Locke Idea for Idea." In a reply, published in a rival newspaper, the *Public Advertiser,* 22 August 1807, Paine affirmed, "It may be so for what I know, for I never read Locke nor even had the work in my hand, and by what I have heard of it from *Horne Tooke* [a legally trained publicist whom Paine knew in London between 1787 and 1791], I had no inducement to read it. It is a speculative, not a practical work, and the style of it is heavy and tedious, as all Locke's writings are."[48]

Paine also distinguished between Locke's notion of elective monarchy and his own theories of representative government. "I suppose Locke has spoken of hereditary and *Elective Monarchy,* but the representative as laid down in Common Sense and Rights of Man is an entirely different thing to elective monarchy."

Two weeks later Paine published a diatribe against his enemy entitled "Farewell Reprimand to James Cheetham," in which he further compared his theories with those of Locke and again denied any direct connection.

> Several writers before Locke had remarked on the absurdity of hereditary succession, but there they stopped. . . .
>
> But I know of no author, nor of any work before Common Sense and Rights of Man appeared, that has exposed and attacked hereditary succession on the ground of illegality, which is the strongest of all grounds to attack it upon; for if the right to set it up does not exist, and that it does not is certain, because it is establishing a form of government, *not for themselves,* but for a future race of people, all discussion upon the subject ends at once. But James Cheetham has not sense enough to see this.
>
> He has got something into his head about Locke, and he keeps it there, for he does not give a single quotation from him to support the random assertions he makes concerning Locke.
>
> "It is to Locke in particular, (says Cheetham) who wrote his incomparable essay on government in 1689, that *we* are almost wholly indebted for those political lights which conducted *us* to *our* revolution."
>
> This is both libellous and false. The revolutionary contest began in an opposition to the assumed rights of the British parliament "*to bind America in all cases whatsoever,*" and there can be nothing in Locke, who wrote in 1689, that can have reference to such a case. The tax upon Tea, which brought on hostilities, was an experiment on the part of the British government to enforce the practice of that assumed right, which was called *the declaratory act.* James Cheetham talks of times and circumstances he knows nothing of, for he did not come here till several years after the war; yet in speaking of the revolution, he uses the words *we,* and *us,* and *our* revolution. It is common in England, in ridiculing self-conceited importance, to say, What a long tail *our* cat has got!
>
> The people of America, in conducting their revolution, learned nothing from Locke; nor was his name, or his work, ever mentioned during the revolution that I know of. The case America was in was a new one without any former example, and the people had to find their way as well as they could by the lights that arose among themselves, of which I can honestly and proudly say, I did my part.
>
> Locke was employed by the first settlers of South Carolina to draw up a form of government for that Province, but it was such an inconsistent aristocratical thing, that it was rejected. Perhaps Mr. Cheetham does not know of this, but he may know it if he will enquire.

Immediately after Paine's death Cheetham published his notoriously unfair biography of his former associate, *Life of Thomas Paine,* in which he substituted sarcasm for his allegation concerning direct influence. Paine's "strongest natural proof" against monarchy, Cheetham now writes, "I should have judged he had clandestinely taken from Locke, had he not told us that he 'read no books, studied no man's opinions.'"[49]

The single paragraph from *Common Sense* which Cheetham here suggests is based on Locke comes immediately after Paine's scriptural demonstration that "the Almighty . . . entered his protest against monarchical government."

> To the evil of monarchy we have added that of hereditary succession; and as the first is a degradation and lessening of ourselves, so the second, claimed as a matter of right, is an insult and an imposition on posterity. For all men being originally equals, no one by birth could have a right to set up his own family in perpetual preference to all others for ever, and though himself might deserve some decent degree of honors of his contemporaries, yet his descendants might be far too unworthy to inherit them. One of the strongest natural proofs of the folly of hereditary right in kings, is, that nature disapproves it, otherwise she would not so frequently turn it into ridicule by giving mankind an Ass for a Lion.[50]

According to Cheetham, this paragraph derives from the following passages from Locke:

> Men being, as has been said, by nature, all free, equal, and independent, no one can be put out of his estate, and subjected to the political power of another without his consent. . . .
>
> It is true, that whatever engagement or promises any one has made for himself, he is under the obligation of them, but cannot, by any compact whatsoever, bind his children or posterity; for his son, when a man, being altogether as free as his father, an act of his father can no more give away the liberty of his son than it can of any body else.

Cheetham's specification of these passages is useful in revealing the flimsiness of the evidence upon which he predicated influence. These passages are separated from each other by over ten pages in the edition from which they are quoted. Also they do not say at all the same things which Paine says. Paine denies that hereditary succession cannot be justified as a matter of right, on the grounds that since all men are equal at birth, no man may set up his own family in a continuing preferential position over others. Locke says in the first passage that since all men are free and equal at birth, no man may have his property taken away from him or be placed under the political power of another without his consent. In the second passage he says that every man must fill the terms of contracts he has made for himself but he cannot make any contracts which are binding upon his posterity. This is by no means the "Idea for Idea" relationship which Cheetham originally proclaimed in his newspaper, and the resemblances are by no means close enough to cast any doubt on Paine's statement that he had never read Locke.

In contrast to these vague and inconclusive resemblances between Locke and Paine, Cheetham provides striking examples of identical expressions in Locke and the Declaration of Independence.

> LOCKE: It is true such men may stir whenever they please, but it will be only to their own just ruin and perdition, for until the mischief be grown general, and the evil designs of the rulers become visible, the people, who are more disposed to suffer than to right themselves by resistance are not apt to stir. [Locke, vol. 5, pp. 574–75]
>
> DECLARATION: Prudence, indeed, will dictate, that government should not be changed for light and transient causes, and accordingly all experience has shown, that mankind are more disposed to suffer, while evils are sufferable, than to right themselves by abolishing the forms to which they are accustomed.
>
> LOCKE: But if a long train of abuses, prevarications, and artifices, all tending the same way, make the design visible to the people, and they cannot but feel what they lie under and see whither they are going, it is not to be wondered that they should then rouse themselves, and endeavour to put the rule into such hands which may secure to them the ends for which government was first erected. [Locke, vol. 5, p. 472]
>
> DECLARATION: But when a long train of abuses and usurpations, pursuing invariably the same course, evinces a design to reduce them under absolute despotism, it is their right, it is their duty to throw off such government, and to provide new guards for their future safety.

These passages provide absolute proof of the direct influence of Locke upon the framers of the Declaration of Independence. Cheetham must have realized how insubstantial by contrast are his allegations concerning Paine.

In the light of Cheetham's parallels, it is amazing that a recent book by Garry Wills arguing against the influence of Locke on the Declaration of Independence has become a best seller. In his book, Wills particularly affirms "no precise verbal parallels have been adduced."[51] Although this is obviously false, Wills's book is otherwise valuable in pointing out the background of moral sense philosophy in Jefferson's thought and parallels between *Common Sense* and the Declaration of Independence.[52] Both documents can be legitimately interpreted as discourses on moral philosophy as well as political statements.

9

Locke: Unraveling the Issues

Two of the basic problems frequently discussed in regard to Locke's *Treatise* are the means of reconciling majority rule with the so-called rule of right and the balancing of public good and individual good.[1] These problems underlie as well Paine's arguments in *Common Sense* concerning the delineation of political power, the definition of civil rights, and the distribution of rights and political power.

Although no modern scholar has as yet compared Locke and Paine in depth, a contemporary of Paine, Thomas Elrington, gave a substantive treatment of precisely the above-mentioned issues as they are found in the two political theorists. Elrington was an Anglican bishop alarmed over the general tendency in Great Britain shortly after the publication of *Rights of Man* to consider Locke and Paine as proponents of the same system. In an edition of Locke's second treatise, published in 1798, therefore, Elrington sought to discredit the parallel between them and to demonstrate that their systems are in reality antithetical. Since Elrington's bishopric was an Irish one and his edition was published in Ireland in the penultimate year of the eighteenth century, there can be little doubt that his comments were intended to counteract sentiments for Irish independence or for social reforms such as had taken place in France. His work is now so rare that only a single copy is listed among library holdings anywhere in the world, that in the University of Leeds, England.[2]

This rarity may perhaps be attributed to the author's dull literary style. That of Locke may be "heavy and tedious," but it is lively and fresh in comparison with Elrington's. As a thinker, however, Elrington is by no means second-rate. Indeed he does more than either Locke or Paine to bring the major issues into focus, and by concentrating on general principles he succeeds in unraveling the major philosophical threads of Paine's polemical discourse. He does not cite particular passages as being related to Locke, and he presumably considers *Rights of Man* rather than *Common Sense* as his target. We have already seen, however, that the same fundamental philosophy is expressed in Paine's two works. The only essential difference is that *Common Sense* emphasizes the members of a political organization conceived as a joint entity whereas *Rights of Man* emphasizes their status as individuals. Elrington's avowed purpose is to show that political power is in essence different from personal rights and that a perfect government is, therefore, not obliged to provide an equality of political power for every individual. In a sense, Elrington anticipated the dichotomy established by modern scholars between the welfare of mankind in general and that of the individual, or between public good and individual good. For Locke, such a discrimination "simply did not exist because he did not draw a distinction between the public good and the particular goods of individuals. For him the one was the same as the other, and though it is true that he was more concerned in some contexts with the particulars and in others with the total, he equated the public good with "the preservation of the property (i.e. the lives, liberties, and estates) of individuals."[3] Paine also never conceived of a dichotomy between public good and individual good, and there is almost nothing on the subject in his system to separate him from Locke.

In his preface, Elrington affirms that Paine teaches that "whatever the people have a mind to do, they have a right to do," even though these are not Paine's actual words in either *Common Sense* or *Rights of Man*. Elrington also affirms that the authority of Locke has been consistently cited in support of this alleged principle of Paine. What Paine actually says in *Rights of Man* is "That which a whole nation chooses to do, it has a right to do,"[4] a completely different statement from that which Elrington accuses him of making. There may be ethical grounds for objecting to such a maxim, but in the presenting of any objections, the maxim should be correctly stated. Elrington's misquotation implies that Paine separates the masses from the government or from the upper ranks of society and that he approves of any action which the broadest segment of the populace may wish to carry out. Paine in reality says that the unanimous will of a nation justifies any action it may carry out, and he implies that the entire nation must be committed to national policy before such a policy is justified.

As a matter of fact, Locke does lend some support to Paine's maxim. He certainly suggests that the right of changing government rests on the will of the people, and even Elrington admits other concessions which the famous seventeenth-century philosopher makes to popular control. "He speaks of the first formation of civil society as a *merely voluntary* act, and scarcely hints at any limitations by which those who establish government are restrained in their choice of its form; and whenever he mentions the supreme power to which every part of the state is subordinate, he describes it as residing ultimately in the people."[5]

Elrington proceeds, however, to affirm two fundamental differences between the system of Locke and that of Paine: first, in their conception of people; and, second, in their conception of supreme power. According to Elrington's interpretation, Paine extends the notion of people in a political sense to the multitude; whereas Locke limits the notion to embrace only those possessing property, and whose interests, therefore, coincide with those of the state and assure their being qualified to evaluate these same interests. In regard to the power of the people, Paine considers it arbitrary; whereas Locke portrays it "as dependent on, and controlled by the law of Nature." It is of some importance to the interpretation of *Common Sense* to decide whether it does indeed raise these issues of political philosophy and, if so, to indicate whether Paine's interpretation is actually different from Locke's.

The issue is significant, transcending both Locke and the American Revolution. One may inquire whether the concept of people represents the entire population, only those persons owning property, or only the multitude, the so-called "common" or vulgar segment of the population. Herder later in the eighteenth century took for granted that the "common people," not the nation as a whole, is "the 'largest and most honorable' part of mankind," and twentieth-century Marxist and existentialist critics have applied this assumption to both society and aesthetics.[6] It if be thus accepted that the "common people" are the focus of society, is it then a corollary that political power should reside with this segment, or must power be distributed throughout all segments of society?

Locke, almost at the beginning of his treatise, defines political power as the right of making laws for the regulating and preserving of property and employing the force of the community in executing these laws and defending it from external injury. These laws would include those bearing the penalty of death. Elrington observes that right must be distinguished from power and accuses Paine of failing to make this distinction in promulgating his "well-known dogma" that "whatever the majority of a nation have a mind to do, they have a right to do."[7] Here we notice that Elrington has changed Paine's words in a slightly different fashion, but since he continues to misquote, his accusation still cannot be considered as damaging. Indeed, in *Rights of Man* Paine seems to base the authority of government on abstract virtue rather than on opinion by characterizing his political system as a return to ethical principles, and the American and French revolutions as representing "government founded on a *moral theory, on a system of universal peace, on the indefeasible, hereditary rights of man.*" In this passage, Paine follows Locke in reconciling majority-will democracy with the existence of objective moral standards.[8]

Elrington not only attributes to Paine words which he never expressed, but completely without foundation affirms that "*Paine* himself has not ventured to give a definition for the word *right.*"[9] This charge is certainly true in regard to *Common Sense,* but not in regard to *Rights of Man,* Elrington's major target, which contains the most famous discussion of the subject in world literature. As we have already indicated, Paine's reference in *Common Sense* to man in the state of nature surrendering up "part of his property" suggests that at this time his conception of rights was very much like Locke's. Although he probably meant by *property* freedom of action as well as material possesions, his actual words do not seem to take basic liberties into account.

The question of rights concerned Paine profoundly, however, for he returned to it over and over after the publication of *Common Sense.* An extensive treatment appears in an unsigned letter originally discovered by Moncure D. Conway in the papers of Thomas Jefferson and subsequently widely discussed by students of Burke, Jefferson, and Paine. This letter, probably written in 1788, is extremely important, not only as a link between Paine and Jefferson, as it has been treated in the past, but also as an intermediate step between *Common Sense* and *Rights of Man.*[10] Neither Rousseau nor any of Paine's other predecessors treated in detail the specific nature of human rights or the distinction between those possessed in the state of nature and those in civil society. In his letter to Jefferson, Paine begins with the supposition he had set forth in *Common Sense* of "a small number of persons settled in some sequestered part of the earth, unconnected with the rest," except that he now specifies a particular number: "suppose twenty persons, strangers to each other, to meet in a country not before inhabited." What follows may, therefore, be considered as an expansion of the relevant passage in *Common Sense.*

Each of the twenty would be "a Sovereign in his own natural right," but his power might not be adequate to protect his right. It would then occur to these twenty persons to exchange their exposed condition to a protected one by joining together "so that each individual should possess the strength of the whole number." They would then distinguish between the rights which they could exercise fully and perfectly as individuals and those which they were not able thus to exercise. "Of the first kind are the rights of thinking, speaking, forming and giving opinions, and perhaps . . . those which can be fully exercised by the individual without the aid of exterior assistance; or in other words rights of personal competency. Of the second kind are those of personal protection, of acquiring and possessing property, in the extension of which the individual natural power is less than the natural right." In the course of the transition into civil society, the first class of rights, "those of personal competency," are retained by the individual, but the second class, "those of defective power," are exchanged for "a right to the whole power produced by a condensation of all the parts." In other words, one class of natural rights, that comprising the perfect ones, is never given up at all. Civil rights consist exclusively in those of "imperfect power," in which the individual agrees not to act wholly in his own person, but "under the guarantee of society." Opinion is divided on whether Locke considered the state of nature as merely an expository device or an actual historical period. Since Paine uses the verb *suppose* in both *Common Sense* and his letter to Jefferson, his portrayal of the passage from the state of nature to society seems to be merely a hypothetical delineation.

Rousseau, who certainly agreed that the state of nature was irretrievable, whether or not it had ever existed in reality, explains in the *Social Contract* that the entrance into civil socity means that each individual places his person and all his power under the supreme direction of the general will and that the social body receives each member as an indivisible part of the whole.[11] According to Conway, Rousseau here describes a trading process whereby man renounces one part of his rights to safeguard the others, whereas Paine maintains that man does not give up any of his rights, but submits a certain class of them to arbitrage as the only means of protecting them.[12] Conway's interpretation is not quite exact, for in some newspaper articles printed in 1777 Paine unequivocally affirmed that "civil government necessarily implies a surrender of something into a common stock, constituting a common property, and to be used for the mutual good of all the proprietors."[13] His distinction between natural and civil rights is essentially the same as that in his letter to Jefferson, but he further explains in 1777 how some natural rights are limited to civil society.

> A *natural* right is an animal right; and the power to act it, is supposed either fully or in part, to be mechanically contained within ourselves as individuals. *Civil* rights are derived from the assistance or agency of other persons; they form a sort of common stock, which, by the consent of all, may be occasionally used for the benefit of any. They are substituted in the room of some natural rights, either defective in power or dangerous in practice, and are contrived to fit the members of the community with greater ease to themselves and safety to others, than what the natural ones could do for the individual in a state of nature; for instance, a man has a *natural* right to redress himself whenever he is injured, but the full exercise of this, as a *natural* right, would be dangerous to society, because it admits him a judge in his own cause; on the other hand, he may not be able, and must either submit to the injury or expose himself to greater: Therefore, the *civil* right of redressing himself by an appeal to public justice, which is the substitute, makes him stronger than the natural one, and less dangerous. Either party likewise, has a natural right to plead his own cause; this right is consistent with safety, therefore it is retained; but the parties may not be able, nay, they may be dumb, therefore the civil right of pleading by proxy, that is, by a council, is an appendage to the natural right and the trial by jury, is perfectly a civil right common to both parties.[14]

It is quite clear that, contrary to Conway's interpretation, Paine does hold that some natural rights are curtailed in the exchange for civil rights.

In *Rights of Man,* Paine draws together elements from his 1777 and 1788 discussions. He defines natural rights, as distinguished from civil, as those which appertain to every man "in right of his existence," that is, merely in consideration of his being alive. This is essentially the same as his statement in 1777–78 that " a *natural* right is an animal right." Natural rights comprise thinking or intellectual activity, including religious belief, and acting as an individual for one's own comfort and happiness provided that the resulting actions are not injurious to the natural rights of others. Civil rights are all founded upon natural rights, but in the natural state the individual lacks the power of enforcing them. These civil rights include all those relative to security and protection. Civil power, in which civil rights reside, "is made up of the aggregate of that class of the natural rights of man, which becomes defective in the individual in point of power, and answers not his purpose, but when collected to a focus, becomes competent to the purpose of every one." Finally, "the power produced from the aggregate of natural rights, imperfect in power in the individual, cannot be applied to invade the natural rights which are retained in the individual, and in which the power to execute is as perfect as the right itself." In his final position, Paine agrees with Locke that some natural rights are given up in exchange for civil rights, but he seems to claim for the individual in relationship to the majority a somewhat greater degree of autonomy than does Locke.[15]

It is obvious that Paine's final analysis of natural and civil rights is far more complex than his cursory statement in *Common Sense* that man "finds it necessary to surrender up a part of his property to furnish means for the protection of the rest." His expanded treatment, nevertheless, does not depart in any way from the fundamental concept of his original statement, but is merely an explanation of it.

Locke specifically mentions the right to seek reparation for injuries sustained, as well as the right of others to join in seeking this reparation. Elrington adds that it is not only the right, but also the duty, of a second party to join in seeking reparation. This leads Locke's commentator to make an original distinction between "those rights which can be renounced at pleasure, and those which cannot," the latter of which are all those "connected with duties."[16] Paine, however, makes an even stronger statement than either Locke or Elrington on the reciprocal relationship of rights and duties. A year before the publication of *Rights of Man,* he explained in an unpublished letter to Thomas Walker of Rotherham, 14 April 1790, "My idea of supporting liberty of Conscience and the rights of Citizens is that of supporting those rights in *other people,* for if a Man supports only his *own* right for his *own sake* he does no moral duty."[17] In *Right of Man* he illustrates this principle in a reference to the French Declaration of the Rights of Man and of Citizens: here he affirms that "a Declaration of Rights is, by reciprocity, a Declaration of Duties also. Whatever is my right as a man, is also the right of another; and it becomes my duty to guarantee, as well as to possess."[18]

Although Paine suggests that civil power is inherently attached to civil rights and its enforcement, he does not, as Elrington alleges, consider right and power as equivalent. Elrington interprets Locke as affirming "that men have not a right to establish a power over themselves which shall dispose *arbitrarily* of their lives and properties" and that, moreover, "their will is not the measure of their rights."[19] There are no passages in either *Common Sense* or *Rights of Man* which indicate that Paine either advances or denies these controverted principles.

A determination of whether rights and political power must in every degree necessarily coincide is fundamental to questions of suffrage and representation. Elrington asserts that "men are free, if governed by just and impartial laws, though in the making of those laws they were not consulted; that is, that the liberty of the people and the power or the independence of the people are perfectly distinct."[20] This doctrine has a good deal in common with a comment of Montesquieu which a colonial opponent of *Common Sense,* Carter Braxton, quoted approvingly: "It is not my business to examine whether the English actually enjoy . . . liberty or not; sufficient it is for my purpose to observe that it is established by their laws, and I enquire no farther."[21]

According to Elrington, "sober" political writers, assume that political power should be distributed to the various classes of men in proportion to their fitness to use it; this is in opposition to those who "contend for the absolute equality of political rights in all the ranks of society." Elrington might have suggested as an example that the American colonies before 1776 possessed liberty even though they were taxed by laws about which they had not been consulted. This proposition Paine would certainly have denied. Elrington might also have maintained as another example that a minor possesses liberty even though he is restricted by laws about which he has not been consulted. This Paine would probably have accepted.

The foundations for the apportioning of political power are to be found, according to Elrington, in the origins of political societies. He objects to Locke's implication that entering into society was a purely voluntary act of will.[22] According to Elrington, if it can be proved that men were under a "direct obligation" to enter society, their subsequent conduct must be under the bonds of liberty, no longer dependent upon their own will, but upon the law of nature. As far as this concept is concerned, Paine is closer to Elrington than to Locke; for he specifically says in *Common Sense* that "necessity, like a gravitating power," forms men into society.[23]

In further comments on the process of conversion from the state of nature to society, Elrington ingeniously demonstrates that the shift from one status to the other necessitates a concomitant adjustment from a condition of social equality to one of extreme political inequality. As he reconstructs the process, the law of nature dictates that every individual "shall act in such a manner as may best conduce to the advantage of all." Natural forces reveal the duty of all "to establish some system by which the mode of conduct proper for each individual, and the degrees of punishment for transgressions of it, might be ascertained."[24] In the establishment of this process only those whose occupations and functions in the society fitted them for the awesome task would participate, and all others would conceive it their duty rigorously to exclude themselves. The excluded elements comprised the young who lack "that judgment and experience necessary to qualify them for giving effectual assistance" and the women, who are disqualified by their "retired habits of life and confinement to the minute details of domestic management." In this way Elrington demonstrates that "it would be the *duty* of the *majority* of the community, (the whole of one sex, and all the youth of the other) to decline any interference in the first act of political power." Here he shrewdly lays the foundation for a regulated society founded upon political distinctions. The duty of the majority of the community voluntarily "to decline any interference in the first act of political power" leads to the separation of *personal rights,* those relating to the security of life, liberty, and property, from *political duties* or political power. Elrington has thus proved to his own satisfaction that "even at the first formation of government," the people as a whole do not possess the right to political power and that they do not possess the "right of doing whatever they have a mind to do." He adds, however, that the right of excluding others from political power should not be insisted upon in the modern world because of "the discontent naturally arising from such restrictions."[25] This is a concession to the common people which even Paine does not make. In *Rights of Man* he surprisingly says nothing whatsoever about the lack of power as a source of dissatisfaction among the common people, but he does mention high taxes and the national debt. "By remitting the taxes of the poor," he observes, "*they* will be totally relieved and all discontent will be taken away."[26] He also affirms that "the riots and tumults, which at various times have happened in England" proceeded not from the lack of government, but from the existing government, which instead of consolidating society, has divided it, and deprived it of its natural cohesion.[27]

Paine, moreover, does not in either *Common Sense* or *Rights of Man* treat the subject of the limitation of suffrage at the origin of society or in an advanced stage of government. Evidence will be presented in a subsequent chapter to show that at the time of writing *Common Sense,* he took for granted that the suffrage base in the English colonies was adequate. It was essentially the same as that defined by Elrington, which excludes "the whole of one sex, and all the youth of the other." In *Rights of Man* Paine objected strenuously to disproportionate representation (rotten boroughs and unrepresented municipalities), but his complaints were directed against geographical rather than class discrimination. This is true of his prior objections in his "Lover of Order" essay to the arbitrary behavior of delgates to the Pennsylvania Assembly. The same principle applies to his recommendations in *Common Sense* for the election of a national congress and to his advocacy of "a large and equal representation."[28]

Other opponents of *Rights of Man* touched upon and vindicated further distinctions which exist in society apart from sex and age, particularly, wisdom, education, and property ownership. There is nothing in either

Common Sense or *Rights of Man* to indicate that Paine would have objected to these qualities as requirements for suffrage. His major statement on rights and distinctions embodies three axioms, which he describes as being "as universal as truth and the existence of man, and combining moral with political happiness and national prosperity."

> I. *Men are born and always continue free and equal in respect to their rights. Civil distinctions, therefore, can be founded only on public utility.*
>
> II. *The end of all political associations is the preservation of the natural and imprescriptible rights of man; and these rights are liberty, property, security and resistance of oppression.*
>
> III. *The Nation is essentially the source of all Sovereignty; nor can any individual or any body of men, be entitled to any authority which is not expressly derived from it.*[29]

In the first of these principles, Paine clearly recognizes "civil distinctions" as being separate from rights, and he bases them on "public utility." His scathing denunciations of privilege in general are based entirely on that arising from inheritance.

In relation to Locke's treatment of the relation between father and son, Elrington takes it upon himself to suggest that limitations other than those of sex and age should be placed upon political power. Locke, in observing that parents have power over their children until the latter attain adequate understanding of their own, was equally insistent to affirm that the son becomes a free man as soon as "he comes to the estate that made his father a freeman." Elrington, however, was interested only in a parallel between children and unsophisticated adults in society. He raised the question, "may not this incapacitating deficiency of understanding exist among adults as well as minors?" And he asked further why such inferiority in intellectual attainments should not be reflected in inferiority of political power in the same proportion.[30]

Locke is clear on the principle that equal representation should be the basis of legislative power, but he places so many qualifications in his statement that Elrington has little difficulty in finding in it a philosophy of elitism. According to Locke, representation should not be based upon "old custom, but true reason, the *number* of *members,* in all places that have a right to be distinctly represented, which no part of the people however incorporated can pretend to, but in proportion to the assistance which it affords to the public."[31] This is, of course, a far cry from universal suffrage, as Elrington recognized. Locke also criticizes the unevenness in borough representation (even in his day some heavily populated districts were given no representatives, and some practically unpopulated were accorded an entire seat in Parliament). Elrington ingeniously interprets this recognition of a gross evil as being tantamount to a recognition that no other evils existed. According to this reasoning, the boldness of Locke's attack on borough representation indicates that he would have been equally vociferous about the qualifications of electors had he believed that any changes of this nature were necessary. "Locke, when speaking of the political power of *the people,* had no idea that he would be interpreted as attributing that power *to the multitude.*"[32] As far as Elrington is concerned, it would be fair to conclude that Locke believed "that those should be excluded from a right of suffrage who, having no property, cannot be considered as sufficiently independent to make a free choice, nor connected with the state by a security strong enough to insure their attention to its interests; and who, being enslaved to their daily necessities, are not possessed of the means or the leisure to obtain such information upon political subjects as is necessary to enable them to judge wisely in the choice of a person to act for them." Although these qualifications are somewhat ambiguous, it would be fair to conclude that Elrington was describing women and the uneducated poor.

When Locke uses the expression "a fair and equal representative" he means, as do both Burgh and Paine after him, a proper geographical distribution of representation. Elrington converts the expression into a prescription against popular government by observing that "the authority of the celebrated Montesquieu is equally unfavourable to those who contend for *universal* suffrage."[33] Strangely enough the only quotation he produces to show the alleged existence of this sentiment in *Esprit des lois* (bk. 11, chap. 5) is completely irrelevant: "*Dans un état libre,* says he [Montesquieu], tout homme qui est censé avoir une âme libre, *doit être gouverné par lui même.*" It is undoubtedly true that Montesquieu, as Elrington says, "had no idea of *power* being a *personal right,* possessed equally by men of every description," but it is equally true that he made no effort to refute such a doctrine.

A careful survey of *Common Sense* will reveal that Paine and Elrington are not actually at opposite poles on the matter of the exercise of political power, no matter how much they differ in regard to theory. Paine not only fails to advocate universal suffrage, as it is now understood, but he also strongly suggests that suffrage should not be extended indiscriminately to the multitude. He makes the significant admission, "It may not always happen that our soldiers are citizens, and the multitude a body of reasonable men; virtue . . . is not hereditary, neither is it perpetual."[34] In one of his works published between *Commnon Sense* and *Rights of Man,* moreover, he recognizes that in a democracy the majority without constitutional checks might tyrannize over the minority, and he uses the pertinent phrase "the despotism of numbers."[35] In *Common Sense* he also recognizes the existence of "the vulgar"[36] and vigorously opposes mob action.[37] Although Paine's objections to hereditary monarchy are based on the principle that all of mankind were "originally equals in the order of creation," he is completely silent on the subject of inequalities of talent. He refers to the natural distinction between male and female, and suggests that the distinction between rich and poor may also be in the nature of things—accounted for at least "without having recourse to the harsh ill-sounding names of oppression and avarice."[38]

In speculating on the origin of government, he seems to assume a parity of reason; the only criterion he offers for the selection of legislators is that of "convenience"; and he assumes that those selected as representatives are not fundamentally different from those being represented.[39] In proposing a continental congress, he suggests that its members be chosen by "qualified voters." He advocates a "large and equal representation" as being an extremely important political matter, but, as we have already said, by "large" he is referring to the number of representatives, not to the electorate, and by "equal," to geographical distribution.[40]

Elrington introduces a fundamental question about the intellectual behaviour of legislators completely separate from the principles of representation—whether the civil law should depend on the law of nature or upon the will of man. In so doing, he presents a theory of the organization of the representative system fundamentally different from that of Paine. According to his theory, the "duty of entering into society" arose from "the weakness of men's reason" and their inability to cope with "the task of determining the conduct they are forced to pursue" in consequence of complex social relationships.[41] Their first object, therefore, becomes the appointing of legislative power or the delegating "the right of determining for them to such persons as may be better qualified for the task than themselves." Paine, as we have already seen, makes no suggestion that legislators are superior to those who elect them to office. It is convenience alone which operates "to leave the legislative part to be managed by a select number chosen from the whole body, who are supposed to have the same concerns at stake which those have who appointed them, and who will act in the same manner as the whole body would act were they present."[42] Furthermore, according to Paine's system, it would be to the best interest of the community to have a constant turnover in the personnel of the legislators by means of frequent elections so that "the *elected* might by that means return and mix again with the general body of the *electors* in a few months." Paine declares that every man by "natural right" has a voice in primitive government, but he makes no observations about more advanced forms.

On the basis of the principle that legislators should have superior qualifications, Elrington argues that each individual legislator must make decisions according to the law of nature, not his individual will, and that these legislative decisions have the same authority over the behavior of each member of society which his own reason would have in the state of nature. The authority of these decisions derives "from the intrinsic fitness of the appointed legislature to discover and promulgate the law of nature, according to the various relations of society by which its obligations are drawn closer and become more numerous."[43] Elrington similarly reasons that if the true excellence of laws is based not on conformity to the will of the majority of people in a community but in conformity to the law of nature, therefore the giving of equal power to every individual in society is not the best method of attaining excellence in government.[44] Elrington's acquiescence to the law of nature—even granting that it may be ascertained in political relationships—still leaves unanswered the question of who is to decide whether or not legislation conforms to this law. The general tenor of his arguments suggests, of course, an intellectual elite or an aristocracy; the general tenor of Paine's arguments suggests the majority of qualified voters. Paine is probably closer on this point to Locke than is Elrington.

Locke affirms that men must follow their own conscience in deciding when to declare that a state of war exists between individuals in a society and unjust magistrates, and when to act accordingly. Elrington objects that "an abstract idea of right" is not a sufficient motive for destroying the peace and order of society, an anticipation of a standard objection to many ideologues in the first decades of the nineteenth century.[45] It is hard to see how Locke's concept of the appeal to conscience, however, is fundamentally different from Elrington's concept of the appeal to the law of nature or why an abstract idea of right (the law of nature) should be accepted as the basis of all government, but not to be deemed sufficient to determine whether a specific government is functioning properly. Locke himself answers the objection that the state would be in constant turmoil if the people have the right "to set up a new legislature whenever they took offence at the old one." In his opinion history had proved an aversion among the English people to quit their old constitutions. According to Elrington's rebuttal, Locke's opinion was clearly founded "on a partial and imperfect experience," and "it would have been better had he stated, that the right of changing their government depended, not on the mere *will* of the people, but on their reason, dictating the *necessity* of it as the only means of removing evils greater than those the change itself would produce."[46]

The same opposition between individual will and the law of nature appears in Locke's effort to define individual freedom. Natural liberty, according to his portrayal, is to have only the law of nature for one's rule; liberty in society is to have a standing rule "common to every one of that society, and made by the legislative power erected in it."[47] But as Elrington points out, it is generally assumed that the laws of the community which are equivalent to this standing rule are enacted with the consent of the majority of the community. The question, therefore, arises whether these laws represent merely the determination of the will of the people or the determination of that which reason approves—in other words, that which is right in nature.

Elrington's insistence on the validity of the law of nature strikes a note completely different from Burke's denunciation in *Reflections on the French*

Revolution of theories of government on abstract principles or, in his words, of the "clumsy subtlety of . . . political metaphysics." Indeed from this perspective, Elrington and Paine seem to belong in one camp; Burke in another. Paine begins the second part of his *Rights of Man* with a parallel between the laws of science and the laws of politics, specifically affirming that "all the great laws of society are laws of nature."[48] Also in *Rights of Man* he repudiates the use of bare power; arguing that the representative system "admits not of a separation between knowledge and power."[49] He further accuses Burke of maintaining that "government is arbitrary power."[50] There is no passage in any of Paine's works to indicate that he would have disputed Elrington's contention that political power should be based on the law of nature rather than arbitrary will (even though Paine opposed the arbitrary will of monarchy and aristocracy while Elrington opposed that of the people). It is also true that Elrington suggests that a large segment of the people is not capable of judging the relevance of most behavior to the law of nature, whereas Paine does not broach this subject at all. He certainly does not, however, make any extravagant claims for the intellectual competency of the masses. The thrust of his argument is in the other direction—affirming the essential simplicity of government when it is organized most closely in conformity with the law of nature.

The parallel between science and politics as twin products of natural law is less obvious in Paine's American works than in *Rights of Man,* despite the passages in *Common Sense* in which Paine compares a metropole and its colonies to a sun and its satellites. Indeed two other themes in *Common Sense* seem to suggest that civil law is not based entirely upon natural law but upon a tension between arbitrary will and the law of nature. These are the themes that political power must have a legitimate source and that government should be established upon natural right. Paine brings the two themes together, first by declaring that in most nations power came first and government was formed subsequently, and then by advocating that in America principles of government should be formed first and men later delegated to execute these principles.[51]

In treating the theme of arbitrary will, Paine accuses George III of arrogating illegitimate power to himself, castigates his "thirst for arbitrary power," characterizes the power of kings in general as arbitrary, and describes the first king as "nothing better than the principal ruffian of some restless gang."[52] In treating natural right, Paine both opens and closes *Common Sense* with reference to the "rights of mankind," declares that "equal rights of nature" will not justify exalting one man so greatly above the rest as kings are, and affirms that "government of our own is our natural right."[53] For Paine, the rights of nature are an essential part of the law of nature. The basic difference between Paine and Elrington lies in the definition of these rights.

The distinction between the will of man and the law of nature as contrary sources of civil law is, moreover, purely an academic one, for in the twentieth century as well as the eighteenth, most, if not all, legislators, regardless of their philosophical beliefs, have based their decisions on personal reactions of the moment rather than on any elusive attempt to determine the law of nature or other abstract standards. Elrington admits as much by recognizing what he calls "the sovereign *power* of the multitude."[54] Right or wrong, it cannot be resisted. The only hope Elrington holds out for just government is through general recognition of the "practical advantages" of adhering to sound principles. Paine in *Common Sense* approaches the same pragmatic recognition of self interest as a prime motivating force in government in his survey of recent votes in the Pennsylvania House of Assembly in which measures were passed in behalf of the whole colony which a majority of the colony would have opposed had they possessed the power to do so.

Underlying all of Elrington's comments is the suggestion that Paine had attempted to advance a system of class conflict—to work for a total equalization in social and economic as well as political areas. Obviously Paine believed in political equality and in the rights of man (which, contrary to the accusation of Elrington, he carefully defined and limited), but he at no time in his life advocated a general leveling. Indeed both *Common Sense* and *Rights of Man,* especially the latter, include strong antileveling passages. In *Rights of Man,* he states that in America, "the poor are not oppressed, the rich are not privileged. Industry is not mortified by the splendid extravagance of a court rioting at its expense. Their taxes are few, because their government is just."[55] Referring to the charge that his work had been called a leveling system, he retorted, "the only system to which the word *levelling* is truly applicable, is the hereditary monarchical system. It is a system of *mental levelling.*"[56] Finally, Paine specifically underlines the existence of widespread intellectual inequities: "Experience, in all ages, and in all countries, has demonstrated, that it is impossible to control Nature in her distribution of mental powers. She gives them as she pleases."[57]

Many others before Elrington had sought to disparage Paine by associating him with leveling systems; Elrington followed a unique path by seeking to disassociate him from Locke. In neither attempt did he succeed. Paine's system of government does not differ fundamentally from Locke's, even though no evidence exists to show that he borrowed directly from his predecessor in any way. In regard to the main principle at issue, the defining of people in a political sense, Paine considers the people to comprise the entire population—not merely those owning property on one side or the so-called common people on the other.

10
Relations with Rousseau

Evidence for Paine's acquaintance with Rousseau is considerably more extensive than that for his knowledge of Locke, which indeed, as we have seen, is entirely negative. Paine makes no reference to Rousseau or his works in *Common Sense,* but in a newspaper article published four months later defending his pamphlet he alludes to a proposal which Rousseau had made for establishing permanent peace in Europe.[1] Rousseau's refurbishing of a plan originally proclaimed by the abbé St. Pierre had been translated into English as *A Project For Perpetual Peace* in 1761. Even if Paine had read this translation, however, it has no direct relevance to *Common Sense.* Many years later, in the first part of *The Rights of Man,* 1791, Paine complimented Rousseau on "the loveliness of sentiment in favor of liberty" in his writings, and in the following year in an essay published in Paris he quoted two sentences from the *Social Contract* on the minimal intellectual qualities possessed by ministers of state.[2] These references late in Paine's career do nothing, however, to prove that he had read Rousseau at the time of writing *Common Sense.* All that these allusions show is that Paine knew about Rousseau as early as four months after its publication, that he quoted from the *Social Contract* many years later, and, most important of all, that he admitted to some knowledge of the writings of the Swiss thinker. This is in sharp contrast to his unequivocal denial of ever having read a page of Locke, whether or not the denial is to be taken at face value.

A remarkable parallelism may be discerned in the personal lives of Paine and Rousseau. As other authors have noticed, both men developed from humble stock, were primarily self-educated, spent their early years in rambling from one place to another, came relatively late to their careers as writers and seriously considered themselves as righteous moralists as well as political theorists.[3] Their general political presuppositions are so close that James Russell Lowell considered Rousseau to be Paine's intellectual father.[4] It is natural, therefore, to look for both resemblances and affinities in their writings.

The works of Rousseau which cover ground similar to that of *Common Sense* are his *Social Contract* and his pair of essays submitted to the Academy of Dijon, now known as his two discourses. In one of the latter he answers the question whether the restoration of the arts and sciences had exercised a purifying effect upon morals, and in the other he attempts to explain the origin of the inequality which exists among men. In order for Paine to have read these books, English translations had to be available in the colonies, for at this time he did not know the French language. Indeed he was unable either to speak or to understand French when he was elected to the French Constitutional Convention, fifteen years after the publication of *Common Sense.*

An American scholar who has devoted an entire book to the influence of Rousseau in eighteenth-century America has discovered that copies in English of the *Second Discourse* and the *Social Contract* were available in a New York City library in 1773.[5] This scholar has also shown that the *First Discourse* was mentioned in the *Virginia Gazette* in 1751, but he nevertheless concludes that Rousseau's treatment of the relation of the arts and sciences to morality "seems to have passed almost unnoticed" in the English colonies. The two discourses together, in this author's opinion, "made little if any impact on eighteenth century America." Even the *Social Contract* was not reprinted in the Western Hemisphere until 1797, and our authority affirms that it "exerted no palpable influence on political thought in the United States in the eighteenth century."[6] In particular reference to the influence of Rousseau on Paine, we are told that the latter remains "a special problem, still unsolved, perhaps unsolvable."

This scholar's study of the impact of Rousseau in America is based almost entirely on external evidence, that is, library holdings, book catalogs, and specific references to the Citizen of Geneva in letters or published works. If we are to come any closer to solving the "special problem" of Paine, we must resort to internal evidence, that is, to a comparison of the language and ideas of the two political writers. The only author who has attempted in any way to do this was, surprisingly enough, one of Paine's contemporaries and acquaintances, William Godwin. In his radical denunciation of social inequities in Great Britain, *Political Justice* (1793), Godwin affirmed that Rousseau's principle "that the imperfections of government were the only perennial source of the vices of mankind" had been "expressed with great perspicuity and energy, but not developed, by Thomas Paine, in the first page of his Common Sense."[7] Godwin adds, however, that this doctrine appears in Paine "probably without being suggested by the writings of Rousseau."

The theme uniting Rousseau's two discourses with his *Social Contract* is that of primitivism, the view that the further away one retreats from civilized society the more to be desired are the conditions of primitive life. This retreat may be either chronological (preferring ancient times to modern) or sociological (preferring simple forms of existence in geographical areas remote from the centers of population to the complications of civilization). Primitivism is a theme which also runs through Paine's political and social ideology.

In a sense Rousseau's denial in his *First Discourse* that the arts and sciences have been a boon to mankind is a *tour de force* comparable to that of Erasmus in his *In Praise of Folly,* but Rousseau maintains a serious rather than an ironical tone throughout. This he establishes by quoting the most learned man among the polite and cultivated Athenians, Socrates, speaking in praise of ignorance. For Rousseau, the happy state for mankind is the state of innocence, and man's efforts to emerge from it, stimulated by his pride, have brought upon him the evils of luxury, profligacy, and slavery. Literature and the arts encourage indolence, vanity, and luxury; the sciences enervate both body and mind and corrupt morals. Virtue, which is engraved on every heart, is to be prized above any of the achievements of the arts and sciences. But virtue not only does not require vast learning, but is even vitiated by it.

Rousseau's attempt to explain the origin of social classes in his *Second Discourse* suggests that since equality was an obvious condition of the state of nature, the state of nature was superior to artificial civilization. His discussion once more emphasizes the good things of primitive life and the bad ones of civilization. The most original contribution of the essay consists of a reconstruction of the stages through which man presumably passed in the development of society: an animal stage in which man is distinguished from wild beasts by little but his free will; an intermediate stage in which he discovers fire and engages in fishing and hunting; and a communal stage in which he possesses a family and private property and recognizes the duties of civility. Private property, for Rousseau, was the origin of both civilization and the inequality of man, and as such the root of the evils of modern life. In an often-quoted sentence he declares, "The first Man who, after enclosing a Piece of Ground, took it into his Head to say, *This is mine,* and found People simple enough to believe him, was the true Founder of civil Society."[8]

Rousseau's notion of the origin of society has much in common with that of Mandeville in the *Fable of the Bees.* Mandeville argues that "in the wild state of nature . . . no species of animals is, without the curb of government, less capable of agreeing long together in multitudes than that of man." A number of crafty or wise men, therefore, perceived that in order to make their fellow creatures submit to being governed, it was necessary to persuade them "that it was more beneficial for every body to conquer than indulge his appetites, and much better to mind the public than what seemed his private interest." These crafty men thereupon preached up "publicspiritedness, that they might reap the fruits of the labour and self-denial of others, and at the same time indulge their own appetites with less disturbance."[9] Rousseau similarly proclaims that the whole human race was subjected to work, servitude and misery for the profit of a few ambitious men. The parallel between Mandeville and Rousseau is particularly significant, since Rousseau throughout his two discourses provides unmistakable evidence of having read *The Fable of the Bees.*

The Mandevillean explanation of the origin of society suggests that man had gone directly from the state of nature to a political society or government, whereas Rousseau describes the transition from an animal to a civilized stage in at least three separate steps. Paine similarly suggests a tripartite process, comprising state of nature, unorganized society, and finally, government. The basic difference among the three theorists is not concerned with the steps in the development of society, however, but with the original nature of man. Mandeville accepts the Hobbesian view that men were fundamentally selfish and quarrelsome in the state of nature; Rousseau and Paine agree with Shaftesbury that man was born with social instincts. A. O. Lovejoy has pointed out that Rousseau declared in the first draft of the *Social Contract* that an ideal state of nature never existed: "l'heureuse vie de l'âge d'or fut toujours un état étranger à la race humain."[10] Although Paine makes no such admission, he probably also considered the depiction of the state of nature as an expository device rather than myth or historical reality. His portrayal in *Common Sense* suggests that he felt that the state of nature actually existed essentially as he describes it, but his letter to Jefferson in 1788, which is described in the preceding chapter, begins with a phrase suggesting that he is dealing merely with a hypothesis: "suppose twenty persons, strangers to each other, to meet in a country not before inhabited." Several thinkers before Paine had implied a distinction between government and society, for example, Locke, Montesquieu, Mandeville, and Rousseau, but Paine in *Common Sense* emphasizes the importance of the distinction more than any of his predecessors.

In a passage in his *Second Discourse* referring to Locke and Barbeyrac, Rousseau condemns those who submit to a tyrannical government and by so doing subject their posterity to the same ignominy of subjection. Here he seems to be looking toward Paine's later doctrine that posterity may not be harnessed by preceding generations, but it is only a hint, not a forthright declaration.

The opening sentence of the *Social Contract* reinforces Rousseau's previous indictment of the inequities of civilized life: "Man is born free; and yet is everywhere enslaved."[11] Even though Rousseau devotes an entire book to the topic of the social contract, he offers in it no specific explanation of how a typical compact or social organization comes into being, but merely analyzes the abstract ramifications of the relationship. He may have felt that he had given a sufficient explanation of the process by means of his previous description in the second discourse of the first man who fenced off a plot of land and affirmed "this is mine." The latter hypothesis for the origin of civil society is, by the way, quite different from Locke's notion of a union of the weak. Rousseau in part resolves his ambiguities in the *Social Contract* by affirming that the original compact covered merely the act of association and not the establishment of government, that the latter came into being with the institution of law. Paine's thought is consistent with this explanation. Rousseau agrees completely with Locke, moreover, that man gives up his natural liberty in exchange for civil liberty or the proprietorship of his possessions; natural liberty is limited only by the individual's strength; civil liberty is restricted by the general will; simple possession in the state of nature is founded on the right of force or priority of occupation, but property in civil society is founded on a positive title.[12] This is essentially Paine's notion, in *Common Sense,* which we have already considered, that man "finds it necessary to surrender up a part of his property to furnish means for the protection of the rest."[13]

One of the features which distinguishes Rousseau's *Social Contract* from the works of previous theoreticians such as Locke is that he describes the origin of society as an agreement among equals rather than an agreement between a master and followers. There accordingly exists a fundamental contradiction between the *Social Contract* and Rousseau's *Second Discourse,* for the latter clearly indicates that the state of nature is replaced with a society in which its members accept the dominance of a leader. That is, the relationship described in the *Discourse* is one of submission; whereas that in the *Social Contract* is one of association.[14] As one of Rousseau's contemporaries observed, it is impossible to cite any work before the *Social Contract* "which has refused sovereignty to kings."[15] That the original compact was one between equals is clearly stated in the sixth chapter of the *Social Contract,* where Rousseau affirms that when each person gives himself to the whole he is not submitting to any individual and that there is no person over whom he does not acquire the same right that he has himself surrendered to the whole. Whether Paine consciously followed the *Contract* or not, he certainly set forth the theory of a society of equals, a doctrine which should be considered a major contribution of *Common Sense.* If it is true that Rousseau was the first in history to affirm the doctrine, Paine was undoubtedly the second.

In Rousseau's system, the sovereign is not an individual ruler as such, but the symbol for sovereignty, which in turn is "only the exertion of the general will."[16] Government is defined as "an intermediate body established between the subject and the sovereign [the collective will] for their mutual correspondence."[17] It is distinct from the people and from the sovereign and intermediate between them.[18] The end of government is the "preservation and prosperity of its members."[19] Paine in an essay published in the *Pennsylvania Gazette* (3 April 1782) as an appendage to *Crisis* No. 10 developed a theory of common interest which strongly resembles Rousseau's theory of the general will. "Members of Congress, members of Assembly, or Council, or by any other name they may be called," he wrote, "are only a selected part of the people. They are the representatives of majesty, but not majesty itself. That dignity exists inherently in the universal multitude, and, though it may be delegated, cannot be alienated. Their estates and property are subject to the same taxation with those they represent, and there is nothing they can do, that will not equally affect themselves as well as others." Paine's term *majesty* seems to represent exactly the same political force as Rousseau's *sovereignty.* But since Paine's essay did not appear until 1782, it does not prove that he had read the *Social Contract* before writing *Common Sense.*

Following Locke and others, Rousseau divides governments into their main types, which for him consist in government of the whole people (democracy), government of a small number (aristocracy), and government of a single individual (monarchy).[20] It is worthy of note that both Locke and Rousseau use the term *democracy,* but Paine in *Common Sense* never does; he employs instead the phrase "Republican materials" to express popular government. Rousseau considers every state which is governed by laws to be a republic.[21] Like Montesquieu and nearly every other eighteenth-century political scientist, Rousseau affirms that democracy is best suited to small states, oligarchy to those of middle size, and monarchy to large ones.[22] Rousseau maintains that "there never existed, and never will exist, a real democracy in the world," on the grounds that it is against nature for the many to govern the few and for the people to remain constantly assembled for the making of political decisions.[23]

This opinion was later frequently brought to bear against *Common Sense.* The "savages of North America," according to Rousseau, have developed an aristocratic system. Paine does not go contrary to Rousseau by arguing that democracies have in fact existed, but he suggests in regard to his imaginary first societies that the pristine parliaments meeting under a tree soon gave way to a legislature "managed by a select number chosen from the whole body." The specific disagreement between the two theorists concerns their attitude toward the principle of representative government; Paine lauds it unequivocally, whereas Rousseau disparages it as a product of the "iniquitous" feudal system.[24] In England, he argues, the people are free only when they perform the act of electing members of Parliament; afterward they are slaves.

As the symbol of ideal and efficient government, Rousseau imagines Archimedes seated on a river bank, pulling with great ease a bulky vessel toward him. Two pages later he declares, "By means of a lever sufficiently long, it were possible with a single finger to move the globe." Strange to say, it has never been pointed out that this symbol and metaphor were later adopted by Paine. He introduces the second part of *Rights of Man* with the following short paragraph: "What Archimedes said of the mechanical powers, may be applied to reason and liberty: *'Had we,'* said he, *'a place to stand upon, we might raise the world.'*" The common source for this anecdote is probably Plutarch, who relates in his life of Marcellus that "Archimedes . . . in writing to king Hiero, whose friend and near relation he was, had stated, that given the force, any given weight might be moved, and even boasted, we are told, relying on the strength of demonstration, that if there were another earth, by going into it he could remove this."[25]

Another striking parallel between the *Social Contract* and *Rights of Man* is revealed in Paine's charge that "the error of those who reason by precedents drawn from antiquity respecting the rights of man, is that they do not go far enough into antiquity. They do not go the whole way."[26] Rousseau in a chapter headed "That One Should Always Go Back to a First Agreement," remarks that "before examining the act by which a people elects a king, it would be well to examine the act by which a people becomes a people."[27]

Rousseau believes that monarchical government is called for in lands "where fertile plains and plenteous values more bounteously reward the labours of the cultivator."[28] He does not, however, accept the monarchical form as the best, but presents a number of specific arguments against it. Those who rise to the top under a king, he affirms, are "men of little minds and mean talents." "A man of real merit is as rarely to be found in the ministry of a king, as a blockhead at the head of a republic."[29] The royal ruler pursues his own ends and ignores those of the people. When succession is supplied by election, the intervals are filled with turmoil; when supplied by inheritance, sometimes children, monsters, and imbeciles are placed on the throne.

In the preceding discussion, we have seen a number of resemblances between Paine and Rousseau, but no parallels close or detailed enough to support the conclusion that Paine drew any direct inspiration for *Common Sense* from the Citizen of Geneva. There is a passage in the fourth book of the *Social Contract,* however, which seems to foreshadow one of Paine's speculative notions. Here Rousseau is praising the local government of his native Switzerland.

> When it is known, that among the happiest people in the world, a number of peasants meet together under the shade of an oak, and regulate the affairs of state, with the most prudential economy, is it possible to forbear despising the refinements of other nations, who employ so much artifice and mystery to render themselves splendidly miserable?
>
> A State thus simply governed hath need of but few laws, while in proportion as it becomes necessary to promulgate new ones, that necessity is universally apparent. The first person who proposes them, takes on himself to speak only what every one hath already thought; and neither eloquence nor intrigue is requisite to make that pass into a law, which every one had already resolved to do, as soon as he should be assured others would do the same.[30]

This passage can be compared to Paine's reconstruction of the process by which primitive peoples form their governments.

> Some convenient tree will afford them a State House, under the branches of which the whole colony may assemble to deliberate on public matters. It is more than probable that their first laws will have the title

> only of regulations and be enforced by no other penalty than public disesteem. In his first parliament every man by natural right will have a seat.[31]

Obviously the closest resemblance between the two passages lies in the imagery of the tree under which primitive people come together for the purpose of making their laws, but the passages are linked as well by the concepts of universal consent given to these laws and universal obedience accorded to them. These resemblances do not conclusively prove a direct link between Rousseau and Paine, but they indicate a strong probability that Paine had read the *Social Contract* at the time he was writing *Common Sense.*

It is quite significant that James Chalmers, author of *Plain Truth,* one of the early replies to *Common Sense,* strongly hinted that Paine derived his imagery from Rousseau. Chalmers writes, "I do not say that our Author is indebted to Burgh's POLITICAL DISQUISITIONS, or to ROUSSEAU'S Social Compact for his definition of Government, and his large Tree; although I wish he had favoured his reader with the following extract from that sublime reasoner."[32] The extract in question from Rousseau affirms that the only beings capable of prescribing the optimum conditions for society "would require the abilities of some superior intelligence," and that it "is the province of Gods to make laws for Men." For Chalmers, in other words, Paine is out of his depth, like all utopian dreamers.

A possibility also exists that Paine's "convenient tree" is not a literary allusion at all, but a topographical one. He may be referring to a famous Philadelphia landmark, "a tall and widespreading elm tree" eight yards in diameter under which William Penn signed his treaty with the Indians, an event celebrated in Voltaire's *Lettres philosophiques.*[33] It may also be that Paine had in mind both Rousseau and the treaty elm.

The chapter in the *Social Contract* containing the above reference to the "happiest people in the world" enables us to perceive a fundamental contradiction in *Common Sense.* Rousseau proceeds in his discussion to show how the weakening of "the bonds of society" leads to the expression of particular interests, and how the voting process brings about "iniquitous decrees which have no other end than private interest."[34] Paine, however, describes the institution of government in the first place as a check on vice and then considers the voting process as a means of carrying out the general will. Rousseau is consistent by portraying vice as a result of the weakening of the social bond; Paine seems to be inconsistent by assuming the presence of vice even before the development of voting. Paine, as we have indicated previously, is even less clear than Rousseau on whether man in issuing from the hands of the creator was completely good and whether the nature of man himself or his association with his fellows is responsible for the evils of society.

Even though we assume that Paine may have been aware of "Rousseau's tree," and even though we also admit a strong similarity of basic attitudes in the two writers, particularly in regard to primitivism, the most that can be said about possible indebtedness in that *Common Sense* shares the basic presuppositions of the Citizen of Geneva. The latter's political system has been epitomized as a choice betwen two incompatible utopias—a primitivistic Golden Age and a Spartan republic.[35] Paine reflects both primitivism and republicanism, but rejects the notion that they are incompatible. In terms of a simple return to nature, Paine has more in common with Crèvecoeur than with Rousseau. The thought of the *Social Contract* has similarly been reduced to two major principles, that sovereignty must rest in the hands of the people and that aristocratic government is the best of all.[36] Paine certainly espoused popular sovereignty with passionate conviction, but held no consistent opinion about whether aristocracy or monarchy is the lesser of two evils.

We must not lose sight of the important fact that Paine was making plans for a type of government which had literally never existed before. His concept of democracy has very little in common with that of Rousseau, who drew all of his illustrations from the republics of ancient Greece or the eighteenth-century ministates of which Switzerland was composed. Rousseau's arguments, moreover, had never been brought to bear against any existing governments. They had not been forbidden in France since it was assumed that they concerned only the Swiss republics. Nobody, least of all Rousseau himself, suggested that his theories of government meant that the Bourbon dynasty should be overthrown. That which had shocked Rousseau's traditionally minded contemporaries primarily was his opinion that a society may exist without being divided into an aristocracy and subordinate orders. Voltaire, for example, called him a madman for maintaining such an absurdity.[37] Although Paine was not, as we have seen, an economic leveler, his major contribution in *Common Sense* consists precisely in advocating the doctrine of social equality in a much more open and explicit manner than Rousseau, which he does by denouncing and rejecting hereditary government.

Paine also for the first time anywhere raised the theory of popular government against the claims of an actual ruling house. He envisioned, moreover, a democracy for a geographically large nation—a circumstance which all preceding theorists, including Locke, Montesquieu, and Rousseau had deemed impossible. Paine also advocated that the people of America should proclaim their independence, an action without parallel in history. Previously nations and territories had undergone changes of rulers or had been fought over by competing ruling houses, but there had never been an example of any group assuming the right to govern itself. Paine was a pioneer in expressing the right to autonomy, and he was original in his manner of expression as well.

The chief tie between Paine and Rousseau is perhaps one of sentiment, that attitude which is reflected in their constant reference to moral principles and to feeling as a mode by which these principles are ascertained and justified. Their ideology was, nevertheless, also considered parallel by Paine's contemporaries. In the midst of the French Revolution, indeed while Paine himself was incarcerated in Luxembourg Prison as an undesirable alien, a publisher in Paris brought out a slim volume containing a précis of Rousseau's *Social Contract* together with a précis of *Common Sense*.[38] The editor made no attempt to point out any parallels, but his joint publication certainly implied that Rousseau and Paine were kindred spirits.

11
Relations with Montesquieu

Although Montesquieu is the third of the triumvirate of great political writers who influenced the ideology of the American Revolution, there has been less attempt among critics to associate Paine with his theories than with those of Locke and Rousseau. Perhaps this is due to the encyclopedic nature of Montesquieu's universally admired treatise *Spirit of the Laws* as compared to the more limited subject matter of Locke and Rousseau. Certainly Montesquieu's works were available to Paine in the colonies had he wished to consult them. The *Spirit of the Laws* was widely known and cited throughout America, and the existence of many copies can be documented. The printed catalog of the Library Company of Philadelphia, 1764, for example, reveals that this institution possessed a copy of the second edition (1752) of an English translation by Thomas Nugent.[1] The Library Company also possessed a commentary entitled *The Source, the Strength, and the True Spirit of Laws,* (London, 1753) a translation of a work by Count Giovanni di Cataneo.[2] There is no question, moveoever, that Paine knew Montesquieu later in his career. In *Rights of Man* he briefly surveys the writings of the French *philosophes*—those which displayed the only signs of "the spirit of liberty" during the reigns of Louis XIV and Louis XV. His comment on Montesquieu is shrewd and appreciative. "Montesquieu, President of the Parliament of Bordeaux, went as far as a writer under a despotic government could well proceed; and being obliged to divide himself between principle and prudence, his mind often appears under a veil, and we ought to give him credit for more than he has expressed."[3]

The major part of *The Spirit of the Laws* is only remotely connected with *Common Sense,* since Montesquieu traces therein the broad history of political institutions and interprets their contemporary operation without indulging in moralistic value judgments. In treating monarchies and republics, Montesquieu accepts them equally as valid forms of government precisely because they exist, and he is not concerned with vindicating one or repudiating the other. There is not a single passage in *Common Sense* that reveals a verbal parallel with *The Spirit of the Laws* or a coincidence of thought close enough to warrant the conclusion that Paine was borrowing from his eminent predecessor. Certain concepts associated with Montesquieu, nevertheless, are reflected in *Common Sense* and must be treated in the light of *The Spirit of the Laws* in order to attain a complete picture of the relationship of Paine's pamphlet to the contemporary climate of opinion.

One of the most famous sections of *The Spirit of the Laws* is that in which Montesquieu describes the British government as a balance of three separate powers, the legislative, the executive, and the judicial.[4] In order that power not be abused, he maintains, the government must so be ordered that one power acts as a check upon another. Montesquieu's admiring survey of the British system is believed to have had much to do with the adoption of the balance of legislative, executive, and judicial powers in the United States Constitution.

Paine's discussion of the separation of powers reveals a major difference from Montesquieu's in that he does not literally consider abstract powers as such but rather particular bodies which exercise powers. The three elements he describes are the king, the lords, and the commons. If anything, Paine's discussion is historically more accurate than Montesquieu's, for British constitutional history reveals that the legislative and executive powers were not separated between king and parliament, but overlapped into both bodies.[5] Paine, almost immediately following his disquisition on the origin of government arising out of the state of nature, examines "the component parts of the English constitution," which he derogates as "the base remains of two ancient tyrannies, compounded with some new republican materials."[6] According to his view, the two ancient tyrannies consist of the king and the peers, or House of Lords. The republican materials are comprised in the House of Commons, "on whose virtue depends the freedom of England." A certain significance attaches to Paine's use of the noun *virtue,* a significance to be revealed later in this chapter. Paine does not mention Montesquieu by name, but he certainly suggests the theory of the balance of powers as he remarks, "to say that the constitution of England is a union of three powers reciprocally *checking* each other, is farcical; either the words have no meaning, or they are flat contradictions." Paine here is in effect repudiating the section of *The Spirit of the Laws* in which the theory of power balance is expressed, but there is no way of knowing that he associated it with Montesquieu.

Paine's demonstration of the absurdity of the British system encompasses only the king and the commons. According to his interpretation, giving the commons a check upon the king presupposes that the king is not to be trusted and that the commons are wiser or worthier of confidence than the king, and giving the king a check upon the commons supposes that he is wiser than the commons. Perhaps it is hardly necessary to observe with Paine's contemporary critics that he misses the point. A system of checks and balances does not necessarily suppose that one force is wiser or less compatible with the interest of the whole than the other, but rather that each is motivated by particular interests and that the mutual checking produces compromise through reciprocal moderating.

Paine next introduces and immediately repudiates an interpretation of the English constitution which he attributes to "some writers" without giving any clue as to who they are. "The king, say they, is one, the people another; the peers are an house in behalf of the king, the commons in behalf of the people."[7] Paine's objection that this represents "an house divided against itself" anticipates his opposition to a bicameral system for the new American nation, both in the proposed continental congress and in the individual colonies.

In *Common Sense* Paine reveals that his main objection to the British system is not to the balance between two forces as such, but to the circumstance that one of these forces is a monarch. It is kingship which is his primary target. He asks the question, therefore, which he prints in italics, *How came the king by a power which the people are afraid to trust, and always obliged to check?* The answer which he provides looks ahead to the subsequent section of his work concerning scriptural arguments against monarchy. "Such a power could not be the gift of a wise people, neither can any power, *which needs checking,* be from God; yet the provision, which the constitution makes, supposes such a power to exist." Having denied God and the people as the source of the power of a king, Paine does not say that it comes from tyranny and arbitrary seizure—but he strongly implies it.

Paine's most convincing argument against a system of checks and balances is that it is virtually impossible to maintain several powers in a condition of absolute equality and that consequently the strongest one will always dominate over the others. As we have already indicated, this argument was later used by Tocqueville. It applies to the British system as portrayed by Montesquieu as well as to the American system as it has developed in the nineteenth and twentieth centuries. "As the greater weight will always carry up the less, and as all the wheels of a machine are put in motion by one, it only remains to know which power in the constitution has the most weight, for that will govern." In expanding his metaphor based on the principles of mechanics, Paine observes that the other powers may clog or hinder the process, but the first moving power will ultimately have its way, "and what it wants in speed, is supplied by time." Paine accepts, nevertheless, the concept of division of powers, which may perhaps not be identical with a balance. In commenting on the manner of choosing members of a future national congress, he warns against allowing this function to become a right of the various colonial legislatures. He puts it "as a question to those who make a study of mankind, whether *representation and election* is not too great a power for one and the same body of men to possess."[8]

In reference to the English constitution, Paine takes as evident that "the crown is the overbearing part," and he attributes its "whole consequence" entirely to its power to give "places and pensions."[9] Here Paine diverges from abstract theory to English practical politics. His portrayal of the King controlling the nation through the bestowal of places and perquisites is based on a doctrine maintained by the Rockingham Whigs, an English Parliamentary group in existence from 1765 to 1782. Edmund Burke in his *Thoughts on the Cause of the Present Discontents* (1770) argued that the policy of the Grenville administration had been to separate the court from the ministry, and "to secure to the court the unlimited and uncontrolled use of its own vast influence, under the sole direction of its own private favor."[10] Paine's concluding summary of his exposition of checks and balances reflects the doctrines which Burke and the Rockingham Whigs had been promulgating for the preceding ten years: "though we have been wise enough to shut and lock a door against absolute monarchy, we at the same time have been foolish enough to put the crown in possession of the key." Although there is not a bit more evidence available to show that Paine had read Burke's *Thoughts on the Present Discontents* than to show that he knew Montesquieu's *Spirit of Laws,* it is hardly conceivable that he would not have been familiar with the public debate between the Grenville administration and the Rockingham dissenters.

In later years, Paine had absolutely nothing to do with framing the Federal Constitution of 1787, but became a vigorous advocate of its adoption and adherence to its principles. His support of the Constitution, which embodies an elaborate system of checks and balances, is not really inconsistent with his denunciation of the British constitution, for the type of balance is quite different in the two modes of government. A balance of executive, legislative, and judicial powers as set forth in the Federal Constitution is by no means the same system as a balance of Crown, Lords, and Commons. Paine did change his mind, however, as we have seen, on the merits of a bicameral system, rejecting it in 1776, but accepting it in 1793 in the course of proposals which he made for the French republic.

Voltaire in a famous essay on Montesquieu maintains that "the author of the *Spirit of Laws* has founded his whole system upon this maxim, that virtue is the principle of a republican government, and honour that of a monarchy."[11] In various places in his published and private writings, Voltaire refutes this maxim concerning virtue and honor which he attributes to his great contemporary. In actuality Montesquieu is somewhat less categorical than Voltaire charges, and he does not establish an absolute dichotomy between monarchy and honor on one hand and republicanism and virtue on the other. Indeed, in his *Lettres persanes,* which preceded the *Spirit of the Laws* by a quarter of a century, he maintains that the ancient republics were the sanctuary of both honor and virtue.[12] In *Spirit of the Laws,* however, he says specifically that virtue is a requirement of popular governments, although he also considers it nearly as important to aristocratic ones.[13] He also says that honor, which in its essence demands preferences and distinctions, is part of monarchies. For practical purposes, therefore, one is justified in accepting Voltaire's view that Montesquieu considered virtue to be the vital characteristic of republican government and honor that of monarchy.

Other French contemporaries besides Voltaire reflected unfavorably on Montesquieu's dichotomy, many pointing out that it was an affront to the government of Louis XV to maintain that virtue was not the mainstay of monarchies. In answer to these critics, Montesquieu himself affirmed in a preface to later editions of his work that he uses the word *virtue* in a restricted sense. "What I call *virtue* in a republic is the love of country, that is, the love of equality. It is not a moral virtue nor a Christian virtue; it is *political virtue;* and the latter is the spring which moves monarchy." Although modern political scientists such as J. G. A. Pocock have accepted at its face value Montesquieu's statement that he considered virtue to be a political rather than a moral quality, his contemporaries accused him of evasiveness. With Paine there is no question. He consistently draws out the moral connotations of the word *virtue* whenever he associates it with either monarchies or republics.

The concept of virtue played a critical role in Anglo-American republican theory. In the debate over the moral nature of man initiated by Shaftesbury and Mandeville early in the eighteenth century, one side held that man is rational and virtuous; the other, that is is passionate and evil. In the political realm, the decision had to be made whether man could be trusted to follow reason and ethical principles or whether the state needed to use coercion of force in molding conduct. According to the classical Whig conception in both England and the colonies, a virtuous citizenry was the essence of the republic. Paine's friends, such as Jefferson, and many of his opponents, including John Adams, believed in man's essential goodness, but other friends such as John Dickinson and opponents such as Gouverneur Morris took the opposite side. As we have already seen, Paine followed Rousseau in the belief that man is inherently virtuous, but that he is corrupted by government or society. Paine's opinion that virtue in an individual is neither hereditary nor unchanging indicates that he would not have sided exclusively with either Shaftesbury or Mandeville had he been pressed. Paine's particular theories of virtue will be treated at length in chapter 18.

In terms of political theory, the Shaftesburian notion of benevolence was translated into republican virtue and the Mandevillean theory of self-interest into British "Court" ideology, "which emphasized that men were guided by interest and passion."[14] J. G. A. Pocock has given a useful summary of recent scholarship concerning the significance of virtue in eighteenth-century political thought. In essence, there existed a tension—sometimes a polarity—between virtue and *virtu* (that is, expediency, prac ticability, or getting things done). Old Whigs and the Country party in England, together with classical republicans (such as John Dickinson) and agrarians (such as Jefferson) in America, believed that government could be established upon principles of virtue. Junto Whigs and the Court party in England, together with Federalists (such as Noah Webster) and patrons of commerce (such as Hamilton) in America, argued that government must take account of self-interest and even allow for corruption as a normal political ingredient. Paine, however, does not fit comfortably into either side, even though he quoted one of the British denouncers of political corruption, James Burgh, and praised the republican rectitude of John Dickinson. There is absolutely no tension between virtue and commerce in *Common Sense,* for Paine assumes that they can and should exist compatibly together.

The notion of virtue as embodied in republican theory required that in the political community each individual give up all private interest not in the interest of the whole body. This doctrine is implicit in one of Paine's tracts of chiefly local concern, *Public Good* (1780), which does not, however, treat abstract questions of ethics in political relationships, but deals entirely with the practical matter of the disposition of territories in the West which were until then under the undisputed control of Virginia. In regard to abstract theory, Paine limits himself to the apothegm that "the governing rule of right and of mutual good must in all public cases finally reside."[15] The title phrase *public good,* however, was a "central tenet of the Whig faith," which, "as much as liberty, defined the goals of the Revolution."[16] Both phrases, "the governing rule of right and of mutual good" and "public good," beg the question of whether matters of state should be settled by a majority or by a responsible governing body.

One cannot be sure whether Paine's references to virtue and honor in *Common Sense* refer to republican virtue in general or to Montesquieu's dichotomy between republics and monarchies, but many of his contemporaries pointedly associated his references with the *Spirit of the Laws.* Several commentaries on *Common Sense,* for example, specifically criticized Paine for not recognizing or sufficiently appreciating the quality of honor in monarchies. In actuality, Paine does closely associate honor with monarchies throughout *Common Sense,* but he consistently does so in a derogatory sense, while attributing virtue to republics in a positive and substantial manner. He very well knew what he was about in attempting to detract from the honor which was conventionally attributed to royalty. He suggests that tradition is mistaken in "supposing the present race of kings in the world to have had an honorable origin."[17] Could the truth be known, he affirms, "we should find the first of them nothing better than the principal ruffian of some restless gang, whose savage manners or pre-eminence in subtilty obtained him the title of chief among plunderers." Since the Norman Conquest, he says, England has known some good kings and a larger number of bad ones, but "no man in his senses can say that their claim under William the Conqueror is a very honorable one." Paine points out that the origin of the British succession is paltry and rascally—"a French bastard landing with an armed banditti, and establishing himself king of England against the consent of the natives." In concluding his comparison of the political doctrine of hereditary succession to the theological one of original sin, Paine concludes in disgust, "Dishonorable rank! inglorious connexion!"[18]

We have already alluded to Paine's reference to the "new republican materials in the persons of the commons, on whose virtue depends the freedom of England." There is a slight ambiguity here, since *virtue* as it was used throughout the eighteenth century suggested both efficiency and integrity, but Paine's context seems to indicate that he has in mind probity of character in a collective sense. Certainly this is the meaning attached to the concept in other parts of *Common Sense.* In reference to the corrupting effect which the Crown's disposing of places allegedly had in England, Paine charges that the monarchical influence had "swallowed up the power, and eaten out the virtue of the house of commons (the republican part in the constitution)." And in consequence, he observes, "when republican virtue fails, slavery ensues."[19] Also he describes the debt which the united colonies would contract in waging a war against England as a future "glorious memento of our virtue." Finally, Paine derides American Tories, those who were opposing resistance to England, as people "who have not virtue enough to be WHIGS."[20] These passages certainly suggest that Paine considered virtue to be a collective characteristic of republican government. Elsewhere in *Common Sense,* however, he describes virtue as a primarily personal quality. In reference to selecting members of a future congress, he reminds his readers that when "we are planning for posterity, we ought to remember, that virtue is not hereditary."[21] A few pages later, in warning against mob rule, he observes that the multitude may not always be a body of reasonable men; "virtue, as I have already remarked, is not hereditary, neither is it perpetual."[22] In a sense this fundamentally conservative observation may be considered as Paine's reminder to fellow advocates of popular government that virtue does not reside continuously in any particular political structure.

The passage in Paine's writings which most directly touches upon the concept of virtue in republics appears in a document which has never been published, a letter from Paine to a Committee of Congress, 26 June 1783, on the subject of a recompense for his services, a matter about which he was forced to write a larger number of communications before any action was taken. "It is the practice of Monarchies, in general," he observes, "to shew their Countenance to flatterers and partizans, but, the principle on which republics are founded, supposes them to be the patrons of Vertue and public spirit, and where this is wanting the principle of a republic is not there."[23] This doctrine can be regarded as pure Montesquieu.

In *Common Sense* there is no attention given to the parallel notion of honor in monarchies, except in the negative perspective toward the hereditary principle already discussed. This is perhaps strange, since Paine's mentor Benjamin Franklin as early as 1769 had interpreted several of the unjust and improper measures of Parliament as devices to preserve its prestige or honor. In Franklin's words, "they cannot bear the Denial of the Right of Parliament" to pass inequitable laws even though "they acknowledge they ought not to have been made. They fear being despis'd by all the Nations around if they repeal them; and they say it is of great Importance to this Nation that the World should see it is Master of its Colonies, otherwise its enemies on a Conceit of its weakness, might be encourag'd to insult it."[24] At the same time Franklin realized that England had to preserve a favorable appearance toward the rest of the world, and he admitted that the redressing of colonial grievances might need to be a gradual process. "You may judge," he wrote to Thomas Cushing in 1771, "whether it will not be prudent in us to indulge the Mother Country in this Concern for her own Honour."[25]

If Paine was silent on British honor in *Common Sense,* he derided it vigorously in various *Crisis* papers, perhaps in reaction to critics of *Common Sense* who had cited the Montesquieu principle. He charged in the *Crisis,* therefore, that it is "the natural temper of the English to fight for a feather, if they suppose that feather to be an affront; and America, without the right of asking why, must have abetted in every quarrel, and abided by its fate. It is a shocking situation to live in."[26] To him, the British idea of national honor seemed to "consist in national insult, and that to be a great people, is to be neither a Christian, a philosopher, or a gentleman, but to threaten with the rudeness of a bear, and to devour with the ferocity of a lion."[27] Paine warned the English people, "If there be any honor in pursuing self-destruction with inflexible passion—if national suicide be the perfection of national glory, you may, with all the pride of criminal happiness, expire unenvied and unrivalled."[28]

Montesquieu's major work, as its title appropriately indicates, is concerned in large measure with the influence of legislation upon human behavior, and by extension it examines the role of social institutions upon the origin of laws or government. Montesquieu was clearly aware of the principle which Paine claims for himself that society precedes government. Montesquieu bases his work, moreover, upon one of the major presuppositions of the Enlightenment—that a source for all human activities may be found in nature. As we have seen, Paine took pride in his own applications of this principle. One of the natural phenomena to which Montesquieu continually traces the origins of human behavior is physical geography, and one of the most discussed of the political principles which he derives is that concerning the physical size of a nation and its government. In his opinion, monarchy is best suited for large nations and republicanism for small ones. "It is the nature of a republic," he says, "that it have merely a small territory; otherwise it could hardly exist."[29] This is a principle highly damaging to Paine's call for the institution of a republic in the vast territories of the thirteen English colonies of America.

Paine in nearly all of his subsequent writings on America is obsessed with the notion of physical grandeur. Several of his purple passages suggest that the magnificence of the landscape must somehow impart lofty sentiments to the inhabitants of an area and sublimity to the institutions they establish. But in *Common Sense* Paine avoids all discussion of a relationship between physical size and a system of government other than admitting that small islands not capable of defending themselves are "proper objects for kingdoms to take under their care." This theme of *imitatio naturae,* however, he exploits *ad nauseam,* according to one critic, with arguments that the governing of a continent by an island is contrary to nature, that a satellite cannot rule a planet larger than itself, and that America covers one-eighth of the inhabitable globe in contrast to the puny extent of 360 miles represented by England.[30]

Paine's failure to discuss Montesquieu's theory of the relationship between geographical extent and form of government may suggest that he had not encountered it in either Montesquieu or Rousseau before writing *Common Sense.* Some of his critics, however, seized upon the doctrine to discredit the republican principles which it contains. Fifteen years later Paine himself specifically treated the argument based upon geographical size, labeling it "one of the absurd notions which the dishonesty or the ignorance of the supporters of monarchy have scattered through the world." In a letter addressed to the editors of a French periodical, *Le Républicain; ou, Le défenseur du gouvernement représentatif* (10 July 1791), Paine put forth the contrary opinion that monarchy may possibly be suited to a small country, but only the republican form is appropriate for a large one. He wrote this letter in collaboration with his friend Condorcet. According to his argument, a government in order properly to fulfill its functions must be "thoroughly acquainted with all the varied interests and all the different parts of the nation."[31] A monarch might possibly become familiar with the affairs of the entire population in a small country, but not in a large one. "His helpless ignorance of matters that affect the people must necessarily lead to the establishment of a tyrannical form of government." The only system which "can insure anything like adequate attention to every portion of an extended territory is the government that has its source in popular representation." Six years later in another French publication, Paine repeated this argument against, in his words, "one of the most vulgar and absurd *sayings* or dogmas that ever yet imposed itself upon the world, which is, *'that a Republic is fit only for a small country, and a Monarchy for a large one.'*" For the first time bringing Montesquieu into the discussion, Paine asserted that the author of *The Spirit of the Laws* did not believe the doctrine himself, but being "strongly inclined to republican government," sheltered himself from the Bastille by pretending that he was not referring to France when speaking of republics.[32]

The theory of geographical size cannot be completely ignored in a discussion of *Common Sense,* because some of Paine's critics cited it to discredit his republican doctrine. Essentially all that need be said now, however, is that the theory was generally considered irrefutable throughout Europe until it was pragmatically proved wrong by the emergence of a successful republic in America.

Perhaps the concept most widely associated with Montesquieu in modern scholarship is the view that climate determines the national character of any people, another notion stressing the influence of geography. Scholars have only recently recognized that Montesquieu borrowed this notion from one or two of his contemporaries and that it actually goes back as far as the Greek classics. *The Spirit of the Laws* had such high prestige and extensive circulation in the eighteenth century, however, that the notion has generally been considered as originating there. The entire fourteenth book of the third part is devoted to the topic "Of Laws in the Relations They Have with the Nature of Climate." Montesquieu introduces this subject with a chapter consisting entirely of the following single sentence, "If it is true that the character of the mind and the passions of the heart are extremely different in various climates, laws should be related both to the difference of these passions and to the difference of these characters." This doctrine is placed in doubt in a passage in *Common Sense* concerning absolutism. In explaining why "the crown is not as oppressive in England as in Turkey," Paine maintains that the relative moderation of the English monarchy "*is wholly owing to the constitution of the people, and not to the constitution of the government.*"[33] Here Paine clearly separates national character from national government, whereas, according to Montesquieu's theory, both should depend upon climate.

There is no further discussion in *Common Sense* of the influence of climate upon character and government, nor does the doctrine appear in Paine's later *Dissertation on the First Principles of Government.* The relevance of the subject to both works is revealed, however, in the introduction to a Spanish translation of Paine's *Dissertation* published in 1819, in London, ten years after Paine's death.[34] The translator, a native of Spanish America, shows a certain resentment at the manner in which the theory of climate has been generally applied to nations in the tropical zone, inhabitants of that region being portrayed as indolent and irresponsible and consequently incapable of self government. He objects that the theory is mechanistic and deterministic, that it denies men freedom of will by considering them to be like a steam machine, the activity of which depends upon the heat of the boiler. In actuality, he maintains, a machine is just the reverse of human beings, active when it is heated and motionless when it is not.

This Spanish-language observer points out that drawing the conclusion that there could not exist republics in the torrid zone of South America, which comprises a major part of the continent, represents a misreading and even a calumniation of Montesquieu. In a most percipient comment on the scope of *The Spirit of the Laws,* Paine's translator quite properly observes that Montesquieu did not propose to treat "principles of government, nor politics according to law, but politics according to the de facto governments existing in that time, and of the spirit which had directed their laws." As Montesquieu isolated the causes which had been influential in the formation of vicious and absurd codes, he found them in the vices and characters of the people, which in turn depended in part upon the influence of climate.[35] Paine's translator adds that even though hot climates may make men indolent and passive and, therefore, more readily susceptible to despotic tyranny, this does not mean that they are incapable of forming a government based on natural rights and even less does it mean that this passivity of character should give one man the right to enslave others.

To defend Paine for not taking up the subject of the influence of climate upon human character, his translator points out that Montesquieu's theory has not been universally accepted. As evidence, he quotes a rebuttal of the theory by Voltaire, together with the latter's conclusion that liberty is dependent not upon climate but upon the structure of society, almost the same principle which Paine had affirmed in *Common Sense* in regard to Turkish absolutism.[36]

Despite the importance of *The Spirit of the Laws* to eighteenth-century political theory and the widespread discussions of many of its principles, no direct influence whatsoever of Montesquieu may be discerned in *Common Sense.* Even indirect influence was at the most minimal, primarily because, as the translator of Paine's *Dissertations* observes, Montesquieu was primarily concerned with particular national governments as they existed in the eighteenth century, not with abstract principles or suggestions for reform. By and large, moreover, Paine found the abstract individualism of Rousseau more congenial than the historical pragmatism of Montesquieu. The prestige of Montesquieu throughout the American colonies was so great, however, that some critics of *Common Sense* felt that the work was deficient in not citing him, and others used Montesquieu, as we shall see, in attempting to undermine Paine's general principles of republicanism.

12
Periodical Polemics

Paine's contemporaries considered pamphlets and newspaper articles to be separate literary genres. One of the writers in the controversy over *Common Sense,* for example, drew a distinction between the two communications media in an imaginary dialogue between an advocate and an opponent of independence.[1] The former remarks, "Our cause will never appear to advantage in a pamphlet. If you begin a series of letters in a news-paper you are at full liberty to say as much or as little as you please, to suspend your operations for a time and strike in again when occasion serves." In writing a pamphlet, he continues, "You are expected to say the best, if not all that can be said on the subject, and if it contains a few weighty arguments the author [being attacked] is despised and the subject suffers. There you are obliged to come to a period, but you may write a twelve month in a newspaper and yet make the public believe that your main argument has not yet appeared." These comments, although appearing in a newspaper article, suggest that the pamphlet is a more solid and substantive form of communication, requiring unity, organization, and a definite conclusion. In contrast, newspaper articles are made to seem random, thin, and ephemeral. There is some truth to this generalization, which by and large describes differences between Paine's *Common Sense* and his *Crisis.* One should state, on the other hand, that many Revolutionary essays, including several of Paine's, appeared in both newspaper and pamphlet form.

The first essay in opposition to *Common Sense* appeared in a newspaper on 28 February 1776 (by "Rationalis"), but prior to this the periodical press had published a good deal in its favor.

On 3 February 1776, an author in the *Pennsylvania Evening Post,* adopting the pseudonym "Candidus," explained that soon after the appearance of *Common Sense* he was informed that at least "three gentlemen of respectable abilities were engaged to answer it." He considered an "oblique essay in *Humphreys*'s paper" and the solemn Testimony of the Quakers as perhaps relevant to the work, but not substantial enough to be considered refutations.[2] "Candidus" himself offers vigorous support of *Common Sense,* but develops some completely different lines of argument.

He begins by affirming that the dependence of the colonies upon Great Britain is absolute and that those who maintain that it is limited in any way have no constitutional authority for their position. If it were true, as pretended, that the people in power in England were "the most just, humane, and affectionate friends" in the world, this would be an encouraging circumstance, but still not a guarantee of liberty and civil rights. In actuality, however, the English leaders have "broken through the most solemn covenants, debauched the hereditary and corrupted the elective guardians of the people's rights"; they have "in fact, established an absolute tyranny in *Great Britain* and *Ireland.*" "Candidus" is virtually the only writer in the controversy over *Common Sense* who recognizes that essentially the same party division existed in England as in the colonies, and that the group in Parliament which supported the extension of civil rights and liberties in England (by and large Franklin's personal friends who were the heirs to the Rockingham Whigs) also defended and supported the interests of the colonists. "Candidus," therefore, affirms that the proposed plan of reconciliation is as unsafe to "the honest party *in England*" as to the colonists themselves. The danger, he points out, exists in the Crown's power of doling out places and perquisites, a power which Paine also denounces in *Common Sense.* "Candidus" asks rhetorically, "what check have they now upon the Crown, and what shadow of control can they pretend, when the Crown can command fifteen or twenty million a year, which they have nothing to say to."

The other main point emphasized by "Candidus" is that the bloodshed and suffering of the colonists will be ineffably less if they declare independence immediately than if they temporize. He uses Paine's argument that other nations have no right to interfere in the dispute as long as the colonists continue to maintain allegiance, to England, and that as soon as independence is declared the maritime nations would in their own interest come to the aid of the Americans. While still dependent, the colonists are merely rebels; after a declaration of separation they would be resisters of tyranny. "Candidus" takes note of a hypothetical threat to internal order which had sometimes been held up, especially in Pennsylvania, that "the Presbyterians, if freed from the restraining power of *Great Britain,* would overrun the peaceable Quakers in this Government." "Candidus," anticipating Paine's reply to the Quakers, indicates that the latter body are a greater threat to liberty than are the Presbyterians. "If they would not pull down Kings," he asks, "let them not support tyrants."

In his final paragraph, "Candidus" agrees with Vattel that a state is "a moral person, having an interest and will of its own," and he affirms that *Common Sense* has clearly demonstrated that the British state is "a monster whose prime mover has an interest and will in direct opposition to its prosperity and security."

A month later, another essay signed "Candidus," presumably by the author of the preceding one, appeared in the *Pennsylvania Gazette* (6 March). Instead of formally replying to the intervening essay of

"Rationalis," whom he mentions, "Candidus" continues to stress European relations. In so doing, he summarizes the major arguments against independence and demolishes them, while all along buttressing the positions of *Common Sense.* The opponents of independence commonly cited the traditional racial, religious, and cultural ties with Britain, the alleged prosperity under British rule in the past, and the continued need of protection against foreign powers. "Candidus" answers that there are limits to the obligations which children have toward their parents; that the demands of Britain have been exorbitant; and that the colonies, like minors coming of age, should have their own rights and property. "Candidus" charges that the colonies have been exploited by a powerful junto which has used them as "the debauched *Romans*" had used their empire, as a source of wealth to be drained to the dregs. The foreign powers now being held up by Britain as potential invaders would actually prefer to be allies and to conclude pacts of mutually advantageous commerce. "Candidus" also observes that the Americans were discharged by the law of nations from allegiance to Britain "the moment the army was posted among us without our consent, or a single farthing taken from us in like manner."

The ministry had promised to send an investigating body to deal with the grievances of the colonies. In regard to "these august Commissioners we hear so much of every day," "Candidus" predicts that because of the attention given to colonial dissensions in courts throughout the world, the commissioners will be instructed only "to receive submission, and grant pardons on the most humiliating terms they can reduce us to" in order that they may "let *Europe* know their great power in reducing their rebellious subjects to a sense of their duty."

Two days before "Rationalis," a writer from New Jersey addressed to *Common Sense* a complimentary letter, 26 February 1776, indicating that he had been persuaded by its arguments of the necessity of independence, to which he had formerly been averse. Writing under the pseudonym "Essex," he contributes several valuable and original ideas to the controversy while developing Paine's contention that the only satisfactory solution to the situation consists in continental unity. Comparing the circumstances of the colonies to the balance of power in Europe, "Essex" maintains that "equality in strength, riches and honours are necessary to safety, mutual confidence, and friendship."[3] In the colloquial vein of *Common Sense,* he draws on popular proverbs to illustrate his point, "the poor is despised of his neighbour"; "the weakest goes to the wall"; and "Aesop's iron and earthen pots cannot swim with safety together." Then striking out in a completely original direction, "Essex" argues that all of the present colonies should be incorporated into the Continental Conference together with Quebec and Nova Scotia; three new colonies should be formed, Montreal, Albany, and Susquehannah; and in addition the colonies of New England should revise their boundaries in order to equalize their size. Were any colonies to object to these changes, "Essex" warns them to consider, in a paraphrase of the language of *Common Sense,* that "the strength and happiness of *America* must be Continental, and not Provincial, and that whatever appears to be for the good of the whole, must be submitted to by every part."

The most valuable contribution of "Essex" consists in a statement concerning voting qualifications in the new government. This statement makes up for the complete neglect of the subject in *Common Sense,* the only significant hiatus in Paine's pamphlet. According to "Essex," suffrage should be granted to "every free man, above the age of twenty-one years, having had a deed for lands for the space of one year, immediately preceding the election, or having in his possession either real or personal estate to the value of one hundred dollars." In an unusual gesture toward the rights of women, "Essex" recommends that widows who pay taxes should have equal voting rights with men of the same property. Finally, he advocates that every person excluded by the above rules from voting should at the same time be exempted from taxes raised for the support of legislation.

Although in *Common Sense* Paine is silent on the subject of property requirements for suffrage, he treated it two years later. In the colony of Pennsylvania before the separation from Britain, a man who wished to vote was required by law to swear or affirm that he was worth fifty pounds in currency, but this qualification deprived very few people of the privilege of the ballot. According to Paine, "every man worth a chest of tools, a few implements of husbandry, a few spare clothes, a bed and a few household utensils, a few articles for sale in a window, or almost anything else he could call or even think his own, supposed himself within the pale of an oath, and made no hesitation of taking it."[4] Probably the fact that the property requirement then in force deprived practically nobody from voting explains why Paine did not consider suffrage a matter of sufficient urgency to be included in *Common Sense.*

The first attack on *Common Sense,* by "Rationalis," already mentioned, is, as its pseudonym implies, a calm, dispassionate, and ordered analysis of Paine's arguments, perhaps the soundest contemporary critique published, despite its relative brevity as a newspaper article. Although "Rationalis" opposes each of what he considers the three major arguments in *Common Sense,* he does not take a determined attitude against independence, but favors delaying action until the outcome of negotiations can be known. When reprinted in the pamphlet *Plain Truth,* "Rationalis" carried an epigraph attributed to Voltaire, "The Republican Spirit is indeed at bottom as ambitious as the monarchical." The three major points which "Rationalis" exposes and attempts to refute are, first, that "the English form of Government has no wisdom in it" and it is not constructed, in Lockean terms, to secure "the happiness of the people, which is the end of all good government"; second, "that monarchy is a form of Government inconsistent with the will of *God*"; and, third, "that now is the time to break off all connection with *Great Britain,* and to declare an independence of the colonies."[5]

"Rationalis" answers the first point by observing that the method of *Common Sense* is to attack the English constitution as an institution by exposing the abuses it has been subjected to, a method which could with equal logic be turned against the Jewish theocracy. "Rationalis," therefore, instead of attacking the English constitution finds fault with the English people. Both profane and sacred history teach, he observes, that even the best laws and the best governments are ineffectual among "a corrupt, degenerate people." It is not the fault of the government but of the people if they are not happy "under an excellent form of civil polity." This "Rationalis" assumes to be "the case of *Great Britain* at this day."

"Rationalis" takes very seriously Paine's scriptural argument against monarchy. In answering it, however, he does little more than quote two authorities on the other side, Trenchard's *Cato's Letters* and Lord Somers's *The Judgment of the Whole Kingdoms and Nations, concerning the Rights of Kings and People.* What is ingenious about these quotations is that they are taken from two celebrated Whigs, whose concepts would ordinarily be associated with hostility toward the abuse of royal power and with support of the commons. Yet "Rationalis" uses them in defense of monarchy. Trenchard, for example, had written in opposition to theories which establish ruling families upon divine right as well as to those associating supernatural power with government. He affirms that "there is no Government now upon earth which owes its formation or beginning to the immediate revelation of God" and "that every Government, which we know, at this day, in the world, was established by the wisdom and force of mere men, and by the concurrence of causes evidently human." Paine, of course, says almost the same thing in his address to the Quakers. In the body of *Common Sense,* Paine, to be sure, does not say that God has established any particular form of government; indeed he affirms the contrary, that God has spoken against monarchy, but this amounts, nevertheless, to an admission of divine intervention in political affairs. The quoting of a Whig authority against an extreme Whig position—the rejection of monarchy as such—serves to discredit the reasoning on which a major part of *Common Sense* depends.

The quotations from Lord Somers, who was even more revered in Whig circles than Trenchard, not only affirm that "mankind is at liberty to choose what form of Government they like," but effectively demolish Paine's biblical argument by evoking "the testimony of the Holy Scriptures" to show that "God permits such magistrate, or magistrates, as the community thinks fit to approve." This is made plain "when *God* said to *Solomon,* 'By me Kings rule, even all the Judges of earth,' Proverbs VIII, 16." Somers also treats in detail the episode of Samuel and the choosing of Saul for king, but cites passages with a contrary meaning from those in *Common Sense.* Most devastating of these is 1 Samuel 12:13, "Now, therefore, behold the King whom ye have chosen . . . ; and behold the Lord hath set a King over you."

In his next section, "Rationalis" goes on to refute the assertion in *Common Sense* that "Monarchy and succession have laid the world in blood and ashes." His method is to demonstrate that the record of republics is just as bad as that of any kingdom. In ancient times, the Athenians often banished their best citizens, fearing their potential power, and the Carthaginian and Roman republics were constantly filled with scenes of blood and devastation. In the Dutch republic, two brothers, Cornelius and John De Witt, were massacred by the people in 1672. "Rationalis" points out that Holland is no longer a republic, but has changed to an aristocracy, and that the people no longer have a voice in the election to the States General nor in the making of laws. In a choice between a hereditary and an elective monarchy, according to "Rationalis," general opinion holds that the system of succession is superior because of the turmoil and confusion which accompany the election of a king. For illustration he points to the elective monarchy of Poland. Continuing to use the language of Whigs, "Rationalis" observes that after the death of the "tyrant" Charles, the Commonwealth also ended in arbitrary power.

"Rationalis" concludes that independence should be considered only as a last resort, but he does not completely rule it out. "If an advantageous accommodation can be had, and a free Constitution for this country be established on mutual agreement and compact, 'twill be better and happier for us; but if justice is still denied us, and we are to contend for liberty by arms, we will meet them in the field. . . . Should the Ministry have recourse to foreign aid, we may possibly follow their example; and if it be essential then to our safety to declare an Independence, I would willingly embrace the necessity."

Despite this moderate conclusion and the high order of debate represented by "Rationalis," the essay was answered in April by an anonymous advocate of independence in New York.[6] He correctly saw the essence of the question as a conflict between monarchy and representative government. After producing further scriptural references in support of *Common Sense,* he asserts, "the plain truth is, the nations, by presumptuously trusting too great power in the hands of one man and one family have caught a Tartar." Tyrannical behavior in these circumstances should be expected because of "the weak and disordered state of human nature." Agreeing wholeheartedly with the contention of *Common Sense* that the institution of hereditary monarchy brings on great strife and confusion, the essayist replies to the objection drawn from the example of Poland that elections are in themselves productive of turmoil and disruption. He answers that the Polish kings are elected not by the people, but by powerful men of the nation who have usurped a tyranny over the people.

Breaking completely with the view that *Common Sense* exposes merely the abuses of the British constitution, not its essence, the essayist insists that *Common Sense* proves that "the great abuses of the government naturally arise out of the errors and defects in the Constitution itself." He admits that the Bill of Rights restrains the crown in a limited manner, but maintains that this is not adequate "to secure the interest and liberty of the subjects." The constitution proposed to America by *Common Sense,* on the other hand, would invest the governing power with full authority "to do all the good to the people they wish them to do," but at the same time restrain them from sacrificing the public interest to their private passions.

The essayist disposes of the arguments of "Rationalis" concerning Athens, Rome, and Carthage by depicting them as tyrannies rather than republics. He uses the same method to explain the arbitrary behavior of the Commonwealth. When Cromwell usurped power from its leaders, "it was only an exchange of many joint tyrants for one." Taking for an illustration a religious sect which was decidedly a minority in the colonies, the Baptists, the essayist suggests that the members of this sect could with half of the men then under arms take over control of the country and call themselves the Commonwealth of America, but in this event the people themselves would actually be a conquered people under a tyranny. The essayist strikes out at the opinion of "Rationalis" that the time is not yet ripe for independence by citing the proverb "After death call the doctor." The program of "Rationalis," he says, amounts to fighting for an accommodation until all the brave men with courage to fight are slain. At that time it will be too late to set up independency.

The answer to *Common Sense* which Paine himself presumably considered to be the most important consists of a series of newspaper articles in the *Pennsylvania Ledger* under the pseudonym "Cato." At least this was the only attack on Paine's work which he answered in return. Cato's letters were written by a prominent citizen of Philadelphia, the Reverend William Smith, president of the University of Pennsylvania, whose Tory opinions eventually became so distasteful that after the Declaration of Independence he was forced to leave the state. During the period before independence, however, he was considered one of the most substantial citizens of the community. Even then, however, he was far from popular. John Adams, who called him one of "the many irregular and extravagant characters of the age," affirmed in April 1776, that he "never heard one single person speak well of anything about him, but his abilities, which are generally allowed to be good."[7]

One of the fundamental acts of the First Continental Congress in 1774 was to call upon all the colonies to set up local committees to carry on activities requisite to the new situation regarding British control. In Philadelphia this body was known as the Committee of Inspection and Observation, and at first it was responsive to the views of the conservative elements in the community.[8] After the holding of a semiannual election on

16 February 1776, however, the committee suddenly developed radical and populist tendencies.

In the midst of this situation, William Smith, using the pseudonym "Cato," addressed the people of Pennsylvania (8 March 1776), defending the Assembly as a body constitutionally superior to the Committee of Inspection. He suggested that some members of the committee were seeking to assume powers which were not rightly theirs, even to the point of attempting to replace the Assembly, which as the traditional body of government should not be forced to surrender any of its power or responsibilities to committees or conventions.[9]

On the very next day, a letter signed "A Lover of Order" appeared in the *Pennsylvania Evening Post* urging that the decision on whether Pennsylvania should declare for independence from Great Britain should be decided by the people precisely through the instrumentality of committees and conventions. The writer uses the strategy of appearing at the outset to be of a conservative disposition and then gradually veering in the opposing direction. Since this is precisely the technique which Paine had used in the previous year in another communication signed "A Lover of Order," one might assume that the letter of 9 March is also from his pen. This would be logical were it not known that Paine left Philadelphia for New York on 19 February and did not return until late in March, when his friends called him back to answer the "Cato" letters.

Exactly one week before the appearance of the "Lover of Order" letters, one of Paine's allies published an essay in the *Pennsylvania Gazette* denouncing the political maneuvers against the colonies which had been taking place in the British Parliament. The pseudonym was that of "Cassandra," and the author was James Cannon, an inconspicuous master in the University of Pennsylvania, organizer and secretary of a Committee of Privates in Philadelphia, and a staunch friend of Paine.[10]

In his essay, which favorably quotes Paine's counsel that "this winter is worth an age," Cannon warns the people of Philadelphia that the promise of Parliament to send commissioners to listen to the grievances of the colonists and to negotiate fair terms of settlement was merely a device to divide and conquer. "Every thinking man on both sides of the question must, and does believe, that their sole errand is to cajole and deceive, and that large promises, lies, bribery, and corruption, are the means they will use." Showing his classical training, Cannon warns that "these Commissioners are the wooden horse which is to take those by stratagem whom twelve years hostility could not reduce."[11]

Smith in his identity of "Cato" answered Cassandra on 9 March, affirming essentially that the latter's hard line toward the anticipated commissioners was based entirely on his having drunk deep "of the cup of Independence." He then admits not being able to understand why the many publications in favor of independence "have passed hitherto unnoticed," that is, without being attacked, apparently not yet having seen *Plain Truth,* which had already been published in Philadelphia. "Perhaps it was thought best," Smith conjectures, "where an appeal was pretended to be made to the common sense of this country, to leave the people for a while to the free exercise of that good understanding which they are known to possess." Although admitting that some men may have harbored the concept of independence from the beginning of the controversy, Smith confidently asserts "nine-tenths of the people of *Pennslyvania* yet abhor the doctrine."

In his next published address (21 March 1776), Smith directly attacks both the "Lover of Order" and *Common Sense.* The former, he alleges, should more appropriately be labeled "an Author of Confusion." Smith's main argument is essentially the same which Paine had previously used in *Common Sense* against the Pennsylvania Assembly, that the sentiments expressed in the newspaper letter did not adequately represent the majority of the people of the colony. Smith says that no committees have ever been entrusted with authority to speak on the subject of independence and that the most important committee then in existence in Philadelphia was chosen by a very few voices. Then he quotes in favor of the instructions given by the Assembly to the delegates to the Continental Congress a section on that subject from *Plain truth,* which he has now read and recommends as "containing many judicious remarks upon the mischievous tenets and palpable absurdities" of *Common Sense.*

Without mentioning either Independents or Moderates as political organizations, Smith divides the people of America into two groups. The advocates of separation are "adventurers who have nothing to lose, or . . . men exalted by the present confusions into lucrative offices, which they can hold no longer than the continuance of the publick calamities." The advocates of reconciliation, on the other hand, are "that great and valuable body of people in *America,* who, by honest industry, have acquired a competency, and have experienced a happier life." Smith also denies from the record of history and all past experience the assertion of *Common Sense* "that the animosities betwen *Great Britain* and the Colonies are now advanced to such a height that reconciliation is impossible." He closes with a capsule summary of the arguments of *Common Sense,* placing them in a ridiculous light.

> It has been further asserted, that we are able, with our land forces to defend ourselves against the whole world; that if commerce be an advantage, we may command what foreign alliances we please; that the moment we declare ourselves an independent people, there are nations ready to face the *British* thunder, and become the carriers of our commodities for the sake of enriching themselves; that if this were not the case, we can soon build navies to force and protect a trade; that a confederacy of the Colonies into one great Republick is preferable to Kingly Government, which is the appointment of the *Devil,* or at least repro-

> bated by *God;* that those denominated wise men in our own and foreign countries, who have been so lavish of their encomiums upon the *English* Constitution were but egregious fools; that it is nothing better than a bungling piece of machinery, standing in need of constant checks to regulate and continue its motions; that the nation itself is but one mass of corruption, having at its head a Royal brute, a hardened *Pharaoh,* delighting in blood; that we never can enjoy liberty in connection with such a country; and, therefore, all the hardships mentioned above, and a thousand times more; if necessary, are to be endured for the preservation of our rights.

James Cannon returned to the fray with another "Cassandra" essay on 20 March, defending the democratic manner in which the Committee of Inspection had been elected and accusing "Cato" of protecting the interest of the royal governor and not of the people. Indeed, Cannon accuses "Cato" of hoping to be the Prime Minister to any future King of Pennsylvania and challenges him to reveal his true identity. He roundly states that the people of Pennsylvania "will ever have the good sense to prefer *Common Sense* to the appeals of any Government tool which may appear in defense of a union with those who know no law, human or divine, but the law of violence and murder."

In the following week, "Cato" accused "Cassandra" of improperly muddling the issues by concentrating on the relatively insignificant matter of the Committee of Inspection instead of the major one of independence. He also charged that it was inconsistent for "Cassandra" to raise questions about his, Cato's, personal identity and to speculate on his station in the community when neither "Cassandra" nor anyone else had objected to the declaration of *Common Sense* that it was "wholly unnecessary to the Public to know the Author of this Production as the Object for Attention is the *Doctrine itself,* not the Man." According to Smith, *Common Sense* and his advocates were not adhering to fair terms by announcing that only ideas are important and then shifting to personal grounds when the ideas of *Common Sense* came under attack.

Smith devotes the remainder of his essay to the final section of *Common Sense,* which sets forth four practical propositions: that no mediation of the dispute can be arranged through a third party while the colonies admit to being subjects of Great Britain; that France and Spain will not afford assistance unless it is clear that such assistance will widen the breach between America and Britain; that continuing to admit to the status of subjects brands the colonists as rebels in the opinion of Europe; and that a manifesto or memorial detailing the treatment which the colonies have received from Britain and justifying their breaking away would produce salutary effects. In answer to the first point, Smith says that mediators are by definition supposed to repair a breach, not to widen it. In regard to the second, he asserts that the colonies would be injured rather than helped by assistance from France and Spain, primarily because these nations would seek to annex the colonies and impose the Catholic religion. Smith does not specifically answer the third point, and about the fourth merely remarks, "We have already declared ourselves independent, as to all useful purposes, by resisting our oppressors upon our own foundation." He concludes that reconciliation has known advantages, whereas the consequences of complete separation remain uncertain.

At this point, Paine, hastily recalled from New York, reenters the battle, answering "Cato" by an essay with the pseudonym "The Forester" (28 March).[12] Here Paine accuses Smith of deliberately and cunningly skirting the main issue by talking about reconciliation but failing to specify what its advantages are or proving them practical. In keeping with Cannon's innuendoes that "Cato" is a Tory place man, Paine taunts him for being unable to specify the terms of reconciliation. "If they be calculated to please the Cabinet, they will not go down with the Colonies, and if they be suited to the Colonies, they will be rejected by the Cabinet."

From Paine's point of view, Cato's addressing his first letter "To the People of *Pennsylvania*" exclusively has a sinister purpose of emphasizing the local situation against the solidarity of all the colonies. "The particular circumstance of a Convention is undoubtedly Provincial, but the great business of the day is Continental; and he who dares to endeavour to withdraw this Province from the glorious Union, by which all are supported, deserves the reprobation of all men."

Paine vigorously objects to Smith's attempts to buttress faith in the promised commissioners by describing them as "Ambassadors coming to negotiate a peace." Following the lead of Cannon, Paine affirms that their business is "downright bribery and corruption," and he denies that they have the power or authority to make peace even if they wish to. According to Paine's interpretation, the present war is different from any preceding one in that it is not carried on under the prerogative of the Crown, "but under the authority of the whole Legislative power united." The barriers to negotiation are not royal proclamations, but acts of Parliament. Even were "the King of *England* here in person, he could not stipulate for the repeal of any acts of Parliament; neither can the Parliament stipulate for him." After thus reducing the authority and responsibility of the king, Paine inconsistently in later passages seems to burden the monarch with total responsibility. In giving a superficial tone of liberal animation to his letter, Smith had stated, "We are contending against an arbitrary Ministry, for the rights of *Englishmen*." Paine answers, "No, *Cato,* we are now contending against an arbitrary King, to get clear of his tyranny. . . . But it suits not *Cato* to speak the truth. It is his interest to dress up the sceptered savage in the mildest colours." This is certainly one of the most serious contradictions (among many) in Paine's writings on American independence. Not only does "The Forester" essay contradict itself by attributing colonial woes to acts of Parliament, but in doing so it goes completely contrary to *Common Sense,* which emphasizes the personal responsibility of the monarch and rhetorically castigates the people of England.

Smith prefaces his next "Cato" essay (No. 5, 30 March) with a humorous epigraph in verse consisting of a parody of Hamlet's "to be or not to be" speech.[13] The lines wittily defend Smith for taking up an unpopular cause and suggest that he is exposing himself to public obloquy for patriotic reasons.

> For who would bear the scoffing of the times,
> The TORY's hated name, the *Tool of Power,*
> The contumely of the *pension'd slave,*
> When he himself might his *quietus* make,
> With a *dry quill?* Who would endure this Pain,
> This foul discharge of wrath from Adam's sons.
> Marshal'd in dread array both old and Young,
> Their pop-guns here, and there their heavy Cannon,
> Our labor'd pages deem'd not worth a Rush
> But that the dread of something worse to come. . . .

The last six lines of the above passage introduce the names of six of the most ardent proponents of independence in Philadelphia, Thomas Paine, John Adams, Christopher Marshall, Dr. Thomas Young, James Cannon, and Dr. Benjamin Rush. A footnote linked to "Pain" by an asterisk explains "*Some writers in imitation of our ancestors yet spell this word* Payne." This comment is significant in revealing that Paine's political sympathies were well known in public by the end of March 1776. This is also the first time that his name appeared anywhere in print in a political connection.[14] Paine later referred humorously to these verses, observing that "Cato's title to soliloquies is indisputable; because no man cares for his company."[15]

Smith's identity as the author of "Cato" had previously been strongly hinted in the press. Cannon as "Cassandra" on 20 March, for example, ostentatiously quoted from "the sentiments of the celebrated Dr. *Smith* . . . in his address to the graduates," a device which a later essayist labeled as "introducing the very name of a private gentleman into his essays, and obliquely glancing at him as the writer of *Cato's* letters."[16]

In the body of his fifth essay, Smith continues to denounce the notion of calling upon France or Spain for help in resolving internal problems within the British empire. He not unreasonably predicts that if one side (Britain or America) should call in foreign assistance, the other would be forced to do so as well, and the result would probably be the expanding of the contest and drawing it out in time. Smith as a parallel direly points to "the scenes of havock and desolation which mark the late footsteps of contending foreign powers" in Poland. The fallacy in Smith's argument, which Paine was soon to notice, is that he confuses mere alliance with foreign powers (which

Britain had many times concluded) with "calling foreigners to decide our quarrels" (which England had never done, and which *Common Sense* does not recommend).

In the second half of his essay, Smith turns to the abstract ideology of *Common Sense* and presents his critique of its first section concerning the origin of government. By drawing attention to alleged verbal contradictions, he assumes that he is demolishing its intellectual structure completely. He takes first of all Paine's rhetorical phrase "The palaces of Kings are built on the ruins of the bowers of Paradise" and applies it in a literal sense to mean that the first governments were monarchies. Then he observes that the subsequent account in *Common Sense* of "peopling the world" in a state of nature presents not a kingdom, but a "pure Republick," and is therefore inconsistent. Smith next summarizes Paine's concepts of dividing a colony into convenient parts, establishing a system of representation, and having frequent elections in order "that the *elected* might never form to themselves an interest separate from the *electors*." These precautions Smith labels as checking. It is, therefore, an easy matter for him to quote from Paine's refutation of the theory that the King and Commons balance each other, the statement "neither can any power *which needs checking,* be from God." There do exist substantive contradictions in *Common Sense,* but this is not one of them. Paine indignantly replied that the explanations which "Cato" endeavored "to impose on the passages which he hath quoted from *Common Sense,* are such as never existed in the mind of the author; nor can they be drawn from the words themselves."[17] Paine is perfectly right in maintaining this, and those modern authors who state that Smith's answer to *Common Sense* is the best one printed must never have read it. Neither fair, nor honest, it is not convincing in its distortions of words and manipulation of ideas.

Turning next to Paine's scriptural argument, Smith makes no attempt for the moment to provide passages vindicating monarchy, as do most other opponents of *Common Sense,* but he contents himself with observing that "there never was a greater perversion of Scripture than our author has been guilty of." Instead of quoting the Old Testament in a serious way, Smith exposes the folly of drawing upon stories of primitive peoples for principles of modern politics. This he does by quoting a section from the thirty-fifth chapter of Ezekiel, ostensibly to prove that the King of France has been particularly rejected by Heaven. "Son of man, set thy face against *Mountseir,* (Heb. *Mounseir,* or *Monseur,*) and prophesy against it, (*Heb.* him) and say unto him, thus saith the Lord *God:* Behold, O *Mountseir* (or *Mounsier*) I am against thee." Obviously Smith meant this biblical interpretation ironically, but even so the device is not very funny. Paine later unctuously accused Smith of turning "the Scripture into a Jest."[18]

In the midst of the debate over *Common Sense,* a new character entered the discussion, "A Common Man," the author of a letter to "Cato, Cassandra, and All the Writers on the Independence Controversy" (31 March). This even-tempered observer called for more precision and documentation in argument and less rhetoric and attention to personalities. As far as he was concerned, he could live contentedly under an emperor, a pope, a king, or the laws of the republic provided he could be convinced "that such or such a state contained the greatest quantity of happiness for the people at large, and for individuals in particular." This "Common Man" deplored the acrimony of both "Cassandra" and "Cato" and their emphasis on personality rather than matter. To him, the identity of neither writer was of any concern at all. Of special interest to twentieth-century students is his interpretation of one of "Cassandra's" aspersions on "Cato," that the latter runs the risk of going too far in "provoking the majesty of the people by the bold flourishes of a pen which pays no respect to truth, lest he may find it expedient to end his days on the principles of dependency." According to "A Common Man," this passage suggests that "Cato," whose identity as Smith has been exposed, is in danger of being hanged by a mob, thus ending his days in a state of "dependency." This interpretation indicates that the modern student is amply justified in occasionally looking beyond the polite or the literal meaning in colonial polemics.

In the rest of his essay—the major part—"A Common Man" calls on the conflicting sides to produce pragmatic evidence of the positive and material advantages to America of either separation or reunion. He asks to be shown alternate prices of imports and local products, the cost of government, the expense of an army or militia, the prospects of international trade, and even the price of rum. Above all he wants these subjects to be treated with calmness and even temper. In the torrid climate of opinion in which he was writing, this was asking too much. Paine later replied that it was unnecessary "to split the business into a thousand parts, and perplex it with endless and fruitless investigations."[19] Major problems of international relations are "not to be settled like a schoolboy's task of pounds, shillings, pence, and fractions." The overriding question, Paine insists, is, "can this Continent be happy under the Government of *Great Britain* or not?" and secondly, "can she be happy under a Government of our own?"

Paine accepts the principle of judging by measures rather than by men in his second "Forester" letter (9 April 1776) and recognizes that he had himself maintained in *Common Sense* that "the object for attention is the doctrine itself, not the man." He points out, however, that in any situation when men are involved the possibility of hypocrisy and dishonesty must also be taken into consideration. As he had already said, the private rank, condition, or fortune of the author of *Common Sense* would not be relevant to the merits of its arguments, "but the political characters, political dependencies, and political connections of men, being of a publick nature, differ exceedingly from the circumstances of private life."[20] Since these political circumstances are closely related to the measures which men propose, we need to be acquainted with the former in order to keep from being deceived by the latter. As an argument this is true enough, but it does not explain why the personal identity of "Cato" is more relevant than that of "Common Sense," since both men were members of political factions in Philadelphia and the personal circumstances of both men undoubtedly influenced their opinions, although perhaps not to an equal degree. Smith himself had used the technique of *ad hominem* argument against Paine by warning against "the foul pages of interested writers, and strangers meddling in our affairs." Paine answered humorously by referring to Smith's own origins in Scotland.

In taking up Smith's attack upon *Common Sense,* Paine challenges him first on the statement that "nine-tenths of the people of *Pennsylvania* yet abhor the doctrine" of independence. In rebuttal he refers to an election held in Philadelphia in the preceding month in which David Rittenhouse, an open advocate of independence, was elected as burgess. Paine next answers Smith's assertion, "we considered our connection with *Great Britain* as our chief happiness. We flourished, grew rich and populous, to a degree not to be paralleled in history."[21] According to Paine, American prosperity was not the result of British rule, but the reverse: the connection with Britain existed only because of the flourishing economic conditions of America; "this is fully proved by the neglect shown to the first settlers, who had every difficulty to struggle with, unnoticed and unassisted by the *British Court.*" The true causes of the greatness of America are internal—agriculture and commerce, Paine affirms, and the true character of the King has been exposed only in the past year; the American people have realized that "*Cato's* Royal Sovereign is a Royal Savage."

Paine exposes Smith's cunning in quoting from *Common Sense* the term "foreign assistance" and converting it into complete surrender to France and Spain. Similarly Smith uses the word "peace" as a synonymn for "reunion with Britain" and repudiates his opponents as being determined "to reject all propositions of peace."[22]

Cato in his next letter (No. 6, 10 April 1776) analyzes in detail Paine's scriptural argument against monarchy, thus acquiring the distinction of being the only critic to take up the specific Old Testament verses on which Paine based his arguments. All other opponents either reject the scriptural argument altogether or bring to bear verses of contrary meaning from other parts of the Bible. Smith agrees with *Common Sense* that God condemned the Jews for rejecting "his just and righteous government," but he objects to the assumption that it is monarchy which the Almighty opposed. He "would have as strongly expressed his displeasure . . . had they rejected his Government for one of their own appointment, whether it had been monarchical or democratical." Smith objects also to the assumption that the narrative in the Old Testament about events in ancient history should be applied to Great Britain. "How then," he asks, "can there be a Scripture protest against a race of men who are not even described in Scripture?" Quoting Grotius and Sidney, Smith affirms that the Book of Samuel does not establish principles governing kings in general, but is limited to the particular situation prevailing in Israel at the time. Smith devotes three long paragraphs to demonstrating, against Paine's contrary assertion, that David is actually presented in the Scriptures as approved by God in the capacity of a monarch rather than as merely the "man after his own heart." In conclusion, Smith quotes a Whig political theorist, Roger Acherley, author of *Britannick Constitutions,* that Jesus Christ left all rulers and subjects of this world to decide their mutual rights by temporal laws "and never intimated what form of Government was most convenient or eligible." Since this is the theme of Paine's "Address" to the Quakers, there is little that he could have said against Acherley and Smith on this point.

Smith's subsequent "Cato" letter is dated the very next day, 11 April (No. 7). He begins with further jibes at Paine's biblical erudition, observing that his study must have begun only after "the fatal 19th of *April,* 1775," for he professed having been prior to that date a warm wisher for reconciliation to monarchical government. Smith then points out a flaw in Paine's rejection of British monarchy on the grounds that it may be traced "to the rascally original of a *French* bastard." Smith objects that one cannot argue against the institution itself merely because of family blemishes among those who have occupied the office. "The family escutcheon that is without a blot, must be but of very fresh date." Here again Smith is accusing Paine of using an argument which he does not use. Paine points to William the Conqueror not to tarnish kings in general, but to show that the notion of hereditary right cannot be justified on the grounds that one family is better qualified than another. Paine clearly admits that England has "known some few good monarchs."

The rest of this particular letter of "Cato" consists almost entirely of a justification of the British constitution drawn from Book 11 of Montesquieu's *Spirit of the Laws.* In essence he establishes through the French author the equity and efficiency in the separation of powers and the balance of the legislative, the executive, and the judicial branches, and argues that republics may be as absolute and tyrannical as are monarchies. He promises that in his next letter he will apply these general doctrines to the British constitution.

By somewhat of a coincidence a masterly refutation of Smith's defense of the British system of government appeared in a letter addressed to the inhabitants of New York dated on exactly the same day.[23] This letter argues that the British constitution may be ingenious in theory, but that it is truly inefficient and inequitable in practice. In a moderate tone, the author observes that "the very general approbation which *Common Sense* and Independence have met with in these Colonies" makes it natural that "some few should rise up and oppose them." It is also logical to suppose "that some of the most zealous opposers of *Common Sense*" should be "Tories in disguise, who finding that toryism is become obnoxious, have chosen dependance as a more advantageous post from which they may promote divisions, and defeat all the measures the Colonies have concerted." The author points out that the British constitution allows "some to wallow in luxury to destroy themselves, and forces the greater part to live in poverty." The landed gentlemen who possess a hereditary seat in the House of Lords know no more about law and legislation than about Arabic and fluxions. The bishops, who sit in the same body, have no competence to justify their being involved with civil government, but merely help to enslave the people by preaching passive obedience. Even the members of the House of Commons are "chosen by a small pitiful handful of the inhabitants." Candidates buy the votes of the electors and then sell their own votes to the Ministry for the highest price they can extort. "Thus bribery and corruption, places and pensions, have subverted any good principles and designs of the Constitution, and reduced the State to an enormous mass of folly and wickedness."

At this juncture, James Cannon, or "Cassandra," once more reenters the controversy, accusing Smith of writing around the main issues and seeking to arouse the passions of his readers rather than to enlighten them.[24] The main point, he insists, is providing "absolute security for the enjoyment of our liberties." The question is liberty or slavery, and for him the British constitution seems to be weighted against the colonies. As he sees the situation, the Parliament through its injust measures has provoked a state of war between England and the colonies. Since the people of Britain and the people of America have acknowledged the same sovereign (the theory of the king as the binding link of Empire), this sovereign should therefore have remained neutral, but by joining on the side of the Parliament, he has become a party against America. This rebuke is mild in comparison to Paine's phrases such as "royal Brute" and "royal Savage." According to Cannon's analysis, the people of England have a great constitutional advantage over the people of America. Magna Charta gives the English the right of waging war against the king any time he infringes their liberties. The people of America, however, are under the rule of governors appointed in England, who are in no way responsive to the popular will. In the remainder of his letter, Cannon refutes Smith's arguments concerning relations with the European continent and closes with the statement that he hopes "to prove every assertion of *Common Sense.*"

Paine returns in his third "Forester" letter (22 April) to expose the deceptive debating techniques of his opponents. He shows how Smith attempts to interpret the call for mediation from a foreign nation as a proposal for union with that power. Smith's dwelling on the alleged danger from the Catholic forces of France and Spain forces Paine to reiterate his formula from *Common Sense* that "it is the true interest of *America* to steer clear of all *European* contentions." In reference to abstract theories of government, Paine taunts Smith for doing little but quoting other authors "without reasoning much on the matter himself." Paine does not abandon the scriptural approach, but quotes a new text against monarchy: "I gave them a King in mine anger." (Hosea 13 : 11).[25] He also refers to Rousseau's plan for establishing a perpetual European peace, which he describes as "forming a kind of *European* Republick."

In reference to local Pennsylvania affairs, Paine clarifies his attitude toward the Assembly and the committees created to deal with the exigencies of the times. Unlike Smith, he prefers the committees as being the more responsive to popular will and the "only constitutional bodies" at present in the province. Their members were duly elected by the people and faithfully carry out the service for which they were elected; the members of the Assembly, on the other hand, even though also elected by the people, exceed their authority by undertaking business for which they were not elected. Still under the impression that Joseph Galloway had written the instructions to the delegates, Paine accuses him of being the same person "who, when the ships now on the stocks were wanting timber, refused to sell it, and thus, by preventing our strength, [forced us] to cry out of our insufficiency."[26] In the concluding section of his letter, Paine introduces a theme which he was later to expand in the *Crisis,* that the aim of Britain is conquest, not retaliation. He also reverts to a theme from *Common Sense,* that of temporal urgency, and assures his readers that America can form a government of her own and be happy under it. "She hath a blank sheet to write upon. Put it not off too long." In a footnote to this passage he appeals, "Forget not the hapless *African.*" Although this passage with its footnote is unusually cryptic for Paine, it seems to be a call for the writing of a constitution, by which the new nation would be governed, as well as an appeal to include in that constitution an emancipation clause or perhaps merely one forbidding the slave trade. The single sentence of the footnote is the first and only declaration of Paine on the subject of slavery which can be demonstrated to be from his pen up to this time, April 1776.

Smith devotes at least half of his next and last "Cato" essay (24 April) to reflections on the personal motives of the author of *Common Sense* and attempts to brand him as a disturber of union and even a tool of the British administration. Defending his own pro-British sentiments, Smith correctly observes that reconciliation is still the theme throughout the colonies "in their publick capacity," that is, in all official communications, and he maintains that as long as this legal situation continues no private individual can be condemned for advocating reconciliation. Identifying the "Forester" as *Common Sense* in a new role, Smith suggests that the latter has neither "character nor connexions" in Philadelphia and that he is the avowed instrument and dependent of those "who, having no concern in our domestick affairs, are nevertheless constantly intermeddling with them, to the great disturbance of the Province, and injury of the publick cause." Here Smith is referring in general to the populist elements in the city and in particular to the organizers of the local committees. Paine answered these personal reflections in the *Pennsylvania Evening Post* (20 April), caustically affirming that it is better to have no connections than bad ones. Admitting that *Common Sense* and "The Forester" were indeed the same, he asserted that he had come from London over a year previously, bearing with him letters of recommendation from Benjamin Franklin. He challenged "Cato" to reveal his own rank and connections, but Smith ignored the challenge.

In the continuation of his letter, "Cato" attempts to discredit popular government in general. Going back to the seventeenth century, he alleges that "the popular leaders who overturned the Monarchy in the last age, were not themselves friends to Republicks." He also maintains that "*Cromwell* exercised the power of a King, and of the most absolute King, under the specious name of a Protector." Smith quotes Sidney at length on the virtues of a mixed government and on the impracticability of primitive republics such as the one imagined in *Common Sense.* "As to popular Governments, in the strict sense (that is, pure Democracy,) where the People in themselves, and by themselves, perform all that belongs to Government, I know of no such thing; and if it be in the world, I have nothing to say for it." The rest of Smith's essay is devoted to other quotations from Sidney, Gordon, and Montagu in favor of mixed governments on the British plan.

James Cannon, returning for his final word, replies that all the panegyrics on the British system are irrelevant to the concerns of America.[27] It matters not "whether the Constitution of their Government answers excellently to the inhabitants of that Island, if dependance on that excellent form of Government is big with slavery and ruin to *America.*" Cannon thereupon offers three constitutional arguments which he feels conclusively demonstrate that the liberties of America would remain uncertain and conditional under any plan of reconciliation. First, according to the constitution of Britain, "the present Parliament can make no law which shall bind any future one," and, therefore, any concessions made now to the colonists could be revoked at a later time. Second, at the time of the ascent of William III, the legislative authority began restraining the elective rights of the people, and upon the principle of allowing the legislature to limit these rights "our Constitution may be one thing to-day, and another thing to-morrow." Third, the King through his power to appoint administrative officials in the colonies "has the whole power of . . . Government in his own hand, and may do with it as he pleases." For Cannon, therefore, only independence could safeguard American liberty.

At this relatively late stage in the debate a new voice appeared, that of "Moderator," presumably a partisan of the political party known as the Moderates.[28] His is one of the most interesting documents in the debate, not because of any intellectual contribution it makes, but because of its percipient analysis of the psychological and esthetic effects of Paine's *Common Sense* and its suggestion that his style depends in large measure on its images of space associated with the sublime. "Moderator" reveals that when *Common Sense* first appeared, "I found myself stagger'd with the high wrought declamations against Monarchy in general, and of Britain in particular; I view'd the 'Royal Brute' with an indignant frown, and began to new-mould my monarchical sentiments, into those of a common-wealth, whose virtue should reign triumphant." On his second reading, he further surrendered the reins of his imagination to the ingenious author. "We soar'd aloft into the wilds of fancy, the dull beaten track of monarchy, we left far behind us, and found a republic amidst the Stars; and though the Sun might seem, to admiring mortals below, the grand monarch of the heavenly bodies, yet we found other suns and other worlds innumerable, who might only be considered as *Presidents,* not *Monarchs,* of the vast system; every where shone a republic, the various constellations which enspangle the sky, united upon the principles of perfect equality, and gravitating toward each other, with wonderful adjustment, mutually attracted and mutually repelled." This seems to be almost a parody of the parallel between science and politics which runs through nearly all of Paine's later works. Although the parallel is merely suggested in *Common Sense,* it apparently came through with sufficient force to intrigue the author of "Moderator." In continuing his critique, this observer recalls that at the end of his second reading, "I could not call to mind a single stage, on which I had given rest to the soal [*sic*] of my foot, the Sun was too hot, Saturn was too cold, the Moon tottered with unsteady motion, Venus held forth deceitful pleasures. Mercury was unfixed, Jupiter had too much the austerity of monarchy about him, and Mars rolled his rivers in torrents of blood." Like the dove of Noah, therefore, "Moderator" returned to the ark and determined to wait for the falling of the waters and the return of the former verdure. This symbolizes the continuance of "opposition to Great Britain till a firm basis of liberty can be established." From a pragmatic perspective, "Moderator" maintains, however, that immediate and total separation will lead to bloody war and provide pleasure and advantage to France and Spain, "natural enemies to every Englishman." He disagrees with the affirmations of *Common Sense* that the time has now come or that the time has found us by observing that all the objections to monarchy and arguments in favor of commonwealths in that pamphlet would have been equally valid half a century previously. He wants to be informed whether after independence he would have any greater guarantees of personal liberty than the habeas corpus act and trial by jury have already given him, whether he would be more secure in property matters and whether the expenses of government would be diminished. These in his opinion are the vital questions.

With this letter, the debate over independence as it was waged in the

Philadelphia press came to an end. The reason for this cessation is that an election took place on 1 May, which seemed to resolve the question constitutionally. In Philadelphia on that day four members were to be elected to the Pennsylvania Assembly, these four seats carrying the power of controlling the entire Assembly. The Moderate candidates campaigned on a platform of reconciliation, more or less identical with the sentiments of William Smith in the "Cato" letters, and the Independents naturally espoused the principles of *Common Sense.* Although the election was close, the Moderates won three of the four seats and thus acquired strength enough to block any measure for independence in the Assembly.[29]

Three days later, Paine published the last of his "Forester" letters, analyzing the results of the election and castigating those responsible for the defeat of the Independent ticket.[30] Here he says nothing further in behalf of independence but predicts the dire results to the community if its protection against British invasion should be left to the Tory leaders of the Assembly. He takes consolation in the fact that the two candidates to receive the largest number of votes were tied, one from the Independent side and one from the Moderate—or dependent as Paine called it. Actually the total number of votes cast for the Moderates was not much greater than that for the Independents, and Paine, therefore, scoffs at "Cato's" earlier pompous boast that "nine tenths of the people were on their side." Paine had a number of reasons to account for the disappointing results. Many good citizens were in the Continental Army fighting "before the walls of Quebec, and other parts of the continent"; many Germans, zealous in the cause of freedom, were excluded for nonallegiance; others were tricked by the electioneering "maneuver of shutting up the doors between seven and eight o'clock, and circulating the report of adjourning, and finishing the next morning."[31] The Moderate vote included not only the proprietary party, but also the Roman Catholics and the Quakers, strangely enough both on the same side. Paine poured out his wrath against "the testimonizing Quakers, who, after suffering themselves to be duped by the meanest of all passions, religious spleen," endeavored "in a vague uncharitable manner to possess the Roman Catholics of the same disease." But in spite of these explanations, the Moderates had won and the sentiments of *Common Sense* were momentarily in abeyance in the province of Pennsylvania.

13
Plain Truth

On 13 March 1776, there appeared in Philadelphia the most devastating, and perhaps the most effective, of all the many attacks on *Common Sense,* the work of a Maryland Tory so obscure that his authorship was not known to the scholarly world until the middle of the twentieth century.[1] This expression of loyalty to the crown bore the title *Plain Truth; Addressed to the Inhabitants of America, Containing, Remarks on a late Pamphlet, entitled Common Sense.* In parts, according to one critic, it belongs "to the best traditions of eighteenth-century rhetoric."[2]

Until the name of the real author was discovered, *Plain Truth* had been attributed to Joseph Galloway, Alexander Hamilton, George Chalmers (the "Oldys" who wrote the disparaging *Life* of Paine in 1791) and William Smith. There is some plausibility in attributing it to George Chalmers, who like the actual author had resided on the Eastern Shore of Maryland, but absolutely none in considering it to be the work of William Smith. Not only is it inconceivable that Smith would duplicate his efforts in "Cato" and in a long pamphlet, but also *Plain Truth* reflects an implicit anticlericalism completely incompatible with Smith's ardent Anglicanism.

The actual author of *Plain Truth* was James Chalmers, a native Scotsman residing in Kent County, Maryland, where he had extensive land holdings. During the Revolution he raised and commanded a corps called the Maryland Loyalists with the rank of lieutenant colonel and as a result suffered the confiscation of his lands at the end of the war.[3] Although eventually indemnified by the British government he expressed disappointment at the meagerness of the compensation. He visited France during the demonstrations of 1789 and was characteristically appalled by "the diabolical arts" there used against monarchy.[4] After Paine in 1796 predicted the utter bankruptcy of the British nation, Chalmers published, in the same year, *Strictures on a Pamphlet Written by Thomas Paine, on the English System of Finance,* in which he disclosed his authorship of the earlier *Plain Truth,* written, he says, "to deter the house of Bourbon" from interfering in American affairs.

Chalmers opposed American independence because he thought it premature and that if it were precipitated, "it would occasion great evils to America, to Great Britain, and the rest of Europe."[5] One would expect, therefore, that much of the argument of *Plain Truth* would be Europe-oriented, and it is. Chalmers argues, for example, that the French and Spanish would be "wretched politicians," if they did not assist England "in reducing her colonies to obedience."[6]

Nearly all of Chalmers's criticism is directed against the pragmatical sections of *Common Sense,* setting him off from most other polemicists, who concentrate on theory. For *Plain Truth,* Chalmers adopts the pseudonym "Candidus," but he is obviously not the same "Candidus" who had supported *Common Sense* in periodical essays in February and March. Chalmers quotes as an epigraph some lines from Thomson, obviously doing so in order to counteract those from the same poet on the title page of *Common Sense.*

> Will ye turn from Flattery and attend to this Side?
> There TRUTH, unlicenc'd, walks; and dares accost
> Even Kings themselves, the Monarchs of the Free.
> THOMSON on the Liberties of BRITAIN.

Apart from the title, this epigraph cannot be considered to be much to Chalmers's purpose. As a matter of fact there is no work by Thomson entitled *On the Liberties of Britain.* The poem from which Chalmers quotes is the same as that cited by Paine, which is simply *Liberty.* The last two lines in Chalmers's epigraph are from book 1 of that poem, (lines 364–65) but the first line is not in Thomson at all. Chalmers also includes on his title page a dedication to John Dickinson, complimenting him on his defense of the constitution and supplicating him to save it "from impending ruin, under the Syren form of delusive Independence." In his text Chalmers defends Dickinson against the attacks in *Common Sense* leveled against the instructions to the Pennsylvania delegates, instructions which Paine thought were composed by Galloway, but Chalmers knew or guessed were Dickinson's. In a separate introduction, Chalmers describes himself as "silver'd with age," somewhat of an exaggeration since he was barely fifty years old at the time.

At the outset Chalmers suggests that Paine's theory of the origin of society is based on Burgh and Rousseau. Then to disparage all abstract political reasoning, he quotes Rousseau to the effect that no one but a supernatural being removed from all human passions and interests could ever succeed in prescribing "those conditions of society which may best answer the purpose of nations."[7] Chalmers admits Paine's charge that no direct line of descent may be established in the British monarchy, but negates the importance of the fact by quoting Hume's "melancholy, but sensible observation," that "there is no property in durable objects, such as lands and houses, when carefully examined, in passing from hand to hand, but must in some period have been founded on fraud and injustice."[8] These introductory remarks establish Chalmers as a cynical realist in contrast to Paine, an optimistic projector.

If it is true that Paine included his assault on monarchy based on Old Testament quotations entirely to please orthodox Christians, Chalmers had no such regard for the opinions of this segment of society. In language as rough and ready as Paine at his most direct, Chalmers brands the Jews as "a contemptible race more barbarous than our savages" and describes their "anti-philosophical story," as a "continued succession of miracles, astonishing our imaginations, and exercising our faith." For good measure, he accuses the Jews of universal misanthropy and charges that, "as destitute of arts and industry as humanity," they had not "even in their language a word expressive of education." He instructs his antagonist that he would be able to elicit many Old Testament texts favorable to monarchy, but does not bother to do so since the Mosaic law has been superseded by the gospel dispensation.

Throughout his discussion, Chalmers clearly appeals to the propertied class of the colonies, whose members were likely to be Anglican or Presbyterian. He insinuates that the author of *Common Sense* is a member of an independent sect, credulous, superstitious, and enthusiastic in religion and demagogic in politics. He does not identify this sect as the Levellers, but this is certainly his meaning. In animadversions on a rather inflated passage in *Common Sense* in which Paine exhorts his readers against reconciliation with the British "murderers" who are responsible for the massacres in New England, Chalmers suggests that such language befits only those who are "drunk with fanaticism," and "perfectly versed in scripture."[9] He also points to the spirit of harmony now prevailing between the English and the Scots "despite the efforts of certain turbulent spirits, tending to rekindle the ancient animosity."[10]

By and large Chalmers does not follow Paine's argument in the order in which it is developed in *Common Sense,* but introduces topics as they occur to him. He answers some of Paine's invective against English kings by historical references designed to show that "the best princes are constantly calumniated by the envenomed tongues and pens of the most worthless of their subjects." He charges that the history of the republics of ancient Greece and Rome proves that democracy is a form of government no less sanguinary than monarchy. And he quotes "a great author" (actually Rousseau) to the effect that "there never existed nor ever will exist a real democracy in the world."[11] He also quotes Montesquieu to the effect that "no government is so subject to civil wars, and intestine commotions, as that of the democratical or popular form." Chalmers provides his own examples to prove against Paine that Holland and Switzerland have been involved in extensive bloodshed and asserts that even if the remarks in *Common Sense* about their tradition of peace were true, this would not be a result of their form of government, but merely of their geographical location.[12]

With Paine's contention that America would have flourished as much as she has even "had no European power taken any notice of her" he agrees, provided that the principle be applied only to the original inhabitants of

America, the Indians. Later in his tract, Chalmers makes another offhand reference to the Indians in connection with Paine's grandiloquent proclamation, "Had right decided, and not fate the cause, Rome had preserved Cato and her laws." Chalmers connects these "fine sounding words" with Paine's scheme of appropriating the back lands, and he suggests sarcastically that envoys be immediately dispatched to the Indians, "praying them to re-enter their former possessions, and permit us quietly to depart to the country of our ancestors, where we would be welcome guests."[13] Chalmers provides a lengthy historical survey to demonstrate that the present colonists are much better off under English rule than they would be under the French, Swedish, or Dutch. Praising "laws, breathing the spirit of humanity," in Jamaica, Barbados and Virginia, he cites Voltaire's opinion "that if ever the golden age existed, it was in Pennsylvania."[14] To Paine's argument that the future prosperity of America is guaranteed by its capacity to export grain to the continent of Europe, Chalmers replies that the market for American grain has opened merely in recent years, that it exists because the usual source of supply in Poland and the Ukraine has been interrupted, and that the market will vanish as soon as normal cultivation is restored in Eastern Europe.

Chalmers next devotes a large section of his work to Paine's comments on military affairs and his predictions that American forces will gain mastery of the British both on land and sea. This is a subject with which Chalmers reveals a professional acquaintance. Since he later took command of the regiment of Maryland loyalists and presumably served in that capacity until 1783, it is probable that he had prior military training before emigrating to Maryland. Certainly he succeeds in making Paine's record of naval service, whatever it may have been, seem trivial. His intention is more comprehensive than this, that is, to show "that our author shamefully misrepresents facts, is ignorant of the true state of Great Britain and her Colonies, [and] utterly unqualified for the arduous task he has presumptuously assumed."[15] On paper Chalmers succeeds in demonstrating that the military might of Britain will prevail; the only drawback to his demonstration is that actual events proved him wrong and Paine right.

Paine had argued that America could overcome Britain at sea with only a twentieth part of the latter's naval force because the Americans would have only their own coast to protect and they could do their refitting and recruiting without sailing three thousand miles back to England.[16] Chalmers turns the geographical argument around by asserting that if the American troops were to concentrate on New England, where military action was then taking place, the British could then desolate the other provinces; if, on the other hand, the Americans were to spread their forces throughout the colonies, they would have no effective power in any one place.[17] Paine had disparaged the British navy by estimating its total worth at no more than 3.5 million sterling and the extent of its fleet as 50 or 60 ships. Chalmers maintains that the British fleet at the close of the previous war comprised 200 ships of the line and 200 frigates or armed vessels and that the naval stores in British arsenals were worth 20 million.[18] If the American fleet is as strong as *Common Sense* represents, Chalmers ironically recommends, it should seize Jamaica and other West Indian islands. In such a venture the American admiral would not be at a loss for personnel, for, according to the optimistic prediction in *Common Sense,* "a few social sailors will soon instruct a sufficient number of active landmen in the common work of a ship." This is the first of a number of sarcastic references to Paine's unhappy phrase "social sailors." Presumably most of his knowledge of naval affairs was based on his own apocryphal period as a "social sailor" at the age of seventeen.

In regard to Paine's suggestion for building merchant vessels to be equipped with guns for temporary naval duty, Chalmers disdainfully states that no European nation depends on such ships for defense, that they would be unfit to contend with capital ships, that they could be easily captured by the enemy on their outward or inward voyages, and that six such ships would be outmatched by one regular British vessel. Chalmers derides Paine's boasting of the abundance of natural products for shipbuilding to be found in the colonies by remarking caustically, "he speaks of forming a fleet as if he could do it by his fiat."[19] According to Chalmers, a third-rate ship would cost 74,000 pounds sterling in Europe and about one-quarter more in America, in contrast to Paine's estimate of £35,553 for a ship of one hundred guns. After a few more digs at Paine's "social sailors," Chalmers takes up the claim in *Common Sense* that the *Terrible* had withstood the "hottest engagement" in the last war with fewer than twenty sailors on board and asks for authority for the statement. "We do apprehend that naval actions very generally depend on seaman-ship, that is, on dextrously working the ship during the combat. Now the judicious reader will remember, that ships of war in engagement cannot be navigated by a few social sailors, nor even by a bare competency, unless such sailors are more invulnerable than was the great Achilles."[20]

In keeping with his interest in military affairs, Chalmers pounces upon Paine's observation "that the more a country is peopled, the smaller their armies are." Chalmer denies the statement categorically on the basis of actual conditions—the armies of nations with large populations, Russia, France, Austria, England, and Prussia being more numerous than those of nations with small populations, Spain, Sweden, Denmark, Portugal, and Sardinia. Since Paine was probably talking about relative population and Chalmers about actual population, the comparison is meaningless. Chalmers also attacks Paine's assertion that "in military numbers, the ancients far exceeded the moderns." Without reference to the Montesquieu-Hume debate, Chalmers supplied evidence strongly indicating his acquaintance with it. "Every man of sense now rejects the fabulous num bers of the army of Xerxes, and other fabled armies of antiquity. . . . The Roman armies never exceeded twenty-five legions, which including auxiliaries, did not exceed two hundred and fifty thousand, a number greatly inferior to the armies of France or perhaps Britain during war."[21]

Chalmers agrees that America should not seek "to set the world at defiance," but strongly denies that her lack of stores of silver and gold will secure her from invasion. He observes that Flanders also possesses no mines of silver or gold, but has, nevertheless, been frequently engaged in bloody wars. He questions Paine's joint appeal to "the nature of things" and "to all examples from former ages" as proof that the American continent cannot long remain subject to any external power. Antiquity offers no parallels, according to Chalmers, and reason indicates that Britain will cling to her colonies and that rather than abandon them she will see them partitioned among the great powers of Europe.[22] Chalmers finds Paine's admission that the fate of war is uncertain, inconsistent with his various predictions of inevitable American victory.[23]

Paine had praised the colonies for their recent "spirit of good order and obedience to continental government." Instead of directly denying the spirit of unity, Chalmers accuses the author of *Common Sense* of being out of touch with the sentiments of many people in the provinces because of his being elevated to the "grand monde" of the city. According to Chalmers, the people in the countryside remember with gratitude the benefits of their connection with Britain, including emancipation from fear of slavery and death; they venerate its constitution; and they reflect with horror on the former English civil wars, particularly the odious crimes of the Independents.[24]

Paine had suggested that Britain was no longer competent to deal with the intricate matters of state in America and had given as an example the dispute then raging between the colonies of Pennsylvania and Connecticut, characterizing the land-seekers as an undisciplined mob set upon ravaging the property of responsible citizens. Chalmers did not dispute this unflattering view of the land-grabbers but used the fact that they had actually been held in check to praise the firm administration of the Empire. According to Chalmers, "the arm of Great Britain alone detained those free booters . . . from seizing the city of Philadelphia, to which without all doubt they have as just a claim as to those fertile regions in Pennsylvania which they surreptitiously have possessed themselves of."[25]

Despite the fact that in the early months of 1776, the major impetus for independence in the Continental Congress had come from the Virginia delegates, men of substance in Philadelphia looked upon the people of New England as the hotheads and radicals. The image of Samuel Adams was more visible than that of Patrick Henry. Chalmers, therefore, found a sinister meaning in Paine's warning that "reconciliation now with Britain . . . it is more than probable . . . will be followed by revolt somewhere."

Paine meant merely that many parts of the colonies were already so committed to the concept of independence that they would no longer submit to British rule even if it were forced upon them by a decision of the majority to remain within the empire. Chalmers converts this simple prediction to an ominous threat that one part of the colonies would attempt to force its will upon the rest, "that if one or more of the middle or southern Colonies reconcile with Great Britain, they will have war to sustain with New England."[26] Chalmers asserts that the weight of Britain would preponderate against the power of New England in either negotiation or arms. He was certainly fomenting intercolonial dissension, in contrast to Paine's emphasis upon continental unity.

Quite out of the sequence of a continued argument, Chalmers introduces the observation from *Common Sense* that "the diminution of trade affords an army, and the necessities of an army create a new trade." In twentieth-century terms this means that commercial recession offers an opportunity for recruiting into the armed services and that supplying the needs of the army stimulates the economy. Chalmers, however, offers in rebuttal the experience of France, which in the eighteenth century had suffered a diminution of commerce, and as a consequence had enlisted nearly one million soldiers, but the addition of this vast number of troops had allegedly bankrupted the nation.[27] Despite Paine's passage favoring trade, Chalmers later attempts to portray him as an inveterate foe of commerce.[28] The absurdity of this attempt may be seen in another economic principle of *Common Sense:* "As Europe is our market for trade, we ought to favor no political connection with any part of it." Chalmers, however, interests himself merely in the paradox of this proposition and exposes the near contradiction it contains. "Our author surely forgets, that when independent, we cannot trade with Europe, without political connections, and that all treaties made by England or other commercial states are, or ought to be, ultimately subservient to their commerce."[29]

After a long quotation from Montesquieu on the advantages of mercantile exchanges, Chalmers points to "our author's antipathy, and extreme aversion to commerce" and explains it on the grounds that after independence international trade would be for America as remote as the philosopher's stone.[30] Perhaps Chalmers acquired the notion that *Common Sense* opposes mercantile affairs from its statement, "Commerce diminishes the spirit, both of patriotism and military defence,"[31] but this is not really antipathy to commerce as such. Other critics of *Common Sense* strangely continued to raise the question of commerce, which became a type of leitmotif in the polemics over independence. We shall see that in later writings Paine presented an almost lyrical portrayal of commerce as a means of drawing the nation together and preserving its economic security and patriotic fervor.

Despite the many passages throughout *Common Sense* indicating that its author does not share the economic philosophy of the Levellers, Chalmers finds a basis for charging him with bias against wealth, a form of aversion to commerce. The passage which Chalmers quotes to support this interpretation concerns the alleged timorousness of English merchants. "The city of London, notwithstanding its numbers, submits to continued insults, with the patience of a coward. The more men have to lose, the less willing are they to venture, and submit to courtly power with the trembling duplicity of a spaniel."[32] The particular insults Paine had in mind are not clear, but Chalmers answers with an apparent reference to John Wilkes. "That an inconsiderable part of the people in London submit to a person not very honourably distinguished in the world is certain, but that the city of London submits to continued insults is certainly a mistake. I suppose our author means, that by submitting to the best laws on earth, they submit to continued insults. The rich, whom he so very honourably distinguishes, can be at no loss for his meaning. An agrarian law would perhaps be convenient for himself and his independents. It may not however be amiss to remind him of that, which in the multiplicity of his projects he may have forgot, viz. that the richest part of the community will always be an overmatch for the poorest part."[33] This is a remarkable passage—not so much because of any light it throws on *Common Sense,* but because it seems to predict the social philosophy which Paine was to develop in *Rights of Man* and *Agrarian Justice.* This attack goes far beyond the traditional tactic of associating nonconformity in religion with leveling in politics. One possible explanation is that Chalmers actually knew that the author of *Common Sense* was Paine and that he also knew through direct contact or through reports of the conversation of others that Paine had entertained schemes such as that hinted at in the "Amicus" article in the *Pennsylvania Magazine.* This is certainly a farfetched hypothesis, but no other seems more plausible.

Chalmers devotes a long section of his pamphlet to repudiating the criticism in *Common Sense* of the Pennsylvania Assembly for its instructions to the Continental Congress. If the resolves of the Assembly had been adhered to, according to Chalmers, a constitutional reconciliation with Britain would probably have already taken place. "Who so proper to instruct the delegates," Chalmers asks rhetorically, "as those chosen by the people," that is, by the members of the Assembly. Without mentioning Dickinson by name or indicating that he was the author of the resolves, Chalmers accords him special praise. "The gentleman whom our author impotently attacks in this and other innuendos, will be long revered by his grateful countrymen and the friends of mankind, as well for his true patriotism and extensive abilities as his unbounded benevolence."[34] In keeping with his extended parallel between the American patriots of the 1770s and the English independents of the 1640s, Chalmers suggests that the author of *Common Sense* is an execrable hypocrite bent upon destroying the king and constitution. "Every virtuous Pennsylvanian," he insists, "must be fired with indignation at the insidious attack made by this independent on the respectable assembly of his province."

Carrying out his purpose of attempting to deter the French government from furthering efforts toward independence, Chalmers predicts that separation from England would weaken the international position of America. Foreign courts would not invest their faith in a disloyal people behaving like an apprentice who declares himself to be free before his contractual period of service has expired; American exports would not find a ready market in Europe and certainly not in England; American ships without the protection of the British navy would be a prey to pirates; and the British would then have the power to annihilate American ships, ports, and commerce.

Chalmers brings his argument to a close by warning the inhabitants of the colonies to weigh carefully "the character, fortune, and designs of our author and his independents, " a further suggestion that Chalmers was aware of Paine's personal history. Quoting Hume to the effect that "all plans of government which suppose great reformation in the manners of mankind are imaginary," he underscores the dangers of allowing the advocates of independence to alter the constitution, a process which he compares to a colonel, engaged in forming his battalion in the face of an enemy, who would stop to write an essay on war.[35] Chalmers predicts that the scheme of independency proposed in *Common Sense* would "very soon, give way to a government imposed on us by some Cromwell of our armies." This prediction he supports by a quotation from Montesquieu indicating that an army will always detest a senate but respect its own officers. In addition to denigrating the supporters of American independence by constant comparison with the religious independents of the English civil war, Chalmers suggests that most of the advocates of revolution belong to the New England region and argues that these fanatics would not respect the religion and customs of the southern and middle colonies. "Notwithstanding our author's fine words about toleration, ye sons of peace and true christianity, believe me, it were folly supreme, madness, to expect angelic toleration from New England, where she has constantly been detested, persecuted, and execrated; even in vain would our author, or our Cromwell, cherish toleration; for the people of New England, not yet arrived in the seventeenth or eighteenth century, would reprobate her." Chalmers even suggests that the New England governments would have no objection to an Agrarian law, that is, to an enforced division of property.

Chalmers concludes by predicting that nothing but "horror, misery and desolation" would come with American independence, and he affirms that true liberty is possible only through reconciliation with the authority of Great Britain. His final sentence, summarizing this perspective, represents one of the greatest paradoxes in the literature of the Revolution, at least when taken literally, "Independence and slavery are synonymous terms."

Plain Truth was published by Robert Bell, who apparently ran into heavy criticism from zealous patriots for thus appearing to oppose independence. In his own defense, and in particular reference to *Plain Truth,* he inserted in another publication a vindication of the liberty of the press which he described as "Extracted from an Old Pamphlet, Published in the Year 1756, Entitled Plain Truth." The author of this "Old Pamphlet," like that of Chalmers named *Plain Truth,* was none other than Benjamin Franklin, and Bell thus cleverly brought the words of a partisan of independence in vindication of a pamphlet against it.[36]

On the day of the publication of Chalmers's pamphlet, one of Paine's Quaker supporters, Christopher Marshall, who had been expelled from the Friends' meeting because of his ardent advocacy of political liberty, visited Dr. Young, another radical in Paine's circle, and, according to his diary, heard Young "read a piece in answer to Common Sense, called Plain-Truth, but very far from coming up to the title."[37] A much higher opinion of the merits of Chalmers's pamphlet was reflected by John Adams, however, who was as much in favor of independence as the Pennsylvania radicals. He indicated in his autobiography that *Plain Truth* "contributed very largely to fortify and inflame the Party against Independence, and finally lost us the Allens, Penns, and many other Persons of Weight in the Community."[38] Paine, however, had nothing but scorn for *Plain Truth,* deriding it as "a performance which hath withered away like a sickly, unnoticed weed, and which even its advocates are displeased at, and the author ashamed to own."[39] Perhaps this is the reason why modern historians tend to diminish the importance of Chalmers and exalt that of Smith. Any objective measure of logic, significance of material, and vigor of style, however, would determine *Plain Truth* to be a far more successful rebuttal of *Common Sense* than the letters of "Cato."

In May an answer to Chalmers, *Remarks on a Late Pamphlet entitled Plain Truth,* bearing the pseudonym "Rusticus," appeared in Philadelphia. Although John Dickinson has been for many years considered to be this "Rusticus," the attribution is extremely doubtful. "Rusticus" makes merely a single allusion to a classical figure; yet Dickinson, one of the outstanding classicists of the colonies, sprinkles all of his known political essays with references to ancient writers. "Rusticus" excuses himself for not having the works of Hume to turn to; yet Dickinson possessed one of the most extensive libraries in the colonies. "Rusticus" also devotes most of his space to a discussion of military prospects and tactics, a subject far from the main interests of Dickinson. "Rusticus," moreover, does not even broach the question of the instructions to the Pennsylvania delegates to the Continental Congress, the only section of *Plain Truth* in which Dickinson was personally involved. "Rusticus" says that he has read *Common Sense* and that as a result he cannot withhold assent to the arguments of the victorious author; yet Dickinson two months later in complete opposition to the arguments of

Common Sense voted in the Continental Congress against independence. "Rusticus" also signs his pamphlet "New-Jersey, May 8th, 1776," whereas Dickinson's residence at that time was Philadelphia. The main reason for assuming that Dickinson is not "Rusticus," however, is that the latter has very little of substance to say, and a feeble effort such as his could hardly be the product of the distinguished penman of the American Revolution.

Perhaps the attribution to Dickinson is a result of confusing his name with that of Jonathan Dickinson Sergeant, a much more likely author of the *Remarks.* Sergeant was a resident of New Jersey and a delegate from that colony to the Continental Congress, and his ideas on government were much like Paine's. "Rusticus" objects to the dedication of *Plain Truth* to Dickinson on the grounds that, while it pretends to disclaim flattery, it is actually filled with adulation and extravagance in the worst taste. Seizing upon *Plain Truth's* characterization of his own style as "crude," "Rusticus" complains that it is an insult to both Dickinson and the public to offer undigested remarks on a subject of vital importance such as American independence. The only observation of "Rusticus" relative to the theory of government concerns the opinion of his antagonist that it is a good thing for the King in England to influence the Commons by means of honours and appointments. *Common Sense,* of course, condemns this practice as bad. "Rusticus," agreeing with Paine, states that most authors on the constitution consider the contrary check which the Commons have on the Crown to be the "supreme felicity" of the system, but he ironically observes that this feature does not work in practice; in his words, we "have not yet fully experienced that happiness of the democratical part of our constitution, which is the admiration and envy of other nations."[40]

The main purpose of "Rusticus" seems to be the correcting of the misconceptions or misrepresentations of *Plain Truth* in regard to the actual and potential military strength of the colonies. He vigorously denies that the number of men capable of bearing arms is no more than seventy thousand and indignantly refutes the charge that American troops in recent actions have failed to exhibit "marks of Spartan or Roman enthusiasm."[41] He supports the proposal of *Common Sense* to equip merchant vessels with guns and observes that all of the objections made to the scheme by *Plain Truth* would be valid only if these defensive merchantmen were to be given full responsibility for maritime protection without the support of a regular naval fleet. Nobody but "Candidus", he affirms, ever assumed that the entire American force would consist of armed merchantmen.[42] In reply to the representations of "Candidus" concerning the extraordinarily high cost of maintaining a fleet, "Rusticus" not only brands them as exaggerated and unreliable but also suggests that vast sums of money which had formerly been contributed to royal revenues could after independence be diverted to naval construction. "Rusticus" bluntly accuses *Plain Truth* of attempting to reduce American military capability by extinguishing "every spark of martial fire." And joining military affairs with the theme of commerce, he rejects as demeaning *Plain Truth*'s dependence upon "the unmanly subtleties of commerce for subsistence."[43] "This may be the policy of Candidus, but I trust it will never be the policy of America: When it is, America should be inhabited only by pedling Jews."

The most damaging accusation against *Plain Truth* is that he has consorted with the enemy and communicated information which could be used against the defense of the colonies. This charge is based on the statement by *Plain Truth* that "in the opinion of the best officers of the navy, *Philadelphia* is accessible to a few 40 and 50 gun ships, in despite of our temporary expedients to fortify the river Delaware." It was quite natural for "Rusticus" to suggest that while "Candidus" was consulting the best officers in the British navy as to "the sufficiency of our endeavours to defend ourselves," he also "pointed out to them those parts wherein he thought us most weak."[44] The whole of *Plain Truth* is similarly considered as an effort "to sow dissentions among the *Rebels*, and throw them and their measures into irretrievable confusion."

"Rusticus" looks scornfully upon the argument of "Candidus" that France and Spain would not aid the colonists out of fear that American love of liberty might infect their own subjects. He answers that these nations would find sufficient advantage in "a free commercial intercourse" to overcome any such fears. In regard to the direful predictions of "Candidus" that some Cromwell will spring up in America and that the people of New England will force puritan doctrines upon the rest of the land, "Rusticus" replies that it would be tedious to obviate in detail all of the difficulties imagined by his adversary. But should the people find a new government necessary, "there is no doubt but they have wisdom and caution sufficient to guard against these threatened evils; and will establish for the people security in their civil and religious rights on a lasting foundation."[45]

Since the Remarks of "Rusticus" have more to do with predicting the military and diplomatic future than with ideology, they have only limited value today. Indeed, the pamphlet has only one truly original notion to recommend it. This is in connection with the commissioners who were then expected from England to make a final effort to negotiate matters with the colonists. "Rusticus" has little faith in the power of such commissioners to do justice, but he offers what he considers the only workable solution: "It is this, that no act of the British Parliament, such only excepted as respect the regulations of our external commerce, shall be valid in America until approved and passed by a *Continental Congress*."[46] Such a solution is considerably short of Paine's call for complete independence, but in the climate of opinion in which it appeared—when the British Parliament had become so intransigent that concessions of any kind were unthinkable—the author might just as well have fully endorsed the program of *Common Sense*.

14
Other Pamphlet Polemics

A. Civil Prudence

Despite the attempt of Chalmers to portray Paine as a foe of commerce, the anonymous author of a subsequent pamphlet which was devoted exclusively to the promotion of trade inscribed his work "*To the most excellent Patriot,* COMMON SENSE, *Defender of the natural Rights and Liberties of Mankind.*" This pamphlet, printed in Norwich, Connecticut, soon after *Common Sense,* was called *Civil Prudence, recommended to the Thirteen United Colonies of North-America* and bore the unidentified epigraph:

> TRADE, *like the genial Sunbeams, spreads around*
> *It's Blessings to enrich the happy Ground.*

In explaining the dedication to *Common Sense,* the author describes Paine's work as a "masterly performance . . . coming forth like a mighty conqueror, bearing down all opposition." He reveals that he had written his own essay shortly after the repeal of the Stamp Act in order to promote the interest of the colonies in the union with Britain, believing the two peoples inseparable. His text confirms this perspective. Great Britain is said to have expended long experience and much blood "to learn the art of gentle government, and due preservation of liberty," and the great advantage of British rule is considered to be its moderating force in regulating affairs between the individual colonies and between civil and religious parties.[1] There can be no question, therefore, of any influence of *Common Sense* upon *Civil Prudence.* The only resemblances between the two works are a result of chance and to a small degree coincidence of subject matter.

The major principle of *Civil Prudence* is that maximum commerce, both internal and external, and maximum circulation of an extensive supply of money will best promote the economic welfare of Connecticut and other parts of America. Nothing in *Common Sense* goes contrary to this principle. The positive resemblances between the two works, however, are scant, limited chiefly to advocacy of the settlement of the back lands, concern for the "poor man's right," and recognition of the advantages of a national debt. In this respect, the author says he is proposing his economic measures in order to "prevent three fourths of the inhabitants of this land from becoming slaves to one eighth."[2] *Civil Prudence* affirms a strong affinity between his own work and *Common Sense* and generously praises it for possessing a wider perspective than his own pamphlet. "When I heard of COMMON SENSE's being out, to promote independence," he says, "I felt disturbed in my mind, concluding it to be the invention of some Tory, to sow discord against us; but reading of it gave me a new set of thoughts, and opened a wider door to the flourishing of trade and common wealth, as well as of the due preservation of liberty, than I ever imagined." What these new set of thoughts may have been, however, must remain undisclosed, since the essence of *Civil Prudence* consists of the economic arguments of the essay as they had existed before Paine's work was published.

B. Zuschrift

Another pamphlet only tangentially related to *Common Sense* was published in the German language in New York in April 1780, *Zuschrift an die Teutschen in Pennsylvanien, und benachbarten Provinzen* [*Address to the Germans in Pennsylvania and Neighboring Provinces*]. This was written by Christopher Saur, the grandson and namesake of the founder of the first German printing press in America. Saur carried on the family publishing business in Germantown, Pennsylvania, but his Tory opinions and sympathies were so extreme that in 1778 he fled to New York, which was then occupied by the British. He cooperated willingly with Crown military and civilian leaders and did all in his power to persuade other Germans to forsake the revolutionary cause. To this end, he published his *Address,* which was revised and approved by General Knyphausen and distributed in Pennsylvania.[3] The pamphlet contrasts the prosperity of the German settlers before the Revolution with the unsettled economic conditions they faced during the war and accuses the supporters of the Congress of being ungrateful to the British government which had treated them kindly and generously. Saur takes notice of *Common Sense,* since a German translation had been published in Philadelphia by the printers Steiner and Cist as early as February 1776, but he devotes to it merely a single page which is translated below.

> The author of the famous work *Common Sense* (a hireling of Congress and restless spirit) has transported you by means of that little work (if I may make use of the metaphor) to the rooftop of the temple to show you the kingdoms of this world and their glories, which were not in his power to give. He prattled to you pleasing fairy stories of fabulous new happiness in future new governments which one can bring into being only with pen and paper. He made independence seem so splendid to you that the brilliance of it blinded you just as the spots in the sun cannot be

> perceived right away because of its dazzling light. He explained to you that it is as easy to change the form of government as it is to clear away trees and roots in a new piece of land. Make up your mind today, however, to read through this marvelous *Common Sense;* weigh its author's advice point by point; follow the thread of the various reasons why his new form of government should be superior; compare his ridiculous predictions with the way events have turned out; judge how far his highly praised independence has failed up to now. Thus you will make a discovery that will astonish you. You will discover that the author is a bribed crook, and his little work a seed of the devil implanted in your midst by the hand of congress. Read the *so-called Common Sense,* now more often than before, especially each time that you see the heads of this unjustified rebellion more and more bowed. As it so easily led you into error at the first reading, it can now just as rapidly open your eyes.

Saur's appeal had very little effect because a majority of colonial Germans were Lutherans and Reformed, whereas Saur was associated in their minds with minor sectarians; also "many Germans, like other nationalities, had through five years of hardship become completely opposed to reunion with England."[4] The Germans, especially those on the frontier, moreover, naturally assumed that their lot would be more favorable under a government which would not necessarily favor a British heritage.

C. Inglis

The answer to *Common Sense* which created most fervor in the colonies was originally entitled *The Deceiver Unmasked* and was printed in New York in March 1776, almost the same time that *Plain Truth* appeared in Philadelphia. The author, an Anglican clergyman of extreme Tory principles, Charles Inglis, took it upon himself to expose or "unmask" what he considered to be the artful and insidious republicanism of *Common Sense.* As soon as his exposé was advertised for sale, a patriotic group known as the Sons of Liberty, but having no official sanction, seized and burned the entire impression of 1,500 copies (18 March 1776) estimated as worth £75. The printer, Samuel Loudon, thereafter bitterly complained to the Committee of Safety of the City of New York and sought reparation for his loss. He not unreasonably maintained that his freedom of speech had been infringed, since the Continental Congress had not yet made a decision on independence and there could be no criminality in publishing arguments either for or against it. Mob action of the kind involved in the invasion of his premises, he protested, meant the annihilation of liberties and would result "in a more miserable slavery than would arise from the most successful execution of all the tyrannical acts of the *British* Parliament."[5]

Inglis sent one of his author's copies to Philadelphia, where it was printed early in June as a second edition under the title *The True Interest of*

America, Impartially Stated, in certain Strictures on a Pamphlet Intitled Common Sense.[6] Before seeking out his second printer, however, Inglis carefully eliminated those passages which had most violently offended the patriots, toned down some others, and inserted a few additional ones to preserve the edition from suffering the same fate as the first one. Without the added moderate passages, he felt, the pamphlet could not have been published. Apparently favorable toward the Congress, these "were intended to soothe the disaffected, gain their confidence and thereby obtain the object principally aimed at."[7] Inglis hoped that his pamphlet would delay a declaration of independence until commissioners should arrive from England who would "probably terminate this unhappy contest."

In his preface, dated 16 February 1776, Inglis condemns the author of *Common Sense* for appealing to "the passions of the populace," giving vent to "his own private resentment and ambition," and exhibiting himself as "an avowed, violent Republican, utterly averse and unfriendly to the English constitution." This personal denunciation, which is in keeping with Inglis's original title, *The Deceiver Unmasked,* reveals that his strategy will consist in large measure in attacking the author's motives, particularly that of promoting "his beloved scheme of Independent Republicanism."[8] In his text, Inglis replies to Paine's arguments concerning the theory of government, but almost entirely evades the fundamental question of independence except in regard to the effect it would have in international relations. Unlike Chalmers, he makes no attempt to vindicate the policies of the British government which the Americans considered objectionable other than suggesting that onerous restrictions are the fault of particular officials and will be rectified in succeeding administrations. Thus he declares that writers on political subjects are likely to "draw general conclusions from particular premises, and form their judgments of human nature, not from a general view of mankind in their various situations; but from the conduct of a few individuals, and the particular state of things at the time they wrote."

He specifically attacks Paine's principle that government and society are different entities by asking rhetorically whether "this gentleman" ever knew of anyone who was born out of society, since "a state of society is the natural state of man." This is a rather weak attack since Paine had never denied that man is born in a state of society; he had merely raised the possibility of the existence of society prior to government. Inglis then more reasonably places the question in the realm of opinion by affirming his own adherence to that of Hooker "that society could not be without government, nor government without law."[9]

In a further misconstruction of *Common Sense,* Inglis charges that it assumes that the only function of government is to punish, and in rebuttal Inglis says that codes of laws have many other purposes. This seems to be a very narrow interpretation of Paine's explanation of government as "a mode rendered necessary by the inability of moral virtue to govern the world." Paine makes no allusions whatsoever to punishment but suggests on the contrary that the major function of government is a regulatory one. Another of the interpretations which Inglis makes of *Common Sense* also seems to be wide of the mark, his assertion that the phrase "first peopling of any country" has the original settlement of the British colonies in view. It may be true, as Inglis argues, that the first emigrants to America were already in a state of society,[10] but this has almost no relevance to Paine's phrase, which concerns the state of nature in the abstract.

Inglis is more logical in pointing out that the maxim in *Common Sense* that the "more simple anything is, the less liable it is to be disordered" fits most precisely absolute monarchy, and yet the pamphlet as a whole favors democracy, the form of government most complex and subject to disorder. Inglis charges that the principle of simplicity was "ushered in, purely to contrast it with the complex nature of the English constitution, and thereby prejudice the reader against the latter."[11] Inglis quite properly observes that a major point in *Common Sense* requiring clarification is the meaning of the phrase in reference to the constitution of England, "the dark and slavish times in which it was intended."[12] As Inglis affirms, the British constitution in the form it possessed in 1776 had been fixed at the time of the Glorious Revolution of 1688—and if *Common Sense* is referring to an earlier period, it is completely irrelevant. This is a valuable observation, for the same ambiguity exists in Paine's subsequent sentence: "When the world was overrun with tyranny the least remove therefrom was a glorious rescue." This seems to have more relevance to the era of Magna Charta than to the Glorious Revolution. Another pamphlet against *Common Sense* nevertheless assumes without question that Paine means by "dark and slavish times" the period of the Restoration, 1660, when the nation "invited the son of the very man they so much complained of to come and be her king."[13] This assumption is probably correct.

Inglis insists that the complexity of the English constitution should not be considered an evil in itself, since it permits anyone who is aggrieved the opportunity of seeking redress, and he cites the case of John Wilkes as proof. Americans, Inglis recommends, should be more concerned about the constitutions of their own colonies, which are indeed very simple, "each being administered by a governor, council and assembly."[14] In reference to the dichotomy in *Common Sense* between alleged tyrannical materials in both monarchies and aristocracies and republican materials in the British House of Commons, Inglis applies the traditional maxim of Montesquieu that "monarchical governments are best adapted to extensive dominions; popular governments to a small territory." He also quotes Harrington to the effect that although "politicans speak of pure aristocracy, and pure democracy, there is no such thing as either of these in nature or example." This is perhaps designed to remind Inglis's more learned readers that

Rousseau had not been the first to deny the existence of a "real democracy."[15]

In reference to the passage in *Common Sense* railing against the absurdity of checks and balances, Inglis objects that it is just as absurd "to suppose, that a man, because he has a constitutional check upon others, must therefore be wiser than those others. A common constable has, in many cases, a check upon his fellow subject," but it does not follow that he is wiser or that the constitution supposes him to be so. Once again Inglis refers to Montesquieu for authority.[16]

In refuting Paine's depiction of the sordid origins of monarchy, Inglis affirms that violence had existed upon the earth long before the institution of kings. Inglis does not say on what authority he bases this statement, but he is certainly correct in affirming that it is supported by the scriptural record which *Common Sense* accepts. Inglis states in addition that the reign of one of the earliest kings, Melchizedek, was a period of patriarchal simplicity and that Holland was a poor example for *Common Sense* to give of a peaceful nation, for Holland had been involved in every general war in Europe for a century. It means nothing against kings when *Common Sense* argues that they were first introduced by heathens—so were the Greek and Latin languages, as well as tobacco, all of which are good.[17]

Inglis devotes ten full pages to refuting Paine's scriptural arguments against monarchy. After asserting that "the Jewish polity, in which the Almighty himself condescended to be a King (and thence called a theocracy) is rather in favour of monarchy than against it," he declares that it is not clear "that any one species of regular government is more acceptable to the Deity now than another; whatever preference may be due to one above another, in point of expediency and benefit." He argues that the passages in Samuel which *Common Sense* cites as condemning monarchy do not really reflect upon the institution in general but merely give an account of "the then despotic monarchies of the East, which Samuel was directed to lay before the Israelites, that they might see how inconsistent such a monarchy was with their peculiar state and circumstances." Eleven other scriptural texts upholding monarchy, which Inglis quotes, give a completely different perspective from Paine's.

Contrary to the insistence of *Common Sense* upon April 19 as the date of the closing of debate between Britain and the colonies, Inglis affirms that the Continental Congress continued long afterward to address petitions to the King and addresses to the inhabitants of Great Britain and Ireland. Then he asks, how George III could be held responsible for the bloodshed at Lexington when he was at the time three thousand miles away. Reconciliation in short was just as possible after April 19 as before. The welfare of the colonies is dependent upon Britain, Inglis affirms, especially Virginia, Georgia, and Nova Scotia; it does not matter whether Britain offers protection on her own account or that of the colonies; it is nonetheless real and necessary.[18] England, Inglis insists, is the real parent of the colonies, for its inhabitants are deemed English subjects and entitled to the privileges of Englishmen, privileges to which emigrants are not entitled until naturalized.

Taking up the hyperbolical claim of *Common Sense* that "our present numbers are sufficient to repel the force of all the world," Inglis does not reject it on the grounds of exaggeration but uses it to show the illogic of predicting connections with other nations; if America can repel the whole world, foreign alliances are not necessary.[19] Inglis pays surprisingly little attention, however, to the proposals in *Common Sense* for erecting a new form of government. "The principal outline of the sketch," he remarks, "seem to be taken from Mr. Harrington's *Rota,* which was too romantic even for the times of *Cromwell.* . . . I may truly say of it, and its author, so far as he may claim author-ship by it, what MONTESQUIEU said of Harrington and his *Oceana,* of which the *Rota* is a kind of abridgment—'For want of knowing the nature of real liberty, he busied himself in pursuit of an imaginary one.' "[20] Inglis follows Montesquieu also in arguing that America is too extensive in territory to be able to adopt republican or democratic forms, but he does not cite *The Spirit of the Laws* as his authority.

Turning one of the arguments of *Common Sense* in a contrary direction, the prediction that reconciliation with Britain would entail unbearable divisiveness, Inglis states that it is a declaration of independence which "would infallibly disunite and divide the colonists." This is one of the few points on which the disputants, taking opposite sides, were both right. Contrary to the optimistic estimates of *Common Sense,* Inglis maintains that the expense of an independent army and navy would be astronomical, far beyond the means of the colonists. He predicts, furthermore, that France would not recognize American independence and points out, apparently without adequate documentation, that France and Spain have already offered to assist Great Britain in a contest with its colonies.[21]

Bernard Bailyn has observed that "when Charles Inglis looked for the source of Paine's anti-monarchism in order to attack it, he found it not in Enlightenment theory, whose exponents he praised, but in an obscure treatise by one John Hall, 'pensioner under Oliver Cromwell.' "[22] One cannot say that Inglis necessarily failed to recognize parallels with Locke or Rousseau. He picked John Hall, a seventeenth-century predecessor, because he deliberately sought to tar *Common Sense* with the brush of religious superstition and leveling. Unlike Chalmers, who sought to do the same thing, but went about it more honestly by rejecting all appeals to scriptural authority, Inglis identified himself with the Puritan tradition to the extent of answering one series of biblical quotations with another group setting forth a contrary doctrine. Ideologically Inglis does not really take a stand against *Common Sense.* His whole method of attack consists, as he admits in his original title, of impugning the author's motives and in uncovering inconsistencies.

Inglis's Philadelphia printer, Humphreys, kept on advertising his *Strictures* against *Common Sense* well into the autumn of 1776, many weeks after the Declaration of Independence, an indication that the discussion stimulated by Paine was not by any means limited to the notion of separation, and that the other issues of government and politics which he had raised were considered to be equally important.[23]

D. John Adams

Of all the authors who wrote rejoinders to *Common Sense* or commentaries upon it immediately after its publication, the most brilliant, learned, and distinguished was John Adams. At first many people believed that he was the author of *Common Sense* itself, and as late as December 1776, a French periodical published in London, *Affaires de l'Angleterre et de l'Amérique,* actually attributed it to him in print.[24] Adams did indeed approve of *Common Sense* when it first came out. Although his own pamphlet entitled *Thoughts on Government* was directly inspired by the suggestions in *Common Sense* for a unicameral national legislature and represents a defense of the contrary system of bicameralism, it contains no other criticism of Paine's pamphlet, direct or implied.

Adams's initial reaction to *Common Sense* and the circumstances of the subsequent composition and publication of his own *Thoughts on Government* are best described by Adams himself in his autobiography.

> The Arguments in favour of Independence I liked very well: but one third of the Book was filled with Arguments from the old Testiment, to prove the Unlawfulness of Monarchy, and another Third, in planning a form of Government, for the seperate States in One Assembly, and for the United States, in a Congress. His Arguments from the old Testiment, were ridiculous, but whether they proceeded from honest Ignorance, or foolish Supersti[ti]on on one hand, or from willfull Sophistry and knavish Hypocricy on the other I know not. The other third part relative to a form of Government I considered as flowing from simple Ignorance, and a mere desire to please the democratic Party in Philadelphia, at whose head were Mr. Matlock, Mr. Cannon and Dr. Young. I regretted however, to see so foolish a plan recommended to the People of the United States, who were all waiting only for the Countenance of Congress, to institute their State Governments. I dreaded the Effect so popular a pamphlet might have, among the People, and determined to do all in my Power, to counter Act the Effect of it. My continued Occupations in Congress, allowed me no time to write anything of any Length: but I found moments to write a small pamphlet which Mr. Richard Henry Lee, to whom I shewed it, liked so well that he insisted on my permitting him

> to publish it: He accordingly got Mr. Dunlap to print it, under the Title of Thoughts on Government in a Letter from a Gentleman to his Friend. Common Sense was published without a Name: and I thought it best to suppress my name too: but as common Sense when it first appeared was generally by the public ascribed to me or Mr. Samuel Adams, I soon regretted that my name did not appear. Afterward I had a new Edition of it printed with my name and the name of Mr. Wythe of Virginia to whom the Letter was at first intended to have been addressed.[25]

What is surprising in Adams's description of *Common Sense* is that it comprises a major misreading of the section entitled "Thoughts on the present state of American affairs." Adams states that it consists "in planning a form of Government, for the separate States in One Assembly, and for the United States, in a Congress," in other words, that *Common Sense* recommends a unicameral system for both the states and the national government. In actuality Paine says nothing whatsoever about changing the existing colonial assemblies from two chambers to one. Indeed he affirms that the urgencies of the time justified the delegates to the Continental Congress being chosen "from the several Houses of Assembly."[26]

It is true that he immediately afterward raises the question "whether *representation and election* is not too great a power for one and the same body of men to possess?" but the doubts here expressed have nothing to do with the nature of the assemblies but rather with the appropriateness of members of assemblies also being delegates to the Continental Congress. It appears, then, that when Adams was writing his autobiography, he did not refresh his memory by rereading *Common Sense.*

Adams expressed his reaction to *Common Sense* shortly after its publication, in a letter to his wife, Abigail, 19 March 1776.

> It has been very generally propagated through the Continent that I wrote this Pamphlet. But altho I could not have written any Thing in so manly and striking a style, I flatter myself I should have made a more respectable Figure as an Architect, if I had undertaken such a Work. This Writer seems to have very inadequate Ideas of what is proper and necessary to be done in order to form Constitutions for single Colonies, as well as a great Model of Union for the whole.[27]

Here we see that Adams is very complimentary in referring to Paine's style and that his reservations concern merely the proposed constitutions both for the new nation and for the individual colonies.

Apparently Adams at this time did not know who was the author of *Common Sense,* for he refers merely to "this writer." Since he customarily expressed himself frankly and fully in his private letters to his wife, he probably would have identified Paine as the author had they been acquainted. The fact that they were strangers is borne out by a note in *Crisis* No. 3 in which Paine remarks that when *Common Sense* made its appearance he did not have "the pleasure either of personally knowing or being known to" Samuel and John Adams.[28]

The full title of Adams's pamphlet was *Thoughts on Government: Applicable to the Present State of the American Colonies. In a letter from a Gentleman to His Friend* (Philadelphia, John Dunlap). According to Adams, he had been asked for his opinion on a suitable state constitution for North Carolina by two delegates to a constitutional convention there, William Hooper and John Perin. He thereupon produced two copies, giving one to each of the delegates. George Wythe, seeing one of these copies, asked to have one of his own, and Adams thereupon wrote another entirely from memory. Shortly after this, Jonathan Dickinson Sergeant of New Jersey also requested a copy, and Adams wrote an enlarged version also from memory. When Richard Henry Lee "requested the same Favour," Adams borrowed Wythe's copy, and Lee prepared it for the printers.[29] The dates of composition and publication can be rather precisely determined. The first version must have been completed prior to 27 March, the date when Hooper and Perin left Philadelphia, and it was already in print on 20 April, when Adams sent a copy to James Warren.

Unlike *Common Sense,* Adams's pamphlet does not exhort the colonists to declare their independence but takes it for granted that this act will take place and that virtual separation from Britain has already been effected. In the manuscript copy given to William Hooper and John Perin, there appears a passage remarkably similar to the following one from *Common Sense* on the unique occasion available to the Americans of forming a new government. "We have every opportunity and every encouragement before us, to form the noblest purest constitution on the face of the earth. We have it in our power to begin the world over again. A situation, similar to the present, hath not happened since the days of Noah until now. The birthday of a new world is at hand."[30] Adams, with less fervor but equal conviction, observes, "It has been the will of Heaven that we should be thrown into existence at a period when . . . a coincidence of circumstances without example, has afforded to thirteen colonies at once an opportunity of beginning government anew from the foundation, and building as they choose. How few of the human race have ever had the opportunity of choosing a system of government for themselves and their children!"[31]

Adams begins the printed version of his *Thoughts* by defining the "divine science of politics" as "the science of social happiness" and affirming that "the blessings of society depend entirely on the constitutions of government." He then quotes a famous couplet from Pope's *Essay on Man* (3. 303–4), which he says flatters tyrants too much.

> For forms of government let fools contest,
> That which is best administered is best.

Adams observes that this doctrine is extremely fallacious, since "some forms of government are better fitted for being well administered than others."[32] Adams may have introduced Pope's couplet in order to refute it, since his main purpose was to expose the weaknesses in a legislature of a single chamber. A unicameral system is less complicated than a bicameral one and could, therefore, be an example of "that which is best administered." He may also have intended to disparage Paine's concept of government in *Common Sense* based on "a principle in nature, which no art can overturn, viz. that the more simple any thing is, the less liable it is to be disordered, and the easier repaired when disordered."[33]

Adams's next stage consists in defining the end of government as "the happiness of society." It follows, according to his reasoning, "that the form of government which communicates ease, comfort, security, or, in one word, happiness, to the greatest number of persons, and in the greatest degree, is the best." This is certainly in full agreement with Paine's quotation from Dragonetti concerning the science of the politician as consisting "in fixing the true point of happiness and freedom. Those men would deserve the gratitude of ages, who should discover a mode of government that contained the greatest sum of individual happiness, with the least national expense."[34] Adams gives no authority for his own prescription, but adds that all inquirers after truth, including Confucius, Zoroaster, Socrates, and Mahomet, have agreed that "the happiness of man, as well as his dignity, consists in virtue." This parade of Enlightenment heroes contrasts sharply with the provincial Christian point of view of Paine's *Common Sense* and for that matter of nearly all other documents in the American independence controversy.

Although Adams observes that "fear is the foundation of most governments," he clearly indicates his opinion that a government with virtue as its foundation is the best "calculated to promote the general happiness." Honor he places lower in the scale than virtue. He does not mention either Hobbes or Montesquieu in connection with these theories, but he lists nearly all of the English Whig worthies—Sidney, Harrington, Locke, Milton, Needham, Neville, Burnet, and Hoadly—in support of three further principles: that "there is no good government but what is republican, that the only valuable part of the British constitution is the republican part," and that "that form of government which is best contrived to secure an impartial and exact execution of the laws, is the best of republics." These concepts are based on the definition of a republic as "an empire of laws, and not of men" which Adams quotes without acknowledgment from Locke. He also maintains that there is an inexhaustible variety of republics "because the possible combinations of the powers of society are capable of innumerable variations."

So far in his pamphlet Adams is either in agreement with *Common Sense* or at least not openly in disagreement. In his next section he takes up the question of the structure of a representive assembly in the individual colonies for the purpose of making laws and vigorously opposes the unicameral system or, as he calls it, a single assembly. He offers six reasons for his opposition. A single assembly, like an individual, is flighty and subject to fits of humor; it is avaricious and favors its own members in financial matters; it is ambitious and may vote itself into perpetuity; it lacks two essential qualities necessary for the executive power, secrecy and dispatch; it is unfitted for the judicial power since it is too numerous and unwieldy; and it is likely to make arbitrary laws and to decide all controversies in its own favor. Adams proposes as a superior plan for each colony in the new American nation the choosing first of all of a representative assembly; this body would then elect a distinct assembly called a council, to have a negative voice over the legislature. These two bodies in joint session would subsequently elect a governor. Other executive officers such as lieutenant governor, secretary, treasurer, and attorney general should also be chosen by joint ballot of both houses. At first these elections should be annual, but in the future the legislature may upon experiment enlarge the terms of office from three years, to seven, or even to life. All judicial officials should be either appointed by the governor or elected by both houses jointly, and their term of office should be during good behavior for life. In addition to prescribing the agencies of government, Adams advocates laws establishing a militia, providing for the liberal education of youth, and regulating luxuries (sumptuary laws). Far from expecting his proposed form of government to be adopted by all of the colonies, he suggests that each one be left to decide upon its own governmental structure. He does not directly advocate any form of national organization, but says that "if a continental constitution should be formed," the resulting congress should have its authority rigidly restricted to "war, trade, disputes between colony and colony, the post office, and the unappropriated lands of the crown."

The diversity in emphasis between Paine and Adams is almost total. One might almost say that they were writing on two completely different subjects. Adams is concerned for the most part with the governmental structure of the individual colonies or states after independence. Paine, on the other hand, inasmuch as he is concerned with affairs after independence, prescribes for the nation as a whole, particularly recommending a continental congress and a constitutional convention. His emphasis in legislative proposals as in all else is continental, not provincial, and he devotes only three sentences to the individual colonies: "Let the assemblies be annual, with a President only. The representation more equal. Their business wholly domestic, and subject to the authority of a Continental Congress."[35] Adams favors concentrations of power in the individual colonies together with a weak national congress; Paine, to the contrary, supports a powerful congress, with the colonies in a subordinate position. Adams wants the individual governments to reflect a conservative philosophy, particularly through a council with a negative voice over the legislature and election of legislative officials by the legislature rather than the people. Paine specifically calls for the representation to be "more equal" and wonders "whether *representation and election* is not too great a power for one and the same body of men to possess."[36]

These differences, major as they are, would not have been apparent, however, to the average reader of *Common Sense* and *Thoughts on Government* in the first six months of 1776. The former would have been generally regarded as an impassioned call for independence, and the latter as a formula for government after independence. Both Paine and Adams, however, fully realized the ideological conflict in their proposals.

Adams in his autobiography has the following intriguing passage concerning Paine's reaction to the publication of *Thoughts on Government.*

> Paine soon after the Appearance of my Pamphlet hurried away to my Lodgings and spent an Evening with me. His Business was to reprehend me for publishing my Pamphlet. Said he was afraid it would do hurt, and that it was repugnant to the plan he had proposed in his Common Sense. I told him it was true it was repugnant and for that reason, I had written it and consented to the publication of it: for I was as much afraid of his Work [as] he was of mine. His plan was so democratical, without any restraint or even an Attempt at any Equilibrium or Counterpoise, that it must produce confusion and every Evil Work. I told him further, that his Reasoning from the Old Testament was ridiculous, and I could hardly think him sincere. At this he laughed, and said he had taken his Ideas in that part from Milton: and then expressed a Contempt of the Old Testament and indeed of the Bible at large, which surprized me. He saw that I did not relish this, and soon check'd himself, with these Words "However I have some thoughts of publishing my Thoughts on Religion, but I believe it will be best to postpone it, to the latter part of Life." This Conversation passed in good humour, without any harshness on either Side: but I perceived in him a conceit of himself, and a daring Impudence, which have been developed more and more to this day. . . . The third part of Common Sense which relates wholly to the Question of Independence, was clearly written and contained a tollerable Summary of the Arguments which I had been repeating again and again in Congress for nine months. But I am bold to say there is not a Fact nor a Reason stated in it, which had not been frequently urged in Congress. The Temper and Wishes of the People, supplied every thing at that time: and the Phrases, suitable for an Emigrant from New Gate, or one who had chiefly associated with such Company, such as "The Royal Brute of England," "The Blood upon his Soul," and a few others of equal delicacy, had as much Weight with the People as his Arguments. It has been a general Opinion, that this Pamphlet was of great Importance in the Revolution. I doubted it at the time and have doubted it to this day. It probably converted some to the Doctrine of Independence, and gave others an Excuse for declaring in favour of it. But these would all have followed Congress, with Zeal: and on the other hand it excited many Writers against it, particularly plain Truth, who contributed very largely to fortify and inflame the Party against Independence, and finally lost us the Allens, Penns, and many other Persons of Weight in the Community.[37]

Adams's reporting of Paine's "contempt" of the Old Testament and of the

Bible at large seems to be contradicted by another passage in the same paragraph of his autobiography, one which was quoted earlier in this chapter. In this passage Adam says that Paine's "arguments from the old Testiment [*sic*], were ridiculous, but whether they proceeded from honest Ignorance, or foolish Supersti[ti]on I know not." Here Adams says he does not know whether Paine was a hypocrite or a fool; yet later in the same paragraph he reports Paine showing open contempt for the Scriptures, in other words, exposing himself as a hypocrite. The editors of Adams's autobiography have revealed that he is not always entirely reliable in his recollections, and the present passage is certainly an example. Since Adams wrote his autobiography after the publication of Paine's *The Age of Reason,* there is considerable room for doubting that Paine actually said in 1776, "I have some thoughts of publishing my Thoughts on Religion, but I believe it will be best to postpone it, to the latter part of Life."[38]

Another indication that Adams in his autobiography is not accurately portraying circumstances as they were in 1776 may be found in his disparaging remarks concerning the style of *Common Sense,* particularly its phrases "suitable for an Emigrant from New Gate, [the London prison] or one who had chiefly associated with such Company, such as 'The Royal Brute of England,' 'The Blood upon his Soul,' and a few others of equal delicacy." In a letter to Jefferson written about the same time as his autobiography, Adams declared in similar vein that in comparison with resolutions of independence proclaimed by a county of North Carolina several months before *Common Sense,* the latter is "a poor, ignorant, malicious, short-sighted crapulous mass."[39] These derogatory estimates of the literary qualities of Paine's work contrast strikingly with Adams's admission in 1776 to his wife, already quoted, "I could not have written any Thing in so manly and striking a style."

Paine, in a public letter of 1802, confirmed that he and Adams had talked about *Common Sense* in 1776, presumably referring to the same conversation that Adams reports in his autobiography. According to Paine, Adams censured *Common Sense* because it "attacked the English form of government. John was for independence because he expected to be made great by it; but it was not difficult to perceive, for the surliness of his temper makes him an awkward hypocrite, that his head was as full of kings, queens and knaves, as a pack of cards. But John has lost deal."[40] This recollection is equally prejudiced and probably no more reliable than Adams's.

As we shall see in a subsequent chapter, Paine attacked Adams's bicameralism shortly before the Declaration of Independence. There is also a cryptic passage in *Crisis* No. 5 which may be a reference to Adams's pamphlet. In this passage, Paine declares "We have equalled the bravest in times of danger, and excelled the wisest in the construction of civil governments, *no one in America excepted.*"[41] Presumably the implied antecedent of "we" in this sentence is the American people as a whole rather than the editorial "we" referring to Paine as an individual, a construction which he never uses in any of his works. He seems to mean that the American government as constituted at the time of writing, March 1778—under the Articles of Confederation—is superior to any other form ever proposed; and he quite conceivably has Adams in mind in his pointed phrase, "*no one in America excepted.*" In the public letter of 1802 which is quoted above, Paine charges that the definition of a republic in Adams's pamphlet is ambiguous. "*It is,* says he, *an empire of laws and not of men.* But as laws may be bad as well as good, an empire of laws may be the best of all governments or the worst of all tyrannies."[42]

Although Adams designed his pamphlet to moderate what he considered to be democratic excesses of *Common Sense,* his own recommendations for a government in Virginia came under fire in a pamphlet by Carter Braxton which also attacked *Common Sense,* particularly the scheme which the latter proposed for the disposal of western lands after the conclusion of the war. The pamphlet, entitled *An Address to the Convention of the Colony and Ancient Dominion of Virginia, on the Subject of Government in General, and recommending a particular Form to their Consideration, by a Native of that Colony,* was described by Patrick Henry in a letter to Adams as a "silly thing. . . . His reasonings upon and distinction between private and public virtue, are weak, shallow, evasive, and the whole performance an affront and disgrace to this country."[43]

Paine never took any public notice of Braxton's pamphlet and continued to favor the continental claims to the western lands as opposed to those of the individual colonies. After independence Virginia maintained its right to the largest share, and Paine considered writing in defense of the claim of the nation as a whole, but refrained from doing so because he lacked documentation and because many of his personal friends and political allies came from the state of Virginia.[44] In 1779, however, some of the directors of the Indiana Company supplied him with the historical records on which their case was based, and Paine thereupon composed *Public Good,* 1780, supporting the land company against the state of Virginia, basically on the ground that national sovereignty supersedes that of the state. From the pragmatic perspective, he argued, that "it is only the United States, and not any single State, that can lay off new States."[45] As a moral principle, he asserted "the governing rule of right and of mutual good must in all public cases finally preside."[46]

E. True Merits

All of the discussions of *Common Sense* which have been treated up to this point were published in America; two other pamphlet replies appeared in

1776 in Great Britain, one designed for an American public, the other for readers at home, particularly in Ireland. The first of these, which was printed in London, bore the title *The True Merits of a Late Treatise, printed in America, intitled Common Sense, Clearly pointed out. Addressed to the Inhabitants of America.* According to the title page, it was written *By a late Member of the Continental Congress, a Native of a Republican State.* No date more precise than the year 1776 is given for the publication of this pamphlet, but it presumably came out shortly before the Declaration of Independence, since a statement is made in the text that the winter has passed without the issuing of such a declaration.[47]

No efforts have ever been made to identify the author, the putative "late Member of the Continental Congress," and it may be that he never existed and that the attribution to such a person is a propaganda trick of the British government. It is possible, on the other hand, that the attribution is genuine. Internal evidence indicates that the author is familiar with events in South Carolina. He states that the best answer to *Common Sense* "has been given by the Congress of *South Carolina,* in the Establishment of a temporary Constitution, which may well be considered as the Counter-Part of the Plan offered by the Author of Common Sense."[48] He also indicates that *Common Sense* has been "lately re-printed at Charles-Town."[49] This in itself is a significant statement, since no copy of a Charleston edition has ever been located, even though such an edition is listed in two reputable nineteenth-century bibliographies.[50] The reference in *True Merits* strengthens the probability that a Charleston edition was actually published. Finally, the author of *True Merits* refers to the neighboring colony of Georgia, where, he reports, if "not greatly mistaken, some of the leading Men in some Provinces already sat, and voted in a Provincial Congress without being chosen by the People."[51] It is significant, moreover, that this pamphlet stresses circumstances concerning America rather than the general theory of government, which would have been more appropriate had the author been writing for a British audience.

The members of the Continental Congress from South Carolina were Christopher Gadsden, Thomas Lynch, Henry Middleton, George Rutledge, and John Rutledge. Of this number, the most conservative was John Rutledge; he did not favor independence but hoped that colonial resistance to British policies would lead to a peaceful settlement negotiated with commissioners from Britain. He resigned from the Congress in February 1776. It is, therefore, possible that John Rutledge was the author of *True Merits.* The self-description which this author presents in his pamphlet seems to fit Rutledge completely:

> The Author always professed, as he now does, a firm Persuasion, that the Acts which gave Rise to the present Dispute are illegal and oppressive; he has no Intimacy with, nor indeed is he acquainted with, a single Person that would take upon him their Defence; he is well persuaded, that the

> Measures taken by the Continental Congress must ensure them the Praises of Nations, and of those yet unborn; he heartily wisheth every Man may exert himself in a proper Manner in so great a Cause, and thinks it would be for the Benefit of *America,* if those who cannot go the same Length with others, while they wish to see *America* redressed, might be treated with Tenderness, and be made useful to the Cause, consistent with their own Principles. He looks upon an entire Separation from *Great Britain* not as a last Remedy, but as a new and more dangerous Disease.

This author points out that independence for the colonies involves a constitutional question which has never been settled, whether subjects who have made a solemn vow of allegiance to a ruler are discharged from their allegiance "because the King, or Legislature, did *one* illegal Act."[52] The American situation, he states, is unique, since all previous constitutional crises in Great Britain have concerned differences between one branch and another, that is, between Crown and subject, nobles and king, or upper house and lower; the present one concerns a dispute between an extensive part of the empire and "the three Branches of the Legislature" [that is, king and both houses of Parliament]. Also involved is the prospect of war "with the more formidable Power of the Universe." Despite the fact that he is releasing his thoughts to the press, the author says that his objections to *Common Sense* represent some of the weaker things that can be said—that the best answer to the work is the temporary constitution of South Carolina, in his opinion a much superior plan of government to that presented in *Common Sense.*[53]

In reference to Paine's distinction between society and government, the author argues that it is impossible to conceive of one without the other; even two persons could not live together without agreeing upon some rule of conduct.[54] Also Paine's imaginary settlers might have had a prior agreement to emigrate and a prearranged destination, and this in itself represents a form of government. As an alternative explanation of the origin of society, the author appeals to the scriptural account of Adam and Eve. Adam's priority of existence and the manner of Eve's formation, he assumes, rendered the woman dependent on the man; from this he concludes "that Government and Society are nearly coeval, and that the very first Mode of Government must have resembled Monarchy." The author, nevertheless, does not accept the contention of Filmer that Adam "was the absolute sovereign of all his Posterity."

He assents without reservation to Paine's maxim "that the more simple a thing is, the less it is liable to be disordered, and the easier repaired," together with its application to government. But he insists that monarchy is much simpler than aristocracy or democracy and that, therefore, all of *Common Sense* is a "constant Contradiction" to its basic principle, for it "proposes a Plan of Government far more complex, and consequently far more unnatural, than those he pretends to abolish." The checking system of the British constitution which *Common Sense* criticizes, he defends as logical and salutary: "it may be very reasonable to put it in a Man's Power to do Good, and yet to restrain him from doing Harm."[55]

The author of *True Merits* labels as "a very levelling Principle" Paine's statement that mankind are "originally equals in the order of creation." He affirms to the contrary that some mortals must submit to rule and obedience.[56] He runs through a number of Scriptural passages to prove against those cited in *Common Sense* that war and murder had existed prior to the institution of kings and that David is actually given the title of king. In regard to the suggestion in *Common Sense* that the Reformation preceded the discovery of America, as if the Almighty meant to create a sanctuary for persecuted groups, he observes that all Protestant settlements had been made by the British. Presumably the author means that this circumstance indicates that victims of persecution on the European continent received no benefit from America. The French Protestants, he admits, had also made an effort to establish a colony, but he adds that these were cut off by the cruelty of the Spanish. Caustically the author suggests by analogy that "Providence, by the late seasonable Discovery of Otaheite . . . graciously meant to open a Sanctuary" for the author of *Common Sense* and his friends.[57]

True Merits adopts a very sober tone in reporting the affirmation from *Common Sense* that "the Almighty hath implanted in us . . . unextinguishable feelings" of resentment and hatred, "the guardians of his image in our hearts." It is true that the preceding words in quotation marks are taken literally from Paine's text,[58] although Paine does not use the inserted words *resentment* and *hatred.* Since he does maintain, however, that there are "injuries which nature cannot forgive" and that the lover cannot forgive the ravisher of his mistress, *True Merits* is not misrepresenting Paine's meaning. Whatever Paine's intention may have been, he certainly does in *Common Sense* attribute undiminished resentment and hatred to God. Yet two decades later he condemned the Old Testament as "a book of lies, wickedness and blasphemy; for what can be greater blasphemy than to ascribe the wickedness of man to the orders of the Almighty."[59] *True Merits* is correct in accusing *Common Sense* of doing essentially the same thing, that is, of attributing to God the implanting of inextinguishable resentment and hatred in the hearts of men.

According to *True Merits,* the "main and leading argument" of *Common Sense* is that the injuries already done to the Americans are too grievous to be forgiven or forgotten. *True Merits* answers first of all by indicating that more husbands and fathers had been killed in the Ministerial Army than in the troops of the Americans. But his main objection is that the principle of unrelenting resentment is a pernicious one, one which would never allow for peace. He points out that the ravages of Indians had in the past always been overlooked and peace concluded—also that the "cause of America" has been pleaded by some of the best men in England.

In answer to the assertion that Europe rather than England is the true parent of America, *True Merits* replies that those who emigrated to America "came into it as an *English* Government" and that they were willing to be naturalized and to maintain their allegiance.[60] In lighter vein, he taunts *Common Sense* for abusing not only the King of England, but also the Pennsylvania Assembly, the City of London, the whole British nation, and all who think well of the European world. *Common Sense* is portrayed as bidding defiance to all mankind by boasting "our present numbers are sufficient to repel the force of all the world." These are indeed Paine's exact words.[61] *True Merits* quotes them four other times in his pamphlet, however, and all four times inaccurately!

"with a Force sufficient to repel all the World."

"*Our present Numbers are sufficient to repel the Force of the whole World.*"

as we have a Force of our own "capable to repel all the World;"

a Force sufficient to repel all the World.[62]

True Merits charges *Common Sense* with serious historical inaccuracy in affirming "that a youth of twenty-one (which hath often happened) shall say to several millions of people, older and wiser than himself, I forbid this or that act of yours to be law."[63] Although Paine does not specifically state that in these words he is referring to England, the context certainly indicates that he is. *True Merits* pertinently points out that no youth of twenty-one had ever made such a remark to millions of people, for "there has been no Minority since *Edward* VI. who was a wise and good Prince."[64] He also sets forth the story of Masaniello in a completely different light from that in which Paine tells it.

> Massanello never was King, but a popular Leader, and his true History is not uninstructive; he headed a Mob, raised on Account of a Duty laid on Fruit, and, driven to Despair by a brutish Answer to the Vice-Re, bidding them to sell their Wives and Children in Payment, at first, while he was moderate, he became very formidable, and a solemn Treaty was entered into by him and the Vice-Re, and publickly sworn to it in the Church; next he became intoxicated with Power, or even delirious, and raved against his own Followers; he was then shot, in or about a Church, and immediately as much execrated by the Mob as before he had been followed and applauded.[65]

Paine's assertions concerning naval affairs are similarly condemned for inaccuracy and illogic. The remark that if America had one-twentieth of the naval force of Britain, she would be an overmatch for the latter represents, according to *True Merits,* a disproportion in favor of Britain ten vessels against two hundred and "the Existence of even these Ten Vessels is still liable to an IF."[66] *Common Sense* also blithely and illogically asserts that at the present the Americans could defeat the entire British navy, while in another passage he admits that twelve months previously one daring pirate ship might have had the whole continent at his mercy.[67]

In regard to the international scene, *True Merits* has a number of objections to the propositions in *Common Sense. True Merits* rejects assistance from France and Spain, since this would mean alliance with "our natural hereditary, Popish Enemies," and it would entail renouncing of the connection "with Protestants, our Parent State." Furthermore, Spain and France cannot publicly espouse the American cause without entering into a war with Britain. If the happiness of America is only of "secondary Object" with Britain, there is no reason for assuming that it would be primary with Spain or France.[68] Also if America were denied the protection of Britain, either Spain or France might decide to make further conquests there.[69] Independence entails other hazards in regard to the internal situation. The fear that one colony would strive for superiority over another, a presentiment which had been ridiculed by some advocates of separation," will not appear so very childish, when the Conduct of some leading Men is duly considered."[70] This is a cryptic remark, but since it undoubtedly refers to colonial leaders, it strengthens the assumption that the author of *True Merits* was indeed a former member of the Continental Congress. Nearly everything in his pamphlet leads up to a plea for delay. "If Time," he says in conclusion, "could be gained for the most violent in *Great Britain,* &c. to cool, it would do more towards healing our Difference, than either Force or Reason has done hitherto." Obviously this author did not believe that the true merits of *Common Sense* were very extensive. In stating this belief, he presented one of the most penetrating critiques which the work has ever received.

F. Reason in Answer

The only pamphlet demonstrably written in the British Isles against *Common Sense* was published in Dublin, Ireland, soon after the appearance of *Plain Truth.* This timing is established by a note to its introductory advertisement indicating that it was "almost ready for publication" before *Plain Truth* appeared. The Dublin pamphlet, entitled *Reason in Answer to a Pamphlet entitled Common Sense,* carries an epigraph of five lines from Shakespeare, including the famous one, "The Devil can cite Scripture for his purpose." It is of considerable significance that this pamphlet assumes that the "author of Common Sense . . . speaks the sentiments of the congress."[71] This, together with the place of publication, suggests that the pamphlet was commissioned by some agency of the British government to counter dissatisfaction with British rule in Ireland. Independence movements had existed there almost since the beginning of English control, and they became particularly strong in the period between 1770 and 1815. This is undoubtedly one of the reasons why the edition of Locke by Bishop Elrington, which attacks Paine as a pernicious advocate of popular government, was later brought out in the same city. It is interesting to observe that not a single edition of *Common Sense* has ever appeared with Dublin on the title page, although Gimbel suggests that some editions attributed to Bradford in Philadelphia may have been printed in Ireland.[72] There were many London editions in 1776 as well as one in Edinburgh. Not surprisingly, a Dublin edition of Chalmer's anti-Paine *Plain Truth* was issued in the same year.[73] There was, on the other hand, a Dublin publication in 1777 favorable to Paine entitled *A Sequel to Common Sense: or, the American Controversy Considered . . . by Theophilus Philadelphus.* Although described as a "Second Edition, corrected and enlarged," it is actually merely a reprint of Bell's *Large Additions to Common Sense,* printed in Philadelphia in 1776, rather than a second edition of a new work printed in Dublin.[74]

Considering the large number of publications in Dublin designed to combat sentiment in favor of Irish independence, it is not surprising that an edition of *The Life of Paine . . . by Francis Oldys* should have appeared in Dublin in 1796 (printed by Zachariah Jackson for Richard White). This is an unscrupulous assault on Paine commissioned by the British government and originally published five years earlier in London.

The probability that *Reason in Answer* was intended primarily for British consumption is suggested by the fact that it tends to ignore the arguments in *Common Sense* bearing on the practical situation in America, precisely the area which Chalmers's *Plain Truth* stresses. The author, described as a citizen of Dublin, states that he had earlier joined his fellow citizens in favor of the colonists, "supposing they had suffered unjustly," but *Common Sense* has opened his eyes to the seditious behavior of those who were attempting to stir up the multitude to unnatural separation. This pamphlet "published under the auspices of the congress, has hurt their cause more on both sides the Atlantic than any thing could be written against them."[75] The most surprising statement in *Reason in Answer* is that Franklin had fled with horror "from their councils at the first mention of a separation."[76] This obviously untrue statement in itself seems to be sufficient proof that the pamphlet was not written in America, where Franklin's political opinions were well known. At least it seems clear that the pamphlet was not intended for circulation there.

A special technique of the Dublin author is to portray American leaders as revolutionary despots. "From the book before us it appears that their leaders exercise most unlimited power: that no man in America dares to avow sentiments different from theirs: that the writer of *Common Sense* and his patrons of the congress, wish to punish with the most bloody and unrelenting severity, those who dare to declare for the British constitution."[77] It is true that Paine deals severely with the Tories, but it is hard to see on what grounds the Dubliner bases his charge that any popular leaders in America exercised arbitrary power. Despite his assumption of coercive force, the Dubliner predicts that if English control should be withdrawn, a civil war will erupt, since the people are greatly divided, particularly in New England, each faction "wishing to be mistress of the rest."[78] According to the Dubliner, the members of congress, having tasted the charms of power and the pleasures of command, do not want reform of constitutional abuses as they profess but insist upon complete separation in order to keep from reverting to their previous condition as private citizens.[79]

The author of *Common Sense* is compared to Shimei in the Old Testament, a dead dog cursing his king, and using Scripture texts in an attempt "to level all distinctions."[80] Also made is the inevitable comparison with Cromwell, who, knowing the aversion of his followers to the name of king, never assumed it, but "exercised a power despotic as the Persian Sophi." The seventeenth-century Commonwealth is, furthermore, described as the "period to which the soul of our author yearns." According to the Dublin pamphlet, England at that time "groaned under the most cruel tyranny of a government, truly military, neither existing by law, or the choice of the people, but erected by those who in *the name of the Lord,* committed crimes till then unheard of."[81] In this vein, the Dubliner indicates that the Jews are the "favourite people" of *Common Sense.* Portraying Old Testament society in the period when Israel had no kings as the prototype of democracy, the Dubliner warns the Americans to "beware how they follow the example of that stiff-necked people, the Jews, in whose dreadful example, we see slavery ever following close upon rebellion; unwilling to submit to laws, even of divine origin, averse to rule and government, they so weaken'd themselves by frequent revolts, and insurrections, that they became the easy prey of foreign or domestic enemies."[82] The author's derogatory reference to that "stiff-necked people, the Jews" is parallel to the explicit disparagement by Chalmers of Jews as "a contemptible race more barbarous than our savages." One cannot deny the element of anti-Semitism in these remarks, compounded by the attempt to associate the independence movement with the Old Testament rigor of seventeenth-century Puritanism.

Toward the conclusion of his pamphlet, the Dubliner points out an inconsistency in the religion of the author of *Common Sense* in that he pretends to be "an utter enemy to all superstitious ceremony" and yet prescribes that the charter of the proposed American nation "be laid upon the bible, and there solemnly crowned."[83] This is indeed a logical flaw in Paine's work. Even today Paine's ceremony represents a problem in interpretation: Is it fanaticism, hypocrisy, clever propaganda, or sincere veneration?

The Dubliner gives a quite thorough treatment of Paine's theory of government, even though rejecting it as "trifling, a mode of arguing, miscalled philosophy." The only society which could exist without government, he affirms, is one of angels. He utterly rejects

> the delightful state of nature, in which it has been lately discovered all men were formed, and to which this author is so fond of sending us back; here every man lives independent of all the rest, subject but to the control of his own will, at full liberty to gratify his wants and appetites, without regard to any other man, not contributing in any thing to the advantage of others, nor receiving assistance from them, unrestrained and undefended from injury; at liberty to attack whom he will, and liable to the assaults of his superiors in strength and cunning; this is a state supremely miserable; the strength of one man is so unequal to his wants, that it many cases he must perish if depending solely on himself, should he even escape the injuries of his own species.[84]

From this dismal portrayal, the Dubliner proceeds to an explanation of the origin of society which is as close to Paine as it is to Locke. In his reconstruction of primitive times, each man renounces mutual injury or engages to restrain his private passions inasmuch as they are injurious to others. This renunciation of mutual injury, which "must be previous to society," leads to a "compact of mutual defense and assistance."[85] The Dubliner agrees with *Common Sense* that when social groups become large and cumbersome, the people may delegate their authority to representatives, but he disagrees with the view that public disesteem has ever been able to keep people from breaking laws made by themselves or their delegates.[86] Since the purpose of the Irish critic is to reinforce the prestige of the monarchy, he argues that the guardians of the laws must be invested with power to enforce them; this is the concept of subordination, "the origin of rulers and ruled coeval with society."[87] According to this reasoning, society cannot exist without government, both spring from the same source, and government is a blessing, not an evil.

Further to explain the origin of monarchy, the Dubliner offers a watered-down version of the patriarchal theory. Since the young of the species are helpless and need the protection of the father, "kingly government then begun in the first man."[88] To counteract Paine's scriptural argument, he asserts that "regal authority has been exercised by many persons approved by Heaven," and he cites three Old Testament passages to prove it. In a novel twist, he draws upon the eighteenth-century vogue for China to portray the beneficent tradition of kingship. In so doing, the Dubliner unwittingly reveals that he shares the principles of deists, who pointed to the antiquity of the laws and traditions of the Chinese and considered them far older than the Hebrews as portrayed in the Old Testament. "In China, whose annals reach to the infancy of our earth, the monarch is considered as the father of all his subjects, bound only by the laws, his power is irrestible, considering his people as children, he can have no interest distinct from theirs."[89] This interesting passage brings together the intellectual currents of patriarchy and Sinology.

In considering the alternatives to monarchy, the Dubliner paints an unfavorable picture of democracy in Athens and of aristocracy in Holland. In the former society, the people, who were fierce, ungrateful, and corrupt, made impossible the existence of private happiness or public security. In the latter, the people would have been powerless to resist the autocratic tyranny of foreign invaders had it not been for the physical nature of their land, allowing them to break the dikes and flood it completely, and had not a single chief, the Prince of Orange, risen to leadership and supreme authority.[90]

The manner of judging the effect of British rule upon the American colonies, the Dubliner asserts, is to compare their degree of prosperity with that of the colonies of Spain and Portugal. Despite the gold and diamond mines of the latter, the commercial colonies of Britain have greater riches. The Hispanic colonies failed to attain "the same pitch of power" as the British colonies "because they did not enjoy the same free constitution."[91]

Although Paine in *Common Sense* does not mention any specific taxes or commercial regulations which the colonies resented, the Dubliner gives the Parliamentary version of the famous destruction of tea in Boston harbor. The fault, according to this interpretation, lay with American merchants who had accumulated large stocks in their warehouses through smuggling. When England removed the export tax in England, these merchants themselves connived at the destruction of further imports in order to reduce the continent to anarchy and confusion.[92]

Like Chalmers, the author of *Reason in Answer* ridicules *Common Sense* for its treatment of naval affairs. Without going into detail, he scorns the author's proposal for raising a naval force as equaled in folly by his false method of valuing the English fleet and his ludicrous recommendation for "defending the American trade by shipping a few guns on each merchantman."[93] The strongest section of *Reason in Answer* consists of its general defense of the English constitution portrayed through admitted viscissitudes as "supporting the people against the oppression of bad kings, and the kings against the rebellion of deluded subjects."[94] In addition to securing British subjects against foreign foes and guaranteeing full internal liberty, "It confines no man in his pursuits, bounds no man's will, or circumscribes the actions of any where they interfere not with the welfare of society, or happiness of individuals; . . . under the English laws, the greatest cannot oppress the least, each individual claims the protection of the whole society; the strength of the whole state becomes the strength of each particular member."[95] This is powerful rhetoric and in the main convincing for home consumption. Readers in the colonies would probably have replied that the description of the glories of the British constitution was irrelevant to them, for its alleged benefits had not been fully extended to America. In rhetoric, *Reason in Answer* was next to Chalmers' *Plain Truth* the best reply ever made to *Common Sense,* but its reasoning, designed primarily for an Irish audience, failed to meet the basic issues of American independence.

PART III

Four Letters and Later Writings on the Revolution

15

Four Letters

In the last of his "Forester" letters in the *Pennsylvania Journal,* Paine took up one of the major threads of *Common Sense,* criticism of the internal British political structure, and applied it to the immediate situation in Philadelphia. In Pennsylvania as well as in England, he declared, "there is no *Constitution,* but only a *temporary form of government.*" In a footnote to this passage he added, "*This distinction will be more fully explained in some future letter.*" Since no further numbers of the "Forester" were published, historians have assumed that Paine never carried out this promise. The truth is that he did bring out his letter on the meaning of a constitution, but he did so in a separate pamphlet of twenty-four pages (nearly half the length of *Common Sense*) rather than in the form of a newspaper article. This pamphlet is now for the first time ascribed to Paine.

Entitled *Four Letters on Interesting Subjects,* it could not have been written earlier than 22 May nor later than 2 July 1776. It was published by a German printing house in Philadelphia, Steiner and Cist, the printers who would a few months later bring out the first three numbers of Paine's *Crisis.* Presumably these German printers were favorably disposed to Paine because of his designation in "Forester" No. 4 of some property-owning Germans in Philadelphia as "zealots in the cause of freedom." "The great body of German farmers," as a contemporary observed, sided with the Whigs or advocates of independence.[1]

Precisely as Paine had promised in his footnote to "Forester" No. 4, one of the sections in the pamphlet is devoted to the distinction between a constitution and a form of government. Not only this circumstance, but parallels of expression in *Four Letters,* "Forester" No. 4, *Common Sense,* and *Rights of Man* prove that Paine was the author of *Four Letters.* The following parallels are conclusive:

"Forester" No. 4. "in England, there is no *Constitution,* but only a *temporary form of government.*"

Rights of Man [1, 382] "From the want of understanding the difference between a constitution and a government, Dr. Johnson, and all writers of his description, have always bewildered themselves. . . . no such thing as a constitution exists in England."

Four Letters No. 4. "A Constitution, and a form of government, are frequently confounded together . . . ; whereas they are not only different, but are established for different purposes. . . . The English have no fixed Constitution."

Rights of Man [1, 390] "Were a bill brought into any of the American legislatures . . . the check is in the constitution, which in effect says, *thus far shalt thou go and no farther.*"

Four Letters No. 4. "That England is governed by the latter [an absolute legislative power], no man can deny, there being, as is said before, no Constitution in that country which says to the legislative powers, 'Thus far shalt thou go, and no farther.' "

Common Sense. "I draw my idea of the form of government from a principle in nature, which no art can overturn, viz. that the more simple anything is, the less liable it is to be disordered, and the easier repaired when disordered."

Four Letters No. 4. "The forms of government are numerous, and perhaps the simplest is the best."

Constitutions, Governments, Charters [2, 990] "Now it does not signify how many nominal divisions, and sub-divisions, and classifications we make, for the fact is, *there are but two powers in any government, the power of willing or enacting the laws, and the power of executing them;* for what is called the *judiciary* is a branch of executive power; it executes the laws; and what is called the *executive* is a superintending power to see that the laws are executed."

Rights of Man [1, 388] "It has been customary to consider government under three distinct general heads: The Legislative, the executive and the judicial.

"But if we permit our judgment to act unincumbered by the habit of multiplied terms, we can perceive no more than two divisions of power, of which civil government is composed, namely, that of legislating, or enacting laws, and that of executing or administering them."

Four Letters No. 4. "GOVERNMENT is generally distinguished into three parts, Executive, Legislative and Judicial; but this is more a distinction of words than things. . . . In short, the distinction is perplexing, and however we may refine and define, there is no more than two powers in any government, viz., the power to make laws, and the power to execute them."

"Forester" No. 3. "Conquest, and not reconciliation is the plan of Britain."

Crisis No. 7. "Reconciliation never appears to have been the wish or the object of administration, they looked on conquest as certain and infallible, and under that persuasion, sought to drive the Americans into what they might stile a general rebellion."

Four Letters No. 1. "Britain . . . would, from motives of political avarice, prefer conquest to any mode of accomodation whatsoever."

Crisis No. 13. "It is with confederated states as with individuals in society; something must be yielded up to make the whole secure."

Four Letters No. 2. "The happiness of individuals is secured to them by the community, and the happiness of the separate Colonies can only be secured by the Continent; and as the former yields up a part for that purpose, so must the latter."

Four Letters even echoes Paine's essay in the *Pennsylvania Magazine* on the salubrious nature of America, in which imported foreign vices lose their vigor and good qualities thrive and increase. In his pamphlet, he contrasts "the proud follies of the old world" with "the simplicity of the new." He also compares Cato, the pseudonym by which Dr. William Smith had attacked the Forester, to "the vicar of Bray, the unprincipled chaplain of every conqueror."

The attention of historians was first drawn to *Four Letters* by Bernard Bailyn, who did not realize that the pamphlet was written by Paine. Bailyn understood, however, its significance in clarifying the nature of constitutional government, and he described it along with another pamphlet printed in Pennsylvania at the same time as "brilliant sparks" that "lit up the final steps of the path that led directly to the first constitutions of the American states."[2] The other pamphlet with similar ideas is *The Genuine Principles of the Ancient Saxon or English Constitution,* which was largely composed of excerpts from Obadiah Hulme's *An Historical Essay on the English Constitution* published in London in 1771.[3] Both tracts are intended as guidelines for the Pennsylvania constitutional convention, but Paine's is critical of the British system whereas *The Genuine Principles* opposes only its elements derived from the Norman tradition. Paine not only distinguishes between a constitution and a government, but continues the attack against the British constitution which he had begun in *Common Sense.*

In order to reach an understanding of the major issues in *Four Letters,* it is necessary to trace briefly the political climate and political events in Philadelphia during the months of May and June 1776.

The election on 1 May in which the Moderates (the party in favor of reconciliation with Great Britain) obtained control of the Assembly did nothing to restrain the increasing sentiment in favor of independence. Twenty days later a public meeting organized by the Independents took place on a field in front of the State House in Philadelphia, attended despite rainy weather by a crowd estimated by contemporaries at between four and seven thousand people.[4] A stage had been erected to accommodate the moderator, Colonel Daniel Roberdeau, and the principal speakers. Among the reasons for the meeting was public dissatisfaction with the instructions to the Pennsylvania delegates to the Continental Congress which the Assembly had issued in the previous November, the same instructions which Paine had attacked in his "Lover of Order" letter and in *Common Sense,* instructions which effectively prohibited the delegates from voting in favor of independence. Since the election of the moderate ticket had erased all hope of the Assembly's recalling these instructions or taking any other positive step toward independence, it was necessary for the advocates of direct action to bypass the Assembly. This became possible on 15 May, when Congress adopted a resolution introduced by John Adams stating that it was an untenable situation for the people of America still to be obliged to take oaths supporting the British Crown and that, therefore, the assemblies and conventions of the United Colonies should establish provincial governments to eliminate this necessity. At the open air meeting at the State House convened for this purpose, the speakers contended that the Assembly's infamous instructions of the previous November specifically prohibited "a change of the form of this Government," and that in so doing the Assembly had kept Pennsylvania from the necessary union with the other colonies. It was argued, moreover, that the present Assembly was not elected for the purpose of forming a new government and that, therefore, a Provincial Convention chosen by the people should be the instrument of carrying out the charge of Congress. A resolution calling for the election of such a convention to comprise at least one hundred members was then carried unanimously.

On the following day, a letter was addressed from the Philadelphia committee to the provincial committees, particularly drawing attention to the evils of proprietary government (the executive control of Pennsylvania by the heirs of William Penn, whose powers rested on a royal charter). The letter brought up the "horrors of the late *Indian* war" and affirmed that "the horrid ravages of that dreadful war were long permitted to spread through this devoted Prinvice, by means of the unjust claims of haughty and 'absolute Proprietaries.'" In like vein, it called upon the county committees to seize their opportunity of ridding themselves forever of the tyranny of the proprietary interest. Finally, it called upon the local committees to send delegates to a meeting in Philadelphia in the next month for the purpose of deciding the manner in which to select members for a Provincial Committee to establish a new form of government "on the authority of the people."[5] According to the general spirit of those who advocated a new government, the issue was simple and clear-cut, whether the province would support the union of all the colonies in opposition to the instructions of the Assembly or support the Assembly against the union of the colonies.

The conservative view was forcibly expressed on the next day, 22 May, in a remonstrance by the Moderates addressed to the Assembly.[6] These partisans of the Assembly openly admitted that it was in their interest "to claim and support our birthright in the Charter and wise laws of *Pennsylvania*," a tacit recognition that they considered themselves as belonging to a privileged group. They argued that the resolve of Congress did not apply to Pennsylvania at all, but only to colonies in which "no Government sufficient to the exigencies of their affairs" had been established. According to their interpretation, the Assembly still carried on all necessary business and had no need of being supplanted. Their civil and religious rights were secured by the charter, they maintained, and there existed no reason for these to be sacrificed.[7]

The provincial committees which had been convened to establish procedures for electing delegates to a constitutional convention paid no attention to the Moderates, but drafted on 22 June an address to the people of Pennsylvania authorizing them to hold elections for the delegates on 8 July. This measure repudiated the stand of the Moderates and the proprietary party and rendered their joint influence minimal. There now remained no doubt that Pennsylvania would both ratify independence and draft a constitution for a new government.

The topics covered by Paine's *Four Letters* look back upon the issues raised by the Moderates and the proprietary party and forward toward the provisions of the proposed constitution. It is possible that parts of the pamphlet were written even before Paine's reference in "Forester" No. 4 on 8 May to the future publication of a letter on the distinction between a constitution and a government. The very earliest date on which the pamphlet could have been published is 23 May, since in Letter 1 Paine refers to the "late Remonstrance" of the Moderates, which had been presented to the Assembly on that date. The latest date is 17 July, when it was advertised in the *Pennsylvania Evening Journal.* No reference is made in the pamphlet to the Declaration of Independence, and the arguments of the first three letters are primarily concerned with the need for a separation from Great Britain. On the inside of the title page, facing Letter 1, appears the following statement:

> *The rapid turn which Politics have taken within the course of a few days, makes it almost impossible for the Press to keep pace therewith; which will account for some few remarks in the first and second of the following Letters, if they should not appear so necessary now as at the time of writing them.*

If this statement were composed by the German printers, Steiner and Cist, it is conceivable that the "*rapid turn which Politics have taken within the course of a few days*" could refer to the Declaration of Independence, but it is much more likely that the statement was written by Paine and that it alludes to the address to the people of Pennsylvania on 22 June authorizing the election of delegates to a constitutional convention. In the last sentence of the fourth letter, Paine explains that "farther observations were intended to have been offered in these letters, but the sudden turn of military affairs hath prevented them." Here Paine is probably referring to the news of the arrival in New York of the British General Howe on 28 June;[8] or he may even have written the passage as late as 2 July, when resolutions were passed in Philadelphia organizing a provincial volunteer militia known as the flying camp, a highly mobile force designed to be dispatched for brief periods to areas of extreme emergency. Paine himself served as secretary to General Daniel Roberdeau, the commander of the Pennsylvania volunteers, or Associators, leaving Philadelphia for Perth Amboy, New Jersey, soon after Congress on 3 July asked Pennsylvania to send troops for the defense of this area.[9]

Paine's letters concern four separate but related topics, and all four attack political attitudes or institutions common to the Moderates. They are directed against (1) the doctrine of reconciliation with Britain, (2) the provincial perspective of placing Pennsylvania above the union, (3) the Pennsylvania charter, and (4) the British Constitution.

I

The first letter begins with an examination of the motives which were keeping the Moderates loyal to the Crown. Without hesitating to oversimplify, Paine suggests that pecuniary self-interest was the primary cause of loyalty to Britain. According to Paine's analysis, every man in public life is subject to inquiry concerning his conduct and his motives, the latter being the key to the former. If a man's conduct has no visible connection with his private interests, one may conclude that he acts from reason and principle; but if his conduct stems from holding a lucrative office and all his measures invariably support the party which keeps him in office, "we may, without hesitation, set that man down for an interested time-serving tool." Paine concludes as his next step that "the same servile principle" produced the Remonstrance of the Moderates of 22 May and "drew together the whole tribe of Crown and proprietary dependents." In this demonstration, Paine follows a method closely related to that which he was to characterize in *Crisis* No. 7, as the study of "the progress of the passions, in order to ascertain the probable conduct of mankind."[10] In his letter, however, he reverses the direction of his inquiry, working backward from conduct to motivation. He argues that the unity and unswerving loyalty of the adherents to the Crown in itself proves them wrong, for "the King and his Ministers could not be for *ever right,* nor the opposition, either in England, or America, for *ever wrong.*" Here his logic is somewhat specious, for elsewhere in his works he suggests that a united front in defense of a cause is a sign of its justice, not that a single "slavish mercenary principle has governed all."

Paine next makes several observations concerning the wealth and station in society of the Proprietary party, a particularly interesting topic in view of the theory that Paine himself belonged to the artisan class and that his writing was strongly influenced by his social position.[11] In a brief paragraph of his letter, Paine diminishes the importance of wealth, affirms that in America moral character counts for more than either birth or property, sketches the economic theory of unearned capital gains, and, after asserting that many in the Proprietary rank have family origins "much beneath the generality of the other inhabitants," concedes that "no reflection ought to be made on any man on account of his birth, provided that his manners rise decently with his circumstances, and that he affects not to forget the level he came from." In reducing the significance of wealth, he points out that the descendants of the early settlers in a new country inevitably become rich merely because of the increase in value of their land through the influx of newcomers. "A capital of ten pounds well laid out in land a century ago, would, without either care or genius either in the heir or the owner, [have] been by this time an estate." This is the germ of Paine's most important economic pamphlet, *Agrarian Justice,* which was to be published twenty years later during the French Revolution. Here Paine argues that the earth in its natural state is the common property of the human race, that the value of land rests entirely in improvements made upon it, and that every owner of cultivated land owes the community a "ground-rent" in compensation for this value. In his Philadelphia letter, Paine is not concerned with economic justice, however, but with political strategy, and he treats the wealth of the proprietary party as less important than "a sound moral character, amiable manners and firmness in principle."

Paine's reduction of the distinctions of rank and class is important in diminishing the role of the establishment in government. Rather than admitting the political preeminence of any class or classes—whether the aristocracy, magistrates or the clergy on one side or farmers, artisans, or laborers on the other—he affirms the absolute equality of all. Officials should be chosen not for their social station, but for their sound moral character, engaging personality, and adherence to principle.

Paine attempts to characterize the Moderates as members of a treasonable conspiracy rather than a mere political organization. "A contest for government," he says, "is not to be considered as an election." Defining a Tory as "every one who contends or argues for the supremacy of the king of England over the colonies," Paine admits of only two categories, Independents and Tories. He considers the latter as equivalent to Traitors and maintains that they should be hanged for their treason. He admits, nevertheless, that there may be some adherents of the Moderates who are honest men deceived by the leaders of the Crown faction into believing that Britain wishes reconciliation. Against this view, Paine cites the series of petitions submitted to Parliament by the colonies and various parts of England, the failure of conciliatory efforts by friends to America in Parliament, and the action of the court in sending commissioners to America while at the same time secretly negotiating for mercenary troops. He concludes, therefore, that the court had wished from the beginning for an open rupture with the American continent so that it might appropriate all its wealth. This it could do by declaring Americans rebels, for all persons so characterized would automatically forfeit their property to the Crown. Britain would "from motives of political avarice, prefer conquest to any mode of accomodation whatsoever." This is a verbal echo of the accusation in "Forester" No. 3, "Conquest, and not reconciliation is the plan of Britain,"[12] and a foreshadowing of an extended treatment of the theme in *Crisis* No. 7.

In response to the anticipated objection that Lord North in February 1775 had proposed a conciliatory plan under which the colonies were allowed to tax themselves, Paine argues that the British never wanted the colonies to accept North's plan, bad as it was, for General Gage was acquainted with it at least three weeks before the military operation leading to Lexington and Concord. This evidence justifies the strong presumption that the plan "was only hung out to amuse the English while an effectual military method was taken to aggravate the Colonies to reject it, till, by driving them to hostilities, she might crush them with arms in their hands, and make them glad to compound for their lives with the surrender of their property." In *Crisis* No. 3, Paine advanced and developed exactly the same argument concerning Lord North's proposal. A single sentence reveals the resemblance: "Degrading and infamous as that motion was, there is, nevertheless, reason to believe that the king and his adherents were afraid the colonies would agree to it, and lest they should, took effectual care they should not, by provoking them with hostilities in the interim."[13]

Echoing the references to the British record in Asia in both *Common Sense* and the "Forester," Paine predicts the vindictiveness which would be exhibited toward the colonies should they ever be subdued. "We have no other mercy to expect from her but a repetition of all those savage and hellish oppressions and cruelties which she so unrelentingly inflicted on the wretched inhabitants of the East-Indies." As the Forester, Paine had affirmed that any foreign troops serving as allies of the colonists could not possibly exceed or even equal "the cruelties practised by the British army in the East Indies: The tying men to the mouths of cannon and '*blowing them away*' was never acted by any but an English General."[14]

In closing the first letter, Paine refers to the constant accusation of the king and his ministers that the Americans had all along been consciously aiming at independence, and he asserts that they would actually have been better off had they made the decision for independence much sooner. Their reliance on reconciliation had prevented them from making necessary preparations, and for this reason any man who henceforth should advocate the doctrine of reconciliation should be treated as a traitor. "Our non-importation agreement ought to have ceased immediately on the breaking-out of hostilities, and instead thereof we ought to have doubled or tribled [*sic*] our imports." This argument is carried over almost verbally in *Crisis* No. 3, along with the accusation that the proclamation of Lord North's plan was insincere. "Had independence been a settled system with America (as Britain has advanced) she ought to have doubled her importation, and prohibited in some degree her exportation."

II

The second letter reinforces the principle of *Common Sense* that the "Continental Belt is too loosely buckled," that is, that the province-centered outlook should give way to a spirit of intercolonial unity. "In the same rank which an individual stands in to the public," he affirms, "do the provinces stand in to the Continent." Later in a newspaper essay belonging to his *Crisis* series, he further maintained this principle of continental unity (*Crisis Extraordinary,* 6 March–3 April 1782): "Each state is to the United States what each individual is to the state he lives in. And it is on this grand point, this movement upon one centre, that our existence as a nation, our happiness as a people, and our safety as individuals, depend." In his *Four Letters,* he similarly joins the condition of the private person to the welfare of the whole. "The happiness of individuals is secured to them by the community, and the happiness of the separate colonies can only be secured by the Continent." In further expanding the analogy, Paine argues that as the individual gives up certain natural rights for the rights he obtains in society, so the provinces yield certain individual rights for the common good.

In economic terms, Paine argues that the prosperity or poverty of one will communicate the same conditions to the others. Trade is like gold from South America; and the first colony which receives it is "only in the state of the Spaniards, who first dig it." The entire continent as well as the colony which directly engages in commerce with other nations will receive the benefits. Just as Britain grows rich or poor in proportion to the economic changes in the nations she trades with, so the conditions in any individual colony will influence the welfare of all. Three years later, Paine expressed the same idea in connection with fishing rights off the coast of Newfoundland: "Whatever is of consequence to any, is so to all; for wealth like water soon spreads over the surface, let the place of entrance be ever so remote; and in like manner, any portion of strength which is lost or gained to any one or more states is lost or gained to the whole."[15] Tocqueville in his *Democracy in America* also applied a theory of the homogenizing influence of commerce upon an international scale. Through commerce, he observed, "it is not only the members of a single nation that come to resemble each other; the nations themselves are assimilated, and one can form the picture of one vast democracy in which a nation counts as a single citizen."[16] In *Four Letters,* Paine similarly concludes that countries at war are benefited by each other's poverty, but commerce leads to mutual prosperity. The economic advantages to be derived from a perfect union of the colonies are adequate proof that "nothing but poverty and destruction can attend their separation."

Conditions of military defense also illustrate the need for union. Britain cannot attack all colonies at once, and each colony is better able to defend itself with the aid of its neighbors. Were any single colony at this stage to proclaim its neutrality or to act separately from the rest, it would be an act of treason toward the union, and that colony would be invaded by the others. The object of the British forces, which is conquest, is more difficult than that of the colonies, merely to retain possession. Britain must either conquer or depart, and to conquer means to occupy the entire coastline. "In short, we may conquer without a battle, but she cannot."

After devoting the major part of the letter to the need of maintaining a "perfect union," Paine seems to reverse himself in the final paragraph by calling for "a disunion," but this is only a rhetorical trick. He uses the term *disunion* to refer to a final and complete separation between Whigs and Tories, the worst of which are the Proprietary party. "We have this consolation, that a union with them would only have weakened us, and produced the same kind of peaceable destruction in the political constitution which opium does in the natural one."

III

Much of the argument in the Remonstrance of the Moderates on 22 May had been concerned with the alleged benefits conferred upon the province of Pennsylvania by the Charter granted to William Penn in 1681 by King Charles II. Paine, therefore, attacks both the charter and the assumptions upon which it is based. First of all, he argues that the charter is established upon "the most villainous injustice," specifically a violation of the rights of the American Indians. Here Paine appears as a defender and advocate of the Indians, even though his defense, as we shall see, is somewhat less than spirited and less than total. He is clearly not as greatly interested in the positive rights of the Indians to the American continent as he is in denying that Charles II had any right to dispose of the land without first settling with them. In his words, "had the kings of England first entered into treaty with the Indians for any part of their lands, and purchased them at ever so small a consideration, they would then have had a fair right either to have granted or disposed of them." Paine ingeniously adds that if the Indian chiefs had attempted to dispose of England in the same manner by a mere declaration of ownership, they would have been subjects for ridicule, but "the right of the one was equally as good as the other." Paine unequivocally treats the Indians as equals by asserting that any individual has the natural privilege to settle in any part of the world which suits him, and the Indian has the same right to settle and purchase land in England that the Englishman has of doing the same in America. But the kings of neither country have the right of claiming land in the other. Paine observes that Penn subsequently made a treaty with the Indians for the purchase of the land at a negligible price, interpreting the transaction as an implied admission that the original charter was invalid. Penn paid two pence half-penny per hundred acres and resold at fifteen pounds the acre along with a half-penny per acre quit rent. Although branding this operation as imposition and extortion, Paine says nothing about the Indians being cheated, but has in mind only later European settlers. The charter forced them to buy the lands from Penn at whatever amount he asked, "when they might have purchased the same of the natives at three or four thousand times less price." Paine is certainly a champion of the Indians, but he places the cause of many other groups so far ahead of them that his gestures in their direction are ineffectual. In the abstract he considers them as the equal of Europeans and insists that their land must be bought and paid for, but he has no objection to their receiving a minimal price, provided that no single proprietor have the monopoly of dealing with them.

This passage is of some significance in the light of a charge made by a French historian that Paine's humanitarian vision extends only to those of Germanic origin and that he completely ignores the peoples of Asia and Africa and all those who are not Christian, specifically, the American Indians.[17] This is an observation which can be easily refuted. Although Paine did not take the pains of Voltaire to acquaint himself with the customs of people in all the remote areas of the globe, his appeals for social justice were certainly universal in application. Apart from his defense of the property rights of American Indians, weak as it may be, he bitterly condemns in his "Forester" letters the cruelties of the British inflicted upon the natives of India, and in a footnote he appeals, "Forget not the hapless *African*."[18]

In further consideration of the original charter, Paine points to one of its major incongruities, that it was granted to Penn, one of the earliest and most influential of the Quakers, a sect which considers the bearing of arms to be sinful, and that it was granted specifically in recognition of a military victory obtained by Penn's father. "Therefore this province was the price of blood." Paine turns next to the fourth section of the charter, which, he maintains, grants the proprietor something which no man can grant, that is perpetual and absolute governance over the people of Pennsylvania. "Where there are no people," Paine replies, "there can be no government; it is the people that constitute the government." As we have already noticed in chapter 4, a similar declaration which Paine made in 1783 that "Government and the people do not in America constitute distinct bodies" seems to go counter to the basic principle of *Common Sense* that government and society are indeed distinct entities. According to his *Four Letters,* the inhabitants of the earth are not property to be bartered, exchanged, and sold. There is "no difference between selling a government and selling the people," and either action violates human rights. Another violation of the rights of nature, according to Paine, is found in Penn's will, in which he disposes of the government of his province of Pennsylvania to "the best advantage and profit." Paine indignantly observes that this amounts to selling to the highest bidder without concern for his abilities or moral character. "He might be of any denomination of religion, or of none; a man of reputation, or not; a gentleman, or a gambler; if he could but raise the money, that was all."

Another objection which Paine finds to the original charter is the ambiguity in its reference to "William Penn and his heirs." Since this seems to give all of Penn's heirs an equal right, it opens the way to rival claims of a host of potential governors should the Penn family be a prolific one. Purchasers of land could never be sure of their title, for it might be challenged by another branch of the family. In Paine's wry and satiricial observation, if Congress had not fortunately suppressed all governments loyal to the Crown, "we might have had heirs and lords coming from every part of Europe, 'whose fathers were the Lord knows who.'" The exact meaning of the concluding phrase, which Paine places within quotation marks, is not clear, but it suggests illegitimacy and seems to be a variant of his joke in *Crisis* No. 1 about the progeny of Hessian soldiers, "whose fathers we shall doubt of."[19]

Paine next turns to Penn's personal behavior as proprietor. In the articles setting forth the laws and government of the province, he was to have had three votes in respect to the passing or rejecting of any bill. Within the space of a year he drew up and substituted a second charter in which he gave up these three votes, but arrogated to himself a major advantage, that is a negative or power of veto over all bills, a far greater power than that which he had in the original articles. Paine objects also to the language of this second charter, which grants to the people of Pennsylvania privileges which never belonged to Penn's disposal in the first place, particularly liberty and liberty of conscience. According to Paine, "Every man who understands the true value of them will disdain to say he receives them in such a narrow line. We hold them immediately from GOD; and though it is our reciprocal duty to guarantee them to each other, we cannot be the givers of them."[20]

Two years later, Paine used the same reasoning concerning religious liberty, but applied it to the English toleration act rather than to Penn's charter. At this time he affirmed that the act "which *granted* liberty of conscience to every man, in religion, was looked upon as the perfection of religious liberty. In America we consider the assumption of such power as a species of tyrannic arrogance, and do not *grant* liberty of conscience as a favor but *confirm* it as a *right.*"[21] This theme is related, of course, to his statement in *Common Sense,* "To God, and not to man, are all men accountable on the score of religion."[22]

In *Four letters,* Paine labels all charters which are acts of a single man a species of tyranny and arbitrary power. He agrees that all constitutions of government should exists in written form, but insists that these documents should represent the act or the consent of all the people, not merely that of a single man. Paine points out the incongruity that not a soul in Pennsylvania would have consented to Penn's assuming the right to make a law entirely by himself, but the whole population accepted a worse kind of tyranny, Penn's unilateral establishing of the constitution of the province. The power of deciding a perpetual form of government is a much higher one than giving out temporary laws. Penn's authority should have been limited to "the making of 'laws with the consent of the freemen;' and all beyond that was arrogance and arbitrary power." Paine charges that Penn continually took advantage of the tremendous authority he exercised by proroguing and dissolving the Assembly and by imposing his negative on laws. For Paine it is an "astonishing absurdity" that the proprietorship and the governorship should be invested in one person. It is like a judge sitting in his own cause with the people powerless to do anything but submit.

In observing that Penn's charter of privileges was accompanied with another one endowing the Corporation of Philadelphia with its authority, Paine attempts to ridicule a provision elevating the town of Philadelphia into a city. Paine insists that this is inappropriate, since the meaning in English of a city is the place where a cathedral is located and consequently the bishop's *see.* According to Paine's etymology, the process of word change was "*See—Seety*—or *City.*" It is not clear whether Paine is here attempting to be humorous or to show off his erudition in the manner in which he later explains in *Rights of Man* the meaning of *Republic* as *res-publica.*[23] At any rate, his effort fails. His readers with a classical background would immediately associate *city* with *civitas.* Paine's primary purpose in introducing the subject is to condemn municipal corporations themselves as "badges of kingly tyranny" which tend "like every other species of useless pomp, to the oppression and impoverishment of the place, without one single advantage arising from them." After observing that the most flourishing towns in England get along without corporations, Paine concludes that the one of Philadelphia "is the most obnoxious, its power resembling that of an hermaphrodite or is at least a kind of aristocratical Corporation made hereditary by adoption." This reflection on the Corporation of Philadelphia does not seem to be highly relevant to Paine's major purpose of building sentiment for a convention to draw up a new charter for the entire province of Pennsylvania. He may have included it to win the favor of farmers in outlying rural districts whose support the Independents counted on in the coming election of delegates.

IV

The most important of Paine's four letters is the last, which sets forth in detail the principles which he hoped would be followed by the Pennsylvania convention in drawing up its constitution. It may be considered as well an answer to the section in Adams's *Thoughts on Government* concerning a unicameral legislature, for Adams's major objections are particularly taken account of.

Paine's letter begins with his promised distinction between a constitution and a government and his accusation, later to become famous in *Rights of Man,* that the English have no constitution. His first proof is that the legislative power in England, which in theory should have its prerogatives or authority limited according to some agreed upon principle, in practice is under no restraints whatsoever. It is important to specify that for Paine in this letter the legislative power does not consist solely of the Parliament, but of the king, lords, and Commons together (essentially the same concept which Rousseau expresses in his *Social Contract*). As examples of the way in which the legislative power circumvents the restrictions ostensibly placed upon it, Paine points out that the Crown may increase the number of lords at pleasure, and may swell or diminish the membership of the Commons by either incorporating or disenfranchising any village or town in the kingdom. There can be no constitution, Paine concludes, when the legislative power has no superior control which says, "Thus far shalt thou go, and no farther." Quoting a phrase used at court, Paine observes that an act of Parliament "can do anything but make a man a woman."

Turning to the abstract, Paine affirms that it is the duty of a constitution, when complete, to decide first on the form of government and, second, on the extent of its power, the second being more important than the first. The constitution should also indicate the areas in which it "does not empower the legislature to act." Repeating a principle from *Common Sense* in a slightly less dogmatic form, he observes, "the forms of government are numerous, and perhaps the simplest is the best." In *Common Sense* he had affirmed with less hesitation, "I draw my idea of the form of government from a principle in nature, which no art can overturn, viz. that the more simple any thing is, the less liable it is to be disordered, and the easier repaired when disordered."

Paine next turns to the question of whether a legislature should have two chambers or merely a single one, and his discussion shows unmistakable signs that it is intended as an answer to Adams's defense of the bicameral system in his *Thoughts on Government.* The two following paragraphs of Adams's pamphlet are clearly refuted by Paine.

> A single assembly is liable to all the vices, follies, and frailties of an individual; subject to fits of humor, starts of passion, flights of enthusiasm, partialities, or prejudice, and consequently productive of hasty results and absurd judgments.
>
> A single assembly, possessed of all the powers of government, would make arbitrary laws for their own interest, execute all laws arbitrarily for their own interest, and adjudge all controversies in their own favor.[24]

Almost as though he were replying directly to Adams, Paine observes that two houses "may fall out about forms and precedence, and check one another's honour [humor] and tempers, and thereby produce petulances and ill-will, which a more simple form of government would have prevented." The printed text reads *honour,* which makes no sense; reference to Adams's remarks on "fits of humor, starts of passion," however, reveals that Paine also is concerned with humor and tempers, and that the printer mistook *humor* for *honour.* Paine observes in addition that a disagreement in a single house "will not retard business" but serve rather to illustrate conditions in the society at large. A disagreement between two houses, however, will provoke serious consequences, and he gives a number of illustrations from English politics. In reference to Adams's charge concerning self-interest and arbitrary conduct, Paine answers that "to say, there ought to be two houses, because there are two sorts of interest, is the very reason why there ought to be but one, and *that one* to consist of every sort [of interest]." Paine admits that the second of the two houses may sometimes mend small imperfections in the laws suggested by the first, but he adds that "there is nearly as much chance of their making alterations for the worse as the better." Bernard Bailyn observes how this passage illustrates the evolving ground of political thought. The essential units of society participating in the constitutional process were no longer formal orders, "derived from the assumptions of late medieval society," or even Montesquieu's categories of Crown, aristocracy, and commoners, but rather factions and parties, "the shifting, transitory, competitive groupings into which men of the eighteenth century actually organized themselves in the search for wealth, prestige, and power."[25] When authorship is ascribed to Paine, however, it seems appropriate to refer also to his principle in *Public Good* that "the governing rule of right and of mutual good must in all public cases finally preside."[26]

Another of Adams's objections to a single assembly is that it cannot carry out the judicial function because the members of a unicameral house would be "too numerous, too slow, and too little skilled in the laws." Also, according to Adams, whatever judicial power it held would not be able to mediate or hold the balance between separate interests in a single assembly, because the judicial power would undermine the legislative. Adams holds that "the judicial power ought to be distinct from both the legislative and executive, and independent upon both, that so it may be a check upon both, as both should be checks upon that." Paine takes the position that there are only two powers in government, the legislative and the executive, that is, "the power to make laws, and the power to execute them; for the judicial power is only a branch of the executive, the CHIEF of every country being the first magistrate." This principle he later developed at length in *Rights of Man*.[27]

Paine's advocacy of unicameralism is far less rigid and contentious than Adams's defense of the bicameral system. Adams positively declares that he thinks that "a people cannot be long free, nor ever happy, whose government is in one assembly." Paine in a spirit of compromise remarks, "let the form of government be what it may, in this, or other provinces, so long as it answers the purpose of the people, and they approve it, they will be happy under it." Whatever a man's private opinion, if he is a "true republican" he will accept and obey the public voice. Indeed, Paine admits that "perhaps most of the Colonies will have two houses, and it will probably be of benefit to have some little difference in the forms of government. Experimentation will make it possible to decide which of the two disputed forms is superior, for "the preference at present rests on conjecture."

Many years later John Adams charged that Paine bore a large part of the responsibility for the single representative assembly in the Pennsylvania constitution of 1776,[28] and Cheetham suggested that Paine was responsible, through his influence over Condorcet, for similarly establishing a unicameral system in the French constitution of 1793.[29] We now realize from Paine's *Four Letters* that he was not completely dedicated to the unicameral system. Here he admits that the system of one house and two houses both have good points, but "when all the supposed advantages arising from two houses are put together, they do not appear to balance the disadvantage." As we shall see in a subsequent chapter, Paine learned in the next few years that the actual single legislative house in Pennsylvania did not work out quite according to theory. It acted in an arbitrary manner by repealing the charter of the Bank of America and in so doing created the apprehension, in Paine's words, "that a single legislature, by having it in its power to act with such instant rashness, and without restraint, was a form of government that might be as dangerous to liberty, as a single person."[30] It was probably because of his disillusion with the Pennsylvania experiment that Paine did not advocate a simple unicameral system for the new French constitution, but rather a single legislature divided into two equal sections.

Each section would discuss some question while the other listened. "Then, after each section had heard the arguments of the other, the debate would be closed, and the subject finally submitted to the decision of the entire legislature."[31]

One of the most important passages in *Four Letters* rejects the theory of a balance of executive, legislative, and judicial powers as a distinction of words rather than things. "However we may refine and define," Paine insists, "there is no more than two powers in any government, viz. the power to make laws, and the power to execute them; for the judicial power is only a branch of the executive, the CHIEF of every country being the first magistrate." This is, in essence, a restatement of the principle in *Common Sense* that a single power predominates over all the others.[32] In *Four Letters,* Paine devotes more space to the legislature than to any other topic included in the constitution, but he believes that other provisions are of more fundamental significance and must, therefore, be set down in a positive and binding manner. "At the forming of a Constitution we ought to have in mind, that whatever is left secured by law only, may be altered by another law." The most important of these provisions, according to Paine, should specify rights. "Perfect liberty of conscience; security of person against unjust imprisonments, similar to what is called the Habeas Corpus act; the mode of trial in all law and criminal cases; in short, all the great rights which man never mean[s], nor ever ought, to lose, should be *guaranteed,* not *granted,* by the Constitution." Paine does not at this time say whether these rights should be set forth in a separate section or included in the constitution proper, but in a later essay, he suggested that they should be part of the constitution.[33]

Nearly all of the other provisions which Paine advocates concern either elections or the manner of keeping the constitution responsive to the needs of the state. In order to prevent the British abuses of rotten boroughs and unrepresented municipalities, he recommends a fixed ratio of representation according to population, "for the right of representation, which is a natural one, ought not to depend upon the will and pleasure of future legislatures." Bailyn interprets this provision as an application of the principle that representatives should vote the will of their constituencies, not their own opinions,[34] but Paine's language falls short of a commitment to this legal principle. He had been slightly more positive in his "Lover of Order" essay in the *Pennsylvania Journal,* in which he declared that "The Delegates in Congress are not the Delegates of the *Assembly* but of the *People.*" Even in *Common Sense,* he did not seem to have recognized the principle of absolute representation, even though he protested against the "undue authority" which the Pennsylvania Assembly obtained over the delegates to the Continental Congress and warned the people of the dangers of trusting power "out of their own hands."[35]

In *Four Letters,* Paine also treats the jury system (a subject not touched by

Adams or the debates in Philadelphia) and recommends that juries be judges of law as well as of fact, a reform which never seems to have been adopted. Attacking the doctrine, which he ascribes to Lord Mansfield, that only the fact is to be proved, Paine argues that if the members of the jury are "not empowered to determine in their own minds, whether the fact proved to be done is a crime or not, a man may hereafter be found guilty of going to church or meeting." Paine also broaches the question of how many persons should constitute a jury. The objections to a jury of twelve which cannot bring in a verdict until all are of one mind are "that the necessity of being unanimous prevents the freedom of speech, and causes men sometimes to conceal their own opinions, and follow that of others; that it is a kind of terrifying men into a verdict, and that a strong hearty obstinate man who can bear starving twenty-four or forty-eight hours, will distress the rest into a compliance." The advantage of the alternate scheme of a jury of twenty-five of which a majority of thirteen may bring in a verdict is that "the dread of the consequences of disagreeing being removed, men will speak freer, and that justice will thereby have a fairer chance." Paine does not come out directly in favor of either system, but since he gives only the objections to the first one and the advantage of the second, we may conclude that he leans toward the notion of a twenty-five-man body with a majority required for conviction.

The remainder of Paine's recommendations all concern matters of election. Local officials, that is, "civil officers for towns and counties," may be chosen by the whole voting population in the relevant district, since these could be convened on the agreed upon day. Provincial officials, however, that is, officers for the entire province of Pennsylvania, must be elected by representatives of the people, since the whole province could not be convened for the purpose. Paine places delegates for Congress into a separate category, since they are not officers but legislators. He does not, however, express an opinion as to whether they should be chosen directly by the voters or by the voters' representative, perhaps because in *Common Sense* he had already suggested the creation of electoral districts for choosing members of the congress. Because of the infamous Assembly instructions to the delegates to the Continental Congress of the previous November, Paine specifically denounces provincial instructions as having a "tendency to disunion" and predicts that, if admitted, they "will one day or other rend the Continent of America." He argues against excluding the military from the legislature because to do so would encourage them to form a distinct party of their own. He has no objection to the creation of "modest and decent honorary titles, so as they be neither hereditary, nor convey legislative authority," for when judiciously conferred they are "badges of merit." Of the 108 members of the Provincial Conference which met in Philadelphia on 18 June to plan the constitutional convention, 58 possessed military titles,[36] and Paine himself later held the rank of major.[37] After the convention had done its work, Alexander Graydon predicted the likelihood of "uniforms and epaulets, with militia titles and paper money, making numbers of persons gentlemen who had never been so before."[38]

To prevent the "encroachments of power," Paine advocates that the elections to the legislature be annual and that no member be allowed to serve "for more than three succeeding years, nor be capable of being returned again till he had been absent three years." The same kind of exclusion, he feels, should be applied toward presidents or governors, a recommendation somewhat contrary to that of Adams, who advocates annual elections for the present but suggests that a term of seven years or even life may be acceptable in the future. Paine observes that no man having filled the highest office in the state should be obliged to descend to a lower one and that the most capable are not necessarily the most wealthy; "some decent provision therefore should be made for them in their retirement, because it is a retirement from the world."

Paine concludes with an important suggestion for keeping the constitution strong and serviceable, for "next to the forming a good Constitution, is the means of preserving it." To protect the constitution from all hazards, including the major one of interference by the legislative power, Paine suggests that machinery be established for continual review and possible modification. "At the expiration of every seven or any other number of years a *Provincial Jury* shall be elected, to inquire if any inroads have been made in the Constitution, and to have power to remove them; but not to make alterations, unless a clear majority of all the inhabitants shall so direct."

When the Pennsylvania Convention met from July to September and finally completed its work of drawing up a constitution, the new document included every one of the major provisions proposed or favored by Paine. It was preceded by a bill of rights. It provided for a unicameral assembly, its members were to be elected annually, and their period in office was to be limited to four terms in seven years. The constitution itself was to be subject to review by "a council of censors" every seven years. This body of censors, which one historian calls "the most singular feature of this singular constitution,"[39] does not seem to have been highly popular. According to the *Pennsylvania Gazette,* 29 April 1789, one waggish member proposed it "as a sort of a joke, disliking the proposed system and wishing to make it as ridiculous as possible."[40]

Actually the Council of Censors may have been introduced into the Pennsylvania constitution in large measure because of Paine's *Four Letters,* even though the idea, like most other features of government, may be traced back to the ancient Greeks and Romans and even though another pamphlet published in Philadelphia during the controversy called for a meeting of delegates every ten years to examine the state of the government and to decide whether the constitution had departed from its first principles.[41]

The constitution provided that the Council of Censors in its septennial review would investigate financial affairs of the government and decide whether the constitution had been preserved inviolate and whether the legislative and executive branches had performed their duties faithfully. It was also to have the more important power of amendment by means of calling a convention for the purpose.

Paine's original proposal for regular amendment of the constitution is closely linked to a problem which he treated formally ten years later in his *Dissertations on Government,* the question of whether it is just and proper for one generation to control future ones by means of the technicalities of politics. In his *Dissertations,* he expressed the concept in clear and precise terms, "As we are not to live forever ourselves, and other generations are to follow us, we have neither the power nor the right to govern them, or to say how they shall govern themselves."[42] Although this great theme is ordinarily associated with Jefferson, who, as Adrienne Koch has pointed out, struggled with it throughout his life, it had been adumbrated by Locke in the seventeenth century.[43] Paine also touched upon it for the second time in a famous letter to Jefferson in 1788 on natural and civil rights,[44] and he treated it at length in *Rights of Man.*

The Pennsylvania constitution embodied another unique feature of Paine's *Four Letters,* his insistence that the judicial power is not coequal with the legislative and the executive but subsidiary to them. The constitution clearly rendered the judicial branch or function subservient to the legislative by giving the single legislature the power to "remove any judge from his office *without* trial, for anything they please to call 'misbehavior.' "[45]

Even though Paine himself was not present during the consitutional convention, doing military service in the "flying camp," his theories were propounded in Philadelphia by associates of the Independent party who served as delegates, including David Rittenhouse, James Cannon and Timothy Matlock. They obviously carried the day. John Adams undoubtedly read Paine's *Four Letters* and could not have failed to realize that they were in part an answer to his *Thoughts on Government.* Adams was in principle quite right, therefore, when he charged in later life, that "it was not Franklin, but Timothy Matlock, James Cannon, Thomas Young, and Thomas Paine," who were the authors "of the Pennsylvania Constitution.[46] There is no question that the principles of Thomas Paine did indeed prevail at the convention. At the same time, Paine himself was also speaking the truth when he maintained in 1777 "I held no correspondence with either party, for or against, the present constitution. I had no hand in forming any part of it, nor knew any thing of its contents till I saw it published."[47] Paine may not have known at the time what was taking place at the convention, but his *Four Letters* reveal that his constitutional theories were of crucial importance to that body. His pamphlet also enables us to see which issues in the debates accompanying the Pennsylvania constitution concerned him the most and to perceive even stronger links between his American ideology and that of *Rights of Man* than are apparent in *Common Sense*.

16

The *Crisis*

Much less has been written about Paine's *Crisis* than his *Common Sense,* probably because it concerns itself primarily with events and circumstances in the military and diplomatic struggle and devotes relatively little attention to ideology.

Its title, like that of Paine's first publication, had previously been used in England. An anti-administration periodical entitled simply *The Crisis* flourished in London throughout 1775 and 1776. A total of ninety-one numbers were published, as well as one *Crisis Extraordinary,* a title which Paine also later adopted.[1] The London *Crisis* vigorously supported the colonies in their struggle for liberty and after July 1776 for independence, and it was widely circulated in the colonies. As a matter of fact, many more separate reprintings of this work throughout America in the one year 1775 are known than of all of Paine's more famous *Crisis* throughout the eight years of the Revolution. Even the London *Crisis Extraordinary* had an American reprinting. If one were to judge by these individual issues alone, one would be forced to conclude that the London *Crisis* had a much greater vogue in the thirteen former colonies than had Paine's *The American Crisis.* This conclusion would be faulty, however, since it would fail to take into consideration newspaper printings. Nearly every number of Paine's *Crisis,* including the first, was reprinted in at least one newspaper, and most of them were reprinted in newspapers all over the continent.

Paine added the adjective *American* to the title of his first five numbers to distnguish them from the London work. These were printed originally as pamphlets or broadsides; later numbers were newspaper articles, some labeled simply *The Crisis* and others having no uniform title.

Although Paine gave the number 13 to his last *Crisis,* symbolizing the number of states in the union, several more than thirteen essays had been published, including some described as "Supernumerary" or "Extraordinary." Paine himself did not assign the numbers 10 or 12 to any of his articles, and to this day one cannot be absolutely sure of what pieces he felt should be included in the complete text of *The Crisis.*

Paine recalled that he wrote *Crisis* No. 1 in "a passion of patriotism,"[2] and like the rest of the series it reflects fervor and propaganda much more than argument and ideas. It opens with one of the most inspiring sentences in

American literature, "These are the times that try men's souls," and concludes with one of the worst jokes, the grim prediction that if the colonists do not resist British troops and German mercenaries, they will see their homes "turned into barracks and bawdy-houses for Hessians, and a future race to provide for, whose father we shall doubt of." Paine, nevertheless, portrays the military situation from an optimistic perspective. He scornfully rejects "the summer soldier and the sunshine patriot" and exhorts his loyal fellow citizens to patriotic dedication, hard work, and sacrifice.

Subsequent numbers of the *Crisis* maintain this tone of cheerful gloom, portraying actual and potential hardships, disadvantages, and defeats as near disasters, but assuring his readers that American right and reason will triumph in the end. As a group, the *Crisis* papers have more in common with exhortatory sermons than with political essays, but they nevertheless embody some segments important in themselves or relevant to Paine's other writings.

Paine embroiders the theme introduced in *Common Sense* of the uniqueness of America and its favored status in the divine dispensation. The theme remains somewhat subdued in *Common Sense* by virtue of the title-page statement on the second and subsequent editions, "Written by An Englishman," and by Paine's insistence that he is writing for all mankind. In the *Crisis,* however, Paine writes as a full-fledged American and addresses himself to particular problems and policies of his country and his countrymen.

He is deliberately ambivalent concerning the extent to which divine providence is entering the military campaign, aware as he is that deciding between the role of the Almighty and that of human enterprise had been a constant dilemma in colonial America. He solemnly affirms that God will not allow a peaceful people to be destroyed and adds even more dramatically, "Neither have I so much of the infidel in me, as to suppose that HE has relinquished the government of the world, and given us up to the care of devils."[3] At the same time he calls upon all America not to throw "the burden of the day upon Providence." He exhorts his readers in proverbial language to "lay your shoulders to the wheel" (Burton, *Anatomy of Melancholy,* part 2, sec. 1, memb. 2). And in biblical style, he urges them to "show your faith by your works."[4]

In *Crisis* No. 8, Paine introduces the theory that the physical size of America exercises a kind of metaphysical influence upon the inhabitants of the country by endowing them with sublime thoughts and superior abilities, a theme which he later developed in *Rights of Man* and which became celebrated in the bombastic phrases of his admirer, Walt Whitman. Paine suggests that "there is something in the extent of countries, which among the generality of people, insensibly communicates extension of the mind. The soul of an islander, in its native state, seems bounded by the foggy confines of the water's edge, and all beyond affords to him matters only for profit or curiosity, not for friendship. His island is to him his world, and fixed to that, his every thing centers in it; while those who are inhabitants of a continent, by casting their eye over a longer field, take in likewise a larger intellectual circuit, and thus approaching nearer to an acquaintance with the universe, their atmosphere of thought is extended, and their liberality fills a wider space."[5] In 1789, Paine wrote in similar vein to Sir Joseph Banks: "Great scenes inspire great Ideas. The natural Mightiness of America expands the Mind and it partakes of the greatness it contemplates."[6] In almost identical terms, he maintains in *Rights of Man* that the scene which America "presents to the eye of a spectator, has something in it which generates and encourages great ideas. . . . The mighty objects he beholds, act upon his mind by enlarging it, and he partakes of the greatness he contemplates."[7]

The notion of the strong effect of sublime natural scenery on the emotions is a commonplace in European aesthetics of the eighteenth and nineteenth centuries, but Paine was the first to give the notion a political connotation, that is, to associate the influence of the landscape with the destiny of a particular nation. It is significant that neither he nor the many Americans after him who exulted in the uplifting effect of the topography of the New World gave any thought to the landscape in South America, the Caribbean, or Canada on the Spanish and French populations in these areas or, perhaps an even greater omission, on the indigenous ones, the Indians. Paine in later works continued to stress the salubrious environment of America with such insistence that one of his critics remarked caustically that he tries to make his readers believe "that every thing began the other day in America, and that nothing really had ever existed before."[8]

In *Crisis* No. 10, Paine affirms that the advantages of America are as much material as spiritual; he initiates, in other words, the myth that the American standard of living is the highest in the world. In his words, "There are not three millions of people in any [other] part of the universe, who live so well, or have such a fund of ability."[9] We have seen that in *Common Sense,* Paine launched another myth associated with America—that of its eternal youth. In *Crisis* No. 5, he interprets the youth or newness of America as aggravating the heinousness of Britain's crime in attacking her. "America was young, and compared with other countries, was virtuous. None but a Herod of uncommon malice would have made war upon infancy."

Paine's obsession with newness and modernity presents a paradox when compared with his rhapsodic portrayal in *Crisis* No. 3 of the pleasures and advantages in the contemplation of history, which he defines as looking back "even to the first periods of infancy," and tracing "the turns and windings through which we have passed." The historical retrospect in America leads to the conclusion that the business of an age has been crowded into a few months. "Never did men grow old in so short a time!"[10]

Too little attention to the past, according to Paine, interferes with our judgment, and the act of comparing the present with the past frequently imparts wisdom. In very modern terms, Paine explains that "it is a kind of countermarch," by which we get into the rear of time, and mark the movements and meanings of things as we make our return." He suggests that a pattern exists in human events; at least explanations are always available if events are properly studied. In reference to "sentimental differences," by which he presumably means the syndrome of romantic love, however, Paine admits that logic is not always effective. Frequently "some striking circumstance, or some forcible reason quickly conceived, will affect in an instant what neither argument nor example could produce in an age."

We have already noticed Paine's early statement concerning the superiority of the moderns over the ancients in the *Pennsylvania Magazine.* He recurs to the theme in *Crisis* No. 5, where he seems to be attempting to overthrow the entire European tradition of historical writing, which uniformly portrays classical antiquity as a kind of golden age. Montesquieu in France and Bolingbroke in England are good examples of this historical classicism, in which, in Paine's words, "the wisdom, civil governments, and sense of honor of the States of Greece and Rome, are frequently held up as objects of excellence and imitation." Paine observes that "mankind have lived for little purpose" if it is necessary continually to go back two or three thousand years for lessons and examples. In his opinion, "could the mist of antiquity be taken away and men and things viewed as they then really were, it is more than probable that they would admire us, rather than we them."[11] The short period of American settlement, Paine maintains, has furnished the world "with more useful knowledge and sounder maxims of civil government than were ever produced in any age before." For this reason Paine refuses to yield "the palm of the United States to any Grecians or Romans that were ever born." He particularly seeks to take away from the ancients the universal acclaim which had been generally accorded to them for cherishing freedom. According to Paine, "the Grecians and Romans were strongly possessed of the *Spirit* of liberty, but *not* the principle, for at the time they were determined not to be slaves themselves, they employed their power to enslave the rest of mankind." This concept was soon versified by David Humphreys, in a brief poem "On the Love of Country."

Perish the Roman pride a world that braves,
To make for one free state all nations slaves;
Their boasted patriotism at once exprest,
Love for themselves and hate for all the rest.[12]

Paine not only denies liberty to the ancients, but actually maintains that "had it not been for America there had been no such thing as freedom left throughout the whole universe." Here we see a further stage of his survey of the progress of freedom. In his poem "Liberty Tree" he had hailed the appearance of the Goddess of Liberty "In a chariot of light, from the regions of day." In *Common Sense,* he had described Freedom as being "hunted round the globe," and had called upon America to "receive the fugitive, and prepare in time an asylum for mankind."[13] Now, in the *Crisis,* he proudly affirms that the present era in America, in contrast to the ancient world, "is blotted by no one misanthropical vice" and the revolution in progress may be styled "the most virtuous and illustrious . . . that ever graced the history of mankind."[14]

Paine echoes his ethical indictment of the ancients in a letter to Henry Laurens in the next year, affirming that "all the histories of ancient wars . . . promote no moral reflection, but like the *Beggar's Opera* renders the villain pleasing in the hero."[15] In similar vein, he charges in *Crisis* No. 13 that "Rome, once the proud mistress of the universe, was originally a band of ruffians" and that her wealth came from plunder and rapine and her greatness from the "oppression of millions." By contrast, everything in America bears the mark of honor, including her birth and the stages by which she has risen to empire. While not discounting the inspirational value of "the remembrance . . . of what is past," Paine calls upon America to look to the future in order to add to "the fair fame she began with," to let the world witness "that she can bear prosperity: and that her honest virtue in time of peace, is equal to the bravest virtue in time of war."[16]

In *Crisis* No. 10, Paine repeats from *Common Sense* the argument that the geographical location of America is a major justification for its independence, suggesting that the eventual military triumph of America over any attempt by an island to conquer her "was as naturally marked in the constitution of things, as the future ability of a giant over a dwarf is delineated in his features while an infant."[17] As British visions of totally subjugating America had been dissipated by military-topographical reality, Paine in *Crisis* No. 12 ridicules the inconsistencies of parliamentary speeches which on one hand boast of the superiority of the British forces and on the other declare that without the economic riches of America the empire is nothing. "Was America, then, the giant of the empire," he taunts, "and England only her dwarf in waiting! Is the case so strangely altered, but those who once thought we could not live without them, are now brought to declare that they cannot exist without us?"[18]

In *Crisis* No. 6 Paine refutes another geopolitical concept, the notion that geographical location in itself inevitably makes certain nations mutually antagonistic. The idea was generally attributed in the eighteenth century to the French writer Mably, who asserted in 1757 that "neighboring states are naturally enemies one to the other."[19] The notion had been introduced into the American context in 1778 by British peace commissioners who attempted to insert a wedge between the Americans and their French allies by issuing a proclamation to the American people describing France as "the late mutual and natural enemy" of both Britain and America. Going back to the concept of the state of nature, Paine vehemently denies that there exists such a principle as natural animosity. "The expression is an unmeaning barbarism, and wholly unphilosophical, when applied to beings of the same species, let their station in the creation be what it may."[20] Paine justifies this assertion on primarily theological grounds, appealing to doctrines which have more in common with Christianity than with deism. Indeed, if his principles in this place can be considered as anything other than Christian, they are pure Manichaeism. "We have," according to Paine, "a perfect idea of a natural enemy when we think of the devil, because the enmity is perpetual, unalterable, and unabateable." But men "become friends or enemies as the change of temper, or the cast of interest inclines them. The Creator of man did not constitute them the natural enemy of each other." Expanding his doctrine to include animals in the chain of being, Paine closes with the statement, "even wolves may quarrel, still they herd together." Here he comes close to repeating an argument which Shaftesbury had used against Hobbes: "Wolves are to wolves very kind and loving creatures."[21]

Readdressing himself to all of the commissioners, Paine condemns England as a barbarous nation the conduct of which is unworthy of comparison to the civilized behavior of France. He closes with a customary barb at the American Tories, whom he dismisses as "a set of wretched mortals, who having deceived themselves, are cringing, with the duplicity of a spaniel."

In the introduction to *Common Sense,* Paine had declared the cause of America to be in great measure the cause of all mankind. In keeping with this pronouncement, he suggests in the opening lines of *Crisis* No. 2 that his remarks there are meant for the world at large even though his subject matter is mainly local. "Universal empire is the prerogative of a writer. His concerns are with all mankind, and though he cannot command their obedience, he can assign them their duty."[22] Several years previously Gibbon had prescribed that "he who writes for all mankind should draw his imagery only from sources common to all, from the human heart and the spectacle of literature."[23] Paine's ability to probe universal experience explains the success and enduring popularity of his writing. As he sees it, "what I write is pure nature, and my pen and my soul have ever gone together."[24] He therefore expresses confidence that this *Crisis,* like *Common Sense,* will make its way to England and inform its people of the design of the Americans to help them.[25]

He affirms that it would be easier for the Americans to bring about a revolution in England than for the British to conquer America, for military expeditions sent to England "with the declared design of deposing the present king, bringing his ministers to trial, and setting up the Duke of Gloucester in his stead, would assuredly carry their point." Paine came back to this notion of an invasion of England many times throughout his career, particularly during and after the French Revolution. It is significant that in the *Crisis* he does not suggest erecting a republican government for the English people, but merely effecting a change in rulers. In other words, he was at this time committed to republicanism in America, but not in Great Britain. His universalism, in other words, did not embrace republicanism. In *Crisis* No. 2 he also touches upon two of his other recurrent themes, British cruelties in India, the Caribbean, and Africa, and the imminent bankruptcy of the British government.

Paine says little in the *Crisis* about the operation of the human intellect except for echoing from *Common Sense* his belief that reason strikes the mind with automatic conviction. He tells his readers in *Crisis* No. 2 that "what I write is pure nature," and in No. 5 he observes that "what we now have to do is as clear as light, and the way to do it is as strait as a line."[26] Paine is almost Cartesian in the metaphors he uses to describe the operation of reason and the beauties of method. According to Paine, the intellectual realm reacts upon reason as the world of objects reacts upon the eye. Reason seems to have visual force as knowledge is imparted with clarity, directness, and distinctness. In *Crisis* No. 10, Paine, with his customary cheerfulness, affirms that "misfortune and experience have now taught us system and method; and the arrangements for carrying on the war are reduced to rule and order."[27] Shortly after this he adds, "I love method, because I see and am convinced of its beauty and advantage. It is that which makes all business easy and understood, and without which everything becomes embarrassed and difficult."[28] In a newspaper article supporting *Crisis* No. 10, Paine repeats his prescription of "order, system and method." "Method," he says, "is to natural power, what weight is to human strength, without which a giant would lose his labour and a country waste its force."[29] These passages share the rapture concerning order of a more famous one in *The Age of Reason* on the attributes of God. "Do we want to contemplate His power? We see it in the immensity of the creation. Do we want to contemplate His wisdom? We see it in the unchangeable order by which the incomprehensible whole is governed."[30] It is not surprising that one of Paine's pseudonyms should be "A Lover of Order."

Paine's political theory, although expressed only fragmentarily in the *Crisis,* is by and large identical with that in *Common Sense.* In *Crisis* No. 3, he suggests that his "creed of politics" is purely pragmatic, embodying a divorce between government and politics. In his words, "if an English merchant receives an order, and is paid for it, it signifies nothing to him who governs the country."[31] This is not quite the same as the dichotomy between government and society, but rather one between government and economic activity. In a newspaper letter following upon *Crisis* No. 10, he makes the assertion, which we have discussed in chapter 4, that "Government and the people do not in America constitute distinct bodies."[32] By this he means merely that the members of Congress and the state governments are drawn from the people and do not lose their identity as citizens by becoming lawmakers. In *Crisis* No. 10, moreover, he describes the war of America against Britain as "the country's war, the public's war, or the war of the people in their own behalf, for the security of their natural rights, and the protection of their own property. It is not the war of Congress, the war of the assemblies, or the war of government in any line whatever."[33] This is certainly a reaffirmation of the principle that government and society are separate.

In his letter following upon *Crisis* No. 10, Paine introduces a concept equivalent to Rousseau's theory that sovereignty in a nation is the expression of the general will. Referring to members of the Congress and the Assembly, Paine explains that they are "the representatives of majesty, but not majesty itself," and that the latter power exists in the "universal multitude." Paine uses the term *majesty* instead of Rousseau's *sovereignty;* otherwise the the theories are the same. In his later *Dissertations on Government,* 1786, Paine adopts the word *sovereignty* in essentially the same context and explains it in some detail.[34] In 1782, however, when Paine was intent mainly upon persuading his readers that increased taxation was the vital need for the survival of the nation, he did not develop the abstract significance of his theory of sovereignty but used it merely to establish a sentiment of national identification or homogeneity.

In *Crisis* No. 7, Paine expands his theories of national honor, perhaps in response to the various references to honor in the polemics over *Common Sense.* He associates personal and national honor by means of his maxim: "That which is the best character for an individual is the best character for a nation."[35] Yet on an international level, according to Paine, mankind seems not to have developed from its primitive origins but to have retained "as nations all the original rudeness of nature." Here, it will be noted, primitive times are not portrayed as being quite so salutary as they seem in *Common Sense.* The British as individuals, Paine maintains, judge other people on the basis of their national origins, their religion, and their wealth. Collectively, they seem to consider honor as consisting in "national insult" and in threatening with the rudeness of a bear and devouring with the ferocity of a lion. Paine completely demolishes the concept of a mother country in reference to Britain's relations with America. Instead of conforming to the natural direction suggested by this image, consisting of "everything that is fond, tender and forbearing," Britain, he says, has intruded its false notions of national honor revealing "the violence of resentment, the inflexibility of temper, or the vengeance of execution." All this is, of course, a repetition of the argument from *Common Sense* that Britain cannot be appropriately termed the parent country since even "brutes do not devour their young, nor savages make war upon their families."[36] In further expanding the connotations of the political term "mother country," Paine observes in the *Crisis* that the metaphor should have taught the necessity of independence, for all children eventually grow into adults and set up for themselves. "Nothing hurts the affections both of parents and children so much, as living too closely connected, and keeping up the distinction too long."[37] Paine states that the natural and the most beneficial policy of Britain would have been to maintain good relations with America and in this way to have preserved her reputation of military strength, which was rapidly being eroded by her impotence in the American campaign. Paine refers to "this method of studying the progress of the passions in order to ascertain the probable conduct of mankind" as a philosophy of politics which the British ministry have no conception of.[3]

Turning to the question of finance, Paine argues that England is so ridden by obligations that the interest on the national debt is almost equal to annual income. In seeking to demonstrate that British financiers count their debt as part of their national wealth but that it is actually a drain on the country which will bring the whole financial system to eventual collapse, Paine anticipates the argument of one of his later pamphlets, *The Decline and Fall of the English System of Finance* (1796). America, unlike England, could easily pay the expenses of the war, Paine maintains, since it has no debt of any kind other than its non-interest bearing paper currency.[39]

In reference to the internal political structure of the British nation, Paine draws attention to a conflict of interest between Parliament and the Crown which would have come to a head had Britain won the war. The fundamental question concerned which political segment could be considered responsible for such a victory and which should reap the benefit. As Paine explains the situation, Parliament claimed a legislative right over America, but the army presumably belonged to the Crown; in the event of subduing the colonies, it would not be clear whether Parliament or the Crown would then be in control. This situation, hypothetical as it is, leads Paine to ask among a series of questions whether the people are not the source of the power and honor of any country, whether there is any such thing as the English constitution, and "whether a congress constituted like that of America, is not the most happy and consistent form of government in the world."[40] Answers to these queries had already been suggested in *Common Sense,* and they were to be further developed in the pages of *Rights of Man.*

Paine addresses the last part of *Crisis* No. 7 to the "mercantile and manufacturing part" of the English nation, for whose benefit he had already observed that it is never worth while to go to war for profit's sake. Attempting to win over this segment of his readers by describing them as the "bulwark of the nation," he embroiders the theme introduced in *Common Sense* that trade is more profitable with an independent nation than with a subjugated one. Since a treaty of alliance had already been concluded with France, Paine warns the English merchants against allowing their government to provoke France into a declaration of war. Having already pointed to a conflict of interest between the Crown and Parliament, Paine now maintains that both forces are inimical to the welfare of the business community. "Your present king and ministry will be the ruin of you; and you had better risk a revolution and call a congress, than be thus led on from madness to despair, and from despair to ruin."[41] In addressing as a final note the ministry and the merchants collectively, Paine characteristically reduces politics to a "simple thought" and describes his own prescription of applying "the domestic politics of a family" to the national scene as an "easy and natural line."

We have already pointed out that Paine in 1776 in his *Four Letters* expressed the doctrine of the supremacy of the union over local governments; the concept is suggested also in *Common Sense* by his warning that "the continental belt is too loosely buckled"[42] and his axiom, " 'tis not in numbers but in unity that our great strength lies."[43] Paine further insisted on the supremacy of the union in his newspaper essay related to *Crisis* No. 10 (*Pennsylvania Gazette,* 3 April 1782) in order to persuade his readers that the central government must maintain its autonomy in financial matters, in other words, that "the expenses of the United States for carrying on the war, and the expenses of each state for its own domestic government" must be kept separate and distinct. In Paine's realistic terms, taxes levied for national defense are "properly our insurance money." To establish the principle, Paine declares that "the union of America is the foundation-stone of her independence, the rock on which it is built, and is something so sacred in her constitution, that we ought to watch every word we speak, and every thought we think, that we injure it not, even by mistake." This warning was needed to avert conflicts between loyalty to state and loyalty to the union, psychological divisions made particularly acute because some states were still bearing the brunt of British attack while others were remote from it. Paine solemnly affirms, therefore, that "with respect to those things which immediately concern the union, and for which the union was purposely established, and is intended to secure, each state is to the United States what each individual is to the state he lives in. And it is on this grand point, this movement upon one centre, that our existence as a nation, our happiness as a people, and our safety as individuals, depend."

Throughout *The Crisis* Paine expounds the primary theme of *Common Sense,* the moral justification of the war of independence. In *Crisis* No. 3, he summarizes the principal arguments in support of independence and concludes that it is "the *moral advantages*" which weigh most with all men of serious reflection."[44] In this section, however, he concerns himself with only one moral issue, that it is wrong for America through its colonial status to be involved in British wars. In *Common Sense,* he had framed the argument in political terms, affirming the principle of isolation from the political affairs of Europe.[45] In *Crisis* No. 3, he stresses ethical considerations: in Paine's words, "America neither could nor can be under the government of Britain without becoming a sharer of her guilt, and a partner in all the dismal commerce of death."[46] According to this train of thought, Britain has a dishonorable record of international belligerence going back for centuries, and the lot of America were she not set free would be to abet in every quarrel. "It is a shocking situation to live in, that one country must be brought into all the wars of another, whether the measure be right or wrong, or whether she will or not."

In *Crisis* No. 11, Paine defends the alliance between America and France on ethical grounds, specifically arguing that "the United States have as much honor as bravery" and that their conduct is based upon firm principle, not hazard or circumstance.[47] At least two years previously, Paine had suspected that the British were considering the notion of abandoning prosecution of the war in favor of seducing America to abandon her alliance with France, and he had written a paragraph denouncing this tactic as revealing "such a disposition to perfidiousness, and such disregard of honor and morals, as would add the finishing vice to national corruption." But Paine held back the paragraph because of the arrival of news indicating British determination to continue with military operations. He later inserted the paragraph in the eleventh *Crisis,* however, because of hints in the New York Tory press that the scheme of dividing America from her allies was reviving in British strategy. He thereupon provides evidence of peace gestures which had been made by the British to the courts of France and warns America to be on guard against the same insidious arts should they be used with her. The mere suggestion of coming to a separate arrangement, he denounces as an insult to America. In a realistic metaphor, he observes that no man attempts to seduce a truly honest woman; the very thought of it is a defamation of her good name.

In a passage highly revealing of his own moralistic mode of thinking, Paine affirms that he will not use the argument of selfish interest to defend the alliance but "go a step higher, and defend it on the ground of honor and principle."[48] Paine argues that since the French have treated America with the same respect which they would have shown to an old, established country, America cannot do less than fulfill her obligations. "Character is to us, in our present circumstances, of more importance than interest." Paine somewhat weakens the nobility of this sentiment by adding that since America is a young nation the rest of the world is observing its behavior to see whether it is worthy of trust. Also he uses a phrase which he had earlier ridiculed as stale and hackneyed, "the eye of the world is upon us."[49] He returns to high morals and vigorous style, however, by affirming that Britain and the world must be shown "that we are neither to be bought nor sold; that our mind is great and fixed; our prospect clear; and that we will support our character as firmly as our independence."

Paine summarizes the moral argument in his *Crisis Extraordinary* of 1782, joining it with the theme of youthfulness. "America is a new character in the universe," he maintains. "She started with a cause divinely right, and struck at an object vast and valuable. Her reputation for political integrity, perseverance, fortitude, and all the manly excellencies, stands high in the world; and it would be a thousand pities that, with those introductions into life, she suffered the least spot or blow to fall upon her *moral* fame."[50]

The thirteenth *Crisis,* symbolic of the number of states in the American union, is dated 19 April 1783, eighth anniversary of the battles of Lexington and Concord. Last of the series which Paine himself considered to constitute the *Crisis,* it begins with the triumphant declaration " 'The times that tried men's souls,' are over—and the greatest and completest revolution the world ever knew, gloriously and happily accomplished." This is the first time Paine uses the word *revolution* to describe the events which had been taking place, although he is equally hyperbolical in *Common Sense* in his reference to beginning the world over again. At the end of the war, he says, America has earned the honor and "power to make a world happy, to teach mankind the art of being so," and "to exhibit on the theatre of the universe, a character hitherto unknown."[51] Echoing the language of the Scriptures, he describes the pastoral scenes now opening for America, comprising not the "cypress shade of disappointment," but "the sweet of her labors, and the reward of her toil" in "her own land, and under her own vine" (Apocrypha 1 Maccabees 14: 12) In this situation, Paine declares, acquiring "a fair national reputation, is of as much importance as independence." A few paragraphs later he observes, "Character is much easier kept than recovered, and that man, if any such there be, who, from any sinister views, or littleness of soul, lends unseen his hand to injure it, contrives a wound it will never be in his power to heal."

Liberal thinkers throughout Europe, particularly in France and England, had supported the cause of the American colonists, but their adherence had been in the main emotional and humanitarian rather than ideological, comparable to the rhapsodic sponsorship which Boswell and Rousseau had accorded to Paoli in the latter's efforts to bring about a new regime in Corsica. There had been little said on ideological grounds about the ramifications of American independence, and one of the most daring depositories of advanced ideas, the abbé Raynal's *Histoire philosophique des deux Indes,* even reflected some doubts concerning the principles which were motivating the American "insurgens." Paine published in 1782, as we shall see later, a reply to Raynal consisting of a detailed vindication of the moral integrity of the American independence movement. The thirteenth *Crisis* offered Paine an additional opportunity of reasserting its ideological significance. He roundly affirms, therefore, that the revolution must be "an honor to the age that accomplished it" to "the end of time" and that it has "contributed more to enlighten the world, and diffuse a spirit of freedom and liberality among mankind, than any human event (if this may be called one) that ever preceded it."[52] Noteworthy in this proclamation is the suggestion of divine guidance or supervision, a religious attitude which conforms to both *Common Sense* and *Age of Reason.*

In a kind of balance sheet for America at the close of the war, Paine finds only one item on the debit side and two on the credit. The single liability consists in the national debt, which he considers as hardly worth mentioning in comparison with the compensating advantages. The two great assets consist of gaining complete freedom in the economic realm and of acquiring an ally, obviously France, "whose exemplary greatness, and universal liberality," according to Paine, "have extorted a confession even from her enemies." In a footnote supporting a principle originally presented in *Common Sense,* that the struggle "never could have happened at a better time," Paine affirms that "the great hinge on which the whole machine turned is the UNION OF THE STATES." Observing that no single state or combination of single states can equal in strength "the whole of the present United States," he stresses the advantages and necessity of "strengthening that happy union which has been our salvation, and without which we should have been a ruined people." Finally, in this footnote, Paine quotes from *Common Sense* the passages concerning the appropriateness of the timing of the struggle for independence—"THE TIME HATH FOUND US"—and the indispensable nature of the glorious union—"It is not in numbers, but in a union, that our great strength lies."[53]

All this is introductory to a forceful argument on the continued necessity of union after America had become a nation and achieved sovereignty, an argument foreshadowing the influential *Federalist* papers to be published a few years later in favor of the new constitution. Paine's major principle is based upon the relationship of the United States to the other nations in the world. The individual states lack the wealth and resources to function by themselves; only as the United States, conceived as a wisely regulated and cemented union, can they obtain the respect of other nations, make treaties, protect their commerce in foreign ports, and provide their security at home. Some measure of local autonomy must in the process be sacrificed. Echoing his *Four Letters,* Paine observes, "It is with confederated states as with individuals in society; something must be yielded up to make the whole secure." Citizenship of a particular state is merely a local distinction, but "citizenship in the United States is our national character. . . . Our great title is, AMERICANS—our inferior one varies with the place."

In the remainder of his remarks, Paine makes a number of personal revelations. In characterizing and vindicating his individual conduct throughout the war, he once more foreshadows a political attitude which became of great consequence in the early years of the republic—the view that political parties are harmful in a nation by fomenting irrational divisions and should, therefore, be avoided if at all possible. This opinion, prevalent in the speeches of George Washington, with whom it is generally associated, is clearly portrayed in Paine's summary of his own political career. "So far as my endeavours could go, they have all been directed to conciliate the affections, unite the interests and draw and keep the mind of the country together; and the better to assist in this foundation work of the revolution, I have avoided all places of profit or office, either in the state I live in, or in the United States; kept myself at a distance from all parties and party connections, and even disregarded all private and inferior concerns: and when we take into view the great work we have gone through, and feel, as we ought to feel, the just importance of it, we shall then see, that the little wranglings and indecent contentions of personal party, are as dishonorable to our characters, as they are injurious to our repose."[54] This statement, apart from its ideological reflection on party divisions, must be considered in the nature of a political appeal and as such interpreted in a very broad sense. In actuality, Paine had served as secretary to the committee on foreign relations of the Congress and as clerk of the Pennsylvania Assembly, and he had several times before the writing of *Crisis* No. 13 appealed to various national leaders to be reimbursed for his services.

Paine reveals his pride of authorship by adding that if he has served the cause of America in the course of more than seven years by opposing "an unnatural reconciliation" with Britain, he has "likewise added something to the reputation of literature, by freely and distinterestedly employing it in the great cause of mankind, and shewing there may be genius without prostitution." He formally takes his leave of the subject—and in a sense of America—speculating upon "whatever country I may hereafter be in"—affirming that "I shall always feel an honest pride at the part I have taken and acted, and a gratitude to Nature and Providence for putting it in my power to be of some use to mankind."

17
Retrospect on 1776

We have seen that during the period when Paine was writing *Common Sense* and the first three numbers of his *Crisis,* a bitter struggle was taking place in Pennsylvania between two opposing factions, represented by the Moderate and the Independent political groupings. For convenience, these opposing factions may be delineated as aristocratic and popular, rich and poor, or conservative and radical. In general, the advocates of the popular side were also the most vigorous supporters of independence. This is not to say, however, that pre-Revolutionary Pennsylvania offered a perfect example of the identification of economic and political interests. Many wealthy and privileged Philadelphians vigorously supported independence, and many members of the artisan and mechanic class opposed it.

In a sense, there existed three major political groups. The Tories, or the ultraconservative force, consisted of Quakers, pietistic Germans, all the people who depended on the proprietary faction, and a large proportion of the wealthy. The Whigs were divided into conservative and radical wings; the conservative Whigs consisted of most of the merchants and a majority of the professional classes, including lawyers and doctors; the radical Whigs consisted of the Irish and Scotch-Irish, the Germans other than pietists, the inhabitants of the western districts, and the disenfranchised segments of Philadelphia.[1] The Tories unequivocally defended the status quo; the conservative Whigs supported every patriotic measure short of independence but were divided over the proprietary charter; and the radical Whigs advocated independence and overthrow of the charter.

One of the groups most vigorous on the side of a new constitution was the local militia, or Associators as they were called. They were particularly bitter against being governed by the charter, since under it they were called upon to fight but for the most part were offered no political representation in return. Historians have shown how Pennsylvania radicals turned to members of the Continental Congress for aid in their efforts to rid themselves of the detested charter government. With Paine it was the other way around; he appealed to radical leaders in local Pennsylvania politics in order to create a sentiment for independence.

During May and July when the movement for a convention to draw up the Pennsylvania constitution was gaining headway, Associators of various districts issued declarations supporting the resolves of the Continental Congress. One of these manifestoes shows how Paine's *Common Sense* influenced both the western provinces and the Associators. It was sent to the *Pennsylvania Evening Post* with the comment that "your inserting the following resolve may convince the public that Common Sense is not altogether destitute of proselytes in Pennsylvania" (4 May 1776).

> At a meeting of Captain James McCandless's company, and a number of other inhabitants of the township of Faun, in York county, Resolved unanimously, That the independent principles of Common Sense are what we wish to see established, as soon as the wisdom of the *Hon. the Continental Congress* shall think proper, as we look upon it to be the only alternative now left us to secure our liberties, and screen us from the disgraceful epithet of rebels in the eyes of all the world.

Paine in most of his writings kept separate the two themes of national independence and Pennsylvania politics, even though in *Common Sense* he particularly condemned the Pennsylvania Assembly for its infamous instructions to the delegates to the Continental Congress. His *Crisis* papers, several of which appeared during the height of the turmoil over the Constitution, are written entirely from the continental perspective. The two strains are interwoven, however, as we have seen, in the "Forester" and in *Four Letters.*

Paine sets the tone of his "Forester" letters by means of a significant statement in the first one, "The particular business of a convention is undoubtedly Provincial, but the great business of the day is Continental."[2] In other words, while committing himself to support a new Pennsylvania Constitution, he affirmed that separation from Great Britain was a vastly more important issue. He proceeded, nevertheless, to justify the call for a local Pennsylvania convention on the grounds that the proprietors had already twice changed the original charters, and that ultimate authority rests in "the body of the people." During the year 1775 a number of committees had grown up in Philadelphia (comparable to parallel ones throughout the colonies) to take care of newly arisen business which the Assembly could not or would not look after. These committees were designed to handle Correspondence (with the other colonies), Elections, Inspection and Observation, and Safety. Smith, writing as Cato, had accused these committees of unspecified crimes. Paine in his third letter replied that they had been "duly elected by the people" and performed the functions for which they were elected; whereas the Assembly, also elected by the people, had taken over powers and functions for which it was not elected and was, therefore, acting in an unconstitutional manner.[31] Here Paine probably had in mind particularly the instructions to the delegates. He concluded the letter by accusing the author of these instructions (whom he still mistakenly believed to be Galloway) of deliberately refusing to sell timber in his possession for the construction of ships to be used against England.

Paine's fourth "Forester" letter cites in a footnote a vigorous remonstrance in 1704 of the Pennsylvania Assembly (then entirely in the hands of Quakers) against the act of the Proprietor in substituting a second charter for the original one.[4] This is clearly an anticipation of the second of his *Four Letters,* in which the subject is developed and amplified. The remainder of the "Forester" letter deals with the election of May 1776, which I have treated in the eleventh chapter. Nearly everything in Paine's subsequent *Four Letters* concerns the situation in Pennsylvania.

During the last six months of 1776, while the Pennsylvania Constitution was being drawn up and adopted, Paine was away from Philadelphia, both serving in the "flying camp" and acting as an unofficial war correspondent. Between January and April of the next year he was back again in Philadelphia, where he published the first three numbers of the *Crisis.* Here he makes absolutely no reference to the Pennsylvania constitutional quarrels because his mission was to bring people together, not only because of the danger of invasion but also because of the debilitating effect of internal dissensions. According to a contemporary observer in December 1776, the people in Philadelphia "appeared all hostile to each other, Whig & Tory in a state little better [than] open Enemies."[5] Much of the dissension was caused by the new constitution, which embodied many of Paine's political notions and was in part the work of his friends James Cannon, David Rittenhouse, and Timothy Matlock, who were all delegates to the convention. Almost from the moment of its adoption, opponents of the constitution complained publicly about its shortcomings, and within a few months a concerted movement had been initiated to convene a new convention, a petition to that effect being presented to the Assembly early in 1777. Many newspaper essays advanced arguments in favor of the convention, one of the best appearing in the *Pennsylvania Packet* of 12 March under the name of Phocion, which was presumed to be a pseudonym for John Dickinson.[6]

It was this essay and another in the *Evening Post* signed Hampden which drew Paine into the controversy. In an essay in the *Packet* of 18 March, he rejected their calls for a new convention but refused to deal in personalities. If either author be a friend, he says, "I spare him out of pity to myself"; if an enemy, "I spare him from a regard to the public peace."[7] In this and all his subsequent writings on Pennsylvania affairs, Paine adopted a tone of moderation, in great contrast to the fury and invective of *Common Sense.* He remarks in one of the last of the series, "This is the age of negotiation, compromise and coalition."[8] In his reply to Phocion, Paine is primarily concerned with healing party tensions and redirecting attention to the danger from the British. "A man may as well talk of loving a wife and a mistress, at one time, with equal felicity, as of jangling with his neighbors and yet joining with them in public defense."[9] To emphasize his own nonpartisan concerns, Paine makes the statement, already quoted, that he had been out of the state during the constitutional convention and that he had no hand in its deliberations. He registers dismay at the deplorable condition in the state at the end of the previous year: "Society had taken its departure: every man's hand seemed against his brother, and all this, for the want of that happy ingredient in life, good temper."

Paine charges that the opposition to the constitution is personal rather than political and that it is inspired by the pique, resentment, and revenge of those who had not been elected to serve in the new government. He admits that the constitution doubtless has errors and defects, but argues that it is good enough to begin with. Since it contains provisions for amendment, Paine affirms that he would have supported it himself even though it were less pleasing than he now finds it merely to ascertain that which should be "retained, reformed or rejected." To clamor for drastic and immediate changes is like "recommending death as a cure for disease."

Paine's sentiments were echoed at a meeting of the Whig Society on 18 March, attended by Charles Willson Peale, its president, Dr. Thomas Young, James Cannon, David Rittenhouse, and Paine, who used his Pennsylvania military title of major. In an address, later published in the *Pennsylvania Gazette* (26 March), the society declared, "A noisy and ill-natured wrangling, about the designs of the framers or opposers of the Constitution, can answer to no other purpose than to injure and disgrace us." The Society's advice to the people of Pennsylvania was essentially that already given by Paine, to protect themselves from the enemy at their gates and within their doors by utilizing the government and laws then in effect and to defer tampering with the constitution until time and experience should have taught them how to make a better one.

Next to enter the fray was Paine's erstwhile collaborator Benjamin Rush, who had in the last months of 1776 come under the influence of John Adams. In a letter published in the *Pennsylvania Journal,* 21 and 28 May 1777, and signed Ludlow, a name hallowed in Puritan circles, Rush castigated the new constitution in the spirit of Adams's *Thoughts on Government.* Paine replied immediately in the *Journal,* 4 June, limiting himself mainly to the Bill of Rights and the question of religious freedom.[10] As we have already pointed out in our discussion of Paine's relationship to Locke, he expands and clarifies in this essay the distinction between natural and civil rights which is merely suggested in *Common Sense.* He observes that civil rights may be alterable and recommends that they be made particular and be included in the body of the constitution, not in the more abstract Bill of Rights which serves as a preamble. Natural rights, according to Paine's scheme, represent inherent liberty whereas laws of any kind, even those designed to protect the individual, represent inherent restraint.

Rush had labeled a constitution "the executive part of the Bill of Rights" and had compared its function in a community to "modes of worship . . . in religion." Paine replies that "a man may be religiously happy without *modes,* but he cannot be civilly happy without a Constitution." After assuming that even his antagonist would admit that religion may exist without modes, Paine denies that laws may be considered parallel to the practice of morality in religion. Paine asks how it is possible "to compare *'Laws'* which are in themselves motionless and have no capacity of action, with the *practice* of morality, which not only implies motion, but the power of continuing it, and even of generating it."

After this essay, Paine devoted his writing exclusively to continental affairs for a year and a half, publishing the fourth number of his *Crisis* on 12 September 1777 and the seventh on 12 November 1778. During much of this period, British troops occupied the city of Philadelphia, and constitutional problems naturally dimmed in importance. But almost as soon as the British evacuated the city in June 1778, the old arguments were revived. Agitation was so great that the Assembly on 28 November 1778 ordered an election to determine whether a convention should be held to revise the constitution.[11] On 1 December, General Joseph Reed was elected president of the Supreme Executive Council of the state.[12] According to Paine, Reed at the time of taking office was so desperate that he talked of resigning and leaving the state unless Paine would publicly come to the defense of the constitution.[13] Whether or not Reed's entreaties represented his only or even his primary motivation, Paine published a series of four articles in the *Pennsylvania Packet* (1, 5, 10, 12 December 1778) which support the constitution. Simply stated, he argued that it was preferable to have it confirmed than altered.[14] In his opening sentence, he expressed unwillingness to have his attention called away from "the great object of the Continent." He had published his last *Crisis*, No. 7, on 11 November 1778, but he was not to put out another one for fifteen months. In order to obviate any charges of self-interest, he revealed that he had not voted on any question since the great one of "independence in seventy-six."

Since the Pennsylvania constitution differed noticeably from the general pattern adopted by the other states, Paine affirms pragmatically that it is in the interest of the states that their constitutions be somewhat diversified from each other. Echoing Franklin's famous injunction, "Let the experiment be made," Paine asserts that "we are a people upon experiments."[15] And reviving from *Common Sense* the theme of newness as a salutary element, he regards the newness or novelty of the Pennsylvania constitution as one of the best things in its favor. In his *Four Letters* he had argued that wealth or poverty flows from one country to another, in other words, that nations communicate and absorb each other's economic condition. In reference to class divisions in Pennsylvania, he asserts that both rich and poor are needed, that they contribute to each other's welfare, and that "the true interest of one is the real interest of both." There is no question that Paine regarded his own approach to constitutional problems as being as new as the Pennsylvania constitution itself. The debate until then, he maintains, had been carried on an abstract and hackneyed level; but the pragmatic effect of a constitution on the best interests of the people had never before been touched.

In his newspaper articles, Paine reveals considerable satisfaction in his observation that in Pennsylvania "the idea of freedom and rights is high." In expanding his somewhat redundant principle that "it is the nature of freedom to be free," he develops an ingenious series of metaphors.

> If the ancients ever possessed her in a civil state, it is a question well worth enquiring into *whether they did not lose her through the bolts, bars, and checks under which they thought to keep her?* An injudicious security becomes her prison, and, disgusted with captivity, she becomes an exile. Freedom is the associate of innocence, not the companion of suspicion. She only requires to be cherished, not to be caged, and to be beloved, is, to her, to be protected. Her residence is in the undistinguished multitude of rich and poor, and a partisan to neither is the patroness of all. She connects herself with man as God made him, not as fortune altered him, and continues with him while he continues to be just and civil. To engross her is to affront her, for, liberal herself, she must be liberally dealt with. In absolute countries she is violated into the concubine of a usurper; and in the motley government of Britain she is held a prisoner of state, and once in seven years let out upon parole. At other times her image only is carried about, which the multitude, a stranger to her person, mistakes for herself.[16]

This metaphorical *tour de force* may be considered as parallel to the portrayal in *Common Sense* of freedom's being hunted round the globe and finding a refuge in America. Paine continues by referring to "the toleration act in England, which *granted* liberty of conscience to every man, in religion." In language almost identical to that in his *Four Letters* he observes that in America "we consider the assumption of such power as a species of tyrannic arrogance, and do not *grant* liberty of conscience as a *favor* but confirm it as a right."

Though Paine considers freedom as a quality inherent in man as he comes from the hands of his maker, he admits that under even a just constitution there are situtations in which the rights of free men may be temporarily suspended, for example, when a man has been convicted of a crime for which he is imprisoned, when he becomes a servant of the state, or when he enters into domestic service.[17] In the last two situations, freedom is curtailed through the loss of the franchise. Paine consider these restrictions perfectly fair, since both the civil and the domestic servant have voluntarily withdrawn from ordinary society and have thereby exchanged their own interests for those of their master. In other words, suffrage need not be universal, but it may be justly denied only to those who have forfeited it by crimes or who have voluntarily accepted a temporary dependence upon another person. Here he is accepting in a limited way Elrington's principle that "men are free, if governed by just and impartial laws, though in the making of those laws they were not consulted."

Paine completely rejects property qualifications for voting, not so much because they separate the rich and the poor but because, in Pennsylvania at least, they tended to make poor people exaggerate the amount of their property. In order to vote in Pennsylvania prior to the 1776 constitution, a man was required to affirm that he owned fifty pounds worth of property. Paine observes that every man with almost any miscellaneous collection of articles would consider himself within the pale of the affirmation. "It is disgraceful that freedom should be made the property of an oath on such *trifling* things, which, whether they are possessed or not, makes scarce any, or no difference, in the value of the man to the community."[18] In treating the principle of representation in *Common Sense,* Paine had advocated an equitable geographical distribution and a large number of representatives. In reference to Pennsylvania, he still insists on the latter, but adds that the electorate should be composed of all classes from rich to poor. His justification is in upward and downward mobility—that the rich man today is a poor man tomorrow and vice versa. For this reason, property qualifications are contrary to the interests of all classes.

In further defending the principle of equality, Paine shows the relationship between democracy and education, or at least an informed public opinion. He predicts, for example, that monarchy will eventually become obsolete—that "in proportion as knowledge is circulated through a country, and the minds of the people become clear of ignorance and rubbish, they will find themselves restless and uneasy under any government so established."[19] The practice of the Old World, he affirms, is to hold up government as a mystery beyond the comprehension of the people, but in America the policy is to make men as wise as possible so that they may be governed rationally. The good citizen, therefore, accepts the principle "that the sense of the majority is the governing sense." It is important to notice that Paine does not affirm that the will of the majority must always be applied, and in later writings he shows himself aware of the possibility of abuses in absolute majority rule.

Continuing his contrast between Europe and America, Paine affirms that "it is the fault of all the governments in the old world, that they GOVERN TOO MUCH."[20] This statement has reference to a proposal by the critics of the constitution to allow the Executive Council to appoint justices of the peace. Paine prefers the method embodied in the constitution by which two candidates are elected for each ward and the President selects one. This combination of election and appointment Paine considers wise and noble, presumably an improvement on his own suggestion in *Four Letters,* "Civil officers for towns and countries [counties] may easily be chosen by election." Similarly, Paine prefers popular election for judges, although he is willing to have judges of the Supreme Court appointed by the Executive Council, since they serve the entire state and since this method of selection is a valid exercise of delegated power.

Despite a promise to treat in subsequent essays other issues such as the Council of Censors and the proposed second house of the legislature, Paine abruptly broke off his newspaper series in December without explanation. In February of the next year, the Assembly repealed its resolution concerning a new convention. This did not necessarily mean, however, that the matter was settled even temporarily. In March, the opponents of the constitution formed a Republican Society and the other side banded together in a Constitutional Society.[21]

Paine maintained his silence concerning the Pennsylvania Constitution during the remainder of the war, but in 1786 he published a major pamphlet reviving the basic issues of the controversy, including some which he had promised to clarify in his earlier essays. This pamphlet was entitled *Dissertations on Government; the Affairs of the Bank; and Paper Money.*[22] Although inspired by the local and ephemeral affairs of Pennsylvania, it deals with many of the fundamental principles of political association, including the problem of how much authority one generation should have to control the destinies of subsequent ones. The work soon penetrated the international area by means of a partial translation into Spanish.[23]

Shortly after the end of the Revolutionary War, the affairs of the Bank of America, which had been chartered in Philadelphia in 1781, became closely identified with the controversy over the constitution. Property values declined sharply at the close of hostilities, and the amount of money in circulation fell off to an alarming degree. Farmers and mechanics who were hardest hit clamored for the issuance of a large amount of paper currency, but the directors of the Bank stood out against it. Obviously if the Bank refused to accept the new currency on the same terms as specie, the paper would have been worthless when issued. The Assembly, nevertheless, authorized the emitting of bills of credit to the amount of £150 thousand and appointed a committee to investigate the Bank. Paine was personally favorably disposed toward the Bank because of its work in financing the Revolution. Indeed, he had been instrumental in its founding and had deposited in it a major part of his own capital.[24] The committee of inquiry denounced the Bank, however, on the grounds that it tended to send specie out of the country in the form of dividends to foreign shareholders, and the charter was repealed in September 1785.

During this same period, the Assembly was taking up the question of reimbursing Paine for his services to the state during the Revolution, and as he was on cordial terms with most of the members of the House he expected to receive a handsome compensation. While both this question and the bank charter were being considered, he accidentally ran into several of the members of the Assembly, who in triumphant tones suggested that the charter would be revoked. Paine immediately saw the situation in a different light, realizing that "this quick rotation of doing and undoing, this facility of making and repealing laws, of granting charters and violating them . . . had a tendency to strike at the constitution." In a phrase he had used originally in 1778 in regard to the constitution, he castigated their proceedings agaisnt the Bank as "a dangerous precedent—that it came under the description of *governing too much.*"[25]

Paine had been in correspondence with one of the founders of the Bank, Thomas Fitzsimmons, who in March 1785 along with eleven others petitioned the Assembly to refrain from issuing paper money. On 19 April 1785, Paine wrote a long letter to Fitzsimmons, reporting his conversation with the Assembly members, setting forth various other reasons for supporting the Bank, and explaining his grounds for opposing the issuing of paper money. The capricious behavior of the Assembly in threatening to revoke the charter of the Bank, Paine considered "a lash of government," endangering the freedom of the generality of citizens, and the proposal to issue paper money he condemned as unconstitutional. The letter to Fitzsimmons was merely a preliminary step, for Paine in the next year published his constitutional principles in greatly expanded form in his *Dissertations on Government.* To his contemporaries, his defense of the Bank may have seemed on the one hand to represent a shift in his party affiliations, since he was on close personal terms with the members of the House who had voted against it, most of whom favored the constitution from which they derived their powers. Paine was equally devoted to the constitution and conceiving that it was threatened by the erratic behavior of the House, he placed abstract principles over party affiliation. In so doing, he consciously took the risk of alienating his friends and supporters and at the same time losing the compensation for his prior services during the war which he expected to receive from the House. According to one conservative interpretation of Paine's economic theories, he was a radical in supporting the constitution, but conservative in defending the Bank.[26] This is a misleading dichotomy, for his basic principles never varied. His only major change in opinion occurred in regard to the number of houses in the legislature. In his *Four Letters,* he was not dogmatic on the subject, but felt that the unicameral system had more advantages than the bicameral. In his writings concerning the Bank, he swung to the opposite position because of the capricious behavior of the single House in Pennsylvania. Since he had been instrumental in establishing both the Constitution of 1776 and the Bank, the second much more directly than the first, one can hardly maintain that there is a tergiversation in ideology involved in his defending them jointly.

There can be no question, however, that he had experienced a definite cooling in his personal relationships with the radical party. Early in 1784, he complained to General Lewis Morris, "The hot-headed whigs of Pennsylvania, many of whom had very little merit to boast of, effectually worked themselves out by attempting too high a hand. Instead of increasing their strength by rendering themselves respectable, they endeavored to monopolize the government in order to be formidable, till at last they lost what they had." Paine opposed power politics and personal aggrandizement, whether on the part of the popular or the aristocratic forces.

Paine launches his *Dissertations on Government* with a discussion of the concept of "sovereign power," the principle common to every form of government. Defined as "a power over which there is no control, and which controls all others," the concept is identical with Rousseau's concept of sovereignty as the exertion of the general will, which Paine had suggested in his *Crisis Extraordinary*, 3 April 1782. In this earlier essay, as we have already seen, Paine uses the term *majesty* instead of *sovereignty*.[27] The use of the latter term in 1786 may mean that Paine had been reading or rereading Rousseau during the interim. In continuing his discussion, however, Paine follows an independent course, treating only two of the possible forms of government, despotic monarchies, or government by a single person, and republics, or government by the people. Paine affirms that "the people in America are the fountain of power."[28] A despotic government has no guiding principle but the will of a single man; whereas a republic is directed by fundamental principles of right and justice, from which there cannot be any deviation. In this broad affirmation, Paine is laying the basis for viewing the revoking of the Bank charter as a turning away from republicanism toward despotism. Declaring that public good is the object of republican government, he carefully explains that public good is not opposed to the good of individuals, but is the good of all: "for as the public body is every individual collected, so the public good is the collected good of those individuals."[29] This distinction has some resemblance to that of Rousseau between the general will and the will of everybody, the first representing a common interest and the second a composite of all private interests,[30] even though Paine talks in terms of good and Rousseau talks of will.

Paine affirms that when a people agree to form a republican government they at the same time concur to seek public good and maintain the rule of equal justice. Then he adds an element which neither Rousseau nor any previous thinker had specified—that the mutual compact renounces "the power of exercising, at any future time any species of despotism." In this sentence, Paine establishes his rejection of capricious and arbitrary action by the government and at the same time prepares for his doctrine that no generation may exert its powers over subsequent ones. According to Paine, the citizens of Pennsylvania made their pledge and compact to this effect by means of the Bill of Rights in their constitution.

Paine clearly sees the potential dangers in majority rule, which he calls "the despotism of numbers." He observes that "despotism may be more effectually acted by many over a few, than by one man over all."[31] As a general principle this is undoubtedly true, but Paine has difficulty in showing how it is related to the revocation of the Bank charter. This is one of the few places in his works when his thought seems tangled and vague. Going back to what he calls "the people in their original compact of equal justice," which he has already identified with the Bill of Rights of the constitution, he declares that they have renounced "a right of breaking and violating their engagements, contracts and compacts with, or defrauding, imposing or tyrannizing over each other."[32] He adds that a despotic monarch could do so, but not a republic nor the legislature of Pennsylvania. The intended application of this is apparent, even though Paine has not yet mentioned the Bank or its charter. His argument is, nevertheless, weak precisely because his general principle is not clearly linked to the practical problem he is attempting to solve. He next admits, moreover, that experience with republicanism is still so limited that many public laws and acts may be discovered to be inconsistent with republican principles. The legislature cannot operate hastily as committees during the Revolution had done to attain the interest of the moment, but it must be governed by rules and principles.

The basic problem is to decide whether such acts as granting a charter are actually inviolable contracts and, if so, how long they must remain in force. Paine states that the powers of the legislature consist of two entirely different categories; first, the making of laws; second, the acting as agents or negotiators for the commonwealth in treating circumstances of the moment. The first category may be changed by succeeding legislatures; the second may not. According to Paine's perspective, all laws are acts, but all acts are not laws. Laws have "universal operation" in the sense that they apply to every individual in the commonwealth; they concern only one party, the public as a whole, but comprise each individual in the whole. Since the entire public is affected by them, they may legitimately be repealed or altered. Acts, however, are individual, not universal. They are contracts between two parties, the state and a second party, and they have the same binding character as contracts between civil parties. Paine does not treat the various classes of laws, but he attempts to classify "acts of agency or negotiation." His distinction between laws and acts is theoretically plausible, but dubious in practical application. He considers, for example, acts of taxation as laws, but it could just as well be argued that these acts are not universal in scope (applying as they do to specified groups, such as landholders, property-owners, or purchases of specific commodities) and that they have two parties rather than one.

Paine establishes two categories of legislative acts; first, those in which matters in the contract are definite and agreed to in a fixed relationship; and, second, those in which only general conditions are stated and particular terms left to be settled at a later date.[33] An example of the first kind would be a state in need of money which passes an act setting forth terms of borrowing and these terms being accepted by a person or persons. Such an act would be binding. An example of the second kind would be a state in need of money which likewise passes an act setting forth terms of borrowing, but in the event of the whole sum not being borrowed, leaves the way open for a subsequent Assembly to make new terms for the remaining amount. Paine's fundamental principle is that "the greatness of one party cannot give it a superiority or advantage over the other." If we grant that an act cannot be changed, it would be even more "inconsistent and irrational, despotic and unjust," according to Paine, to make one "with the professed intention of breaking up a contract already signed and sealed."[34]

Finally applying his theory to the situation in Pennsylvania, Paine affirms that a charter such as that extended to the Bank is a contract or joint act, which cannot be dissolved unilaterally. Paine reminds his readers of the financial history of the Revolution, that in the dark days of 1780, when the only resource was private credit, Paine and others had subscribed their funds, for the organizing of a Bank, having as its primary purpose the supplying of the governmental treasury. The members of the House, including those who later turned against the Bank, were then only too glad to take advantage of the sudden restoration of public and private credit which took place. Paine maintains that the attack on the Bank has been organized by the Assembly members themselves, and not their constituents, the people at large. The Assembly was charged to investigate the workings of the Bank, he further claims, but they had made inquiries only among themselves and reached predetermined conclusions.[35] The only section in the report of the committee of investigation to which Paine attaches any value is the objection that the Bank according to its charter is "to exist forever." This concept gives Paine the occasion of developing the theme of the political power of one generation extending to future ones, or governing "beyond the grave." He analyzes the subject at much greater length than in his more famous communication to Jefferson two years later, which has been interpreted as the first treatment of the topic in American intellectual history.[36] His major principle—the concept which was to become the keystone of his later argument against Burke's theory of precedent—is succinctly set forth in the following sentences:

> As we are not to live forever ourselves, and other generations are to follow us, we have neither the power nor the right to govern them, or to say how they shall govern themselves. It is the summit of human vanity, and shows a covetousness of power beyond the grave, to be dictating to the world to come.[37]

Paine suggests that the Constitution should have a clause mandating that all acts and laws should cease of themselves at the expiration of a period of "about thirty years" and then either be reenacted or go into oblivion. In England he later revised this period to twenty-one years.[38]

Paine is not at all clear as to whether he means that the Bank charter should exist for only thirty years or whether the charter is an act of perpetual duration. All of his pragmatic arguments tend toward removing the

Bank from government interference. "If corporate bodies are, after their incorporation," he says, "to be annually dependent on an assembly for the continuance of their charter, the citizens which compose those corporations are not free." Even though he is specifically opposing merely annual dependence, this comment seems to advocate a perpetual arrangement. Yet a few pages later, Paine unequivocally says that the determination of whether the charter is a law of universal operation or a contract between the public and the Bank "is a question of law and not a question of legislation, and must be decided on in a court of justice and not by a house of assembly."[39]

In turning to the question of paper money, Paine combines the labor theory of value which he had suggested in *Common Sense* with the scarcity theory, that is, the view that certain objects or commodities are considered precious merely because they are in short supply. In essence, he argues that gold and silver always retain their value, but paper money without security behind it has no inherent value at all and loses whatever associated value it may have in proportion to increases in the amount issued. Paine denounces the Assembly for making paper money legal tender, describing all tender laws as "tyrannical and unjust, and calculated to support fraud and oppression." As a major reform, he advocates that the security of the bank and that of the government be merged for the purpose of issuing specie notes, that is, paper money which could be exchanged for hard money at stated periods and quantities.

Even though Paine's compensation was being considered by the Assembly at the time of the publishing of his *Dissertations,* he makes no effort to conceal his disenchantment with the behavior of that body. He affirms that the dire mistake of the unicameral legislature in passing a legal tender bill has caused him to rethink his previous advocacy of a single legislature. He now considers that a single house may be more easily manipulated by parties than a legislature of two houses. "When party operates to produce party laws, a single house is a single person, and subject to the haste, rashness and passion of individual sovereignty. At least, it is an aristocracy."[40] This may seem to be relatively mild criticism, but we need to remember that for Paine aristocracy is worse than monarchy. He was soon to make his objections to a single house even more vigorous and vehement.

Paine apparently felt that the somewhat formal and theoretical treatment accorded to the Bank in his *Dissertations* was not sufficient in itself to rally public opinion, and so he contributed a number of supplementary essays on the subject to Philadelphia newspapers between March 1786 and March 1787.[41] These for the most part reflect his opinion that the controversy over the Bank has nothing to do with political principles or political parties, but that the turmoil has come about because of the selfish expectations of the opponents of the Bank to derive personal gain from its downfall. In April 1786, he observes that no subject treated by the legislature of Pennsylvania ever drew such a large audience as that of the Bank and that the debate went on for four days.[42] He again criticizes a single legislature, considering it as good for carrying on a war, but not for regulating the affairs of peace. "That which was then its blessing is now its curse. Things are done too rashly."[43] He shows the interrelationship between the constitution, the single legislature, and the attempt to overthrow the Bank, by affirming that the revoking of its charter "could not fail to create an apprehension which would grow into a belief, that a single legislature, by having it in its power to act with such instant rashness, and without restraint, was a form of government that might be as dangerous to liberty, as a single person."[44] In keeping with his charge that greed, not principle, lay behind the opposition to the Bank, he accuses various "monied men" of seeking its downfall because it places smaller businessmen on an equal level with them.

This accusation takes no account of the actual circumstance that much of the antagonism to the Bank came from the frontier settlers, who had previously made common cause with Paine in the struggle against the proprietary interests. Paine disposes of the frontier parts of the state by observing that under present conditions the settlers have no need of commercial facilities, but the time will come when they will turn into farmers, have products to sell, and then need the Bank. He also cites the flourishing manufacturers and mechanics of New England, attributing their prosperity to their having banished paper money. In language which seems strange from the pen of one of America's greatest ideologues, he concludes that the experience of the New England states "is preferable to all the reasoning that can be offered on the subject."

In an essay in the *Pennsylvania Gazette,* 20 September 1786, which has never been reprinted, Paine comes out unequivocally against a single legislature, exploring at length the disadvantages of unicameralism. He bitterly condemns the revoking of the charter of the Bank as proof that a single legislature ruled by party prejudice "is capable of being made a compleat aristocracy for the time it exists." Because of "the superabundance of its power, and the uncontrouled rapidity of its execution," he charges that it may become "as dangerous to the principles of liberty as that of a despotic monarchy." In a following essay in the *Gazette,* 8 November 1786, which also has not been reprinted, Paine declaims against legal tender acts which place paper money on the same footing as specie. These acts cannot be justified under the principles of civil government, he maintains, for they take away a man's share of civil and natural freedom and render his property insecure. This would be the actual effect of forcing a man to accept paper money as payment of a debt which had been incurred with hard money.

Paine's last discussion of the Bank took place in the spring of 1787, when a bill had been introduced in the Assembly to restore its charter, but its opponents brought various delaying tactics into play. In an essay in the *Pennsylvania Gazette,* 7 March 1787, Paine summarizes the sordid history of the struggle over the Bank and concludes that a country under the management of the crazy-brained politicians who conducted the opposition to it "would be a perpetual scene of distraction and poverty."[45]

18
The Circle of Civilization

Shortly after the publication in May 1782 of the *Crisis* No. 11, which was devoted in large measure to a defense of the American alliance with France, Paine published a far more ambitious work concerned with the same subject, as well as what he described as the enlightened field of philosophical reflection." This work was the longest single one which Paine had written up to that time, a pamphlet entitled *A Letter to the Abbé Raynal on the affairs of North America: in which the Mistakes in the Abbé's Account of the Revolution of America are Convicted and Cleared Up*. Raynal was an influential French *philosophe*, now considered to be, along with Voltaire, Rousseau, and Diderot, one of the four most important intellectual predecessors of the French Revolution. Paine's enemy George Chalmers, however, dismissed Raynal as "one of the metaphysical statesmen of the age, who writes history, as men take cathartics, for discharging crudities, or for the pleasure of evacuation."[1] In his magnum opus, *Histoire philosophique et politique des . . . deux Indes*, to which Diderot is supposed to have contributed generously, Raynal lavishly sprinkled elements of progressive religious and political philosophy. Paine's attention was drawn, not by these advanced ideas, which he undoubtedly would have found congenial, but by a somewhat superficial account of American political history which appeared in a supplementary volume entitled *Révolution de l'Amérique*.

Before making his trip to France during the summer of 1781, Paine had the idea of writing a pamphlet for circulation in England treating political questions from the American point of view. This was to appear anonymously "as from a person who had made the Tour of America" incognito.[2] When he arrived in Paris, he confided his scheme to Franklin, who agreed that it "might be done with advantage." The brevity of his sojourn in France, however, prevented him from carrying out the project. Paine later confided to Robert Livingston in 1789 that the appearance of Raynal's history had afforded him "some opportunity," or pretext for issuing his pamphlet, but not as full or complete as he would have wished. He added his conviction that "so far as the press can be employed toward completing the System of America that it can be used to much greater advantage at this time in Europe than here."[3]

Paine borrowed an English translation of Raynal's work in the fall of

1781, soon after returning from France, and immediately realized that a reply on ideological grounds could both advance the cause of the American Revolution abroad and enhance his personal literary reputation. As he later revealed, the abbé's mistakes "afforded me, in part, the opportunity I had wished for, of throwing out a publication that should reach Europe, and by obtaining a general reading there, put the affairs of America and the revolution in the point of light in which they ought to be viewed."[4]

Paine's answer to Raynal, therefore, represents the beginning of a third category of his writings: those intended primarily for an international market, or readers outside of the United States. His first category obviously consists of those works written for America, including *Common Sense* and the *Crisis;* and his second, those written for Pennsylvania alone, including *Four Letters* and polemics over the Bank. It does not follow, however, that the letter to Raynal represents Paine's first literary use of international materials or his turning away from a purely nationalistic perspective to think in international terms. Among many other notable passages in prior works incorporating a worldwide perspective, he affirms in *Common Sense* that "we claim brotherhood with every European Christian and triumph in the generosity of the sentiment," and in *Crisis* No. 7 he maintains that "My principle is universal. My attachment is to all the world, and not to any particular part."[5] In the same number of the *Crisis* he attacks the principle of national pride which leads to war, and in *Crisis* No. 8 he condemns a nationalistic spirit in science and learning. Paradoxically, his writings intended primarily for American readers deal with principles of government in abstract terms; whereas the letter to Raynal is the first of Paine's writings which gives detailed treatment to particular American grievances against Great Britain, such as the tax on tea.

Although Paine certainly considered his *Letter to the Abbé Raynal* as a means of obtaining a reputation as an international literary figure, he also had a more immediate object in mind—to gratify the Chevalier de la Luzerne, the French minister to the United States. It was this French diplomat who urged Paine to write his *Crisis* No. 11 in May 1782 and paid him an undetermined amount for doing so.[6] La Luzerne also wanted Paine to write a history of the American Revolution, setting forth the United States, France, and England in their true light, naturally to the advantage of the first two. In a sense Paine's reply to Raynal consists of a preliminary attempt to write such a history, for it contains a good deal of information concerning military, financial, and diplomatic affairs of America since 1776. On 28 August 1782, La Luzerne wrote to his superior, the Count de Vergennes in Paris, enclosing a copy of Paine's pamphlet with the following explanation: "the attached work having as its purpose the refutation of the rash principles contained in the work published under the name of the Abbé Raynal and of demonstrating the falsity of his assertions in regard to the causes and aims of the alliance, I have remitted to Mr. Payne 50 guineas, and I have exhorted him to exercise his pen on objects of the same kind."[7] It is clear that Paine had both financial and literary reasons for his commentary on Raynal. Like *Crisis* No. 11 it could legitimately be described as the product of his "*frenchified* politics."[8]

Paine was actually more concerned about the reception of his work in Europe than in the United States, and he carefully left out any republican propaganda which might have proved offensive. His plan envisaged that "all partiality to forms of government or defence of any one in preference to another should be omitted, and the facts of the revolution only attended to, with such reflections on them as may serve to promote the general good and peace of mankind without disturbing their modes of government."[9] This is consistent with the implication in *Crisis* No. 2 that he had no interest at that time in interfering with the monarchical form of government in England.[10]

Paine introduces his letter with a discussion of literary ethics, plagiarism, and the need for a copyright law. The English translator of Raynal's *History* had encountered a manuscript copy of the text even before it had been printed in any form in France. He had immediately gone to work on the translation and published it with encomiums on the author and protestations that he had been motivated solely by thoughts of the benefit that his own beloved country would receive from Raynal's material. Condemning the translator's work as embezzlement and rejecting his professions of patriotism as hypocrisy, Paine labeled his action "a breach of civil manners and literary justice." He also affirmed that the circumstance of France and England's being at war was no apology for literary depredation. In a footnote, Paine drew attention to the need for protecting literary property in America, called for future legislation on the subject, and praised Russia in his times and France in the reign of Louis XIV for the "close attention" and "wide encouragement" given by these nations to every branch of science and learning.[11] After the Revolution, Paine made personal efforts to obtain a copyright law, a further example of his pioneering in social reform.

In his letter to Raynal, Paine observes that he has not been deterred by the French author's "distinguished reputation" from revealing where he has "extolled without a reason, and wounded without a cause." Raynal, as a philosopher, would wish the truth to be known, and therefore Paine, instead of offering a complimentary apology, affirms his motives—which are merely those of doing justice. He admits that it is too early to write the history of the Revolution, for "things, like men, are seldom understood rightly at first sight," an echo of the statement in *Common Sense* that it is "seldom that our first thoughts are truly correct."

Paine's primary reason for writing against Raynal is that the latter denied that the colonists had a valid reason for their revolt—that all of their grievances boiled down to a slight tax. Paine quotes the offending passage:

> None of those energetic causes, which have produced so many revolutions upon the globe, existed in North America. Neither religion nor

> laws had there been outraged. The blood of martyrs or patriots had not there streamed from scaffolds. Morals had not there been insulted. Manners, customs, habits, no object dear to nations, had there been the sport of ridicule. Arbitrary power had not there torn any inhabitant from the arms of his family and friends, to drag him to a dreary dungeon. Public order had not been there inverted. The principles of administration had not been changed there; and the maxims of government had there always remained the same. The whole question was reduced to the knowing whether the mother country had, or had not, a right to lay, directly or indirectly, a slight tax upon the colonies.[12]

No doubt Raynal derived this interpretation of the Revolution from reading John Dickinson's *Farmer's Letters,* which had experienced a certain vogue in France and had particularly impressed Raynal's collaborator Diderot. Dickinson's work is primarily pragmatic, and he confines himself to such particular and specific issues as taxation without representation, the authority of Parliament to regulate trade but not to raise revenue, the distinction between external and internal taxes, and the relationship between virtue and liberty.[13] This is in sharp contrast to the abstract reasoning of *Common Sense,* which assumes as its primary object the moral justification of American independence, which is carried over as the theme of Paine's *Letter* to Raynal.

Before returning into the area of abstract reasoning, however, Paine takes Raynal's list of valid and concrete causes and argues that in order to carry weight they must be located in a specific period of time. He grants that they may not have existed before 1763 but insists that they had all emerged before 1776. Indeed all the inequities of despotism were comprised, according to Paine, in the Declaratory Act which affirmed the right of Parliament "to bind America in all cases whatsoever." According to Paine, this is the only instance in the history of mankind in which tyranny has been established by law. It is undoubtedly significant that in *Common Sense,* in which Paine's primary target is the monarchy, he plays down the role of Parliament, denying that it is worthwhile "to expend millions for the sake of getting a few vile acts repealed," whereas in his answer to Raynal, Parliamentary oppression assumes a position of central importance.[14]

He argues that the Declaratory Act in itself had the effect of displacing or nullifying all the original charters or compacts within the colonies. Had this single act of legislation been applied to England, it would have had the same effect as revoking the Magna Charta, the Bill of Rights, and the right to trial by jury. For Paine, this was ample proof that the Revolution was not being waged, as Raynal asserted, over "a *slight* tax." It was not a question of tax, but of principle. Raynal would have been right, according to Paine, had he asserted that the causes which produced the Revolution in America were different from those which had caused upheavals in other parts of the world. In America, the Revolution came as a result of knowing the principle of "the value and quality of liberty, the nature of government, and the dignity of man."[15] Later in life Paine admitted that independence would have been inevitable for America sooner or later, but he informs Raynal that it could have taken place only at "the exact time it was."[16] A Declaration of Independence after July 1776 would have been too late. Previous revolutions, Paine adds, had been primarily changes in dynasties and had not been accompanied, as was the one in America, by reformation in either government or manners. Paine repeats from his *Four Letters* and *Crisis* No. 7 his charge that Parliament deliberately provoked the Americans to rebel in order to establish absolute control over their property and revenue. "It was the fixed determination of the British Cabinet to quarrel with America at all events."[17]

Proceeding next to Raynal's summary of the military history of the Revolution, Paine rejects it as short, barren, and full of omissions. He therefore recounts in some detail the events taking place between the retreat of the American forces from Long Island and the defeat of the Hessians, probably because he had himself been either an observer or a participant during much of this action. In the course of his narrative, he glorifies Washington for taking Trenton and subsequently retreating from it. He observes that the "combination of equivocal circumstances, falling within what the Abbé styles *'the wide empire of chance,'* would have afforded a fine field for thought."[18] Here Paine suggests the possibility of a strong element of chance or gratuitous circumstances in human events, whereas in his other major writings, particularly *Common Sense,* and even *Age of Reason,* he attributes crucial happenings to divine providence.

From the military campaign, Paine abruptly turns to a vindication of Congress for issuing paper money in such large quantities that it depreciated to a fraction of its face value. Paine ingeniously compares this decrease in value of an entire currency to a system of taxation which would likewise have an effect on the entire population. According to Paine, "every man depreciated his own money by his own consent."[19] The currency was issued for the purpose of carrying on the war, and nobody expected it to turn into gold and silver. Although Paine terms the currency experiment an example of the "majesty of the multitude," he also admits that the plan was not intentional, that it was not foreseen that the expenses of the war would be met in this manner. Significantly, when he later wrote in 1786 against the emission of paper money by the Pennsylvania Assembly, he conveniently made no mention of his theory of a depreciated currency as a type of voluntary taxation. Paine assures Raynal that despite the heavy debt which the United States accumulated, it now has ample supplies of merchandise and a monetary system based on gold and silver. He admits that it is hard to explain how this stable condition arose, but affirms pragmatically "they are facts, and facts are more powerful than arguments." This is the same anti-ideological sentiment which he would utter four years later in the Bank controversy: "We have the experience of the New England states before us, which is preferable to all the reasoning that can be offered on the subject."[20]

Paine next answers Raynal's assertion that the Americans rejected a British peace proposal in 1778 only because their confidence had been restored by promises of forthcoming aid as a result of a treaty of alliance with France. Paine demonstrates that, to the contrary, the British proposals had been repudiated eleven days before knowledge of the French treaty had arrived in the United States. The Americans had never considered yielding and never would have. Having the record set straight in this way was important to Paine's patron La Luzerne. If Raynal were right concerning the decisive effect of the French alliance, La Luzerne might have been reproached in Paris for treating the United States as an equal and not demanding material concessions to France. The English, moreover, might have been expected to show more hostility in prosecuting the war against France if it were true that the French-American alliance alone had lost them their colonies.

At this point, Paine passes from the facts of history to pure ideology, or what he calls the "enlightened field of philosophical reflection."[21] Here he enters the final stages of his effort to prove that the American revolution has a moral purpose, a parallel aim to that in *Common Sense* of persuading the Americans themselves that independence would be morally justified. Paine expresses his disappointment at the "cynical complexion" in Raynal's statement that in an alliance between a monarchy and a people defending their liberty "the happiness of mankind has no part in it." In reply, Paine makes the astounding declaration that "it is not so properly the *motives* which *produced* the alliance, as the *consequences* which are to be *produced from it,* that mark out the field of philosophical reflection."[22] Paine does not quite come to the point of saying that the virtue of an action must be judged from its results rather than its intentions, but he certainly does not affirm the opposite, that intention is paramount. His statement is a very pragmatic one—that intentions are difficult, if not impossible, for an observer to judge, whereas consequences are visible and objective.

Here Paine is touching on an important controversy in eighteenth-century ethical thought that had been initiated by Shaftesbury in his *Inquiry concerning Virtue.* The English philosopher had maintained that both reason and affection must be present for the production of a virtuous act, that virtue consists in the affections stimulating an act which reason pronounces to be good. In short, the virtue of an act consists in its intention, not its result. Pragmatists such as Bernard Mandeville took the opposite side, that results are all-important. Although Paine does not anywhere in his works take up this abstract problem, he for the most part agrees with Shaftesbury that individual virtue proceeds from the working of benevolent affections. Also he strongly suggests in many places that it is possible to perceive a direct connection between motivation and conduct.

Paine's clearest formulation of the latter opinion appears in the first paragraph of his *Four Letters* in the affirmation that every man in public life must expect to be severely examined in regard to his motives and his conduct. Paine specifically asks how a man's motives are to be known and provides the following reply: "I answer, by tracing his conduct back on himself, as you would a stream to the fountain-head, and comparing the measures he pursues with his own private interest and dependencies; and the conclusion will be, that if no visible connexion appears between them, we are obliged, on the grounds of justice and generosity, to believe that such a man acts from reason and principle; for if this criterion be taken away, there is no other general one to know men by." This explanation can be considered as an extension of the argument in his second "Forester" letter that it is legitimate and necessary to consider personalities in political debate. He had been forced to defend this position by William Smith, who had answered Paine's first letter by quoting the affirmation in *Common Sense* that "the Object for Attention is the *Doctrine itself,* not the *Man.*" Paine replied that he had been referring in *Common Sense* merely to the rank or social position of the man, "but the political characters, political dependencies, and political connections of men, being of a public nature, differ exceedingly from the circumstances of private life; and are in many instances so nearly related to the measures they propose that to prevent our being deceived by the last, we *must* be acquainted with the first." In *Crisis* No. 7, he affirms that "the probable conduct of mankind" may be ascertained by studying "the progress of the passions."[24] In his writings on the Bank, moreover, Paine suggests that the knowledge of a man's economic situation will in large measure explain his thinking processes and behavior. "As a man's ideas are generally produced in him by his present situation and condition," Paine says, "it will naturally follow, that if you investigate his situation you will get into the channel his throughts run in, and find out their source, direction and extent."[25]

In these passages, Paine seems confident that it is possible to work back from conduct to motives and that a man's social and political status reveals the motives for his conduct. In his "Address to the People of Pennsylvania," however, he admits that these connections may possibly be obscured or concealed by false ones erected by a man's enemies. "I well know," he admits, "that when men get into parties, and suffer their tempers to become soured by opposition, how tempted they are to assign interested reasons for other people's conduct, and to undermine the force of their reasonings by sapping the reputation of the person who makes them."[26]

All this is relevant to Paine's rejection of Raynal's statement that the happiness of mankind had no part in the motives which brought about the French-American alliance. He objects that to declare this "a man must be possessed of the mind of all the parties concerned, and know that their motives were something else."[27] According to Paine, the motives of France were less interested and more philanthropic than those of America, but both nations were concerned with the happiness of mankind. America had in mind not only the advantages to herself, but numerous benefits to all humanity and a continued good to all posterity. France, however, had no need of seeking a friend, "and therefore her motive in becoming one, has the strongest evidence of being good." Turning again to generalizations, he affirms that "as a bad cause cannot be prosecuted with a good motive, so neither can a good cause be long supported by a bad one."[28] This may not flatly contradict his previous statement that it is the consequences which produced the alliance rather than the motives which count, but it is, nevertheless, hard to reconcile the two attitudes.

As though in apology, Paine observes that Raynal's observations on motives have led him "unintentionally into a train of metaphysical reasoning," and as a kind of antidote he repeats his principle that it is the consequences of the alliance that "mark out the field of philosophical reflection." In his subsequent remarks, Paine offers the American Revolution as evidence of the validity of the doctrine of progress. By way of introduction he refers to "an observation I have already made in some former publications, that the circle of civilization is yet incomplete."[29] Apparently the expression "circle of civilization" has no reference to a cyclical theory of history which it might seem to imply, but concerns a particular aspect of the doctrine of progress, the process in social evolution by which mutual wants force individuals to form national societies. Paine felt at the time of writing that the "progress of civilization has stopped." He looks forward to a future completing of a civilization of nations, however, a type of international society. No precise statement concerning this "circle of civilization" is to be found in any of Paine's previous works known at the present time, and it may be that there are others such as his *Four Letters* remaining to be discovered. He may, on the other hand, be alluding merely to a variety of passages in earlier writings in which he suggests the formation of future compacts among nations without fully explaining his concept or using the expression "the circle of civilization." One such passage in *Common Sense* argues that all Europeans meeting each other in other continents such as America consider themselves as countrymen, "for England, Holland, Germany, or Sweden, when compared with the whole, stand in the same places on the larger scale, which the divisions of street, town, and county do on the smaller ones."[30] Another passage in the "Forester" letters refers approvingly to Rousseau's proposal for a perpetual European peace, the forming of "a kind of European Republic."[31] *Crisis* No. 7 concerns the false concept of national honor which keeps nations apart: "In a Christian and philosophical sense, mankind seems to have stood still at individual civilization, and to retain as nations all the original rudeness of nature."[32] Paine also discerns an "easy and natural line" between "the domestic politics of a family" and those of a nation. In another *Crisis,* written after the letter to Raynal, he affirms that "each state is to the United States what each individual is to the state he lives in."[33] The emphasis in *Crisis* No. 13 upon the union of the American states is in the same vein: "It is with confederated states as with individuals in society; something must be yielded up to make the whole secure. In this view of things we gain by what we give, and draw an annual interest greater than the capital."[34] None of these passages, however, specifically advocates an international union and only one uses the word *civilization*.

In his letter to Raynal, Paine does not state precisely the nature of the international alliance or collaboration which he would like to see, whether international cooperation, an association of nations, or world government. He concentrates instead on practical measures for attaining international understanding and avoiding war. As the times in which he is writing had been ripe for the formation of the United States of America, there was also "a greater fitness in mankind to extend and complete the civilization of nations with each other . . . than there was to begin it with the unconnected individuals at first. . . . The wants of the individual, which first produced the idea of society, are now augmented into the wants of the nation, and he is obliged to seek from another country what before he sought from the next person."[35] The first sign of advancing civilization which Paine specifies is the growth of letters, science and philosophy. In the barbarian world, hunting and war were the only occupations of mankind, but in the modern world man studies "arts, sciences, agriculture and commerce, the refinements of the gentleman, the principles of society, and the knowledge of the philosopher." Here Paine echoes the sentiments of "An Act for Incorporating the American Philosophical Society," which he had transcribed two years earlier in 1780 as clerk of the Pennsylvania Assembly, as well as his *Crisis* No. 8 in the same year, setting forth the principle that the study of "universal science" carries the mind from the boundaries of a single nation to the entire creation.[36]

Turning to the evils of war as a vestige of barbarism, Paine explains why, in his opinion, the modern world is ready to abandon warfare as a political instrument. Commerce, for example, has not only widened man's horizons, but given him a method of obtaining exotic productions different from the barbarian one of war. Indeed Paine is so optimistic concerning the mutual advantages of trade and commerce that he maintains that "experience has exploded the notion of going to war for the sake of profit," almost a direct quotation from *Crisis* No. 7 where he says that mankind in general believe "that it can never be worth their while to go to war for profit's sake."[37] Unfortunately this state of affairs seems never to have existed outside of Paine's mind, and his assurance of its reality tends to discredit his primary thesis of human progress.

He is perhaps on firmer ground when he specifies national prejudice as a major cause of war, and the eradication of unfounded opinions concerning the vices and odious behavior of other nations as a means of establishing peace. "Prejudice, like the spider, makes every place its home. It has neither taste nor choice of situation, and all that it requires is room. Everywhere, except in fire or water, a spider will live."[38] Paine suggests that perhaps no two events in the history of the world had done so much to expel prejudice from the world as the American Revolution and the French-American alliance, resulting as they had in social and cultural interchange. The Americans, as colonists of the British, had lived "at a distance from, and unacquainted with the world" and had absorbed all the prejudices of their governors, but after the outbreak of hostilities their minds opened out toward the world and their prejudices, like their oppressions, became subject to rational examination. The alliance with France continued the process of intellectual liberation, with the result that the French and American peoples experienced a union of mind as well as interest.

Paine clung to his theory of combating national prejudices as a means of attaining international peace, and it figured significantly in his intellectual preparation for writing *Rights of Man.* In 1787 Paine made a trip to Paris with the hope of obtaining backing for the erection of an iron bridge of his design. While there he made the acquaintance of Abbé Morellet, a *philosophe* in the confidence of Archbishop Loménie de Brienne, at that time minister of finance. Paine wrote a long letter to Morellet on the subject of bringing about permanent peace between England and France, a letter which Morellet showed to the minister and answered in writing with Brienne's knowledge.[39] Paine, in his letter to Morellet, affirms that the major obstacle to harmony between the two nations consists in the "vulgar passions and prejudices" of the common people, and he explores at great length the reasons for the British errors and prejudices against the French nation. He later sent this correspondence to Edmund Burke with the expectation that Burke would use it as the basis of negotiations for a permanent peace. In *Rights of Man,* Paine describes his correspondence with Morellet and castigates Burke for failing to pursue the opportunities it had provided for diplomatic action.

In his reply to Raynal, Paine considers the French-American alliance as a step toward universal union. He embarks, therefore, on a long defense of the compact, not only supporting his ideology, but also showing La Luzerne that the latter's financial investment has been justified. He denies Raynal's opinion that the British are praiseworthy for having rejected an offer on the part of Spain in 1779 to act as a peace negotiator. According to Raynal, the British felt that negotiations at that time would have been a sign of weakness and being faced with the choice between ruin and dishonor determined to sacrifice their existence rather than their glory. Paine bluntly retorts that the British were prompted by vanity, not fortitude, since they still expected to win. Raynal should have praised instead the Americans for their having rejected British proposals in 1778, an action which revealed their courage, willingness to experiment, and zeal for freedom. Paine also objects to Raynal's habit of caricaturing national traits, for example, depicting the Frenchman as light and disdainful, the Spaniard jealous and shy, and the American envious and vindictive. Instead of drawing foolish portraits, according to Paine, Raynal should have dwelt upon the greatness of character and superiority of heart revealed by France in her conquests.[40]

Paine even had a personal grievance against Raynal—that he had taken from *Common Sense* without acknowledgment the fundamental distinction between government and society. To back up his accusation, Paine prints what he considers to be parallel passages in his footnotes.[41] The resemblances between the two passage are not particularly close, and it is more likely that Raynal had derived his notions from Rousseau's *Second Discourse* rather than from Paine. The fact that Paine believed that Raynal was drawing upon *Common Sense,* however, is perhaps the best proof that Paine had not read Rousseau before January 1776. His rebuke of Raynal indictate that even in 1782 he was not aware how clearly his own thought parallels Rousseau's.

Parenthetically there is a striking passage in Raynal's *History* which actually seems to have been taken from *Common Sense,* but which Paine did not notice. It appears in Raynal's discussion of the attitude which people in other parts of the world should take toward the American colonies. According to Raynal, "The name of liberty is so sweet that all those who struggle in its behalf are certain of interesting our secret vows. Their cause is that of the entire human race; it becomes our own. We obtain vengeance from our own oppressors in at least breathing out in liberty our hatred against foreign oppressors."[42] This is certainly an echo of Paine's sentiments in his "Introduction": "The cause of America is in a great measure the cause of all mankind. Many circumstances have, and will arise, which are not local, but universal, and through which the principles of all lovers of mankind are affected, and in the event of which their affections are interested."[43]

The next section of the *Letter* to Raynal is a reworking of two themes from *Crisis* No. 8, the weakening of American ties with Britain and the necessity of an international perspective in politics as well as science. The "rising generation in America," he says, no longer cares about the British Parliament or whether certain ministers have a potentially favorable attitude toward America. People in America, Paine asserts, will not agree to any terms from friendly ministers which she has disdained from unfriendly predecessors. England, therefore, needs a total reformation, "an expanded mind—a heart which embraces the universe." "Instead of shutting herself up in an island, and quarreling with the world, she would derive more lasting happiness, and acquire more real riches, by generously mixing with it."[44]

Paine looks for the day when prejudices would be removed and England would adopt friendly relations with France and Spain. Although his language is somewhat ambiguous, he seems to envision more than friendship and cooperation between nations, even an international federation. "The true idea of a great nation, is that which extends and promotes the principles of universal society; whose mind rises above the atmosphere of local thoughts, and considers mankind, of whatever nation or profession they may be, as the work of one Creator. The rage for conquest has had its fashion, and its day. Why may not the amiable virtues have the same?"[45] Such a happy state of affairs would be what Paine describes earlier in his letter as completing "the circle of civilization." This was not to Paine an unrealizable goal—it had been in his mind ever since his "Forester" letters in 1776. Paine concludes his optimistic forecast with a stylistic echo of a famous passage in *Common Sense:* "Of more worth is one honest man to society and in the sight of God, than all the crowned ruffians that ever lived."[46] He assures Raynal: "Of more use was *one* philosopher, though a heathen to the world, than all the heathen conquerors that ever existed."[47]

In an appended postscript concerned with negotiations for the treaty of peace which would bring the American Revolution to an end, Paine combines his ultimate aim of preparing the ground for international understanding with his immediate one of creating a favorable climate of opinion for French diplomacy, further to gratify his patron La Luzerne. In regard to the coming negotiations, he remarks that independence is already established and that America must be treated as a sovereign nation. Although a young country, America possesses both military strength and moral integrity. In estimating the power and worth of a nation, it is not age which counts. A right which originates today has as much validity as one which is a thousand years old. Once more introducing the relations between motives and consequences with which he began his letter, Paine observes that frequently in ordinary life as well as in politics "people complain that such or such means produced an event directly contrary to their intention." Paine replies that their fault lies in not judging correctly, "for the means produced only its proper and natural consequences."[48] There is a certain logical flaw here in that Paine confuses motives and means: it may be that a particular means will lead to a particular consequence through a chain of cause and effect, but one can never be sure of the consequences or results which will follow from the motives of an act—for example, one might fire at an intruder but hit one's father. Paine's intention, however, is not to treat a metaphysical problem, but a diplomatic one. His basic point is that Britain does not understand American psychology or the realities of the military situation. He argues that England in the negotiations should not hold out for Canada and that Gibraltar would prove a burden to her, obviously points on which the British diplomats failed to concur. Finally, Paine proposes that there should be an article in the eventual peace treaty concerning disarmament. To be sure, the limitation he suggests is far short of universal disarmament, merely that "no nation should, in time of peace, exceed a certain number of ships of war."[49]

Paine continued to reflect on measures for completing the circle of civilization, and in 1797 he published a lengthy pamphlet in both French and English setting forth an additional step toward that end. The pamphlet entitled *Compact Maritime* proposed that in time of war all neutral nations should associate and declare publicly that if any belligerent power should disturb a vessel belonging to any of the associated nations, they would all close their ports to the offending nation.[50] In his letter to Raynal, however, England is his primary target, and he concludes with the admonition that she should "reform her manners, retrench her expences, live peaceably with her neighbor and think of war no more."[51] The elements of this advice had first been manifested in *Common Sense.* Paine obviously felt that "the circle of civilization" might be rendered complete were his idealistic principles to encompass the world at large.

Most English readers no doubt passed over Paine's rhapsodies concerning the desirability of completing the circle of civilization to concentrate on the threat to the empire implied in Paine's disparaging assessment of British military power. The only published answer to the letter to Raynal came, therefore, not from Raynal himself or one of his countrymen, but from an Englishman, who in a country newspaper in 1792 and in a pamphlet of the same year attempted to answer Paine's "unjust reflections" on Great Britain.[52]

According to the author, he had written his criticism of Paine in 1783, immediately after reading Paine's pamphlet, but reflecting on the sufferings of America brought on by England and the services which Paine as the author of *Common Sense* had done for his adopted country, had kept his strictures to himself and would never have published them had Paine "not come over to Europe to propagate *his wild and dangerous notions.*" The final straw had been the republication in England in 1792 of *Common Sense* and the *Letter to the Abbé Raynal.* In reference to the concept of individual motives, which, as we have seen, Paine considered to be of great importance, the anonymous author cites the observation of Sir Brooke Boothby that those of Paine "contain the most positive and unequivocal declaration of *eternal* and *implacable* hatred" toward England. This author does not attempt to justify British treatment of the American colonies, however, but concentrates on international politics at the close of hostilities. He argues that the retention of Gibraltar, Canada, and Halifax is requisite for the future protection of British interests and points out that the brutal treatment by the French of the Corsicans proves that French policy does not reflect the principles of equity and generosity which Paine had attributed to it.

Conclusion

When the American Revolution finally came to an end, Paine proudly affirmed that it had "contributed more to enlighten the world, and diffuse a spirit of freedom and liberality among mankind, than any human event (if this may be called one) that ever preceded it."[1] Despite this emphasis upon universal enlightenment, historians have tended to overlook Paine's contribution to the intellectual foundations of the Revolution in their quite understandable concentration on his rhetorical skills. It is true that Paine's stirring words had a great deal to do with the decision of the colonies to separate from Great Britain and with upholding morale during the various crises of the struggle. But, as Paine himself has pointed out, political independence itself would probably have come about at one time or another without the great events which took place in the years immediately following July 1776. The unique character of the American Revolution as it actually occurred consisted in the complex of ideas with which it was accompanied, and the enduring elements in Paine's writings are precisely those which established or clarified these ideas.

Paine has certainly given the most penetrating discussion in American Revolutionary literature of theories concerning the origin of government, especially those related to the state of nature and the social contract. Like Rousseau, he considered the first governments to be associations of equals, and, also like Rousseau, he maintained that the general will is the sovereign power of the nation. His concept that each human being has natural rights which it is the duty of society to protect is as relevant two hundred years later as it was when he first expressed it, particularly his exposition of the relationship between natural rights and civil rights. One of the problems which Paine foresaw is becoming of major concern at the end of the twentieth century, that is, the unfortunate consequences of one generation's running future ones into debt, a problem now acute in both a literal and a figurative sense. To Paine, governing beyond the grave is an institutional injustice to which democracies and despotic governments are equally susceptible. Another potential flaw in democratic organization which Paine warned against is, in his own wording, "the despotism of numbers," a realization which indicates that Paine was not a naïve republican radical, as he has been portrayed by many personal enemies.

He did not believe that the ordered universe of natural law is necessarily reflected in political and social relationships, but rather that government would be most just and efficient if it were to be structured on orderly principles. He was fully aware of the emotional as well as the rational side of human beings. In his opinion, the best character for an individual is also the best character for a nation. He based his extensive program of social and political reform upon the opinion that man is an inherently gregarious, rational, and moral being.

Paine enunciated—and as far as he was concerned—made clear for the first time in any political discussion in America the distinction between a government and a constitution and laid the foundation for the debate over the essence of a constitution which he later waged in *Rights of Man*. Most of Paine's writing in America was concerned with the struggle for independence and the building of a new nation, but he also expressed principles of internationalism. Just as he considered each state in the United States to be what each individual is to each state, he hoped that each nation would eventually consider itself as a member of a world society. When this should happen, "the circle of civilization" would become complete. Paine realized that economic conditions spread from one nation to another and that nations are as much affected by the prosperity or lack of it in their neighbors as single states are by the welfare of the nation as a whole. He preached isolation from the European continent in regard to military and political alliances but strongly advocated international cooperation and even universal society as steps toward the eventual attaining of peace.

Less visible or distinguishable, but almost equally important in Paine's intellectual history as these single concepts, are his attitudes toward primitivism, the quarrel of the ancients and the moderns, and the doctrine of progress. Primitivism appears in Paine's thought in his association of the state of nature with virtue, his portrayal of the earliest generations in the scriptural record as happy ones, his dictum that the simplest government is the best one, and his protests against governing too much.

In the quarrel of the ancients and moderns, he sided unequivocally with the moderns and, therefore, logically accepted the doctrine of progress in nearly all of its forms. But to praise the moderns and to exalt progress cannot be reconciled with primitivism. This combination of mutually exclusive elements was by no means unusual, however, in the eighteenth century any more than it is now, for many people in all historical periods long for the quiet and beauty associated with a rural retreat while insisting on all the advantages, social and material, of modern civilization. Paine's attack on the ancients is both implied and explicit. He admitted that the Greeks and Romans possessed the spirit of liberty in the abstract, but accused them of using their power in practice to enslave the rest of mankind. He ridiculed the notion that man must continually "go back two or three thousand years for lessons and examples" and maintained that if things could be viewed in their true light, the ancients "would admire us, rather than we them."

There is scarcely a page in all of Paine's writing which does not suggest faith in general progress in one way or another. Attacking the ancients and eulogizing the American scene were both elements in his unique portrayal of the doctrine. "Improvement and the world," he announced, "will expire together." In several places he depicts the flight of liberty from Europe to the West, and in keeping with his pronouncement on improvement he asserts that when liberty "quits America she quits the world." Paine also embraced the closely related theme of the moral and physical superiority of America, almost literally maintaining his adopted land to be God's own country. He affirmed that "degeneracy here is almost a useless word," suggested that providence had deliberately provided the New World as a refuge for Europeans fleeing religious persecution, and pointed to the topographical extent and impressiveness of America as reasons for her destined greatness as an independent nation. In relation to both time and topography he contrasted the rest of the world so unfavorably with America that, as a contemporary critic objected, he seemed to believe "that every thing began the other day in America, and that nothing really had ever existed before."

Many of Paine's patriotic assumptions belong more to the area of mythology than of ideology. Blending the millenial view of America as a garden spot for a chosen people with the secular theory of progress, he argued that American prosperity derives from honest toil and the blessing of heaven. He originated claims still being put forth that the standard of living in America is the highest in the world, that its public opinion is unusually well informed, and that it has a high level of education resulting from the application of democratic principles to government. And with more fervor than logic, he promised eternal youth to America through its "power to begin the world over again."

Although somewhat equivocal in his use of Christian symbols, Paine consistently praised religious values and religious toleration. He espoused the principle of the separation of church and state and applied it to the political problems of the nation and the community. In all of his writings, moreover, Pain proclaimed the need for a high degree of morality. In *Common Sense,* he proved that independence may be justified ethically, and in each number of the *Crisis* issued during the war which followed, he consistently drew attention to the idealism of America and to the contrasting deficiencies of Great Britain. He likewise used moralistic appeals in advocating measures for international peace.

Much of his argument is simply rhetoric and propaganda, but every one of his works, nevertheless, rests upon a substantive ideological foundation. As Abigail Adams said of *Common Sense,* "everyone assents to the weighty truths it contains."[2] To be sure, Paine's writings are filled with logical incompatibilities—some of which may be resolved but others of which must be recognized as absolute contradictions. These contradictions are not apparent on the surface, however, and they in no way detract from the importance of Paine's role in the history of ideas. Nowhere does he pretend that his works represent a logically coherent philosophical system. They are brilliant examples of the use of ideology to promote social ideals and of ethical persuasion to inculcate, as Paine himself expressed it, "the idea of freedom and rights."

Appendix
Paine's Publications before *Common Sense*

Although more than a dozen newspaper and magazine pieces published in Pennsylvania between January and November 1775 have been attributed to Paine, there is not a single one which was originally published with his name. Nor is there a single one which he refers to in any later work, or which can in any other way be conclusively demonstrated to be his. Essays and poems from this period which appear in editions of Paine's works are there only because some associate of Paine has attributed them to him or because of their style or subject matter.

Most of these early works appeared for the first time in the *Pennsylvania Magazine,* on which Paine served as editorial assistant. A Philadelphia printer, Mathew Carey, in the "Advertisement" to his edition of Paine's *Works* in 1797 indicates that he had asked Aitken, Paine's employer, to identify all of the pieces in the *Pennsylvania Magazine* which were written by Paine. Following Aitken, Carey mentions, but does not reprint, a description of a new electrical machine (January) and a description of a method of building frame houses in England (April). He reprints "To the Public" and "To the Publisher" (January), "The Snow Drop and the Critic" and "New Anecdotes of Alexander the Great" (February), "Account of the Burning of Bachelor's Hall (March), "Liberty Tree" (July), and "Farmer Short's Dog Porter" (July). Many, but not all, of these pieces were published over the pseudonym "Atlanticus."

The only other contemporary attempt to ascertain Paine's early writings was that of a nineteen-year old English admirer, W. T. Sherwin, who published a list of Paine's contributions to the *Pennsylvania Magazine* in the appendix to his *Memoirs of the Life of Thomas Paine* (London, 1819). He presumably obtained his information from a "political friend" in the United States, William Clark. (Harrison T. Meserole, "W. T. Sherwin: A Little-Known Paine Biographer," *Papers of the Bibliographical Society of America* 99 [1955: 270–72). Sherwin lists all of the pieces mentioned in Carey except the description of the electrical machine and the method of building frame houses. He mentions in addition "Useful and Entertaining Hints on the Internal Riches of the Colonies" (February) and "Reflections on the Life and Death of Lord Clive" (March).

All of the above pieces may be accepted without much doubt into the

Paine canon with the possible exception of "Reflections on the Life and Death of Lord Clive." Even though Benjamin Rush also attributes the latter to Paine (in a letter to James Cheetham, 17 July 1809, L. H. Butterfield, *Letters of Benjamin Rush* [Philadelphia, 1951], 2:1008), there are circumstances which place the attribution in doubt. The essay as it appears in the March issue has no signature, but editorial comments at the end of the number (page 144) explain that "the piece entitled Reflections on the life and death of Lord Clive, on page 107, by our correspondent ATLANTICUS, had no signature to it, and was printed off before we received his directions to add it thereto." This comment, which would seem to be by Paine himself in his capacity as editor, does not suggest that Paine was the author of the piece, but the contrary.

A problem exists also in regard to the two essays in the January number, the description of an electrical machine and "To the Public." In a letter to Benjamin Franklin on 4 March 1775, Paine refers to the second number (February) which had just come out and then flatly declares, "the first I was not concerned in" (*Writings,* 2:1131). The probable explanation is that Paine in his letter is limiting himself to his post as editor and that he had written for the January number merely as a contributor. This explanation is borne out by the poem "The Snow-Drop and the Critic" in the February number, recognized as Paine's by both Carey and Sherwin, which asserts that the author of the poem and the author of "To the Public" are the same person. We are reasonably safe in concluding, therefore, that "To the Public," one of Paine's best, is actually from his pen.

There remain other essays from the *Pennsylvania Magazine,* which have been printed as Paine's by Moncure D. Conway (*The Writings of Thomas Paine,* [New York, 1894–96]) and by Philip S. Foner (*The Complete Writings of Thomas Paine* [New York, 1945]) but which are probably not by Paine at all. An essay entitled "Cupid and Hymen" in the March issue has no connection with Paine whatsoever except that it is signed "Esop," the same signature which is used for "New Anecdotes of Alexander the Great," which Carey and Sherwin accept as Paine's. The early issues of the magazine contain a series of essays entitled "The Old Bachelor." The only connection with Paine consists in the poem in the March issue "An Account of the Burning of Bachelor's Hall" also signed "The Old Bachelor," which Carey and Sherwin assign to Paine. Although none of the prose essays has any resemblance to Paine's style, a part of one of them, "Reflections on Unhappy Marriages" (June) has been printed by Conway and later editors, but with no evidence to support the attribution to Paine. Conway also accepts as Paine's an essay "Reflections on Titles" (May) signed "Vox Populi" apparently on the grounds of style and subject matter. On style all that can be said is that it is not unlike that in some of Paine's works. The theme is the absurdity of pompous titles bestowed upon unworthy men, but the essay does not by any means, as many writers have suggested, denounce titles themselves or the system of aristocracy, and it is in no way a foreshadowing of the attacks upon monarchy in *Common Sense* or upon hereditary aristocracy in *Rights of Man.* Conway prints as Paine's another political piece, "The Dream Interpreted" (May) for no apparent reason except that it summarizes the political and economic situation of the colonies. Its signature, "Bucks County," however, would seem clearly to indicate that Paine had nothing whatsoever to do with it.

For over fifty years it has been known that an "Occasional Letter on the Female Sex" (August), which Conway attributes to Paine, was actually written by a French friend of Voltaire, and that it was translated and published in London by an obscure Englishman. (Frank Smith, "The Authorship of 'An Occasional Letter on the Female Sex,'" *American Literature* 2 [1930]: 277–80.) Foner, nevertheless, declares with no authority whatsoever that "some of the language" is Paine's. Even more surprising, three of Paine's latest biographers, together with the editor of a mass printing of *Common Sense,* have persisted in attributing the entire essay to him. Despite this effort to portray Paine as a defender of women's rights, the point must be stressed that he did not write a single word of this essay.

Four other pieces printed by Conway, however, are almost certainly Paine's. His most famous poem, "The Death of General Wolfe," originally composed while he was a resident of Lewes, England, appeared in the March issue of the *Pennsylvania Magazine* with the signature Atlanticus and a musical accompaniment. According to Paine's friend Thomas Clio Rickman, the poem had been written immediately after Wolfe's heroic death and intended as an entry into a competition for an epitaph, but growing too long was entitled an "Ode" (*Life of Thomas Paine* [London, 1819], p. 257). Another poem in the March issue also with the signature Atlanticus bears the title "The Tale of the Monk and the Jew Versified." This was identified as Paine's in an early nineteenth-century English collection made by William Dugdale of *The Theological Works of Thomas Paine.* This is the only work in Conway which Foner does not carry over into his edition, but he gives no explanation for not doing so. An unsigned review in the May issue of a book against dueling, *Cursory Reflections on the Single Combat,* can be assigned to Paine on the reasonable assumption that any anonymous book review would be from the editor's pen. The essay by "A Lover of Peace" (July) can be linked to Paine, as demonstrated in chapter 2 above, by parallels in subject matter and style.

There are two other pieces in the *Pennsylvania Magazine* not reprinted in any Paine edition which may be attributed to Paine on the basis of internal evidence. First of these is the "Amicus" essay (June) which is treated in chapter 2 above.

An apparent echo of Paine's biography appears in an unsigned poem in the April number bearing the title "O What a Pity!" In a style strongly imitative of "The Deserted Village" of Goldsmith, Paine's favorite contemporary poet, the first stanza discusses the depopulation of Britain, through mass emigration to India in the East and America in the West. The rest of the poem concerns the slaughter of Americans by British troops, a reference to the Battles of Lexington and Concord. After depicting the forces of hell "exulting in the mischief" and crying, "There drops a Briton, there a Buckskin dies," the poet calls on heaven to stay "the hasty hand" of barbarous power lest future generations "brand a BRITON with a NERO's name." In the final stanza the poet calls on American armies to resist should the parent nation proceed to murder and destroy,

> Whilst I disown the place that gave me birth,
> And call my native home *A hell on earth.*

The poet, like Paine, had come to America from England as a result of overpopulation, had been horrified by the attacks of British troops on American provincials, and had disowned his native land. If Paine and the nameless poet are not the same, one wonders if there was any other literary Englishman in Philadelphia at that moment whose career and feelings could have produced "O What a Pity!" Paine reveals in *Common Sense* that the instant the events of the nineteenth of April were made known, he "rejected the hardened sullen-tempered Pharaoh of England forever"; he disdained "the wretch, that with the pretended title of FATHER OF HIS PEOPLE can unfeelingly hear of their slaughter, and composedly sleep with their blood upon his soul" (*Writings,* 1:25). This personal antipathy toward George III, which Paine later made even more explicit in his most widely circulated poem, "To the King of England" (A. O. Aldridge, "The Poetry of Thomas Paine, PMBH 79 [1955]: 93), is suggested in "O What a Pity!"

> Ye, one, or all, whatever be your name,
> Look kindly down, and check the barb'rous flame.
> Teach British hearts the power of nature's law,
> And kings to know a murder from a war.

Perhaps the most widely discussed of all the works attributed to Paine before *Common Sense* is an antislavery essay signed "Justice and Humanity" which appeared in the *Pennsylvania Journal,* Postscript to 8 March 1775. This has been accepted as Paine's by Conway as well as subsequent editors and biographers because of a passage in Benjamin Rush's autobiography describing his first acquaintance with Paine.

> About the year 1773 I met him accidentally in Mr. Aitkin's bookstore, and was introduced to him by Mr. Aitkin. We conversed a few minutes and I left him. Soon afterwards I read a short essay with which I was much pleased, in one of Bradford's papers, against the slavery of Africans in our country, and which I was informed was written by Mr. Paine.

> This excited my desire to be better acquainted with him. We met soon afterwards in Mr. Aitkin's bookstore, where I did homage to his principles and pen upon the subject of the enslaved Africans. He told me the essay to which I alluded was the first thing he had ever published in his life. After this Mr. Aitkin employed him as the editor of his *Magazine*, with a salary of fifty pounds currency a year. (L. M. Butterfield, ed., *Letters of Benjamin Rush* [Princeton, N.J., 1951], 9:1007).

Rush gave this account in 1809 to James Cheetham, long after he had become bitterly alienated from Paine because of the latter's attack on the Bible in his *Age of Reason*. Cheetham, who was even more hostile toward Paine and who had publicly declared his enmity, had asked Rush for materials to be used in his life of Paine, which was eventually published and can be considered the first muckraking biography in American literature. Rush's chronology is inaccurate, since Paine did not set foot in Philadelphia until November 1774. Also there is no essay by Paine on slavery in the newspaper published by Thomas Bradford, the *Pennsylvania Journal and the Weekly Advertiser,* prior to Paine's becoming editor of Aitken's enterprise, the *Pennsylvania Magazine*. Cheetham, who lists in his biography many of Paine's miscellaneous works, makes no mention of any essay on slavery by Paine, apart from quoting Rush's letter, nor do Paine's contemporary English biographers or editors.

Conway, however, identified as Paine's essay "against the slavery of Africans in our country" the "Justice and Humanity" piece in the March 1775 *Pennsylvania Journal*. Although no subsequent writer on Paine has doubted this attribution, there is absolutely no valid reason for assuming that this essay is Paine's. Apart from the fact that it appeared after he had begun to work for Aitken, is subsequent to other essays from his pen, and could not possibly be "the first thing he had ever published," even in America, it has no resemblance in style to any of Paine's acknowledged works. The author seems to be an evangelical Christian, possibly a Quaker, who is not sympathetic to the political grievances of the colonists. He asks them to consider whether they can with decency or consistency "complain so loudly of attempts to enslave them, while they hold so many hundred thousands in slavery." He also uses a number of phrases typical of evangelical Christianity such as "divine religion," "the common Lord of all," and "Redeemer's cause," a vocabulary completely alien to Paine even in those works in which he attempted to appeal to the tradition of his Christian readers. The essayist also cites a number of English ecclesiastics such as Ames, Baxter, and Durham, whom it is very doubtful Paine ever read. Conway and other scholars have tried to explain away the chronology of this essay—its appearing in print several weeks after Paine's becoming editor of the *Pennsylvania Magazine*—by theorizing that Rush saw the essay in manuscript before its publication. Rush actually says, however, that he saw it in "one of Bradford's papers."

Conway also attributed to Paine a subsequent newspaper piece against slavery, this one signed "Humanus," which appeared in the *Pennsylvania Journal,* 18 October 1775, and no subsequent writers on Paine have rejected it. Certainly it has more claim that "Justice and Humanity" to be considered Paine's. Its style resembles that of Paine, and Conway maintains that a certain "Mr. Moreau mentions it as Paine's in his M S. notes in a copy of Cheetham's book, now owned by the Pennsylvania Historical Society" (*The Life of Thomas Paine* [New York, 1892], 1:59). Mr. Marc S. Gallichio of the Manuscript Division of the Society informs me in March 1978, however, that "I have checked the only copy of Chetham's *Life of Thomas Paine* in our possession, and did not find any pencilled notations in the entire volume." The chief importance of the "Humanus" essay lies not in its references to "the horrid cruelties exercised by Britain in the East Indies" or to her ravaging "the hapless shores of Africa, robbing it of its unoffending inhabitants to cultivate her stolen dominions in the West," significant as these themes certainly are, but in the author's expressed belief that "the Almighty will finally separate America from Britain. Call it independence or what you will, if it is the cause of God and humanity it will go on." This prediction was published 18 October 1775, nearly three months before *Common Sense.*

In revealing the inadequacy of the evidence for Paine's authorship of the "Justice and Humanity" essay, I am not seeking to deprive Paine of the distinction of being an early opponent of slavery, for he did speak out on the subject. It is important, however, to distinguish between works which are clearly his and those which are improperly attributed to him. The earliest known antislavery pronouncement which can positively be assigned to Paine is the cryptic sentence, "Forget not the hapless *African,*" which he published as the Forester in April 1776. Paine is sometimes given credit for drawing up the Preamble to an act emancipating slaves which was passed by the Pennsylvania Assembly, 1 March 1780, but there is no valid reason to assume that he was the author. He was not a member of the Assembly, but merely the copyist.

The most explicit defense of black people attributed to Paine is found in a manuscript poem written during the French Revolution and now in the Morgan Library. The following is the third stanza:

See Afric's wretched Offspring torn
From all that human heart holds dear,
See Millions doomed in Chains to Mourn,
Unpitied even, by a Tear.
See Asia and her fertile plains
Where once the Bramin dwelt serene,
Now ravaged by the thirst for Gain,
Till Famine ends the dismal Scene.

Notes

Chapter 1. **Common Sense** *and the History of Ideas*

1. James Cheetham, *Life of Thomas Paine* (New York, 1809), p. 24.

2. Talcott Parsons, *The Social System* (New York, 1951), pp. 354, 349.

3. Quoted by Audrey Williamson, *Thomas Paine, His Life, Work, and Times* (New York, 1973), p. 190.

4. Foner, ed., *Writings,* 1:46. A humorous portrayal of the similarities between *Common Sense* and *Rights of Man* is given in a late edition of one of the most effective attacks on Paine ever published. This is a putative defense of his writings by George Chalmers under the pseudonymn Francis Oldys. Here Chalmers accuses Paine of plagiarisms upon himself. "Much of *Rights of Man* is obviously borrowed from his own *Common Sense.* This treated of society and civilization, so does that; this gave the origin and design of governments, so does that; this writes of monarchy and succession, so does that . . . . The sentiments of the last are merely the echoes of the first; and thus Paine performs the office of his own magpie." *The Life of Thomas Paine* . . . 5th ed. (London, 1792), pp. 120–21.

5. Theodore Besterman, ed., *Voltaire's Correspondence* (Geneva, 1953–65), Document no. 8133.

6. *Writings,* 1:397.

7. *Writings,* 1:45.

8. *Writings,* 2:956.

9. Letter from Hartford, 19 February 1776, in *New York Constitutional Gazette,* 24 February 1776.

10. *Writings,* 1:88.

11. *The Literary History of the American Revolution 1763–1783* (New York, 1897), 1:8.

12. *An Economic Interpretation of the Constitution* (New York, 1935), p. viii.

13. *Main Currents of American Thought* (New York, 1930), 1:329.

14. Gordon S. Wood, "Rhetoric and Reality in the American Revolution," *William and Mary Quarterly,* 3d ser., 23 (1966): 15.

15. *Pamphlets of the American Revolution 1750–1766* (Cambridge, Mass., 1965), 1:90.

16. Wood, "Rhetoric and Reality," p. 23.

17. *Ideological Origins of the American Revolution* (Cambridge, Mass.), p. 302.

18. Christopher Lasch, as quoted by Gene Wise in "The Contemporary Crisis in Intellectual History,"5 *CLIO* 5 (1975):59.

19. (New York, 1976), p. xiv.

20. Ibid., p. xvii.

21. *Writings,* 2:426.

22. Lawrence Stone, "The Ninnyversity," *New York Review of Books,* 28 January 1971.

23. Richard Carlile [?] *Aphorisms, preceded by an Essay on the Life and Genius of Thomas Paine* (London, 1826), pp. 8–9.

24. *Writings,* 1:214.

25. *Writings,* 1:496.

Chapter 2. Paine's Political Writing before Common Sense

1. Paine's denial: *Writings,* 1:72; text of *Case of the Officers: Writings,* 2:3–15.
2. *Writings,* 1:143.
3. *Writings,* 2:956. He makes the same declaration in *The Age of Reason, Writings,* 1:496.
4. L. H. Butterfield, ed., *Diary and Autobiography* (Cambridge, Mass., 1961), 3:334.
5. Moncure D. Conway, *Life of Thomas Paine* (New York, 1892), 1:58.
6. These problems are treated in detail in the Appendix.
7. *Writings,* 1:12.
8. This evidence is discussed in the Appendix.
9. Audrey Williamson, *Thomas Paine, His Life, Work, and Times* (New York, 1973), p. 37.
10. "On the Laboring Poor," in William B. Willcox, ed., *Papers of Benjamin Franklin,* vol. 15 (New Haven, Conn., 1972), p. 104.
11. *Writings,* 1:924.
12. *(Philadelphia, Printed . . . for B. F. Bache*]1797]).
13. James Eayre, "The Political Ideas of the English Agrarians, 1775–1815," *Canadian Journal of Economics and Political Science* 18 (1952): 298–302.
14. *Writings,* 2:52–55.
15. *Writings,* 1:23.
16. *Writings,* 1:12.
17. None of the biographies of Paine mentions that he was chosen by Congress as the representative from Pennsylvania along with one from every other colony to serve on a committee "to consider of farther ways and means of promoting and encouraging the manufactures of Saltpetre, Sulphur and Powder in these Colonies." *Pennsylvania Evening Post,* 24 February 1776.
18. That Paine, although a native Englishman, had voting rights in Philadelphia before July 1776 is shown in his address to the people of Pennsylvania in 1778. *Writings,* 2:280. He also specifically states that he had exercised the privilege of voting in Pennsylvania, but had not done so after "the great question of independence" had been settled in seventy-six. *Writings,* 2:278.
19. *Writings,* 1:38.
20. *Writings,* 1:44.
21. *Writings,* 1:29.
22. *Writings,* 1:55.
23. 22 November 1775, reprinted in *Pennsylvania Ledger,* 25 November 1775.
24. The instructions were actually drawn up by John Dickinson.
25. *Writings,* 1:38.

Chapter 3. A Runaway Best Seller

1. Autobiography of John Adams, cited by William Jay, *Life of John Jay* (New York, 1833), 1:97.
2. Whitehead Humphreys, *Pennsylvania Evening Post,* 9 July 1779, reprinted in Deane Papers, *Collections of the New-York Historical Society* (New York, 1890), 22:4–5.
3. "A Friend to Cato and to Truth," *Pennsylvania Evening Post,* Deane Papers, 22:13–14.
4. Cited by David Freeman Hawke, *Paine* (New York, 1974), p. 96.
5. A. O. Aldridge, *Man of Reason: The Life of Thomas Paine* (Philadelphia, 1959), p. 75.
6. *Writings,* 2:1234.
7. George W. Corner, ed., *The Autobiography of Benjamin Rush* (Princeton, N.J., 1948), p. 113.

8. L. H. Butterfield, ed., *Letters of Benjamin Rush* (Princeton, N.J., 1951), 2:1008.

9. W. Duane, ed., *Memoirs of . . . Benjamin Franklin,* p. 326.

10. 19 February 1776. A. H. Smyth, ed., *Writings of Benjamin Franklin,* vol. 6 (New York, 1906), 440.

11. *Writings,* 2:67.

12. *Writings,* 2:928.

13. *Writings,* 2:125.

14. *Writings,* 2:1151.

15. *Writings,* 1:144.

16. *Writings,* 2:1227.

17. 9 June 1809, *Commonplace Book,* in Corner, ed., *The Autobiography of Benjamin Rush,* p. 323.

18. *Writings,* 2:1162.

19. *Writings,* 1:406.

20. *Writings,* 1:496–97.

21. New York *Public Advertiser,* 22 August 1807. Reprinted by A. O. Aldridge in "Thomas Paine and the New York *Public Advertiser,*" *New-York Historical Society Quarterly* 37 (1953): 376–77.

22. *Pennsylvania Evening Post,* 30 January 1776. Reprinted by A. O. Aldridge in "Some Writings of Thomas Paine in Pennsylvania Newspapers," *American Historical Review* 56 (1951): 837.

23. The manuscript of this letter is to be found in the New York Historical Society.

24. Richard Gimbel, *Bibliographical Check List of "Common Sense"* (New Haven, Conn., 1956), p. 17.

25. *Writings,* 2:1239.

26. Gimbel, *Check List,* p. 25.

27. Gimbel, *Check List,* p. 27.

28. Gimbel, *Check List,* p. 28.

29. In a letter by William Smith in the *Pennsylvania Ledger.* Full details appear in chapter 11, below.

30. Isaiah Thomas, *History of Printing in America* (Worcester, Mass., 1810), 2:346.

31. Reprinted in *The Echo; Printed at the Porcupine Press by Pasquin Petronius.* This has no date on title page, but the copyright is assigned to Noah Bailey, New York, 1807.

32. Newspaper sources of these pieces are indicated in Gimbel, *Check List,* pp. 36, 39.

33. Masaniello is a Neapolitan revolutionary or demagogue mentioned in *Common Sense. Writings,* 1:29.

34. *Writings,* 2:1163.

35. The Richard Gimbel Thomas Paine Collection in the American Philosophical Society contains a partial outline or précis of *Common Sense* in a contemporary hand as well as a folio manuscript of Bell's entire second edition, including the title page. The latter had presumably been copied in England, since it was presented to Samuel Clay Harvey, J.P., of Lodge Hill, Kent.

36. *Mémoires* (Paris, 1830–32), 3:65.

37. "American Independence: The Growth of an Idea," *Publications of the Colonial Society of Massachusetts,* no. 43 (1956): 4.

38. Norman Philbrick, ed., *Trumpets Sounding* (New York, 1972), p. 61.

39. *Writings,* 2:1189.

Chapter 4. Theories of Government

1. *The True Merits of a Late Treatise . . . intitled Common Sense* (London, 1776), p. 2.

2. *Writings,* 1:34. C. S. Lewis has traced the term *common sense* to medieval psychology. He

observes that in this early period it "must not be confused either with *communis sensus* (the common opinion of mankind) or with common sense as gumption or elementary rationality—a much later usage. Albertus gives it two functions: *(a)* 'It judges of the operation of a sense so that when we see, we know we are seeing'; *(b)* it puts together the data given by the five senses, or Outward Wits, so that we can say an orange is sweet or one orange is sweeter than another. Burton, centuries later, says 'this common sense is the judge or moderator of the rest, by whom we discern all differences of objects.'" *The Discarded Image* (Cambridge, Eng., 1964), p. 164.

3. *Characteristics of Men, Manners, Opinions, Times* (London, 1711), 1:104. Typography has been modernized in the above quotation. Significant is Shaftesbury's phrase "the common rights of mankind," a precursor of later formulations such as Diderot's "droits de l'humanité," and Paine's in *Common Sense*, "RIGHTS *of* MANKIND." *Writings*, 1:46.

4. An acute discussion of the controversy and of the development of what is now known as the Scottish common sense school was given by Samuel Miller in his *Brief Retrospect of the Eighteenth Century* (New York, 1800), 2:12ff.

5. The ambiguities in the phrase *common sense*, involving consensus or the received opinion as opposed to sound reasoning, exist also in the French translation of the title of Paine's pamphlet, *Le Sens commun*, which like the English derives from the Latin. These ambiguities do not exist in German translations, which unequivocally refer to thinking as a process. One appeared in Philadelphia in 1776, *Gesunde Vernunft* [sound reasoning], the other in Hamburg, 1848, *Gesunder Menschenverstande* [sound human judgment]. The latter work does not appear in Gimbel's bibliography. Its complete title is as follows: *Republik oder Monarchie? Beantwortet durch Thomas Paine's "Gesunder Menschenverstand" und "Menschenrechte." Nach der Originalquellen bearbeitet von John Greis* (Hamburg: Hoffmann und Campe, 1848). Another edition appeared in America in the next year: 2. Auflage (Chicago: Charles Petersen, 1849). The same title, *Der gesunder Menschenverstand*, was also used in *Die politischen Werke von Thomas Paine* (Philadelphia, Maass und Cursch, 1852).

6. *Writings*, 1:5.

7. Jacob E. Cooke, ed., *The Federalist* (Middletown, Conn., 1961), p. 349.

8. *Writings*, 1:5.

9. "Que l'Europe moderne vaut mieux que l'Europe ancienne," in *OEuvres complètes*, vol. 36 (Basle [Kehl], 1785).

10. *Writings*, 1:6.

11. *Writings*, 1:6.

12. *Pennsylvania Gazette*. The relationship of this essay to the *Crisis* is explained in chapter 14 below.

13. *Writings*, 2:283.

14. *Writings* 1:6.

15. 1:50.

16. Early in the nineteenth century, Charles Botta affirmed that "the excellence of the British constitution" had never been "called in question" until *Common Sense*. *History of the War of Independence of America*, trans. G. A. Otis (New Haven, Conn., 1834), 1:343. Gordon S. Wood in *The Creation of the American Republic* (Chapel Hill, N.C., 1969), p. 224, in a footnote to a quotation from *Common Sense* attacking the British constitution, supplies a further reference: "'Paine may well have been the first Englishman during the classical age of the constitution to ridicule its maxims publicly.' Weston, *English Constitutional Theory*, 192."

17. Phillips Bradley, ed., *Democracy in America* [vol. 1, chap. 15] (New York, 1948), 1:260.

18. *Writings*, 2:374.

19. *Writings*, 1:9.

20. James Chalmers, *Plain Truth* (Philadelphia, 1776), p. 2.

21. *Writings*, 1:10.

22. *Writings*, 1:12.

23. *Writings*, 1:14.

24. Peter Laslett, ed., *Two Treatises of Government* (Cambridge, 1960), p. 69.
25. *Writings,* 1:253.
26. *Writings,* 1:14.
27. *Writings,* 1:16.
28. A copy of this letter is to be found in the Gimbel Collection of the American Philosophical Society from the original in the Public Library, Rotherham, England.
29. Statistics on this point are available in Leonard W. Labaree, *Royal Government in America* (New Haven, Conn., 1930), passim.
30. L. H. Butterfield, ed., *Adams Family Correspondence* (Cambridge, Mass., 1963), 1:381.
31. A. H. Smyth, ed., *Writings of Benjamin Franklin,* vol. 6 (New York, 1906), p. 144.
32. Richard Bland, *An Inquiry into the Rights of the British Colonies* (Williamsburg, Va., 1766); James Wilson, *Considerations on the Nature and the Legislative Authority of the British Parliament* (Philadelphia, 1774).
33. A. O. Aldridge, *Benjamin Franklin Philosopher and Man* (New York, 1965), p. 247.
34. *Writings,* 1:368.
35. *Writings,* 1:45.

Chapter 5. The State of American Affairs

1. *Writings,* 1:21.
2. *Writings,* 1:53.
3. *Writings,* 1:17.
4. *Writings,* 1:36. Much of the effectiveness of Paine's rhetoric may be attributed to his metaphors. These have been analyzed from a Marxist viewpoint by André Ladousse in "La rhétorique comme idéologie dans *Common Sense,*" *Annales du Centre de recherches sur l'Amérique anglophone,* Université de Bordeaux III, vol. 3 (1974), no. 1, pp. 100–116. Paine's imagery in *Rights of Man* has been studied with occasional reference to *Common Sense* by Ronald Paulson in *Representations of Revolution (1789–1820)* (New Haven, Conn., 1983), pp. 73–79. The latter analysis is eclectic, with references ranging from Miltonic and biblical to Freudian. It should be stated that Paine's metaphors were striking and frequently brilliant, but they were not systematic. They may, of course, be grouped according to categories such as the family, biological nature, theology, and ancient history, but no valid conclusions can be drawn concerning any conscious link between them. Take, for example, three examples, all from the same page of *Common Sense* (*Writings,* 1:30). Paine's description of freedom as "hunted round the globe" (repeated in *Rights of Man, Writings,* 1:354) may call up visions of a virgin beauty fleeing a potential rapist and, therefore, be compared as sexual imagery to his question "Can ye give to prostitution its former innocence?" or his affirmation "As well can the lover forgive the ravisher of his mistress, as the continent forgive the murders of Britain." These images, however, have absolutely no connection with each other. Paine obviously uses his famous metaphor of spring as seed-time to refer to new beginnings, and he may also have associated it with the Christian doctrine of resurrection, with the concept of natural progress, or with a plea for sexual liberty, but there is no proof that he did. His metaphors are discrete, occasional, and usually expressed in biblical, proverbial, or colloquial language. Two of his best similes describe the Quakers' quest for the mammon of this world "with a step as steady as time, and an appetite as keen as death" (*Writings,* 2:58). These images, like the others in *Common Sense,* stand by themselves and do not need to be related to Miltonic echoes or Marxist economics.
5. *Writings,* 1:21.
6. *Ibid.*
7. *Writings,* 1:251.
8. *Writings,* 1:23.

9. *Writings,* 1:22.
10. *Writings,* 1:23.
11. *Writings,* 1:24.
12. A. H. Smyth, ed., *Writings of Benjamin Franklin,* vol. 6 (New York, 1906), 460.
13. *Writings,* 1:18.
14. This passage is quoted in *New York Journal,* 31 August 1775.
15. *Writings,* 1:19.
16. Charles Inglis, *The True Interest of America Impartially Stated* (Philadelphia, 1776), p. 39.
17. *Writings,* 1:19.
18. *Writings,* 1:19–20.
19. "A Search into the Nature of Society," in *Fable of the Bees* (London, 1777), 1:260.
20. *Writings,* 1:20.
21. *Writings,* 1:136, 396.
22. *Writings,* 1:24.
23. Glenn Negley and J. Max Patrick, eds., *The Quest for Utopia* (New York, 1952), p. 345.
24. *Thoughts on the Revival of Religion in New England* (New York, [1845?]), p. 194.
25. *Magnalia Christi Americana,* "General Introduction" (London, 1702), no page number. Robert C. Winthrop, *Life and Letters* (Boston, 1864), p. 309. The notion of America as a divinely appointed haven has been extensively treated by modern scholars. See Ernest L. Tuveson, *Redeemer Nation: The Idea of America's Millenial Role* (Chicago, 1968) and Sacvan Bercovitch, *The Puritan Origins of the American Self* (New Haven, Conn., 1975), especially chap. 3, "The Elect Nation in New England."
26. *Miscellaneous Works* (New York, 1804), p. 47.
27. In *Crisis* No. 5, Paine compares a military engagement, "the attack and defence of Mud Island," to "the fable of Bender realized on the Delaware." *Writings,* 1:116. This reference to Charles XII of Sweden defending himself at the Turkish city of Bender against an entire army indicates that Paine was familiar with Voltaire's *Histoire de Charles XII* in which the episode is narrated at length. René Pomeau, ed., *Œuvres historiques* (Paris, 1957), pp. 198–221.
28. *Writings,* 1:25.
29. *Writings,* 1:24.
30. *Writings,* 1:27.
31. "A Settled Citizen," *Pennsylvania Ledger,* 4 May 1776.
32. *Civil Prudence, Recommended to the Thirteen United Colonies of North America* (Norwich, 1776), p. 14.
33. *Writings,* 1:28.
34. *Writings,* 2:490.
35. Vittorio Gabrieli, "Thomas Paine fra l'America e l'Europa," *Studi americani* 1 (1955): 14.
36. Eric Foner, *Tom Paine and Revolutionary America* (New York, 1976), p. 115.
37. *Writings,* 1:29.
38. *Writings,* 1:30.
39. Garry Wills, *Inventing America* (New York, 1978), p. 312.
40. *Writings,* 1:30–31.
41. *Writings,* 2:284.

Chapter 6. "The Time Hath Found Us"

1. *Writings,* 1:31.
2. *The True Merits of a Late Treatise* (London, 1776), pp. vi, 22, 32, 36, 43.
3. Jean Brethe de la Gressaye, ed., *De l'Esprit des loix* [bk. 39, chap. 18] (Paris, 1955), 3:394–95.
4. *Writings,* 1:32–33.

5. James Chalmers, *Plain Truth,* p. 14.
6. William Fox, *An Examination of Mr. Paine's Writings* (London, 1793), p. 6.
7. *Writings,* 2:1239.
8. Entick's *New Naval History* does raise a question concerning a subsequent passage in *Common Sense* referring to the "Terrible privateer, Captain Death" (p. 45). In *Rights of Man,* Paine volunteers the additional information that he himself attempted at the age of sixteen to enlist on the *Terrible.* Entick twice lists the *Terrible* as being in commission, but both times he indicates the commanding officer as a Capt. Philip Durell, not the Captain Death cited by Paine (pp. 846, 853). In another work, *The General History of the Late War* (London, 1763), Entick includes a long footnote describing a battle between the *Terrible* and the French vessel the *Vengeance,* but does not mention the captain by name (2:110–13). Yet in the index under "Death, Captain," this location is cited. The most recent and complete account of Paine's maritime career appears in an article "Thomas Paine, Privateersman" by Alyce Barry, *Pennsylvania Magazine of History and Biography* 101 (1977): 451–61. This author, in addition to giving the basic facts about the engagement between the *Terrible* and the *Vengeance,* points out that Paine could not have signed on the *Terrible* at the age of sixteen, as he states. This would have been in 1753 when England was at peace, and there are no records to indicate that the *Terrible* was commissioned as a privateer until some months after war was declared in May 1756. Rather than assuming that Paine allowed his father to dissuade him from serving on the *Terrible* at sixteen and that he actually signed on another vessel, the *King of Prussia,* three years later, Barry believes that both episodes occurred at the age of nineteen. Although reporting that no documentary evidence exists to show that Paine either did or did not sail on the *King of Prussia,* she concludes that he probably did so because the episode fits into the known facts of his life.
9. Barry, "Thomas Paine, Privateersman," p. 455.
10. Paine specifically admits that "a common pirate, twelve months ago, might have come up the Delaware, and laid the city of Philadelphia under contribution for what sum he pleased." *Writings,* 1:34. Yet in a *Crisis* (1780) he indignantly rejects Sir John Dalrymple's affirmation in 1775 that "*two twenty-gun ships, nay, says he, tenders of those ships, stationed between Albemarle sound and Chesapeake bay, would shut up the trade of America for 600 miles.*" *Writings,* 1:182.
11. Solomon Lutnick, *The American Revolution and the British Press, 1775–1783* (Columbia, Mo., 1967), p. 47.
12. Ibid.
13. A. O. Aldridge, *Man of Reason* (New York, 1959), pp. 84–85.
14. *Writings,* 1:43.
15. A. O. Aldridge, "Population and Polygamy in Eighteenth-Century Thought," *Journal of the History of Medicine* 4 (1949): 129–48.
16. *Writings,* 1:36.
17. *Writings,* 1:37.
18. John Paul Selsam, *The Pennsylvania Constitution of 1776* (Philadelphia, 1936), p. 99.
19. *Writings,* 1:38.
20. (Philadelphia, 1775), 1:48–49.
21. *Writings,* 1:39.
22. *Writings,* 1:40.
23. *Writings,* 1:43.
24. *Writings,* 1:6.
25. *Writings,* 1:43.
26. *Writings,* 1:44.
27. Ibid. A more extensive discussion of this subject appears in A. O. Aldridge, "The Influence of New York Newspapers on Paine's *Common Sense,*" *New-York Historical Society Quarterly* 60 (1976): 53–60.

28. A correspondent in another newspaper, the *New York Journal* (14 November 1775), preceded Paine in denouncing "this vile letter," and he attributed it with some plausibility to Dr. Myles Cooper (1737–85), a notorious Loyalist, who had sailed for London at precisely the right moment to have had the time to discern the sentiments of the ministry and communicate them to the colonies by means of a letter dated in late July.

29. *Writings,* 1:44

30. John Heywood, *Proverbes,* pt. 1, chap. 8, "Reckeners without their host must recken twice."

31. *Writings,* 1:45.

32. John Conington and Henry Nettleship, eds., *The Works of Virgil* (Hildesheim, 1963), 4:56.

33. Renato Poggioli, *The Oaten Flute* (Cambridge, Mass., 1975), p. 323.

34. *A Poem on the Rising Glory of America* (Philadelphia, 1772), p. 4.

35. *Writings,* 2:956.

36. Editorial page, *New York Times,* 29 December 1976.

37. Printed in *Pennsylvania Ledger,* 27 January 1776.

38. *Writings,* 2:55–60.

39. *Writings,* 2:1500.

40. A. O. Aldridge, *Man of Reason* (New York, 1959), p. 315.

41. *The Life of Thomas Paine* (Dublin, n.d. [1793]), p. 24.

42. Ibid., p. 25.

43. E. A. Payne, *Times Literary Supplement,* 31 May 1947, p. 267.

44. This manuscript is part of the Richard Gimbel Thomas Paine Collection of the American Philosophical Society.

45. Nehemiah Curnock, ed., *Journal of the Rev. John Wesley* (London, 1916), 8:31n. I am indebted to Mr. G. Hindmarch for this information.

Chapter 7. Levellers and Puritans

1. *The Ancient Constitution and the Feudal Law* (New York, 1967), pp. 125–26.

2. (Philadelphia, 1776), p. 8.

3. *John Locke and the Theory of Sovereignty . . . in the Political Thought of the English Revolution* (Cambridge, 1979), p. 126.

4. *Reason in Answer to a Pamphlet entitled Common Sense* (Dublin, 1776), p. 9.

5. Rev. John Riland, *The Rights of God, occasion'd by Mr. Paine's "Rights of Man," and his other publications* (Birmingham, 1792); *A Defence of the Constitution of England* (1791), p. 74 [cited by D. F. Hawke, *Paine* (New York, 1974), p. 224]; *Rights of Citizens* (London, n.d. [1791]), p. 105.

6. *Writings,* 1:18.

7. *Writings,* 1:617.

8. L. H. Butterfield, ed., *Diary and Autobiography* (Cambridge, Mass., 1961), 3:333.

9. A. S. P. Woodhouse, ed., *Puritanism and Liberty, Being the Army Debates . . . with Supplementary Documents* (London, 1950), p. 230.

10. *Writings,* 1:10.

11. *Grounds and Reasons,* pp. 1–2.

12. *Grounds and Reasons,* p. 10.

13. *Grounds and Reasons,* p. 15.

14. *Grounds and Reasons,* p. 17.

15. *Grounds and Reasons,* p. 13.

16. *Writings,* 2:1000.

17. "Negotiations in London for Effecting a Reconciliation," in A. H. Smyth, ed., *Writings of Benjamin Franklin,* vol. 8 (New York, 1906), pp. 459–560.

18. A. O. Aldridge, "Thomas Paine and the New York *Public Advertiser*," *New-York Historical Society Quarterly* 38 (1953): 380.

19. "Salus Populi," 7 March 1776, in Peter Force, ed., *American Archives*, Fourth Series, 5 (1844): 96.

20. Henry Yorke, *These are the Times that Try Men's Souls! A Letter to John Frost* (London, 1793), p. 34.

21. This particular quotation is from John W. Derry, "Tom Paine: An International Radical," in *The Radical Tradition: Tom Paine to Lloyd George* (London, 1967), p. 41.

22. *Writings*, 1:19.

23. *Writings*, 1:41.

24. *Writings*, 1:8.

25. *Writings*, 1:10.

26. *Writings*, 1:28.

27. *Writings*, 1:21.

28. *Writings*, 1:29.

29. *Writings*, 1:30.

30. Ibid.

31. *Writings*, 2:59.

32. *Writings*, 1:274. On the basis of these passages an opponent unfairly accused Paine of founding "the most extravagant political doctrines on the first chapter of Genesis and the genealogy of Christ" and then declaring "for pure deism" in the rest of his work. Sir Brooke Boothby, *Observations on the Appeal from the New . . . Whigs* (London, 1792), pp. 228–32.

33. *Writings*, 1:442.

34. *Writings*, 1:12.

35. Boothby, *Observations on the Appeal from the New . . . Whigs*, p. 99.

36. L. H. Butterfield, ed., *Diary and Autobiography of John Adams* (Cambridge, Mass., 1961), 3:333.

37. Photostat in the Richard Gimbel Thomas Paine Collection American Philosophical Society. The original passed at a Parke-Bernet sale in New York in April 1978.

38. *Four Letters* (Philadelphia, 1776). See chapter 13 for a demonstration that this work is by Paine.

39. *Writings*, 1:17.

40. *Writings*, 1:23.

41. *Writings*, 1:123.

Chapter 8. Relations with Locke

1. *Plato and Milton* (Ithaca, N.Y., 1965), p. 3.

2. L.H. Butterfield, ed., *Diary and Autobiography* (Cambridge, Mass., 1961), 3:330.

3. John Dunn, "The Politics of Locke in England and America in the Eighteenth Century," in John W. Yolton, ed., *John Locke: Problems and Perspectives* (Cambridge, 1969), p. 80.

4. *Writings*, 2:73.

5. A. O. Aldridge, *Man of Reason* (Philadelphia, 1959), p. 309.

6. James Tyrrell to Locke, 18 March 1680, quoted in Peter Laslett, ed., *Two Treatises of Government* (Cambridge, 1960), p. 73. This work will be cited henceforth as *Two Treatises*.

7. *Two Treatises*, p. 41.

8. *Two Treatises*, pp. 50, 65.

9. *Two Treatises*, p. 68.

10. F. B. Kaye, ed., *The Fable of the Bees* (Oxford, 1924), 1:40.

11. *Writings*, 1:10.

12. *Two Treatises*, pp. 160–61.

13. *Two Treatises,* p. 190.
14. *Writings,* 1:14.
15. *Two Treatises,* p. 220.
16. *Writings,* 1:14.
17. A. O. Aldridge, "The State of Nature: An Undiscovered Country in the History of Ideas," *Studies in Voltaire and the Eighteenth Century* 98 (1972): 8.
18. Mordecai Roshwald, "The Concept of Human Rights," *Philosophy and Phenomenological Research* 19 (1959): 358.
19. *Two Treatises,* p. 287.
20. *Two Treatises,* p. 293.
21. *Two Treatises,* p. 313.
22. *Two Treatises,* p. 343.
23. *Two Treatises,* p. 347.
24. *Two Treatises,* p. 435.
25. *Two Treatises,* p. 228.
26. *Two Treatises,* p. 360.
27. *Two Treatises,* p. 371.
28. *Two Treatises,* p. 364.
29. *Two Treatises,* p. 359.
30. *Two Treatises,* p. 430.
31. *Two Treatises,* p. 405.
32. *Two Treatises,* p. 360. Laslett traces the Latin Tag to Ovid, *Metamorphoses* 1.131.
33. *Two Treatises,* pp. 368–69.
34. *Writings,* 1:5.
35. "The Moralists," in John M. Robertson, ed., *Characteristics* (New York, 1900), 2:83.
36. *Writings,* 1:6.
37. *Two Treatises,* p. 364.
38. *Writings,* 1:13.
39. *Two Treatises,* p. 359.
40. *Writings,* 1:11–12.
41. *Two Treatises,* p. 405.
42. *Writings,* 1:14.
43. *Two Treatises,* p. 356.
44. *Writings,* 1:6.
45. *Two Treatises,* sec. 20.
46. *Two Treatises,* pp. 369, 228, 435.
47. *Writings,* 1:6. As has been previously noted, Paine in the third section of *Common Sense* alludes to Tommaso Aniello, the Neapolitan revolutionary. Locke in his first treatise also refers to "Massanello's Government" and describes him as a "King, who was but the Day before properly a Fisherman" (p. 219). This common reference does not demonstrate a necessary link between Locke and Paine, however, for Aniello's revolt in 1647 "became a symbol for mob rule all over Europe for the next few generations." Also Paine provides additional information about the Neapolitan not available in Locke.
48. The controversy is described in A. O. Aldridge, "Thomas Paine and the New York *Public Advertiser,*" *New-York Historical Society Quarterly,* 38 (1953): 375–85.
49. (New York, 1809), p. 51.
50. *Writings,* 1:13.
51. *Inventing America* (Garden City, N.Y., 1978), p. 173.
52. Ibid., pp. 315, 329–30.

Chapter 9. Locke: Unraveling the Issues

1. Willmoore Kendall, *John Locke and the Doctrine of Majority-Rule* (Urbana, Ill., 1965), pp. 132–36; J. W. Gough, *John Locke's Political Philosophy* (Oxford, 1973), pp. 52, 74).

2. *An Essay concerning the True Original Extent and End of Civil Government. By John Locke. Salus populi suprema lex esto. With notes.* Cited henceforth as Elrington.

3. Gough, *John Locke's Political Philosophy,* p. 38.

4. *Writings,* 1:251.

5. Elrington, page v.

6. Armand Nivelle, *Les Théories esthétiques en Allemagne de Baumgarten à Kant,* 2d (German) ed. (Berlin, 1971), p. 176, quoted by S. S. Prawer, *Comparative Literary Studies: an Introduction* (New York, 1973), p. 164.

7. Elrington, p. 3.

8. *Writings,* 1:356. Kendall, *John Locke and the Doctrine of Majority-Rule,* p. 134. Another twentieth-century scholar has duplicated Elrington's argument by affirming that "when the need arises" Paine "is quite willing to argue that might makes right." This charge is based entirely on the statement in *Common Sense* concerning England's rule over America, "if they cannot conquer us they cannot govern us." Evelyn J. Hinz, "The 'Reasonable' Style of Tom Paine," *Queen's Quarterly* 79 (1972): 238. This accusation has no more substance than that of Elrington, for in the specified passage Paine is not at all affirming that might makes right. What he actually says is simply that the absence of might means the inability to exercise the privilege of right, or that power is a requisite of government. Paine is affirming no right whatsover nor is he making a moral judgment. Throughout *Common Sense,* Paine, like Locke, maintains that "right is what the majority wills," which, as Willmoore Kendell observes is not precisely the same as "the majority always will what is right" (p. 133). Paine no more than Locke identifies the majority with the common segment of the population, but neither does he any more than Locke precisely define the constituency of the majority.

9. Elrington, p. 3.

10. The letter is reprinted in *Writings,* 2:1298–99.

11. Bk. 1, chap. 6.

12. *Thomas Paine (1737–1809) et la révolution dans les deux mondes* (Paris, 1900), p. 159.

13. *Writings,* 2:295.

14. *Writings,* 2:274–75.

15. *Writings,* 1:276. Kendall, *John Locke and the Doctrine of Majority-Rule,* p. 104.

16. Elrington, p. 9.

17. Copy in the Richard Gimbel Thomas Paine Collection at the American Philosophical Society, from the original at the University of Texas.

18. *Writings,* 1:316.

19. Elrington, p. 3.

20. Elrington, p. 48.

21. *An Address to the Convention of the Colony . . . of Virginia* (Philadelphia, 1776), p. 21. The passage is found in *Esprit des loix,* bk. 11, chap. 5.

22. Elrington, pp. 83–84.

23. *Writings,* 1:5.

24. Elrington, p. 85.

25. Elrington, p. 87.

26. *Writings,* 1:444.

27. *Writings,* 1:359.

28. *Writings,* 1:37. Locke used a similar phrase, "a fair and equal representation" (sec. 158, Elrington, p. 141), but the verbal resemblance does not reveal a necessary connection between the two writers since Paine presumably adopted his phrase "a large and equal representation" from James Burgh.

29. *Writings,* 1:342.

30. Elrington, p. 50.
31. Elrington, p. 141.
32. Elrington, p. 140.
33. Elrington, p. 141.
34. *Writings,* 1:45.
35. *Writings,* 1:374.
36. *Writings,* 1:14.
37. *Writings,* 1:37.
38. *Writings,* 1:9.
39. *Writings,* 1:39.
40. *Writings,* 1:37–38.
41. Elrington, p. 117.
42. *Writings,* 1:6.
43. Elrington, p. 177.
44. Elrington, p. 12.
45. Elrington, p. 20.
46. Elrington, p. 192.
47. Elrington, p. 23.
48. *Writings,* 1:358.
49. *Writings,* 1:372.
50. *Writings,* 1:319.
51. *Writings,* 1:37.
52. *Writings,* 1:8, 25, 13.
53. *Writings,* 1:3, 46, 10, 29.
54. Elrington, p. 12.
55. *Writings,* 1:360.
56. *Writings,* 1:364.
57. *Writings,* 1:367.

Chapter 10. Relations with Rousseau

1. *Writings,* 2:79.
2. *Writings,* 1:299; 2:543.
3. R. R. Palmer, "Tom Paine Victim of the Rights of Man," *Pennsylvania Magazine of History and Biography,* 66 (1942): 163.
4. "Rousseau and the Sentimentalists," *Writings* (Boston, 1897), 2:237.
5. Paul M. Spurlin, *Rousseau in America 1760–1809* (University, Ala., 1969), p. 36. Nothing but general parallels in subject matter are indicated by Harry H. Clark in "Thomas Paine's Relations to Voltaire and Rousseau," *La Revue anglo-américaine* 9 (1932): 305–18, 393–405.
6. Spurlin, *Rousseau in America,* pp. 43, 45, 57, 68.
7. F. E. L. Priestley, ed., *Enquiry concerning Political Justice* (Toronto, 1946), 2:129.
8. Part 2, line 1. This quotation and others in the present chapter from Rousseau's second discourse are taken from the translation which would have been available to Paine in the eighteenth century: *A Discourse upon the Origin and Foundation of the Inequality among Mankind. By John James Rousseau, Citizen of Geneva.* London: Printed for R. and J. Dodsley, 1761.
9. "An Enquiry into the Origin of Moral Virtue," in *Fable of the Bees.* (Edinburgh, 1772), 1:22, 25.
10. *Essays in the History of Ideas* (Baltimore, Md., 1948), p. 34.
11. Quotations are taken from a translation which Paine could have used, *A Treatise on the Social Compact; or, The Principles of Political Law* (London, 1764).
12. Bk. 1, chap. 8, pp. 28–29

13. *Writings,* 1:5.

14. B. Gagnebin and M. Raymond, eds., *Du Contrat social. Ecrits politiques.* Vol. 3 of *OEuvres complètes.* Pléiade ed. (Paris, 1964), pp. 1355–56.

15. Ibid, p. xvii.

16. Bk. 2, chap. 1, p. 36.

17. Bk. 3, chap. 1, p. 92.

18. Bk. 3, chap. 1, p. 98.

19. Bk. 3, chap. 4, p. 142.

20. Bk. 3, chap. 3, p. 107.

21. Bk. 3, chap. 6, p. 59. In *Rights of Man,* Paine considers as forms of government only "the democratical, the aristocratical, the monarchical," and he defines a republic as not any particular form of government, but the object of government, "*res-publica,* the public affairs, or the public good." *Writings,* 1:369.

22. Bk. 3, chap. 3, p. 109.

23. Bk. 3, chap. 4, p. 110.

24. Bk. 3, chap. 15, p. 164.

25. Rousseau: Bk. 3, chap. 6, p. 120. Paine: *Writings,* 1:353; A. H. Clough, ed., *Plutarch's Lives. The Translation called Dryden's* (New York, 1911), 2:279.

26. *Writings,* 1:273.

27. Bk. 1, chap. 5.

28. Bk. 3, chap. 7, p. 133.

29. Bk. 3, chap. 6, p. 122.

30. Bk. 4, chap. 1, pp. 179–80.

31. *Writings,* 1:5–6.

32. *Plain Truth* (Philadelphia, 1776), p. 2.

33. Benjamin Rush described this tree in a letter to Robert Barclay, 9 May 1810. L. H. Butterfield, ed., *Letters of Benjamin Rush* (Princeton, N.J., 1951), 2:1046–48. Further details are given in the editor's notes.

34. Bk. 4, chap. 1, p. 1.

35. Judith N. Shklar, *Men and Citizens. A Study of Rousseau's Social Theory* (Cambridge, 1969), p. 5.

36. Ibid., p. 19.

37. Theodore Besterman, ed., *Voltaire's Correspondence* (Geneva, 1953–65). Document No. 9721.

38. Jean-Etienne Judith Forestier Boinvilliers, *L'Esprit du Contrat social, suivi de l'esprit du Sens commun, de Thomas Paine, présenté à la Convention par le Citoyen Boinvilliers.* Paris, Cailleau, An II [1793–94].

Chapter 11. Relations with Montesquieu

1. Paul Spurlin, *Montesquieu in America 1760–1801* (University, La., 1940), p. 62.

2. Ibid., p. 62.

3. *Writings,* 1:298.

4. Book 11, chapter 6.

5. Jean Brethe de la Gressaye, ed., *De l'Esprit des loix* (Paris, 1955), 2:347.

6. *Writings,* 1:7.

7. *Writings,* 1:8.

8. *Writings,* 1:38.

9. *Writings,* 1:8.

10. Peter J. Stanlis, ed., *Edmund Burke: Selected Writings and Speeches* (Garden City, 1963), p. 12.

11. *Annual Register for the Year 1772,* 15:178. The reference is to Voltaire's *Commentaire sur l'Esprit des lois.*
12. Brethe de la Gressaye, ed., *De l'Esprit des loix,* 1:256.
13. Bk. 3, chap. 4.
14. J. G. A. Pocock, *The Machiavellian Moment. Florentine Political Thought and the Atlantic Republican Tradition* (Princeton, N.J., 1975), p. 525.
15. *Writings,* 2:304.
16. Gordon S. Wood, "Republicanism as a Revolutionary Ideology," reprinted by John R. Howe, Jr., in *The Role of Ideology in the American Revolution* (New York, 1970), p. 85.
17. *Writings,* 1:13.
18. *Writings,* 1:14.
19. *Writings,* 1:16.
20. *Writings,* 1:46.
21. *Writings,* 1:38.
22. *Writings,* 1:45.
23. Copy in the Richard Gimbel Thomas Paine Collection at the American Philosophical Society from the original in the National Archives. Record Group No. 11.
24. To Joseph Galloway, 9 January 1769. William B. Wilcox, ed., *Papers of Benjamin Franklin,* vol. 16 (New Haven, Conn., 1972), p. 11.
25. 10 June. A. H. Smyth, ed., *Writings of Benjamin Franklin,* vol. 5 (New York, 1905), pp. 323–24.
26. *Writings,* 1:82.
27. *Writings,* 1:147.
28. *Writings,* 1:162. Paine in *Common Sense* also touched on another polemical subject of the eighteenth century which had been brought to the fore by Montesquieu, the question of the relative population of the ancients and moderns. In *The Spirit of the Laws,* Montesquieu maintained that the numbers of the ancients had far exceeded those of modern times and that population reached its peak during the period of Julius Caesar. Bk. 23, chaps. 17–26. He was supported in the general principle of the superior populousness of the ancients by Robert Wallace, a Scotsman, in a *Dissertation on the Numbers of Mankind, in Ancient and Modern Times* (1753). The opposing side was taken by Hume and Voltaire, who maintained that the populousness of the ancients had been grossly exaggerated. Paine's position is equivocal, but he seems to support Hume and Voltaire rather than Montesquieu. "It is a matter worthy of observation," he declares, "that the more a country is peopled, the smaller their armies are. In military numbers, the ancients far exceeded the moderns; and the reason is evident, for trade being the consequence of population, men become too much absorbed thereby to attend to any thing else" (*Writings,* 1:36). The declaration that ancient armies contained greater numbers than modern ones seems to support the opinion that ancient countries were more populated than modern ones, but taken with the principle that the smaller the country, the greater the army, it has the opposite meaning.
29. Pt. 1, bk. 8, chap. 16.
30. Antonelli Gerbi, *The Dispute of the New World. The History of a Polemic, 1750–1790* (Pittsburgh, Penna., 1973), p. 246.
31. *Writings,* 2:1316.
32. *Writings,* 2:598–99.
33. *Writings,* 1:9.
34. *Disertación sobre las primeros principios del gobierno por Tomás Pain; traducido* [*sic*] *por un ciudadano de la Nueva Granada* (London, 1819). The British Museum Catalogue attributes this translation to José Maria Vergara. A. Owen Aldridge, "El granadino que tradujo la obra de Tomás Paine," *Revista interamericana de bibliografia* 31 (1981): 538–42.
35. Paine's translator cites bk. 14, chap. 1; bk. 15, chap. 8; bk. 16, chap. 14.
36. The translator does not mention Voltaire by name but cites him merely as author of

Commentaries on the Spirit of Laws. This may be because Voltaire was still considered a dangerous heretic in Spanish-speaking countries.

Chapter 12. Periodical Polemics

1. "Conversation between Cato and Plain Truth," in *Pennsylvania Packet,* 25 March 1776, cited by T. R. Adams, "American Independence: The Growth of an Idea," *Publications of the Colonial Society of Massachusetts* 43 (1956): 8.

2. "*Humphreys*'s paper" was a weekly of Tory sympathies, the *Pennsylvania Ledger.* The "oblique essay" was an extract from a pamphlet, *Sentiments of a Foreigner, on the Disputes of Great-Britain with America,* which appeared 20 January 1776. This pamphlet, advertised in the *Ledger,* 17 June 1775, six months before the appearance of *Common Sense,* consists entirely of a translation from abbé Raynal. The "Testimony" of the Quakers is the document of 20 January to which Paine replied in the third edition of *Common Sense.* Gimbel attributes the "Candidus" essay to James Chalmers with a question mark after his name, presumably because Chalmers was the author of a pamphlet *Plain Truth,* which also bears the pseudonym "Candidus." But since *Plain Truth* is a rejection of independence from an extreme Tory point of view, and the essay by "Candidus" is an enthusiastic vindication of independence, it is obvious that the latter was not written by Chalmers.

3. Peter Force, ed., *American Archives,* Fourth Series, 4: 1496–98. This collection will be cited henceforth as Force.

4. *Writings,* 2: 1945.

5. Force, Fourth Series, 4: 1527–30.

6. Force, Fourth Series, 5: 974–77.

7. Force, Fourth Series, 5: iiii.

8. Hawke, *In the Midst of a Revolution,* p. 18.

9. The "Cato" letters together with Paine's answers as "The Forester" appeared originally in the *Pennsylvania Ledger* and were reprinted in other newspapers throughout the thirteen colonies. In the present discussion, the text cited will be that of Force. The letter now under discussion appears in Fourth Series, 5: 125–27.

10. Hawke, *In the Midst of a Revolution,* p. 105.

11. Force, Fourth Series, 5: 42–43.

12. "The Forester" essays are reprinted in *Writings,* 2: 60–87.

13. This epigraph is not reprinted in Force.

14. After the publication of *Common Sense,* Paine consistently adopted the form of his name which is now in universal use, but it was spelled *Pain* in the *Pennsylvania Journal,* 22 November 1775, and in the records of his sister's birth in England it is spelled *Payne.* See A. O. Aldridge, *Man of Reason,* p. 19.

15. *Writings,* 2: 74.

16. "A Common Man," 31 March 1776.

17. *Writings,* 2: 67.

18. *Writings,* 2: 81.

19. *Writings,* 2: 82.

20. *Writings,* 2: 66.

21. *Writings,* 2: 68.

22. *Writings,* 2: 73.

23. Force, Fourth Series, 5: 854–56.

24. *Pennsylvania Ledger,* 13 April 1776.

25. *Writings,* 2: 78.

26. *Writings,* 2: 83.

27. *Pennsylvania Ledger,* 27 April 1776.

28. Ibid.
29. David Hawke, *In the Midst of a Revolution* (Philadelphia, 1961), p. 10.
30. *Pennsylvania Journal*, 4 May 1776.
31. *Writings*, 2:86.

Chapter 13. Plain Truth

1. Thomas R. Adams, "The Authorship and Printing of 'Plain Truth,'" *Papers of the Bibliographical Society of America* 49 (1955): 230–48.
2. Ibid., p. 235.
3. Lorenzo Sabine, *Biographical Sketches of Loyalists of the American Revolution* (Boston, 1864), 2:301.
4. *Strictures on a Pamphlet Written by Thomas Paine* (London, 1796), p. 35.
5. Ibid., pp. 64, 65.
6. *Plain Truth*, p. 12.
7. *Plain Truth*, p. 1.
8. *Plain Truth*, p. 3.
9. *Plain Truth*, p. 27.
10. *Plain Truth*, p. 28.
11. *Plain Truth*, p. 5. This is almost an exact rendering of the text of the English translation of the *Social Contract* then available in the colonies: *A Treatise on the Social Compact* (London, 1764), p. 100 (book 3, chapter 4). It is also parallel to the quotation from Sidney in William Smith's final "Cato" letter.
12. *Plain Truth*, p. 7. Chalmers completely changed his opinion about the relative influence of social conditioning and the physical environment in his later *Strictures on a Pamphlet written by Thomas Paine* (London, 1796). Here he maintains "that in our climates courage and discipline are accidental circumstances, entirely dependent on the chiefs of mankind; consequently the Flemish boors may be rendered as excellent soldiers as the Dutch are acknowledged to be seamen" (p. 39).
13. *Plain Truth*, p. 16.
14. *Plain Truth*, p. 8.
15. *Plain Truth*, p. 10.
16. *Writings*, 1:35.
17. *Plain Truth*, p. 10.
18. *Plain Truth*, p. 14.
19. *Plain Truth*, p. 19.
20. *Plain Truth*, p. 23.
21. *Plain Truth*, p. 25.
22. *Plain Truth*, p. 18.
23. *Plain Truth*, p. 16.
24. *Plain Truth*, p. 19.
25. *Plain Truth*, p. 20.
26. Ibid.
27. *Plain Truth*, p. 21.
28. *Plain Truth*, p. 26.
29. *Plain Truth*, p. 24.
30. *Plain Truth*, p. 26.
31. *Writings*, 1:36.
32. Ibid.
33. *Plain Truth*, p. 27.
34. *Plain Truth*, p. 34.

35. *Plain Truth,* p. 35.

36. *The Rights of Great Britain Asserted against the Claims of America . . . Said to be written by Lord George Germaine. London Printed: Philadelphia Re-Printed, and Sold by R. Bell 1776.* The extracts from Franklin's *Plain Truth* appear on unnumbered pages, which would correspond to 95–96.

37. William Duane, ed., *Extracts from the Diary of Christopher Marshal . . . 1774–1781* (Albany, N.Y., 1877), p. 62.

38. L. H. Butterfield, ed., *Diary and Autobiography* (Cambridge, Mass., 1961), 3:334.

39. *Writings,* 2:69.

40. *Remarks,* pp. 6–7.

41. *Remarks,* p. 10.

42. *Remarks,* p. 20.

43. *Remarks,* p. 23.

44. *Remarks,* p. 25.

45. *Remarks,* p. 28.

46. *Remarks,* p. 30.

Chapter 14. Other Pamphlet Polemics

1. *Civil Prudence,* pp. 11–13.

2. *Civil Prudence,* p. vi.

3. Oswald Seidensticker, *Der deutsche Pionier,* vols. 12–13 (1880–81), 10 ff. and passim; James O. Knauss, "Christopher Saur, the Third," *American Antiquarian Society Proceedings,* n.s., 41 (1962): 246.

4. Knauss, "Christopher Saur," p. 247.

5. Force, Fourth Series, 5:439–40.

6. The first advertisement appeared in the *Pennsylvania Ledger,* 8 June 1776.

7. The information in this paragraph is obtained from the author's handwritten dedication to William Eden, first baron Auckland, on the flyleaf in the copy now in the John Carter Brown Library.

8. *True Interest,* p. 10.

9. *True Interest,* p. 11.

10. *True Interest,* p. 14.

11. *True Interest,* p. 15.

12. *Writings,* 1:7.

13. *Reason in Answer to a Pamphlet entitled Common Sense* (Dublin, 1776), p. 20.

14. *True Interest,* p. 16.

15. As we have already seen, William Smith quotes Sidney to the same effect in his final "Cato" letter.

16. *True Interest,* p. 20; *De l'Esprit des lois,* bk. 11, chap. 6.

17. *True Interest,* p. 23.

18. *True Interest,* p. 39.

19. *True Interest,* p. 45.

20. *True Interest,* p. 54.

21. *True Interest,* pp. 64–66.

22. *Pamphlets of the American Revolution 1750–1776* (Cambridge, 1965), p. 25.

23. In issues of the *Pennsylvania Ledger* beginning with 14 September 1776, it was regularly stated, "A few Copies of the Second Edition of Strictures on Common Sense, May be had of the Printer."

24. L. H. Butterfield, ed., *Diary and Autobiography* (Cambridge, Mass., 1961), 2:351. Adams refers only to himself, but the French journal mentions also Franklin and Dickinson as coauthors. *Affaires de l'Angleterre et de l'Amérique,* 1776, pp. 85–86.

25. Butterfield, ed., *Diary and Autobiography,* 3:332–33.
26. *Writings,* 1:38.
27. L. H. Butterfield, ed., *Adams Family Correspondence* (Cambridge, Mass., 1963), 1:350.
28. *Writings,* 1:88.
29. Butterfield, ed., *Diary and Autobiography,* 3:331–32.
30. *Writings,* 1:45.
31. C. F. Adams, ed., *Works of John Adams* (Boston, 1850–56), 4:203.
32. An interesting parallel exists in a later comment on the same couplet by James Sullivan, Attorney General of the Commonwealth of Massachusetts. Sullivan affirms that "it is a maxim which serves as an apology for not thinking, and it has no foundation in nature or politics." *Observations upon the Government of the United States of America* (Boston, 1791), p. 9.
33. *Writings,* 1:6.
34. *Writings,* 1:29.
35. *Writings,* 1:28.
36. *Writings,* 1:38.
37. Butterfield, ed., *Diary and Autobiography,* 3:333–34.
38. In his autobiography, Adams has a strikingly similar passage portraying himself as rebuking Jefferson for sacrilege: "The most Speech he ever made in my hearing was a gross insult on Religion, one or two sentences, for which I gave him immediately the Reprehension, which he richly merited." Ibid., 335.
39. C. F. Adams, ed., *Works of John Adams,* 3:380.
40. *Writings,* 2:915–16.
41. The Foner reprint of this passage (*Writings* 1:124) is incomplete. The accurate text may be found in the original or in a reprint by Dolphin Books, *"Common Sense" and the "Crisis"* (Garden City, N.Y., n.d.), p. 147.
42. *Writings,* 2:912–13.
43. C. F. Adams, ed., *Works of John Adams,* 4:202. Contrary to Paine's suggestion of selling the western backlands in order to raise money to help meet continental military expenses, Braxton advocates that all areas not already granted to land companies be sold for the use of the colony of Virginia and for the payment of its debt incurred in the war. The proposal set forth in *Common Sense* of "seizing all unappropriated lands for the use of the Continent" was to Braxton a design in which he saw "as few traces of justice, as in many other of his schemes."
44. Aldridge, *Man of Reason,* p. 84.
45. *Writings,* 2:327.
46. *Writings,* 2:304.
47. *True Merits,* p. 40.
48. *True Merits,* p. vi.
49. *True Merits,* p. 1.
50. Richard Gimbel in his *Thomas Paine: A Bibliographical Check List of Common Sense* (New Haven, Conn., 1956), p. 79, cites W. T. Lowndes, *Bibliographer's Manual,* ed. H. G. Bohn, p. 1761, and Justin Winsor's *Narrative and Critical History,* vol. 6, p. 269. Gimbel assigns the Charleston edition the number CS-20 in his own bibliography.
51. *True Merits,* p. 42.
52. *True Merits,* p. iv.
53. For the opinions of John Rutledge on the temporary constitution of South Carolina see Force, Fourth Series, 5:651.
54. *True Merits,* p. 3.
55. *True Merits,* p. 7–8.
56. *True Merits,* p. 10.
57. *True Merits,* p. 24.
58. *Writings,* 1:30.
59. *Writings,* 1:529.

60. *True Merits,* p. 21.
61. *True Merits,* p. 43.
62. *True Merits,* pp. vi, 32, 36, 43.
63. *Writings,* 1:26.
64. *True Merits,* p. 28.
65. *True Merits,* pp. 31–32.
66. *True Merits,* p. 34.
67. *True Merits,* p. 33.
68. *True Merits,* pp. 36–38.
69. *True Merits,* p. 20.
70. *True Merits,* p. 30.
71. After the promulgation of the Declaration of Independence, *Common Sense* continued to be regarded in Britain as representing the opinions of the American Congress. An anonymous London attack on the Declaration described *Common Sense* as "a book which has been in some sort *adopted* by the Congress; many of the most striking passages of the Declaration being borrowed from it." *An Answer to the Declaration of the American Congress. . . ,* 5th ed. (London, 1776), p. 9.
72. *Bibliographical Check List,* CS-14, CS-15, CS-66.
73. *Bibliographical Check List,* CS-209.
74. Gimbel has given this so-called "Second edition" of *A Sequel* the code CS-226 and reserved CS-225 for the first edition, "the existence of which is indicated on the title page of CS-226." Since the latter is not a new work at all, Gimbel's CS-225 is probably a ghost.
75. *Reason in Answer,* p. 25.
76. *Reason in Answer,* p. 26.
77. *Reason in Answer,* p. 1.
78. *Reason in Answer,* p. 24.
79. *Reason in Answer,* p. 17.
80. *Reason in Answer,* p. 9.
81. *Reason in Answer,* p. 20.
82. *Reason in Answer,* pp. 10–11.
83. *Reason in Answer,* p. 23.
84. *Reason in Answer,* p. 130.
85. *Reason in Answer,* p. 47.
86. *Writings,* 1:6.
87. *Reason in Answer,* p. 5.
88. *Reason in Answer,* p. 6.
89. *Reason in Answer,* p. 7.
90. *Reason in Answer,* p. 13.
91. *Reason in Answer,* p. 14.
92. *Reason in Answer,* p. 15.
93. *Reason in Answer,* p. 16.
94. *Reason in Answer,* p. 21.
95. *Ibid.*

Chapter 15. Four Letters

1. Alexander Graydon, quoted by J. P. Selsam, *The Pennsylvania Constitution of 1776* (Philadelphia, 1936), p. 96.
2. *Pamphlets of the American Revolution* (Cambridge, Mass., 1965, 1:48.
3. Ibid., 104–5.

4. Peter Force, ed., *American Archives,* Fourth Series, 6:1022.
5. Force, Fourth Series, 6:521.
6. Dated 22 May 1776 and presented to the Assembly 23 May.
7. Force, Fourth Series, 6:552.
8. Force, Fourth Series, 6:1124, 1135.
9. J. Thomas Scharf and Thomas Westcott, *History of Philadelphia, 1609–1884* (Philadelphia, 1884), 1:329.
10. *Writings,* 1:148.
11. This is the theory set forth in Eric Foner, *Tom Paine and Revolutionary America* (New York, 1976).
12. *Writings,* 2:81.
13. *Writings,* 1:85.
14. *Writings,* 2:77.
15. *Writings,* 2:191.
16. George Lawrence, trans., *Democracy in America* (New York, 1966), p. 454.
17. Elise Marienstras, *Les Mythes fondateurs* (Paris, 1976), p. 110.
18. *Writings,* 2:82.
19. *Writings,* 1:57.
20. Thomas Jefferson has received fame and praise for saying in his *Notes on the State of Virginia* in 1785, "Our rulers can have authority over such natural rights only as we have submitted to them. We are answerable for them to our God" (William Peden, ed. [Chapel Hill, N.C., 1955], p. 15). Paine clearly deserves the distinction of priority.
21. *Writings,* 2:285.
22. *Writings,* 2:56.
23. *Writings,* 1:370.
24. C. F. Adams, ed., *Works of John Adams* (Boston, 1850–56), 4:195, 196.
25. *Pamphlets of the American Revolution,* 1:188.
26. *Writings,* 2:304.
27. *Writings,* 1:388.
28. *Works* (Boston, 1854), 9:622–23.
29. *The Life of Thomas Paine* (London, 1817), p. 165.
30. *Writings,* 2:422.
31. *Writings,* 2:526. A discussion of this text is found in A. O. Aldridge, "Condorcet et Paine, leurs rapports intellectuels," *Revue de littérature comparée* 32 (1958):58–60.
32. *Writings,* 1:8.
33. *Writings,* 2:274.
34. *Pamphlets,* 1:97.
35. *Writings,* 1:38.
36. J. P. Selsam, *The Pennsylvania Constitution of 1776* (Philadelphia, 1936), p. 137.
37. *Pennsylvania Gazette,* 26 March 1777.
38. Alexander Graydon, *Memoirs* (Philadelphia, 1846), p. 285.
39. Samuel B. Harding, "Party Struggles over the First Pennsylvania Constitution," *Annual Report of the American Historical Association,* 1894, p. 377.
40. Ibid., p. 379.
41. Selsam, *Pennsylvania Constitution,* pp. 199n, 175.
42. *Writings,* 2:314.
43. *Jefferson and Madison: The Great Collaboration* (New York, 1964), pp. 62–96.
44. *Writings,* 2:1298–99.
45. Selsam, *Pennsylvania Constitution,* p. 224.
46. *Works* (Boston, 1854), 9:622.
47. *Writings,* 2:270.

Chapter 16. The Crisis

1. Paul Leicester Ford, "The Crisis," *Bibliographer* 1 (1902): 139–52.
2. *Writings*, 2:1164.
3. *Writings*, 1:51.
4. *Writings*, 1:55.
5. *Writings*, 1:164.
6. A. O. Aldridge, *Man of Reason*, p. 109.
7. *Writings*, 1:354.
8. William Lewelyn, *An Appeal to Men against Paine's Rights of Man* (London, 1793), p. 43.
9. *Writings*, 1:203.
10. *Writings*, 1:74.
11. *Writings*, 1:123.
12. *Miscellaneous Works* (New York, 1804), p. 132.
13. *Writings*, 1:30–31.
14. *Writings*, 1:123.
15. *Writings*, 2:1179.
16. *Writings*, 1:231.
17. *Writings*, 1:193.
18. *Writings*, 1:224.
19. *Des Principes des négociations* in *Collection complète des oeuvres* (Paris 1794–95), 5:93.
20. *Writings*, 1:136.
21. *Characteristics of Men, Manners, Opinions, Times* (London, 1711), 2:320.
22. *Writings*, 1:58.
23. "The Study of Literature," in J. W. Spadden, ed., *Miscellaneous Works* (New York, 1907), p. 10.
24. *Writings*, 1:72.
25. *Writings*, 1:71. As a matter of fact, the first four numbers of the *Crisis* appeared in Almon's *Remembrances . . . For the Year 1778*, and later issues of this periodical published the rest of the *Crisis* with the exception of Nos. 10, 11, and 12.
26. *Writings*, 1:125.
27. *Writings*, 1:195.
28. *Writings*, 1:205.
29. *Pennsylvania Gazette*, 3 April 1782.
30. *Writings*, 1:483.
31. *Writings*, 1:72.
32. *Pennsylvania Gazette*, 3 April 1782.
33. *Writings*, 1:198.
34. *Writings*, 2:369. See chap. 15 below.
35. *Writings*, 1:147.
36. *Writings*, 1:19.
37. *Writings*, 1:154.
38. *Writings*, 1:148.
39. *Writings*, 1:149.
40. *Writings*, 1:152.
41. *Writings*, 1:155.
42. *Writings*, 1:44.
43. *Writings*, 1:31.
44. *Writings*, 1:81.
45. *Writings*, 1:20.
46. *Writings*, 1:81.
47. *Writings*, 1:209.
48. *Writings*, 1:214.

49. *Writings*, 2:65; 1:215.

50. *Pennsylvania Gazette*, 6 April 1782. This paper, which was intended as a continuation of *Crisis* No. 10, has never been republished. See A. O. Aldridge, *Man of Reason*, pp. 92–93.

51. *Writings*, 1:231.

52. *Writings*, 1:232.

53. *Writings*, 1:232–33.

54. *Writings*, 1:234–35.

Chapter 17. Retrospect on 1776

1. J. P. Selsam, *The Pennsylvania Constitution of 1776* (Philadelphia, 1936), p. 95.

2. *Writings*, 2:62.

3. *Writings*, 2:80n.

4. *Writings*, 2:83.

5. General John Lacey, quoted in Selsam, *Pennsylvania Constitution*, p. 239.

6. Scharf and Westcott, *History of Philadelphia*, 1:338.

7. *Writings*, 2:270.

8. *Writings*, 2:425.

9. *Writings*, 2:270.

10. *Writings*, 2:273–77.

11. Scharf and Westcott, *History of Philadelphia*, 1:396.

12. Ibid.

13. *Writings*, 2:1183.

14. *Writings*, 2:278–302.

15. A. O. Aldridge, *Benjamin Franklin Philosopher and Man* (Philadelphia, 1965), p. 97; *Writings*, 2:281.

16. *Writings*, 2:284.

17. *Writings*, 2:287.

18. *Writings*, 2:288.

19. *Writings*, 2:290.

20. *Writings*, 2:293.

21. Scharf and Westcott, *History of Philadelphia*, 1:396.

22. *Writings*, 2:368–416.

23. "Disertación acerca del Gobierno, los asuntos de Banco y papel-moneda," in Manuel García de Sena, *La Independencia de la Costa Firma, justificada por Thomas Paine treinte años ha* (Philadelphia, 1811) pp. 67–156. The translation is treated by Pedro Grases and Alberto Harkness in *Manuel García de Sena y la Independencia de Hispanoamérica* (Caracas, 1953), pp. 33ff.

24. A. O. Aldridge, "Why Did Thomas Paine Write on the Bank?" *Proceedings of the American Philosophical Society* 93 (1949):309–315.

25. Paine to Thomas Fitzsimmons, 19 April 1785, quoted in ibid., p. 311.

26. Joseph Dorfman, "Economic Philosophy of Thomas Paine," *Political Science Quarterly* 53 (1938:372–86.

27. See chapter 4, note 12.

28. *Writings*, 2:369.

29. *Writings*, 2:372.

30. *Social Contract*, bk.2, chap. 3.

31. *Writings*, 2:374.

32. *Writings*, 2:375.

33. *Writings*, 2:378.

34. *Writings*, 2:380

35. *Writings*, 2:389.

36. Julian P. Boyd, ed., *The Papers of Thomas Jefferson,* vol. 13 (Princeton, N.J., 1956), pp. 6–8.
37. *Writings,* 2:397.
38. *Writings,* 2:509.
39. *Writings,* 2:404.
40. *Writings,* 2:409.
41. *Writings,* 2:415–39.
42. *Writings,* 2:417.
43. *Writings,* 2:420.
44. *Writings,* 2:422.
45. *Writings,* 2:435.

Chapter 18. The Circle of Civilization

1. *The Life of Thomas Paine . . . The Fifth Edition* (London, 1792), p. 29. The complicated bibliographical record of Raynal's *History* has never been thoroughly traced. The first edition consisted of six volumes: *Histoire philosophique et politique des établissements et du commerce des Européens dans les deux Indes* (Amsterdam, 1770). The separate volume on the American Revolution came out concurrently in French and English editions, both published in England: *Révolution de l'Amérique, par . . . auteur de l'Histoire philosophique. . . . Ouvrage qui peut servir de supplément à la dite Histoire philosophique* (London, 1781). *The Revolution of America, by the abbé Raynal* (London, 1781).
2. *Writings,* 2:1232.
3. Unpublished manuscript in American Philosophical Society Library.
4. *Writings,* 2:1236.
5. *Writings,* 1:19, 146.
6. Paine's relations with French diplomats are sketched in A. O. Aldridge, *Man of Reason,* pp. 93–98. Record of La Luzerne's payment for *Crisis* No. 11 is found in a letter from La Luzerne to Vergennes, in the archives of the Ministère des Affaires Etrangères, 21:171.
7. Ministère des Affaires Etrangères, 22:162.
8. *New York Royal Gazette,* quoted by William W. Stinchcombe, *The American Revolution and the French Alliance* (Syracuse, N.Y., 1969), p. 128.
9. *Writings,* 2:1240.
10. He remarks that it would be feasible for a military mission to depose George III and set up the Duke of Gloucester in his stead. *Writings* 1:71. He does not here suggest erecting a republican government for the English people, but merely effecting a change in rulers.
11. *Writings,* 2:213.
12. *Writings,* 2:216.
13. A. O. Aldridge, "Paine and Dickinson," *Early American Literature* 11 (1976): 125–38.
14. *Writings,* 1:31–32. Paine also declares in *Common Sense,* "The removal of North, or the whole detestable junto, is a matter unworthy the millions we have expended; . . . 'tis scarcely worth our while to fight against a contemptible ministry only." *Writings* 1:24. Finally, he says in *Common Sense,* "the taking up arms, merely to enforce the repeal of a pecuniary law, seems as unwarrantable by the divine law, and as repugnant to human feelings, as the taking up arms to enforce obedience thereto." *Writings* 1:45.
15. *Writings,* 2:219.
16. *Writings,* 2:956, 219.
17. *Writings,* 2:221.
18. *Writings,* 2:224.
19. *Writings,* 2:229.
20. *Writings,* 2:428.
21. *Writings,* 2:235.

22. *Writings,* 2:239.
23. *Writings,* 2:66.
24. *Writings,* 1:148.
25. *Writings,* 2:246.
26. *Writings,* 2:279.
27. *Writings,* 2:238.
28. *Writings,* 2:239.
29. *Writings,* 2:240.
30. *Writings,* 1:20.
31. *Writings,* 2:79.
32. *Writings,* 1:146.
33. *Writings,* 1:204.
34. *Writings,* 1:234.
35. *Writings,* 2:240–41.
36. *Writings,* 2:39–40; 1:164.
37. *Writings,* 2:242; 1:145.
38. *Writings,* 2:242.
39. Background information and proof that the letter is addressed to Morellet appears in A. O. Aldridge, "Thomas Paine and the French Connection," *The French-American Review* 1 (1977): 240–48. The text of the letter, August 1787, appears in A. O. Aldridge, "Thomas Paine, Edmund Burke and Anglo-French Relations in 1787," *Studies in Burke and His Times* 12 (1971): 1851–61.
40. *Writings,* 2:247–49.
41. *Writings,* 2:251–52.
42. *Histoire philosophique et politique* (Geneva, 1781), 9:233.
43. *Writings,* 1:3.
44. *Writings,* 2:255.
45. *Writings,* 2:256.
46. *Writings,* 1:16.
47. *Writings,* 2:256.
48. *Writings,* 2:257.
49. *Writings,* 2:262.
50. A French edition, *Pacte maritime,* was printed by Paine's friend Nicolas de Bonneville in 1800; the American edition, *Compact Maritime,* was printed in Washington in 1801 under Thomas Jefferson's supervision. Neither version has ever been included in an edition of Paine's works, although excerpts appear in the seventh of his letters "To the Citizens of the United States." *Writings,* 2:940–46.
51. Paine had his *Letter to the Abbé Raynal* printed at his own expense, sent fifty copies to George Washington for distribution to the American army, and dispatched one hundred copies to La Luzerne for use in France. The *Letter* was almost immediately given four different French translations, including one carrying a preface asserting that Paine had been inbued with the ideas of French thinkers such as Montaigne, Montesquieu, and Rousseau. A. O. Aldridge, "La Signification historique, diplomatique et littéraire de la *Lettre adressée à l'Abbé Raynal* de Thomas Paine," *Etudes anglaises* 8 (1955): 223–32.
52. His refutation in the form of letters was published under the signature IVOR in the *Kentish Gazette* during May and June and in a pamphlet with the title *Observations on a Letter of Mr. Thomas Paine, to the Abbe Reynal* [*sic*]. *1783 . . . By a Country Gentleman* (Brighton, 1792).

Conclusion

1. *Writings,* 1:232.
2. L. H. Butterfield, ed., *Adams Family Correspondence* (Cambridge, Mass., 1963), 1:350.

Bibliography

There is no complete edition of Paine's works. The two most useful editions are Philip S. Foner, editor, *The Compete Writings of Thomas Paine* (Garden City, New York: Citadel Press, 1945), 2 vols., and Moncure D. Conway, editor, *The Writings of Thomas Paine* (New York: Putnam, 1894–96), 4 vols. The Foner edition has more of Paine's writing, but is flawed by inaccuracies. The Conway edition is more reliable textually, but lacks many twentieth-century additions to the Paine canon. Thirty years of Paine scholarship are analyzed by A. Owen Aldridge in "Thomas Paine: A Survey of Research and Criticism since 1945," *British Studies Monitor* 5 (1975); 3–27.

Adams Family Correspondence. Edited by L. H. Butterfield. 2 vols. Cambridge, Mass.: Harvard University Press, 1963.

Adams, John, *Diary and Autobiography.* Edited by L. H. Butterfield. 4 vols. Cambridge, Mass.: Harvard University Press, 1961.

———. *Thoughts on Government.* Philadelphia: J. Dunlap, 1776.

———. *Works.* Edited by C. F. Adams 10 vols. Boston: Little, Brown, 1850–56.

Adams, Thomas Randolph. "The Authorship and Printing of 'Plain Truth.'" *Papers of the Bibliographical Society of America* 49 (1955).

———. "American Independence: The Growth of an Idea." *Publications of the Colonial Society of Massachusetts,* no. 43 (1956).

Aldridge, A. Owen. *Benjamin Franklin Philosopher and Man.* New York: J. B. Lippincott, 1965.

———. "Condorcet et Paine, leurs rapports intellectuels." *Revue de littérature comparée* 32 (1958).

———. "El granadino que tradujo la obra de Tomás Paine." *Revista interamericana de bibliografia* 31 (1958).

———. "La Signification historique, diplomatique, et littéraire de la Lettre adressée à l'abbé Raynal de Thomas Paine." *Etudes anglaises* 8 (1955).

———. *Man of Reason: The Life of Thomas Paine.* Philadelphia: J. B. Lippincott, 1959.

———. "Paine and Dickinson." *Early American Literature* 11 (1976).

———. "Population and Polygamy in Eighteenth-Century Thought." *Journal of the History of Medicine* 4 (1949).

———. "Some Writings of Thomas Paine in Pennsylvania Newspapers." *American Historical review* 56 (1951).

———. "The Influence of New York Newspapers on Paine's *Common Sense.*" *New York Historical Society Quarterly* 60 (1976).

———. "The Poetry of Thomas Paine." *Pennsylvania Magazine of History and Biography* 89 (1955).

———. "The State of Nature: An Undiscovered Country in the History of Ideas." *Studies in Voltaire and the Eighteenth Century* 98 (1972).

———. "Thomas Paine and the French Connection." *French-American Review* 1 (1977).

———. "Thomas Paine and the New York *Public Advertiser*." *New-York Historical Society Quarterly* 32 (1953).

———. "Thomas Paine, Edmund Burke and Anglo-French Relations in 1787." *Studies in Burke and His Times* 12 (1971).

An Answer to the Declaration of the American Congress. 5th ed. London, 1776.

Bailyn, Bernard. *Pamphlets of the American Revolution 1750–1776.* 3 vols. Cambridge, Mass.: Harvard University Press, 1965.

Barry, Alyce. "Thomas Paine, Privateersman." *Pennsylvania Magazine of History and Biography* 101 (1977).

Beard, Charles A. *An Economic Interpretation of the Constitution.* New York: Macmillan, 1935.

Bercovitch, Sacvan. *The Puritan Origins of the American Self.* New Haven, Conn.: Yale University Press, 1975.

Bland, William. *An Inquiry into the Rights of the British Colonies.* Williamsburg, Va., 1766.

Boinvilliers, J.-E. J. F. *L'Esprit du Contrat social, suivi de l'esprit du Sens commun, de Thomas Paine.* Paris: Cailleau, An II [1793–94].

Boothby, Brooke. *Observations on the Appeal from the New . . . Whigs.* London, 1792.

Botta, Carlo G. G. *History of the War of Independence of America.* Trans. G. A. Otis. 2 vols. 3d ed. New Haven, Conn.: N. Whiting, 1834.

Braxton, Carter. *An Address to the Convention of the Colony . . . of Virginia.* Philadelphia: J. Dunlap, 1776.

Carlile, Richard [?]. *Aphorisms, preceded by an Essay on the Life and Genius of Thomas Paine.* London, 1826.

Chalmers, George. *The Life of Thomas Paine.* 5th ed. London: John Stockdale, 1792.

Chalmers, James. *Plain Truth.* Philadelphia: R. Bell, 1776.

———. *Strictures on a Pamphlet Written by Thomas Paine.* London, 1796.

Cheetham, James. *The Life of Thomas Paine.* New York: Southwick and Pelsue, 1809.

Civil Prudence. Recommended to the Thirteen United Colonies of North America. Norwich, Conn.: Spooner, 1776.

Clark, Harry H. "Thomas Paine's Relations to Voltaire and Rousseau." *La Revue anglo-américaine* 9 (1932).

Conway, Moncure D. *Life of Thomas Paine.* 2 vols. New York: G. P. Putnam, 1892.

———. *Thomas Paine (1737–1809) et la révolution dans les deux mondes.* Paris: Plon-Nourrit, 1900.

Deane, Silas. "Papers." *Collections of the New-York Historical Society* 22 (1890).

Dorfman, Joseph. "Economic Philosophy of Thomas Paine." *Political Science Quarterly* 53 (1938).

Eayre, James. "The Political Ideas of the English Agrarians, 1775–1815." *Canadian Journal of Economics and Political Science* 18 (1952).

Edwards, Jonathan. *Thoughts on the Revival of Religion in New England.* New York: American Tract Society [1845].

Entick, John. *New Naval History.* London, 1757.

———. *The General History of the Late War.* 5 vols. London, 1763.

Foner, Eric. *Tom Paine and Revolutionary America.* New York: Oxford University Press, 1976.

Force, Peter, ed. *American Archives.* Fourth Series. 6 vols. Washington, D.C., 1837–53.

Ford, Paul Leicester. "The Crisis." *Bibliographer* 1 (1902).

Fox, William. *An Examination of Mr. Paine's Writings.* London, 1793.

Franklin, Benjamin. *Papers.* Various editors. New Haven, Conn.: Yale University Press. In process since 1959.

———. *Writings.* Edited by A. H. Smyth. 10 vols. New York: Macmillan, 1905–1907.

Franklin, Julian H. *John Locke and the Theory of Sovereignty . . . in the Political Thought of the English Revolution.* Cambridge: Cambridge University Press, 1979.

Freneau, Philip, and Hugh Henry Brackenridge. *A Poem on the Rising Glory of America.* Philadelphia: Crukshank, 1772.

Gabrieli, Vittorio. "Thomas Paine fra l'America e l'Europa." *Studi americani* 1 (1955).

García de Sena, Manuel. *La Independencia de la Costa Firma, justificada por Thomas Paine treinte años ha.* Philadelphia, 1811.

Genuine Principles of the Ancient Saxon, or English Constitution. Philadelphia: Bell, 1776.

Gerbi, Antonelli. *The Dispute of the New World. The History of a Polemic, 1750–1790.* Pittsburgh, Penna.: University of Pittsburgh Press, 1973.

Gibbon, Edward. *Miscellaneous Works.* Edited by J. W. Spadden. New York: F. De Fau and Company, 1907.

Gimbel, Richard. *Bibliographical Check List of Common Sense.* New Haven, Conn.: Yale University Press, 1956.

Godwin, William. *Enquiry concerning Political Justice.* Edited by F. E. L. Priestley. Toronto: University of Toronto Press, 1946. 3 vols.

Gough, John W. *John Locke's Political Philosophy.* Oxford: Clarendon Press, 1973.

Grases, Pedro, and Alberto Harkness. *Manuel García de Sena y la independencia de Hispanoamérica.* Caracas: Publicaciones de la Decima Conferencia, 1953.

Graydon, Alexander. *Memoirs.* Philadelphia: Lindsay & Blakiston, 1846.

Harding, Samuel B. "Party Struggles over the First Pennsylvania Constitution." *Annual Report of the American Historical Association.* 1894.

Hawke, David Freeman. *Paine.* New York: Harper & Row, 1974.

Hinz, Evelyn J. "The 'Reasonable' Style of Tom Paine." *Queen's Quarterly* 79 (1972).

Howe, John R., Jr. *The Role of Ideology in the American Revolution.* New York: Holt, Rinehart & Winston, 1970.

Inglis, Charles. *The True Interest of America Impartially Stated.* Philadelphia: Humphreys, 1776.

Jay, William. *Life of John Jay.* New York: J. & J. Harper, 1833.

Jefferson, Thomas. *Notes on the State of Virginia.* Edited by William Peden. Chapel Hill: University of North Carolina Press, 1955.

———. *Papers.* Edited by Julian P. Boyd. Princeton, N.J.: Princeton University Press. In process since 1950.

Kendall, Willmoore. *John Locke and the Doctrine of Majority Rule.* Urbana: University of Illinois Press, 1965.

Knauss, James O. "Christopher Saur, the Third." *American Antiquarian Society Proceedings,* n.s. 41 (1962).

Koch, Adrienne. *Jefferson and Madison: The Great Collaboration.* New York: Knopf, 1964.

Labaree, Leonard W. *Royal Government in America.* New Haven,Conn.: Yale University Press, 1930.

Ladousse, André. "La rhétorique comme idéologie dans *Common Sense.*" *Annales du Centre de recherches sur l'Amérique anglophone.* Université de Bordeaux III. Vol. 3 (1974).

Latnick, Solomon. *The American Revolution and the British Press 1775–1783.* Columbia: University of Missouri Press, 1967.

Lewelyn, William. *An Appeal to Men against Paine's Rights of Man.* London. 1793.

Lewis, Clive S. *The Discarded Image.* Cambridge: Cambridge University Press, 1964.

Locke, John. *An Essay concerning the True Original Extent and End of Civil Government.* Edited by Thomas Elrington. Dublin, 1798.

———. *Two Treatises of Government.* Edited by Peter Laslett. Cambridge: Cambridge University Press, 1960.

Lovejoy, Arthur O. *Essays in the History of Ideas.* Baltimore, Md.: Johns Hopkins University Press, 1948.

Lowell, James Russell. *Writings.* 11 vols. Boston: Houghton, Mifflin, 1898–1900.

Mably, Gabriel Bonnot de. *Collection complète des oeuvres.* 15 vols. Paris, 1794–95.

Madison, James, and others. *The Federalist.* Edited by Jacob E. Cooke. Middletown, Conn.: Wesleyan University Press, 1961.

Mandeville, Bernard. *The Fable of the Bees.* Edinburgh: J. Wood, 1777.

———. *The Fable of the Bees.* Edited by F. B. Kaye. 2 vols. Oxford: Clarendon Press, 1924.

Marienstras, Elise. *Les Mythes fondateurs.* Paris: F. Maspero, 1976.

Marshall, Christopher. *Diary.* Edited by William Duane. Albany, N.Y.: J. M. Munsell, 1877.

Mather, Cotton. *Magnalia Christi Americana.* London, 1702.

Meserole, Harrison T. "W. T. Sherwin: A Little-Known Paine Biographer." *Papers of the Bibliographical Society of America* 99 (1955).

Miller, Samuel. *Brief Retrospect of the Eighteenth Century.* 2 vols. New York: T. & J. Swords, 1800.

Montesquieu, Charles Louis de Secondat, baron de La Brède et de. *De l'Esprit des loix.* Edited by Jean Brethe de la Gressaye. 3 vols. Paris: Belles Lettres, 1955.

Negley, Glenn, and J. Max Patrick, eds. *The Quest for Utopia.* New York: H. Schuman, 1952.

Observations on a Letter of Mr. Thomas Paine, to the Abbe Reynal [*sic*]. 1783 . . . By a Country Gentleman. Brighton, 1792[?].

Oldys, Francis [George Chalmers] *The Life of Thomas Paine.* 5th ed. London, 1792.

Palmer, R. R. "Tom Paine Victim of the Rights of Man." *Pennsylvania Magazine of History and Biography* 66 (1942).

Parrington, Vernon L. *Main Currents of American Thought.* 3 vols. New York: Harcourt, Brace, 1927–30.

Parsons, Talcott. *The Social System.* Glencoe, Ill.: Free Press, 1951.

Paulson, Ronald. *Representations of Revolution (1789–1820).* New Haven, Conn.: Yale University Press, 1983.

Philbrick, Norman, ed. *Trumpets Sounding.* New York: Benjamin Blom, 1972.

Plutarch. *Parallel Lives.* Edited by A. H. Clough. 3 vols. New York: E. P. Dutton, 1911.

Pocock, J. G. A. *The Ancient Constitution and the Feudal Law.* New York: Norton, 1967.

———. *The Machiavellian Moment: Florentine Political Thought and the Atlantic Republican Tradition.* Princeton, N.J.: Princeton University Press, 1975.

Poggioli, Renato. *The Oaten Flute.* Cambridge, Mass.: Harvard University Press, 1975.

Prawer, Siegbert S. *Comparative Literature Studies: An Introduction.* London: Duckworth, 1973.

Raynal, Abbé G. T. F. *Histoire philosophique et politique des établissements et du commerce des Européens dans les deux Indes.* 6 vols. Amsterdam, 1770.

Reason in Answer to a Pamphlet entitled Common Sense. Dublin, 1776.

Rickman, Thomas Clio. *Life of Thomas Paine.* London, 1819.

Rights of Citizens. London, n.d. [1791].

Riland, John. *The Rights of God, occasion'd by Mr. Paine's 'Rights of Man,' and his other publications.* Birmingham, 1792.

Roshwald, Mordecai. "The Concept of Human Rights." *Philosophy and Phenomenological Research* 19 (1959).

Rousseau, Jean-Jacques. *A Discourse upon the Origin and Foundation of the Inequality among Mankind.* London: R. and J. Dodsley, 1761.

———. *OEuvres complètes.* Pléiade edition. Edited by B. Gagnebin and M. Raymond, 4 vols. Paris, 1959–69.

———. *A Treatise on the Social Contract.* London, 1764.

Rush, Benjamin. *Autobiography.* Edited by George W. Corner. Princeton, N.J.: Princeton University Press, 1948.

———. *Letters.* Edited by L. H. Butterfield. 2 vols. Philadelphia and Princeton, N.J.: Princeton University Press. 1951.

Sabine, Lorenzo. *Biographical Sketches of Loyalists of the American Revolution.* 2 vols. Boston: Little, Brown, 1864.

Samuel, Irene. *Plato and Milton.* Ithaca, N.Y.: Cornell University Press, 1965.

Scharf, J. Thomas, and Thomas Westcott. *History of Philadelphia.* 3 vols. Philadelphia: L. H. Everts, 1884.

Seidensticker, Oswald. *Bilder aus der deutsch-pennsylvanischen Geschichte.* New York: E. Steiger, 1886.

Selsam, John Paul. *The Pennsylvania Constitution of 1776.* Philadelphia: University of Pennsylvania Press, 1936.

Shaftesbury, Anthony Ashley Cooper, 3d earl of. *Characteristics of Men, Manners, Opinions, Times.* Edited by John M. Robertson. 2 vols. London: G. Richards, 1900.

Shklar, Judith N. *Men and Citizens: A Study of Rousseau's Social Theory.* Cambridge: Cambridge University Press, 1969.

Smith, Frank. "The Authorship of 'An Occasional Letter on the Female Sex.'" *American Literature* 2 (1930).

Spurlin, Paul M. *Montesquieu in America 1760–1801.* University, La.: University of Louisiana Press, 1940.

———. *Rousseau in America 1760–1809.* University, Ala.: University of Alabama Press, 1969.

Stinchcombe, William O. *The American Revolution and the French Alliance.* Syracuse, N.Y.: Syracuse University Press, 1969.

Sullivan, James. *Observations upon the Government of the United States.* Boston: Hall, 1791.

Thomas, Isaiah. *History of printing in America.* 2 vols. Worcester, Mass.: Press of Isaiah Thomas, 1810.

Tocqueville, Alexis de. *Democracy in America.* Edited by Phillips Bradley. 2 vols. 1945. Reprint. New York: Vintage Books, 1948.

———. *Democracy in America.* Translated by George Lawrence. New York: Harper & Row, 1966.

True Merits of a Late Treatise . . . intitled Common Sense. London, 1776.

Tuveson, Ernest L. *Redeemer Nation: The Idea of America's Millenial Role.* Chicago: University of Chicago Press, 1968.

Tyler, Moses Coit. *The Literary History of the American Revolution.* 2 vols. New York: G. P. Putnam, 1897.

Voltaire. *Correspondence.* Edited by Theodore Besterman. 107 vols. Geneva: Institut et musée Voltaire, 1953–65.

Voltaire. *Oeuvres complètes.* 70 vols. Basle [Kahl]: Société littéraire-typographique, 1784–1789.

Wallace, Robert. *Dissertation on the Numbers of Mankind, in Ancient and Modern Times.* Edinburgh: G. Hamilton, 1753.

Wesley, John. *Journal.* Edited by Nehemiah Curnock. 8 vols. London: R. Culley, 1909–16.

Williamson, Audrey. *Thomas Paine, His Life, Work, and Times.* New York: St. Martin's Press, 1973.

Wills, Garry. *Inventing America.* New York: Doubleday, 1978.

Wilson, James. *Considerations on the Nature and the Legislative Authority of the British Parliament.* Philadelphia: Bradfords, 1774.

Winthrop, Robert C. *Life and Letters.* 2 vols. Boston: Ticknor and Fields, 1864–67.

Wise, Gene. "The Contemporary Crisis in Intellectual History," *CLIO* 5 (1975).

Wood, Gordon S. "Rhetoric and Reality in the American Revolution." *William and Mary Quarterly,* 3d ser. 12 (1966).

———. *The Creation of the American Republic.* Chapel Hill: University of North Carolina Press, 1969.

Woodhouse, A. S. P., ed. *Puritanism and Liberty, Being the Army Debates . . . with Supplementary Documents.* London: J. M. Dent, 1950.

Yolton, John W., ed. *John Locke: Problems and Perspectives.* Cambridge: Cambridge University Press, 1969.

Yorke, Henry. *These are the Times that Try Men's Souls: A Letter to John Frost.* London, 1793.

Index

I. Names and Titles

II. Themes and Topics